Praise for *NO SUCH THING AS A BAD KID...*

"'Behave well and we treat you great—if you don't, it won't be much fun here.' This reactive mindset is still widely used with behaviorally challenging children and youth, as Charles Appelstein observes in his new edition of *No Such Thing as a Bad Kid*. While current professional literature is awash with 'strength-based' platitudes, this book turns positive psychology rhetoric into reality. Tapping decades of practice wisdom, Appelstein shows how dedicated adults break through barriers of distrust and defiance to unleash hidden potentials in our most vulnerable young people."

—Larry Brendtro, PhD
Senior training consultant, CF Learning (cflearning.org) and
coauthor of *Reclaiming Youth at Risk*

"I have sat across from many troubled and violent people in my work as a psychological expert witness in murder cases. How I wish their caregivers had made use of Appelstein's prescriptions for nurturing the humanity in these traumatized children so they would not have reached the terrible point at which I came their lives."

—James Garbarino, PhD
Maude C. Clarke Chair in Humanistic Psychology, Loyola University Chicago
and author of *Lost Boys* and *Listening to Killers*

"Appelstein's lectures, seminars, and writings have demystified the behavior of at-risk kids for thousands of parents and professionals. This revision of his 1998 classic builds on his original work with an abundance of fresh material to help a new generation of educators and others better connect with today's challenging youth."

—Richard D. Lavoie, MA, MEd
Author of *The Motivation Breakthrough* and
It's So Much Work to Be Your Friend

"This book offers a compelling framework for navigating the research and practices required to help at-risk children get back 'on the rails.' Its practical strategies inspire and empower parents, educators, youth and social workers, therapists, and other caring adults."

—Rick Miller
Founder of Kids at Hope and author of *Youth Development*

"Full of familiar vignettes and scenarios, this easy-to-read guide provides a multitude of strategies that can be implemented immediately by a student teacher or first-year counselor as well as an experienced professional. It also offers direction on how to sustain our efforts as we foster powerful relationships with kids and, in so doing, change the way they view themselves."

—Jessica Minahan, MEd, BCBA
Coauthor of *The Behavior Code* and author of *The Behavior Code Companion*

"Charlie Appelstein has written a tool in the guise of a book for those working with traumatized children and youth. It is essential reading for anyone who wants greater insight in how to be an effective 'child-guider.'"

—Analyn Einarson, PhD
Clinical director, Marymound School, Winnipeg, MB

"Equipped with Charlie Appelstein's theory and the toolbox of practices found in this book—like raps, metaphors, modifying activities to enhance success, jokes, amplifying and squeezing strengths into positive pursuits, and more—our dedicated volunteers have been pointing promising youth toward a better future. Remember, as Charlie says, little changes can ripple into big solutions. This book can form the origin for many of our society's big solutions."

—Daniel McNeil
Grand Area Mentoring, Moab, Utah

"This timely and important book helps educators and others better respond to the SOS signals being sent by too many students. It should be mandatory reading for anyone who touches the lives of children."

—Alvin L. Garrison
Superintendent of Schools
Covington Independent Public Schools, Kentucky

"This book is a compendium of Charlie Appelstein's uncommon wisdom, insight, compassion, talent, and skill in working with troubled children and training others who work with them, including parents and teachers. It is a welcome treasure to the field."

—David A. Crenshaw, PhD, ABPP
Author and clinical director of Children's Home of Poughkeepsie, New York

"Appelstein has taken what is arguably the definitive book on youth-care work and made it even stronger and more encompassing. I highly recommend this enriching volume for those who are either new or experienced in the field."

—Bob Bertolino, PhD
Author of *Thriving on the Front Lines* and
Working with Children and Adolescents in Residential Care

"'No such thing as a bad kid' is a phrase I repeat frequently, not only because I believe it's true based on the latest research in the neurosciences but because I *know* it's true from years of watching young people previously considered 'unhelpable.' Charlie Appelstein offers practical strategies for finding this proof and the hope that comes with it. He also provides terminology for better understanding and responding to trauma in language residential youth-care workers, therapists, and parents can understand. A must read."

—Robert Lieberman, CEO, Kairos and
former president of the Association of Children's Residential Centers

"This book can change lives. Educators will be highly engaged in learning what they can do to build transformative relationships with their most challenging students."

—Elaine T. Brown, PhD
Executive director, Student Intervention and Support Services
Ann Arbor Public Schools

"These useful tools and techniques are highly recommended for anyone looking to expand their strength-based skills to help in their youth advocacy work."

—Justin Allen
CASA/ CAPS GAL director, Elkhart County, Indiana

"If working with troubled kids has always baffled you, this book is the key to unlock its mysteries. Full of fresh ideas and practical interventions, it should be read by every youth-care practitioner."

—Dave Purpur
Director of Group Care
Knowles Centre, Winnipeg, MB

No Such Thing as a Bad Kid

Also by Charles D. Appelstein:

The Gus Chronicles I: Reflections from an Abused Kid
The Gus Chronicles II: Reflections from a Kid Who Has Been Abused

No Such Thing As a Bad Kid

Understanding and Responding to Kids with
Emotional & Behavioral Challenges
Using a Positive, Strength-Based Approach

CHARLES D. APPELSTEIN, MSW
FOREWORD BY ROBERT BROOKS, PhD

SOARING
WINGS
PRESS

Salem, New Hampshire

Published by:

SOARING WINGS PRESS

A division of ATR

12 Martin Avenue

Salem, NH 03079

www.charliea.com

Editor: Ellen Kleiner

Book design and production: Angela Werneke

Second Edition

PUBLISHER'S CATALOGING-IN-PUBLICATION DATA

Names: Appelstein, Charles D., author. | Brooks, Robert B., writer of foreword.

Title: No such thing as a bad kid : understanding and responding to kids with emotional and behavioral challenges using a positive, strength-based approach / Charles D. Appelstein, MSW ; foreword by Robert Brooks, PhD.

Description: Revised and updated edition. | Salem, New Hampshire : Soaring Wings Press, [2018] | Revision of the 1998 1st ed. (Weston, Mass. : Gifford School). | Includes bibliographical references and index. | Contents: Part I. Using a strength-based perspective to better understand kids with emotional and behavioral challenges — Part II. Preventing challenging behavior — Part III. Responding to challenging behavior.

Identifiers: ISBN: 978-0-9845897-4-6 (print) | 978-0-9845897-4-0 (eBook) | LCCN: 2017907605

Subjects: LCSH: Problem children--Education. | Problem children—Behavior modification. | Problem children--Counseling of. | Positive psychology. | Problem children—Discipline. | Success—Psychological aspects. | Child psychology. | Resilience (Personality trait) | Teacher-student relationships. | Classroom management. | Parents of problem children. | Child care workers. | Child development. | Social acceptance in children. | Parenting. | Self-esteem in children. | Psychic trauma in children. | Children and adults. | Child psychology--Methodology. | BISAC: EDUCATION / General.

Classification: LCC: LC4801 .A67 2018 | DDC: 371.93—dc23

1 3 5 7 9 10 8 6 4 2

For my mother, Tiby Appelstein . . .
I wish every kid could receive the kind of love,
humor, and warmth she has bestowed on me my entire life.
Thank you, Ma. This one's for you!

Acknowledgments

THIS BOOK IS A CULMINATION of forty years of work in the trenches with kids at risk. Along the way, numerous individuals have guided and inspired me, helping to not only shape my career but bring this book to life.

I would like to express particular thanks to Ellen Kenney, my first supervisor in residential care, whose wisdom, passion, and commitment to at-risk kids is ensconced in my brain. Also, special thanks to Bernard Levine, PhD, who opened up new worlds to a dubious social work intern; Dave Villiotti, a great professional, leader, and friend, who allowed me to spread my practice wings; my special friend Neil Pare, who proved that miracles can happen when you don't give up on a kid; my special friend Jill Hopkins, perhaps the most gifted child-care professional I've ever observed; Ed O'Brien, all my co-workers, and the kids at St. Ann's Home in Methuen, Massachusetts, which provided an invaluable foundation for my career; and the amazing kids and staff at New Hampshire's Nashua Children's Home—I will forever cherish my time there.

A huge, heartfelt thank you to Michael Bassichis, the former executive director of The Gifford School in Weston, Massachusetts. After hearing me speak almost twenty-five years ago, Mike convinced his board to fund the writing and publication of the original version of this book. I will be forever in his debt and grateful to his staff members Mandy Irwin and Barbara Selwyn for skillfully guiding me through the entire process.

I extend my thanks, as well, to Ellen Kleiner, my fabulous editor—a true wizard of words who consistently makes me sound smarter than I am—and to Angela Werneke, whose cover design is incredible and whose graphics enhance every page of this book. And a big, hearty thank you to Steve Baron, PsY, my clinical editor, without whom I could not have written this book. He was with me through every sentence, offering astute criticism and tremendous support. A rising, gifted, strength-based clinician and author, Steve is making his mark in this field.

And a very special thank you to Jessica Minahan. In my humble opinion, Jessica is one of the most gifted and brilliant experts on behavior analysis and management in our field. Her books are a must read, and this book was greatly enhanced when she agreed to write a section for chapter 14.

Many of the new techniques introduced in this revised and updated version are outgrowths of my work as a part-time behavior consultant for the Newton, Massachusetts, public schools. During my eighteen years in Newton I was fortunate to work for two very special educators, Mozelle Berkowitz, EdD, and Robin Fabiano, MEd, CAGS, who displayed an unwavering commitment to the district's most vulnerable students. Their passion, empathy, wisdom, and grit inspired me to step outside my comfort zone to explore new approaches for reaching students most at risk. Among the other gifted professionals in Newton whom I wish to thank are Joan Berk and Suzanne Flaherty, phenomenal educators whose support and friendship created an amazingly effective synergy. Ladies, I think we performed a little magic in that learning center!

I am incredibly grateful, as well, to Robert Brooks, PhD, who, for countless years, has been an inspiration to me and many others. He is a man whose brilliance is matched by his warmth. His support during the writing of this book was invaluable.

Last but not least, I extend love and a big family hug to my wife Cheryl and daughter Julie. Blessed to have them in my life, I am grateful to Cheryl for her unbridled compassion and for marrying me, and to Julie for her spirit, originality, and drive that energizes everyone around her—and also to my little canine pal Riley, whom I miss.

Contents

Part I

Using a Strength-Based Perspective to Better Understand Kids with Emotional and Behavioral Challenges

Part II

Preventing Challenging Behavior

Part III

Responding to Challenging Behavior

List of Figures

Chapter 17

Chapter 18

Chapter 19

Foreword

When I read the first edition of Charlie Appelstein's *No Such Thing as a Bad Kid*, I was flooded with thoughts. My first thought was: "I wish this book had been available early in my career as a clinical psychologist. Charlie is so insightful, open, informative, and creative. His strategies for working with challenging youth are practical and brilliant. How helpful they would have been to me."

My second thought was: "It is such a pleasure to read the words of someone who believes in identifying and reinforcing the strengths and beauty of children and teens rather than focusing on their deficits or faults. Charlie truly appreciates that if we are to touch the hearts and minds of challenging youth, while addressing their problems we must never lose sight of their strengths, or what I call their 'islands of competence.'"

My third thought was: "This book is an impressive resource to use in guiding our interactions not only with children dealing with emotional, cognitive, and behavioral struggles but with all children. It will be read and reread, continually adding insights into how we intervene with youngsters who have faced many adversities."

This revised and updated version of *No Such Thing as a Bad Kid* has me marveling at Charlie's skill in significantly enriching the content of the first edition by elaborating on the ideas and strategies presented, providing additional clinical vignettes, and injecting even more wisdom, humor, and empathy. As a result of his efforts, people he refers to as "child-guiders," whether they are novices or seasoned veterans in working with challenging youth, will surely gain from the views of this master clinician who so eloquently describes his journey, his doubts and setbacks, and his adherence to a strength-based approach promoting hope and resilience.

Reading this expanded edition of Charlie's impressive first book prompted me to reflect on my own career working with at-risk youth in the inner city of Boston, as principal of a school in a locked-door unit of a child and adolescent program in a psychiatric hospital, and as a therapist consulting with many children and their families. Over the course of my career I became increasingly interested in the concept of resilience, wondering: "What prevention and intervention measures can we adopt to help children and teens become more self-disciplined, responsible, caring, and hopeful in order to better cope with the many challenges they have faced and will continue to face?" I eventually shifted my focus from a so-called "medical model," with its emphasis on "fixing deficits" in individuals, to a perspective that emphasizes identifying and utilizing an individual's strengths in treatment and educational plans.

The shift to a strength-based perspective impacted all facets of my relationships with challenging youth, including my patterns of communication, my ability to be empathic, and my appreciation of their capabilities. I had realized that, as Charlie so eloquently says, "there is no such thing as a bad kid" but rather kids in such emotional pain and turmoil and, lacking sufficient inner controls, resorting to such impulsive, counterproductive, and self-defeating behaviors that they push away the very people attempting to help them.

Numerous studies seeking to identify the key ingredients necessary to nurture resilience in youngsters reveal that those who are resilient have at least one adult in their troubled lives who believes in and encourages them. The late psychologist Julius Segal referred to such individuals as "charismatic adults," defining them as "adults from whom children gather strength." Curious about what charismatic adults say and do to achieve that role, I often think back on my early interest in how particular theories guide the interventions clinicians use in interacting with patients. One of my most beneficial learning experiences as both a psychology trainee and a supervisor and training director came from observing actual clinical encounters through a one-way mirror. While I did not always agree with the interventions I observed—nor did people observing me always agree with my techniques—I learned a great deal from the ensuing discussions.

For me, Charlie's book is like an observation seminar, providing a first-hand account of the work of a gifted clinician. It articulates a theoretical framework for a successful strength-based approach; cites research findings supportive of those endeavors; and generously acknowledges the contributions of pioneers who played a significant part in formulating the approach. Especially illuminating are the book's numerous concrete examples of what one can actually say or do during interactions with challenging youth to cultivate trusting, therapeutic relationships. Not only do these clinical vignettes delineate what prompted Charlie to apply the interventions he used, but throughout he is refreshingly candid in detailing mistakes he may have made and what he learned from them.

It is as if Charlie has invited us into his world and given us an intimate view of all that we might accomplish as child-guiders. In the process, he has handed us some specific tools for replacing the suspiciousness, despair, self-defeating behaviors, and hopelessness of struggling youth with a sense of trust, optimism, and resilience. Charlie's deep respect for youngsters who face a myriad of problems, as well as for the child-guiders in their lives, is conveyed page after page through empathy, compassion, humility, and humor.

I applaud Charlie for all that he has accomplished in this new version of *No Such Thing as a Bad Kid*. The experience and insights he shares here, combined with his ability to express such breadth of knowledge in a reader-friendly fashion, earn him the laurels of "charismatic adult." I have no doubt this book will quickly become one of the most respected works in the child-care field.

Robert Brooks, PhD
Faculty, Harvard Medical School (part-time)
Coauthor of *Raising Resilient Children* and *The Power of Resilience*

Preface

I WAS COMMISSIONED TO WRITE the original edition of *No Such Thing as a Bad Kid* in the late 1990s by Mike Bassichis, the former executive director of the Gifford School of Weston, Massachusetts, who had attended one of my workshops and was enamored with the approach I taught. I am gratified and humbled to report that twenty years later the original edition still resonates with readers throughout the world. I recently posted a message on LinkedIn about my revision of the original edition and received the following reply from William Brill: "That book helped us take our program from 300 restraints a year to zero in six months. It's been restraint free for 10 years now. Thank you for your guidance!"

Over the years, I have received many similar messages and have witnessed equally impressive transformations in my own work with kids using the principles and techniques in this book. It's been a wonderful career. After all, nothing compares to the joy and satisfaction a child-guiding professional experiences when kids struggling to make it in life—perhaps for a long time having felt like giving up—turn the corner to better days. What I didn't know twenty years ago was that the approach that enthused Mike Bassichis, one that I have practiced almost instinctively from the first day I began working with kids, has a name: it's called "strength-based practice."

This revised and updated edition of *No Such Thing as a Bad Kid* defines what strength-based practice is and supports its usage with a plethora of evidence based on science and practice. Like the original edition, it was written to help educators and child-welfare professionals—child-guiders—who work with children and youth struggling with emotional and behavioral challenges to better understand and respond to those they serve. This book provides child-guiders with a strong relationship- and strength-based foundation for responding to kids with emotional and behavioral issues.

Child-guiders assisting kids with more serious behavioral issues who want to build on the knowledge presented, are advised to read *The Behavior Code* by Jessica Minahan and N. Rappaport and *The Behavior Code Companion: Strategies Tools and Interventions for Supporting Students with Anxiety-Related or Opposition Behaviors* by Jessica Minahan.

As in the first edition of *No Such Thing as a Bad Kid*, this edition often takes complex material and synthesizes it into user-friendly, easy-to-understand theories and techniques to help readers better comprehend how to respond to kids calling out for help. Also, more attention is devoted to understanding how various forms of abuse (sexual, physical, and neglect) affect the brain and why and how to respond using positive, trauma-informed, strength-based strategies. In the original edition, I presented a host of tools to help kids with emotional and behavioral challenges change their negative mindsets and improve their functioning. In this revised and updated edition, I include many more tools and a good deal of research and theory that explains why using a positive, strength-based approach is so effective.

The original edition was written for professionals on the front lines dealing with kids struggling with emotional and behavioral challenges, including teachers, parents, child and youth care workers, foster and adoptive parents, after-school workers, mentors, juvenile detention counselors, social workers, clinicians, and probation officers, and not specifically for parents facing the usual vicissitudes of child rearing. Over the years, however, many parents have benefited from the book, and I now conduct numerous workshops for them using much of the material in this edition. At first, I was somewhat surprised that the material in *No Such Thing as a Bad Kid* was being so well received by parents, but then I figured out it was at least partly because of the following principle: "The healthier a kid is, the more you can screw up with him; the more troubled he is, the more you've got to do it right." During evening workshops, I tell parents that if you've raised your kids in a pretty good way, they are wired properly, and they have a good sense of self, you can go home tonight and yell at them, unfairly punish them, or talk rudely to them and they'll be fine. They'll think: "Mom or Dad must have had a bad night. That workshop must have sucked." However, if a kid in foster care with a very fragile sense of self who is hypersensitive to power being misused against her is yelled at, unfairly punished, or verbally demeaned, she'll likely go ballistic and trash your house. The same adult behavior would bring about a radically different reaction because, given her history, the kid in foster care has little tolerance for adults who do not treat her in a respectful, fair, and compassionate way.

I began my career working with kids with serious trauma histories who acted out if they felt in any way mistreated. They forced us to develop interventions that were respectful, fair, positive, and energizing because such kids tolerate nothing less. Twenty years later I figured out that high-functioning kids also want to be guided in a respectful, fair, and energizing manner; and just because they will tolerate less is no reason to give them less.

Actually, I believe that if we treated all kids in the world as if they were seriously troubled kids they'd all be healthier and happier. From the day my daughter, now seventeen, was born, my wife and I have treated her as if she were an emotionally disturbed child and used techniques I would use with at-risk kids, including all the strength-based theories and tools presented in this book: We try not to yell. We use consequences instead of punishment. We establish routines. We normalize mistakes and failures. We try to say please and thank you every time we make a request. We are appropriately affectionate and use a lot of humor. We encourage her to help others, and we encourage her to pursue activities in which she is genuinely interested. As a result, she's on track for a good life and we're very proud of her.

Consequently, even though this revised edition is written for professionals who guide kids with emotional and behavioral challenges, many of the tools and theories described here work wonderfully with higher-functioning kids, and much of the material should also be of assistance to typical parents.

In sum, I hope this book will make child-guiders get up each day with an even greater passion for the work they do—and with an even larger toolbox. And I especially hope the book will help child-guiders decode the messages behind problem behavior and respond in ways that elevate children and youth to higher levels of functioning and happiness.

Introduction

I TRULY BELIEVE THERE IS no such thing as a bad kid, just bad luck and bad choices. If we label kids as bad, we're essentially giving up on them. We're not listening to the messages they are sending. Behavior is a message. When kids misbehave, they are sending a message loud and clear: "Help me." Of course, kids who commit horrific acts should be held accountable for their actions. But these are kids who made terrible choices, and they don't need to be labeled pejoratively.

The approach used in this book, called strength-based practice, is a positive and inspiring way of assisting kids struggling with emotional and behavioral challenges. In the initial chapters, the approach is defined and a plethora of cutting-edge research is presented that supports its effectiveness. The material in subsequent chapters serves as a solid foundation for understanding and responding to kids sending big messages. The many tools described have all been used successfully to reduce or eliminate problem behavior and enhance the functioning of kids struggling to succeed.

At the heart of this book is the need to change the way kids with emotional and behavioral challenges view themselves to promote their success. Many techniques presented involve altering negative mindsets, changing kids from the inside out to get them to believe in themselves, after which they often succeed.

The precursor to getting kids to believe in themselves is a trusting and inspiring adult-child relationship. One positive figure in the life of a vulnerable youth can produce amazing changes. Thus, although this is often promoted as a book about behavior management in reality it's about creating powerful relationships with kids. Sure, some kids with serious behavioral challenges need to learn skills that will help them navigate their lives better. But these kids will be more open to learning such skills if the adults teaching them know how to engage them and form strong connections.

With at-risk children, there are no quick fixes. To the contrary, these children require great patience, fortitude, sacrifice, and sustained caring. Because they want to believe in us, they often "test" us to see if we are worthy of their confidence, to make sure our actions support our words. When we stay true to our words, the children connect to us and grow stronger.

That is what happened with Al, a man I met many years ago. After spending a decade as a businessman, Al discovered that the corporate world did not jibe with who he really was. Making a radical change, he took a job at a residential school for at-risk kids. Two years into it he still loved the work and knew he had found his true calling. Around this time, Billy, an angry and resistant twelve-year-old, entered the program. One Friday afternoon Billy began acting out, whereupon Al kept him after school to work through the problem. When school let out, Billy refused to speak and continued to act in a rude and belligerent manner.

"Billy, I'm going to keep you here until we talk about what is going on with you," Al calmly asserted.

Billy scowled, laughed mockingly, then shot back, "Go ahead, keep me here. I live here, you idiot. You're the one who goes home at three o'clock. I'll keep you here all night!"

Al replied, "Billy, I love it here. Working with you guys is the best job in the world. I'm never going to leave. If I need to stay late tonight, that's okay. In fact, I've already called your unit, and they'll be sending your dinner down in an hour."

Billy grew silent. Soon afterward he began talking about his day and some of the pressure he was under.

Two years later Al was ready to leave the program. Used up and feeling as though he had nothing left to offer, he gave notice. On his last day on the job, Billy volunteered to help him move his things to the car. As they made their final trip to the parking lot, Billy suddenly looked him square in the eye and asked, "Do you remember that day a few years ago when you kept me after school?"

"Yes, I think so," Al replied.

"You said you loved this job and would never leave. Why are you leaving?" Billy insisted on knowing.

Al looked into Billy's eyes and saw heart-wrenching despair. After a few ponderous seconds, he announced, "Put all the stuff back in my office." As Billy asked his question, Al was given a rare glimpse into the soul of a despondent young man and heard his message: "Don't leave me, Al. I need you." Al stayed a few more years before moving on. He was able to see Billy graduate with a proud smile on his face, a bounce in his step, and a future of endless possibilities.

This story attests to the power of relationship. It reminds us of the degree to which kids with emotional and behavioral challenges want to believe in adults and of how critical it is to stay the course with them. It is easy to get angry at kids and act impulsively. It is equally easy to walk away from behaviors that push us away. Yet those behaviors are silent calls for help, and when child-guiders listen for the messages and stay in control of themselves they can transform lives. The following chapters offer many principles and tools that help child-guiders make a difference with children, especially those with emotional and behavioral challenges.

—— PART I ——

*Using a
Strength-Based Perspective
to Better Understand Kids
with Emotional and Behavioral
Challenges*

— CHAPTER 1 —

Understanding Challenging Behavior Using a Positive, Trauma-Informed, Strength-Based Perspective

WHEN WE WORK WITH or raise kids who struggle with ongoing emotional and behavioral challenges, the highs can be very high and the lows can gut us. However, if we stay the course and have the right mix of passion and skill, every now and then we experience a precious moment when we realize there's a young person standing in front of us who has recognized what we've known all along: he or she is one heckuva kid and is capable of accomplishing untold feats in life. To experience more of these priceless moments, it's critical for anyone who guides at-risk children and youth to first have a firm grasp of the origins of problem behavior. In this chapter and the next, we explore the roots of challenging behavior and explain an uplifting approach that can reshape troubled lives.

Behavior Is a Message

Caring professionals and parents often become exasperated with kids who chronically misbehave. It hurts when our best efforts fail to produce the behavioral changes we desire. Far too often comments like the following reverberate through the halls of schools, homes, and programs: "That kid enjoys being sent to the office; the secretary gives him candy and treats him nice," "He likes skipping school and smoking weed," "She got off on beating up that kid and was braggin' about it," and "She loves getting in my face and spewing crap at me."

In reality, the behaviors described probably provide a short-term respite from the ongoing stress, anger, and anxiety the kids experience, but they don't like what they're doing. This would be evident if we could inject a truth serum into any kid who chronically acts out and ask, while identifying a successful kid as a comparison, "Who would you rather be—you, the kid who is always acting out, or that kid, the one with many friends, a loving home life, lots of talents, and a great future ahead?" There isn't a challenging young person in the world who would pick the first option. Many such kids loathe their actions and, in fact, misbehave with the intent of getting the help they sorely need but, in many cases, can't ask for directly. Misbehavior is a message, a neon light flashing over a child's head signaling: "Something is wrong. I need help!"

Behaviorists believe kids act out to avoid a difficult situation or to get attention. It's true that misbehavior is their attempt to cope with an immediate need, but it is also generally symptomatic of the incessant hurt and pessimism that often pervade their lives. In my first book, *The Gus Chronicles: Reflections from an Abused Kid,* I created the character of a young teen named Gus Studelmeyer, who was a composite of all the kids with whom I had worked in residential care. I asked Gus to write about his life as a trauma victim. Early in the book Gus writes: "The kid who's pushing you away the most is probably the one who needs you the most."[1] This is a helpful line to think about when dealing with kids who push your buttons and are hard to engage. Behavior is a message, and the goal of a strength-based practitioner is to understand that good kids sometimes send harsh messages.

The hurt and pessimism that often pervades the lives of at-risk kids can originate from a number of sources, including psychological, neurological, social, and developmental. Therefore, effective child and youth care should focus on why such kids with endless potential possess such negative, self-defeating mindsets, and generate interventions and environments that inspire and revitalize their souls. And the way we do this is by adopting a strength-based perspective and approach.

Strength-based practice is an emerging approach to guiding children and youth, particularly those experiencing ongoing emotional and behavioral challenges, that is exceptionally positive and inspiring. Its focus is on building strength rather than fixing flaws—on what kids do right instead of what they do wrong. It begins with the belief that all young people are resilient, have or can develop strengths, and draw on past successes to make good decisions and enhance functioning and happiness.

More specifically, strength-based practice is about two things: *attitude* and *action*. It begins with the uplifting attitude a professional presents to an at-risk young person or group, which conveys the message "I believe in you. And, although I know the road won't always be easy, I'm convinced you will succeed and am thrilled to be part of your life." Subsequently, every action a professional takes—everything he says or does—with an at-risk child or group needs to be an extension of this critical affirmation.

Let's examine three major reasons why believing in at-risk kids is so important.

Believing Cultivates Positive Relationships

The first reason for believing in at-risk kids is that it cultivates positive relationships that make kids happier, prompting enhanced functioning. When at-risk kids know there are child-guiders in their lives who truly believe in them and are excited to see them every day, it makes them feel good. And when they feel good *due to the sustenance of a positive relationship*, they are more likely to behave well. Later in this chapter we will present neurological evidence that ties positive emotions to enhanced functioning.

James Garbarino, PhD, one of the world's preeminent youth-care authors, told a group of a thousand professionals in Las Vegas: "We can now predict with almost 100 percent certainty whether a youth with a history of aggression prior to entering high school, will commit another act of aggression while he or she is at the school. If that student can wake up every day knowing there is at least one adult at the school who 'thinks I'm terrific,' the odds of this student acting aggressively drop to about zero."[2] Garbarino speaks to the power of a positive relationship to transform a child's life.

As a part-time behavior consultant to a number of school systems over an eighteen-year period, I've worked with roughly 250 very challenging yet wonderful kids, some incredibly difficult to engage. I would like to believe that every one of them woke up every day thinking, "Mr. A can't wait to see me. I must be his favorite kid." Was that true? No. Yet I always tried my best to approach all 250 with the enthusiasm expressed in the following exchange:

"My man, it's great to see you. Slap me five!"

"I don't want to meet with you today, Mr. A!"

"C'mon, let's play some soccer, bro!"

If you're currently working with at-risk kids, ask yourself this question: Does every one of them wake up every day thinking you think they're terrific? If the answer is no, find out what you can do to improve your relationships.

The child- and youth-guiding field is replete with research and wisdom that emphasize the importance of positive relationships to kids' success. Rick Miller, the founder of Kids at Hope (KidsatHope.com), in his seminal book *Youth Development: From the Trenches* cites a plethora of interdisciplinary research that supports the transformative power of strong adult-child connections. In summing up his findings, he notes a number of essential truths, the following being the most critical:

- Children who succeed seem to do so when they have people in their lives who believe they can succeed.

- Children who succeed have meaningful relationships with caring adults.[3]

Miller also mentions the work of researcher Emmy E. Werner, who followed a group of students from 1955 to 1985 and reported, "Resilient children had at least one person who unconditionally accepted them as they were."[4]

Edward Hallowell, MD, one of the world's leading experts on understanding and responding to kids with attention deficit disorder (ADD), writes about the power of positive adult-child connections in helping kids with ADD: "While medication makes the biggest difference immediately, as time goes by other factors come significantly into play, including the skill and knowledge of the doctor providing treatment, as well as the positivity of the connections in the life of a child. It is time for all of us to take the force of connection in life far more seriously than we have."[5]

The power of positive adult-child connections is also reflected in the following anecdote. Ruth, one of the most difficult teenagers with whom I've ever worked, lived at a group home run my friend Jill. Cognitively challenged and a trauma victim, Ruth was prone to explosive outbursts and verbal tirades. Yet no matter how extreme she acted, Jill remained loving and supportive to this vulnerable adolescent. We all worried about how Ruth would fare after she left our treatment setting. After being discharged, Ruth bounced from program to program, but as she entered adulthood she settled into a comfortable life at an assisted-living facility and has been relatively happy for over thirty years. Since 1983 she has placed a phone call to Jill every week. Jill and Jim, another of my heroes, take Ruth out for her birthday each year.

Believing Confronts Self-Doubt

The second reason for believing in at-risk kids is that it confronts their self-doubt. Kids with emotional and behavioral issues often struggle with self-doubt. Years ago, I saw a movie on TV about Degas, the great French impressionist whose paintings of ballerinas hang in many prominent museums. In the movie Degas, while counseling a young ballerina who was obviously struggling with her confidence, remarked, "Self-doubt kills ability!"[6] Randall S. Sprick, who writes invaluable books on classroom management, believes a major reason students misbehave in school is because they don't believe they can do the work.[7]

Strength-based practitioners believe every young person has untold potential but will not develop their abilities if they are riddled with self-doubt. When such practitioners hold this belief so deeply that they focus on kids' strengths instead of their weaknesses, create environments offering ample success opportunities, trumpet accomplishments and normalize mistakes and occasional failures, teach kids new skills, and change their self-defeating thought processes, self-doubting kids start to believe in themselves. When we employ a positive, strength-based approach and create living and learning environments that are in sync with kids' strengths and challenges, we begin to erase the debilitating insecurity with which so many at-risk kids struggle and we see significant changes in self-confidence, initiative, and performance.

Self-doubt is widely known to compromise a person's ability. In many cases, the self-doubt and accompanying behavioral issues are due to kids not being properly diagnosed or responded to. I've worked as a part-time behavior consultant in numerous schools over the past twenty years. I'd be rich if I had a nickel for every time I was asked to help a student acting out who was later diagnosed with ADHD, a learning disability, sensory integration issues, Asperger's syndrome, or an anxiety disorder—each riddled with self-doubt.

Additionally, too many kids who struggle with emotional and behavioral issues are trauma victims who have experienced some degree of sexual, physical, or emotional abuse, significantly impacting every facet of their lives, including their self-confidence, initiative, and creativity. In their article "The Resilient Brain," Larry K. Brendtro and James E. Longhurst suggest that the brain is like a library, continually storing information. When I first read this, I immediately imagined kids with trauma histories as having library wings filled with pain, shame, and humiliation in the lower regions of their brains, which Brendtro and Longhurst call the survival brain. So filled were they with these emotions that they could not deal with any more of them, just as library wings filled to the brim with books cannot take on one more. Citing the work of Bruce Perry, who has found that children traumatized by neglect and abuse overuse this part of the brain, Brendtro and Longhurst state that due to the children's fears regarding safety, "their survival brains are chronically stimulated and they are at high risk of engaging in behaviors which hurt themselves or others."[8] The phrase "fear, fight, or flight" is often used to describe the reaction of abuse victims when feeling threatened and thinking. "What if I'm hurt? What if I'm embarrassed, feeling ashamed? I can't handle any more of that. All I can do is react."

Brendtro and Longhurst further explain that kids who have suffered trauma don't properly utilize the higher regions of their brains, called the emotional and logical brains, which involve more advanced thought processes such a problem-solving, creativity, ingenuity, perspective, tolerance, and empathy. "Many of these youngsters have not had the nurturance and learning experiences to fully develop brain pathways for self-control. Thus their heightened impulsivity, frustration, and motor hyperactivity combine with an underdeveloped capacity to accurately perceive situations and problem solve. This unfortunate combination severely limits the child's ability to maximize his or her potential."[9]

As a result, when we ask a young person who has incurred abuse to try a difficult assignment, speak up in class, get a job, go to therapy, or sign up for a sport, often they act out or refuse due to self-doubt and fear of failure, saying such things as "That's stupid!" "I hate basketball," "I don't want to do that," "I don't want to work there! It's dumb!" They think: "What if I fail? What if I stumble? What if I don't know what to do? I could be embarrassed, humiliated, shamed—and I don't have any more room in that wing as it's already bursting at the seams! No, I ain't doing that!" Reactions like this come directly from the survival brain, which is on alert 24/7.

When I first read Brendtro and Longhurst's article, I couldn't help but think about my experience going on Safari in Tanzania years before. Occasionally we'd approach a herd of elephants spread over acres of land. Some herds, sensing danger, given prior traumatic experiences with humans, would rapidly form a tight circle with the parents on the perimeter and their young safely protected in the middle, behavior triggered by a hyper-vigilant survival brain (see figure 1–1). Such elephants might even die protecting their young in this way rather than moving along existing pathways to higher regions of the jungle to find water holes they desperately need for hydration or a new food supply. Given their history, they stay in the lower regions of the jungle, overly concerned with safety. Similarly, many trauma victims, due to their incessant fears, will not properly access their more highly evolved emotional and logical brains, which help with critical thinking, perspective, and problem-solving. That's the bad news.

Here's the good news: while on safari, every now and then we'd come across a herd of elephants that would not quickly form a protective circle but would continue to roam new and existing pathways because they had pos-

Figure 1–1

Elephant Circle

itive memories of humans. "Hey, guys, the humans are back! They like us. Treat us well." Likewise, new neural pathways can be created in humans to enhance functioning. Brendtro and Longhurst write: "Neuroplasticity refers to the reality that the brain is malleable and can therefore change through-out its existence. Positive and frequently occurring experiences can create new neural pathways that enhance functioning and produce growth."[10] Bingo! Consequently, when kids who have suffered trauma function in settings with adults who are positive, safe, respectful, and energizing—strength-based— neural pathways to richer lives are opened, and their troubled lives are trans-formed.

Shannon, Simone, and Rhonda lived at a residential program for ado-lescents with abuse histories. Each was more than capable of holding a part-time job in the community. But no matter how hard the staff encouraged them the girls wouldn't pick up job applications. They were called lazy by some; others felt they preferred the daily activities of the program. But Candace, the unit director, knew their histories and surmised that the girls felt working in the community and getting accustomed to a cash register would cause them fear, anxiety, and shame—feelings that were intolerable. So she did two things. First, she invited some managers from a local restaurant that was hiring to brunch one Sunday morning, during which they explained the job to the girls, answered their questions, and assuaged their fears. Afterward, Candace told each one, "Okay, you've met the managers. The job sounds cool. You each can do it. You know that. So if any or all of you fill out the application, go for the interview, get hired, and work one week, I'll give you a fifty-dollar gift certificate to any clothing store in town." All the girls ended up working at the upscale restaurant; and Shannon, having worked there for over fifteen years, is now one of their most valued employees and has become the first member of her family to own a house.

Believing Generates Hope

The third reason for believing in at-risk kids is that knowing there are adults in their lives who believe in them generates hope. Hope is humanity's fuel. Without fuel, even a Mercedes-Benz parked in your driveway would go nowhere. Strength-based practitioners believe every challenging kid is a Mercedes-Benz—a talented individual creature—whose fuel gauge is on or near empty. They are not broken down, dysfunctional kids who need to be fixed. If we think they are, then they think so, too, and won't travel far. Instead, they are more often amazing kids who simply lack the sustenance of hope.

Rolodex Imagery. When most of us go to bed at night, as we toss and turn trying to fall asleep we flip through a Rolodex of cards creating images in our heads.

FIRST CARD: Friends.

"Hey, we're seeing Bruce and Carmalita on Saturday night. That'll be fun. I wonder if he's still working at the shop."

NEXT CARD: Money.

"Our finances are a bit tight right now. But my job is safe, and I should get a bump up in the spring. Not so bad. Better than most."

NEXT CARD: Family.

"My daughter is sixteen. She can only be a teenager for three more years. We can do anything for three years."

And then we slowly drift off to sleep.

But bedtime is often dreaded by kids who have suffered any form of trauma because at nightfall suddenly all stimulation ceases and they're left alone with the terrible thoughts and feelings that still haunt their psyches. Kids with adverse histories will stay up all night listening to music, doing drugs, or playing video games to avoid going to bed. Yet if and when they make it to bed and flip through their Rolodex cards the images they see are very different.

FIRST CARD: Friends.

"Shit, I don't have any friends!"

I've asked more than five hundred thousand educators and child-care professionals over the past twenty years, "Have you ever worked with a troubled kid who had a best friend, a meaningful, reciprocal relationship with another kid?" Rarely does a hand go up. Often the source of problem behavior is loneliness resulting from a lack of meaningful friendships.

In chapter 5, we will explore in more depth why at-risk kids often have trouble making and sustaining friendships and what to do about it. The quick and easy answer is that such kids are often too egocentric, a behavior necessary to their survival. The message of a kid who is overly self-centered is: "I've learned I can't trust others and can better take care of myself."

I periodically ask workshop attendees, "Have you ever worked with a troubled kid who was not overly egocentric?" Rarely does a hand go up. Yet it's a mistake to criticize these kids for their self-centered ways. The egocentrism they display isn't self-love; it's usually self-protection.

Who wants to make friends with a kid who lacks empathy and is self-absorbed? If we don't help these kids learn friendship skills earlier in their lives, the ramifications are often dire. Young people who enter adolescence too self-absorbed, lonely, and dispirited are at greater risk of cutting themselves, joining gangs, getting pregnant, bullying, having sexual relations with random partners, abusing drugs and alcohol, and even getting weapons and killing—anything to express or avoid facing the loneliness and estrangement they frequently endure.

People are sometimes shocked by the number of school shootings that occur annually. Frankly, I'm shocked that we don't see more given the vast number of kids who lack meaningful friendships, and the anger and mental deterioration as a result.

A few years ago I had a brief stopover at LaGuardia Airport in New York. I picked up the New York Times and read the following passage from an article on school shootings: "When Mark Barden considers Adam Lanza, the young man who murdered Barden's 7-year-old son and 25 others in the Sandy Hook massacre, he is struck by what he calls 'a sad parallel.' In his short life, Daniel made a habit of seeking out and befriending youngsters he spotted sitting alone, a virtue his teachers praised at Sandy Hook Elementary.

"'The young boy that killed my son was the little boy that sat alone,' said Mr. Barden with rueful certainty. 'Maybe if there was a little Daniel Barden that came along in his growing up, perhaps things could be different.'"[11]

Kids with adverse histories are also likely to respond differently to the other Rolodex cards.

SECOND CARD: School.

"School sucks. I've got all these learning disabilities, and the vice principal hates my guts. Damn, I've got to get up in four hours to catch the bus."

THIRD CARD: Family.

"Man, I haven't seen my father in a year, and my mother might be using again. And I don't know where the hell we'll be living next month."

Strength-based practice is about caring adults positively altering the experience for kids deprived of hope and giving them incentives to enthusiastically rise in the morning, as reflected in the following Rolodex response: "Wow. I love Doris, my foster mother. I beat her in chess today, and she got real pissed off. She said no one beats her in chess—particularly a kid.

She said she was a chess champion at her college and has written books on the subject. She said I must be a forty-seven-year-old midget and chess master from Russia hiding out in her home. I love this lady! Oh, and she said something nice about my father today. No one ever says anything good about him. Most of the time I hear, 'Keep it up and you'll end up just like your father.' Doris said, 'I never met your dad. But I know all dads love their kids, though sometimes life gets in the way and they have trouble showing it. I bet a day doesn't go by that he doesn't wish he could have been there for you.' Oh, and she told me today that when I'm a successful video game designer I've got to come back and buy her a car—a convertible. I love this woman. She makes me feel like a million bucks!"

Doris has pumped twenty gallons of fuel, or hope, in this young man, making it more likely he will work harder at school, control his anger, engage in difficult endeavors, and succeed in life. Hope is about the future, and at-risk kids are often so consumed with the here and now that they can't envision a positive life down the road, and so they desperately need people to talk about the wonderful possibilities that lie ahead.

Envisioning the Future. James Garbarino has stated that "terminal thinking," the inability to envision one's future, may be a clue to why some children succeed while others fail.[12] And Rick Miller, founder of Kids at Hope, believes, according to his extensive research, that for children to be successful they must be able to talk about the future in four domains: home and family; education and career; community and service; and hobbies and recreation. When we talk about the future with at-risk kids in positive terms, we make any desired outcome more possible, as reflected in the following story.

Todd was a challenging adolescent at a special education high school. He came to school every day with a big chip on his shoulder and was often merciless toward his teacher, Mary. Stubborn, rude, and defiant, he knew how to get under an adult's skin. But Mary understood that underneath Todd's bravado was a scared, insecure kid desperate for adult nurturance, support, and guidance. No matter how terrible he acted, she consistently responded to him in a warm and encouraging manner—always reminding him of his talents and the positive future that lay ahead for him. She would send him from the room from time to time but in a respectful manner, and always greet him the next day with a big smile. Shortly after Todd graduated from the school, he began calling Mary on a semi-regular basis because he needed to hear her voice. Two or three years after graduating, Todd called with exciting news, saying, "Hey, Mary, my landscaping company signed a twenty-thousand-dollar contract with a big client today. Can you believe it?"

She replied, "Oh, Todd! That's fantastic news. I'm so proud of you. I always knew you'd be successful!"

There was a long pause at the other end of the line, then Todd said, "Yeah, that's why I've been calling you all these years."

Hope is humanity's fuel.

Positive Emotions and the Brain

Brain research has added irrefutable evidence about why a positive, strength-based approach is so effective in work with kids struggling with emotional and behavioral issues. Shawn Achor, a Harvard professor and author of the landmark book *The Happiness Advantage*, cites empirical evidence that points to the transformative effects of a positive, strength-based modality:

> New research in psychology and neuroscience finds: "We become more successful when we are happier and more positive. Students primed to feel happy before taking math achievement tests far outperform their neutral peers. It turns out our brains are literally hardwired to perform at their best not when they are negative or even neutral, but when they are positive. . . ." Recent research shows that the broadening effect (how positive emotions broaden the amount of possibilities we process, making us more thoughtful, creative, and open to new ideas), is actually biological. Positive emotions flood our brains with dopamine and serotonin, chemicals that not only make us feel good but dial up the learning centers of our brains to higher levels. Positive emotions help humans to organize new information, keep that information in the brain longer, and retrieve it faster later on. And they en-

able us to make and sustain more neural connections, which allows us to think more quickly and creatively, become more skilled at complex analysis and problem solving, and see and invent new ways of doing things. Brain change, once thought impossible, is now a well-known fact, one that is supported by some of the most rigorous and cutting-edge research in neuroscience.[13]

This is irrefutable evidence that when kids are happier they function better.

A few years ago I was flying from Boston to San Francisco and reading Rick Miller's book *Youth Development*, in which he questions why schools can't be happy places. I laughed and immediately conjured up some of the lovably irascible teachers I'd dealt with over the years who had said such things as: "Schools aren't supposed to be happy places. They're places to learn. We work students hard. We're not their friends. Be nice to them and they'll walk all over you!"

But why *can't* schools be happy places? A happy place doesn't need to be a setting where expectations are lowered and limits aren't established. Surely, whether a place is happy depends partly on the attitudes and communication found there. For example, there is a huge difference between the directive "Go to the office! I'm tired of dealing with you!" and "Could you please head to the office. I'm uncomfortable with the choices you're making. We'll talk about this later. Thanks."

Achor, like many experts before him, cites two factors that all happy people have in common: meaningful social connections and strong social support networks.[14] To assess a client's level of support according to these criteria, child-guiders, when first working with a kid or family, could use the ecological tool shown in figure 1–2.

Each area of this "eco map" is a potential source of strong support for a kid or family and, when missing, can have obvious consequences. In particular, kids with emotional and behavioral challenges often lack friends, do not have hobbies or play sports, do not have jobs (if they are teens), do not have a mentor, have conflicted family relationships, do not volunteer to help others, and so forth. An effective child-guider will rate each area from -3 (serious

Figure 1–2
Eco Map for Rating Kids' and Families' Level of Support

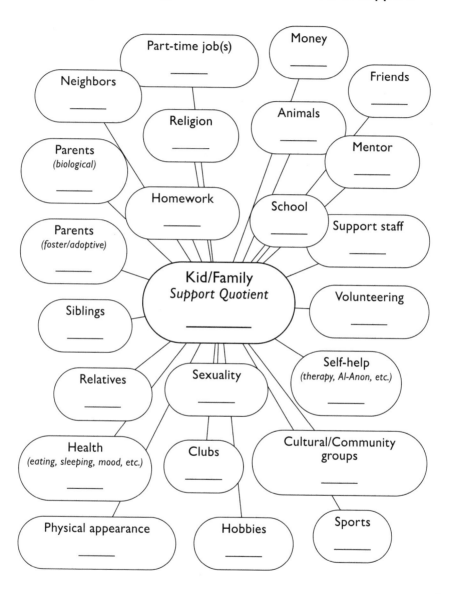

SUPPORT CONTINUUM

-3   0   +3
Serious lack of support   *Strong support*

lack of support) to +3 (strong support), tabulate the scores to arrive at a support quotient, and plan ways to improve each area with a score of less than +3. Every area in which the score is ultimately raised increases the odds for the client's improved happiness and higher functioning.

A few years ago I was working with a spirited fifth grader, Bart, who was being returned to his mainstream classroom from a self-contained setting. Early on I assessed his eco map and immediately began to increase his levels of support. I was assigned to see him once a week, which allowed me to give him a +3 for the mentor category. During our first meeting, I asked him what he wanted to be when he grew up. He replied, "A professional wrestler or a kindergarten teacher." Within minutes I had arranged with the school's kindergarten teacher to let Bart volunteer once or twice a week, and it turned out that the kids loved him. Every time he entered the room they'd yell out, "Bart!" And after scanning the room he'd shout, "If you got to do it—" And they'd yell back, "Just hop to it!" This experience significantly boosted his self-esteem and positive connections throughout the school. Further, Bart couldn't throw a football very well, so I taught him to throw a mean spiral, which raised the sports score on his eco map. He didn't have a lot of friends, so every now and then we'd invite kids to join us. I kept a line of communication open with his parents, sustaining a good number in that area. I also taught him self-talk—"Step after step, that's the prep; make a list—it will assist"—to help with his functioning issues, raising his school support number. All year we sang:

> I'm a mainstream guy. This year I'm gonna fly!
> I'm a mainstream guy. This year I'm gonna fly!
> Learning is my ticket to a really good life
> It's going to get me a job . . . and a really cute wife!

Increasing Bart's level of support eliminated the need for incentive charts or other similar tools. We got him feeling happy, and he did the rest.

In his book *Residential Treatment*, Michael Durant states that the goal of his residential setting is to have each youth leave feeling better about herself. The logic is simple: if kids leave with a more positive self-image, they're more likely to develop their strengths to make better choices in life.[15] Part II of this book addresses methods for transforming environments such as schools, homes, and programs into happier places while maintaining high standards for behavior and performance.

*** Reality Check ***

Employing a positive, strength-based approach doesn't mean ignoring the unpleasant realities of situations and circumstances. Gabrielle Oettingen, a psychology professor at New York University and the University of Hamburg, and the author of *Rethinking Positive Thinking*, writes: "Positive thinking is pleasurable, but that doesn't mean it's good for us. Like so much in life, attaining goals requires a balanced and moderate approach, neither dwelling on the downsides nor a forced jumping for joy."[16]

She recommends the process of "mental contrasting," explaining: "Think of a wish. For a few minutes, imagine the wish coming true, letting your mind wander and drift where it will. Then shift gears. Spend a few minutes imagining the obstacles that stand in the way of realizing your wish."[17] If we apply her research to Rick Miller's findings (To be successful, kids must be able to articulate their futures in four domains), as well as to Garborino's conclusions (Terminal thinking, the inability to articulate a positive future, might be a clue to why some kids make it and some don't), then imagine a dialogue between a teacher and student based on these views, we get:

TEACHER: What do you want to be when you grow up?

STUDENT: A video-game designer.

TEACHER: Hey, that's cool. Will you work for a big company or will you start your own?

STUDENT: I'll start my own.

TEACHER: Well, that's going to take a lot of work, won't it? You'll have to take some challenging courses in college. And you'll need to arrange financing.

STUDENT: Yeah.

TEACHER: There will be a lot of ups and downs, but I think you can do it. I'll buy your first game!

STUDENT: Thanks!

Current research on trauma and the brain not only emphasizes the importance of employing a positive, safe, and empowering approach with children struggling with emotional and behavioral challenges but suggests that encouraging them to think positively about their futures, which we now know is critical to individual success, will produce even greater results if we simultaneously present the challenges they will face on the road to meeting their goals.

Andrew Denholm, a teacher from Falkirk, Scotland, related the following story, which attests to the incredible power of positivity and hope:

> I saw your post on Facebook and thought I would share a story from sunny Falkirk. I attended your training in Falkirk last spring and have subsequently changed my whole approach to behavior management. I am now reviewing and implementing a whole-school, strength-based system to build positive relationships and change the culture of our school in a very deprived area of Falkirk.
>
> My real success story has been my class this year. I was asked to move from p2 (six-year-olds) to p5/6 (ten- to eleven-year-olds) to deal with the pupils that others had been struggling with. One boy in particular, Angus, spent his entire year out of class and had every agency look at him as he was off the wall. I read his psychologist's report and didn't know where to begin. He didn't work well in groups, wouldn't read out loud, and refused to do division in math. He suffered from sore heads due to stress and refused to work. I think you get the picture.
>
> Before the summer holidays, I went up to him and all of his troubled classmates and said, "I picked you. I want to be your teacher." They couldn't believe it! I subsequently put a positive system in place, greeting them every day with a big morning smile! Always saying

please and thank you! Never raising my voice. Externalizing their behaviors! I built great relationships with all of them. And now the pupil
with all the difficulties, Angus, is transformed. I reviewed his psychologist's report and realized he is now doing everything she had said he
would not do. He now loves division in math, has won the class award
twice. And what moved me the most occurred on parents' night. His
teary-eyed mother took me aside and said, "I now have a happy boy,
and that's amazing."

Is it?

The Impact of Acting

Based on the incredible impact one strength-based practitioner or parent
can have on a child or group, like Andrew from Falkirk or my buddy Jill
from Massachusetts, it's clear that for adults to be successful with at-risk
kids they must be great actors. Teachers, parents, and other child-welfare
professionals should start every interaction with challenging kids looking
like they are excited to see them: "Good morning, ladies and gentleman!
I am thrilled to see all of you and excited to begin the day! Let's go, my
friends!" When adults begin every interaction in such a manner, they send
an important message: "I'm excited to be around you, and I know you are
capable of doing great things."

From a neurological perspective, presenting in a positive manner opens
up pathways in kids' brains, triggering biochemical reactions that enhance
performance. Psychologically, it instills hope, inspiring thoughts like "This
lady really looks forward to seeing me. I must be special to her and capable
of doing good things."

When actors perform, they can be in a bad mood, but when the lights
dim and the curtain opens they play their roles. And parents and professionals who guide at-risk kids are far more important than actors. While actors entertain people for a few hours, the central figures in challenging kids'
worlds are trying to save lives. Consider the following scenarios, which illustrate the impact of a central figure in a challenging kid's life acting versus
not acting.

SIMPLETON ELEMENTARY SCHOOL *8:13 a.m. (before her students arrive)*

"Mrs. Jones, this is the secretary. Billy Strathmore won't be in today. He's sick."

Mrs. Jones switches off the intercom, raises a clenched fist to the sky, and says, "Yes! That kid drives me nuts. That's a bad kid! Oh baby, a day without Billy. We're gonna get some work done today!"

Eighteen minutes later, Billy strolls into class and explains, "I'm feeling better. My mother made me come."

Honest reaction

MRS. JONES: What? You're here! Ah, for crying out loud. Look, we just started math, and I know you hate it. Go disrupt one of the groups. Don't wait. Let's get it over with.

Positive, strength-based reaction (acting)

MRS. JONES: Billy, my man, slap me five. I thought you were out today. This is great. You got here just in time for math. Hey, I've added a new math sheet to your folder. I made some of the changes we talked about. I know you can get this one done. Just take it one problem at a time.

Billy gets it done.

Interestingly, minutes after faking a good mood one's mood often changes for the better. I remember years ago driving through Colorado and listening to pianist and composer John Tesh on the radio talking about moods and science. He reported a study showing that when people fake a smile the act actually produces a chemical change in the brain that makes them happier.

I've often encountered a kid or group while in a lousy mood yet faked being in a great mood, and minutes later I thought to myself, "Hey, you're having fun!"

Years ago an attendee at one of my workshops asked me a question that led to a revealing dialogue.

ATTENDEE: You seem to be really pumped up about this training. How do we know you're not faking it?

CHARLIE: If I'm doing my job correctly, you should have no clue whether I'm genuinely excited about being here today or whether this is my fifth full-day training in a row and I can't wait to get home.

ATTENDEE: But can't kids tell if you're faking a positive attitude? They don't want phonies in their lives.

CHARLIE: Sure they can—which means you need to be a great actor. Of course, if someone close to you dies the night before and you actually come in the next morning, you can't be expected to be bubbly. But, in general, you should start every interaction looking like you care and want to be with the kids or family members you're guiding. Now let me ask you a question: Do you think there's a big difference between the most troubled kid you work with and any one of us in this room?

ATTENDEE: Maybe.

CHARLIE: I don't think so. Say you were being wheeled into open-heart surgery tomorrow, and minutes before they put you under, your surgeon approaches and says: "Excuse me, Mr. Mathis, I'd like to be honest with you before I cut your heart open. I'm kind of in a bad mood this morning. I was working all night on a research paper, and my computer was freezing up so I didn't get a lot of sleep. And then this morning, while I was driving in my broker told me I lost ten thousand dollars on IBM. I told the sucker no tech stocks! So I'm pissed, tired, and irritable, but I can still operate on your heart this morning." Are you going to say, "Cut, doctor?"

ATTENDEE: No!

CHARLIE: Now you might be thinking: "What a ridiculous analogy, comparing open-heart surgery to what I do every day with kids." And I would agree. Because what you do every day with your kids is far more important than the surgery. Your heart will be a piece of meat on slab to this doctor two weeks from now. But the kids you're currently working with will only be ten, fourteen, sixteen years old on October twenty-third one day in their lives, and they are running out of time. If you choose to start a class, an interaction, a phone call with anything less than an I'm-thrilled-to-be-around-you attitude, you take away a little bit of the probability of that kid, parent, or group having a good day.

This dialogue emphasizes how, in reality, working with or raising at-risk kids is, to a great extent, about one thing: probability. The better we do, the better they'll do. There are no guarantees in the child-guiding world. At the end of every day, when I play my day over in my head, I never judge my success based on the behavior of the challenging kids I was working with that day. Sure, I like it when the kids improve their behavior. In fact, if they didn't I'd lose my job. But the first questions I ask every night are: Did I treat every kid in a positive, uplifting manner? Did I use the strength-based strategies I teach? And if I screwed up did I apologize? If I can answer yes to each question, I know I increased the odds that tomorrow will be a better day for the kids whose lives I touched.

By the way, I'm not saying that if a kid spits on your face your reply should be: "Hey, great aim! You got me dead center on the cheek." Instead, the appropriate response would be: "I'm angry about the choice you just made. Could you please chill out on the bench. In a little while we'll discuss what just happened." In other words, show controlled anger at the choice not the child.

The Power of Passion

As a former program director at a midsize residential program, I hired numerous child-care workers over the years. In interviews, I had basic questions that I would ask potential employees, but I usually knew within minutes of speaking with someone if I was going to hire the person. My criteria had nothing to do with age, gender, size, skin color, or experience. I was looking for only one thing: passion. Give me the twenty-year-old who is bouncing off her chair and can't wait to shoot hoops with the kids over the twenty-eight-year-old with six years of experience who seems burned out, since, while I can teach technique, I can't teach passion.

Near the end of the movie *Serendipity,* after one person makes a life-altering decision to follow his dreams his best buddy utters these words: "You know, the Greeks didn't write obituaries. They only asked one question after a man died: 'Did he have passion?'"[18]

In 1979, Neil was the unit director of a twelve-bed group of latency-age boys at a large East Coast residential treatment setting, while I was the activities director. Early in the year, Carl, a severely traumatized ten-year-old, was admitted to the program. Carl had endured an unfathomable amount of sexual, physical, and emotional abuse in his life. Right away his behavior was out of control. He would openly masturbate, smear his feces, defy all requests, and gaze at kids and adults with a bizarre affect. During his first few months, he was physically restrained multiple hours every day. Initially, he was placed on the short-term unit on the top floor of our building. But after three months it was decided that he needed to be transferred to one of our long-term units. After careful deliberation, he was assigned to Neil's unit. Neil, one of the most hardworking, passionate, and dedicated youth-care professionals I'd ever met, had a strength-based perspective, and the kids he worked with all knew this and loved him for it. Neil treated his kids as if there were nothing wrong with them, literally using his passion and demeanor to will kids into behaving well and maximizing their talents; and he started every interaction with a "you can do this" attitude. Yet I didn't think Carl would succeed with Neil, believing Carl was too damaged and needed a more sophisticated therapeutic treatment setting.

So what did Neil do with this feces-smearing, masturbating, out-of-control, defiant young man? He immediately placed a big apron over Carl's head and put him in charge of the kitchen, telling Carl that he was going to cook every meal and clean up afterward. Early on I'd sometimes hear a scream coming from their unit. Carl would be trying to run from the little, square-shaped kitchen, yelling, "I ain't gonna clean this fucking kitchen! You can't make me!" Neil would place his big frame in the doorway to stop him and say calmly, "Carl, you will clean this kitchen. It's going to look great, and I'll be here to help. Let's go."

A few months after Carl arrived on Neil's unit my job at the agency got very busy, and I temporarily lost track of them. Then one day when I visited right before dinner I observed all the kids and Neil on couches watching TV about ten feet from the kitchen. Apron-clad Carl was inside diligently preparing the meal. A few minutes later the phone rang, and Neil, a husky man with a distinctive walk, got up and answered it. Two minutes later I observed Carl walking from the kitchen to the TV stand to check *TV Guide* for shows that night. I did a double-take when I saw he was walking exactly like Neil. I then entered the kitchen to talk with him briefly, which he didn't seem to enjoy, given how busy he was. "Okay, good-bye," he said, mimicking a funny habit Neil had of blurting out these same words midway through a conversation. I realized that Carl had become Neil. In thirty-eight years of work, I had never witnessed such an amazing success story. I heard later through the grapevine that Carl made it, and wondered if he became a cook.

— CHAPTER 2 —

Misbehavior
A Coded Message

CHAPTER 1 DESCRIBED the importance of viewing behavior through a positive, strength-based lens and described this modality from a number of perspectives. In this chapter, we examine in greater depth the notion that misbehavior is always a coded message.

Some years ago I was driving along Elm Street, a heavily traveled road, with my twelve-year-old passenger Andy, a resident at a treatment center for at-risk youth. Before coming to the center, Andy had been severely abused by his parents. His behavior was described as provocative, rude, wild, and aggressive. He trusted no one. As the social work intern assigned to Andy, I was taking him out for his fourth therapy session. Our first three sessions had gone well, though he had tested me a bit. Even so, I liked him; he had spunk. With each session, it had become easier to see through his tough facade. I sensed a lonely and hurting boy underneath, someone longing to connect but fearful of relationships.

As we passed a busy intersection, Andy began rummaging through my glove compartment. Inside was a stack of bills I had just paid, neatly wrapped in an elastic band and ready to be mailed. I tried to stay calm while he removed the elastic band.

"Hey, Andy," I said with as much composure as I could muster, "why don't you put those back. They're just crummy old bills."

Ignoring me, he studied the sealed envelopes in his hands, then glanced out the side window and asked with a provocative glint in his eyes, "What would you do if I threw these out the window?"

My mind flooded with the consequences I would administer. "Throw those out the window and we won't be driving together for a l-o-n-g time!"

I imagined saying to him. A moment later I silently added, "Because you'll be grounded for a month!"

"Get control of yourself," a familiar inner voice chimed in my head. "What you say will make a difference." I took a deep breath, analyzed the situation, and changed my tune. "Andy," I explained, "you're my friend, and I don't think you would do such a thing."

He stared at me for a while, looked at the letters, then quietly returned them to the glove compartment. I started to breathe again. We never discussed the incident. As far as I could tell, he forgot about it. Yet I never did, for I could see that beneath Andy's bravado was a kid seeking to connect and needing to test our relationship.

Looking beyond Behavior

Children like Andy, who push our buttons, are usually attempting to tell us, "Something isn't right. I need help!" But when we've just been verbally assaulted or asked to picture our bills flying one by one out the car window, anger and frustration surge to the fore, temporarily overriding any inclination we may have had to decode the underlying message. When our buttons are pushed, the natural tendency is to focus our attention on what the child did and what should be done about it rather than on why a good kid would make such a bad decision. In the incident with Andy, his threat to toss the bills out the window was symptomatic of a deeper issue. Andy lacked trust in adults and wanted to know if I would turn on him like his parents had.

To grasp the difference between symptoms and core issues, imagine an athlete who has torn the cartilage in his knee and is experiencing pain. A strong painkiller may temporarily ease the situation, but it will not remedy the underlying problem. The pain is a symptom—a message that something is wrong. If the athlete's doctor treats only the symptom, the condition may worsen. Good treatment entails both appropriate symptom management (pain relief) and sophisticated problem resolution (surgery). Disciplining children without considering the cause of their problematic behavior is like dispensing medication to people without searching for the cause of their symptoms. If a problem is significant, symptom management alone will not be enough. Andy, for one, needed more than behavioral limits; he needed to know he could count on me not to hurt him.

Decoding the Message

To get to the root of troubling behavior, we must decode its underlying message, as in the following scenario. Linda, an elementary school art teacher, was having a tough time holding the attention of her fourth-grade class. Tommy, a defiant student seated at the back of the room, kept disrupting the others. When Linda stopped to think about the boy behind the behavior, she realized that Tommy had trouble drawing as well as the other students, never seemed satisfied with his work, and appeared to have low self-esteem. The message behind his unruly behavior was: "I can't draw like the other kids, and I'm sick and tired of being the worst at everything. Help me!"

Consequently, to improve his chances of succeeding, Linda decided to let him tackle less-complicated projects while she privately helped him expand his drawing skills. At the start of each class, she presented her students with the exercise for the day, inviting Tommy to choose from a number of simpler ones. Over time he stopped acting out. By the end of the year, he was able to work on the same projects as his classmates, with satisfactory results.

In addition to modifying the work and encouraging Tommy to practice his art skills, Linda also worked on Tommy's thinking, knowing that kids often misbehave because of the negative way they perceive themselves or a situation. Linda helped Tommy replace his faulty thinking, suggesting he get more pumped about the *effort* he was putting forth than the *end result*. She told him, "Tommy, it takes courage to try things we're not good at, and you're one courageous kid." She explained that all kids have strengths and weaknesses and that to live a happier life it's really helpful to see challenges as opportunities for learning something new. She then relayed some of the challenges she had faced in school, normalizing this dynamic for Tommy.

It was also essential to decode the misbehavior of Mary, a young teenager with a traumatic history of mistreatment who had recently been placed at a residential treatment center. Socially immature, she was incessantly ridiculed by her public school classmates and would often return to the center in tears. Mary wanted desperately to switch schools and attend a local special education facility with some of the other residents. The staff agreed that the change would make sense. Weeks later, while the paperwork was still in process, Mary's therapist, Eileen, reported a serious problem: Mary was running away in the middle of their psychotherapy sessions. Eileen suspected that from Mary's perspective the staff had not acted quickly enough, and that she was turning her back on her therapist in much the same way that she felt the staff had turned its back on her. When confronted with this interpretation of events, Mary acknowledged that she was indeed running away because her request to change schools had not initially been taken seriously. Eileen relayed this message to the administrators, who more promptly arranged for Mary's transfer. Assured that her needs were being addressed, Mary stopped running from her therapy sessions.

In both these scenarios, the adults in charge were able to decode the message behind the misbehavior. As a result, they addressed the issue troubling each child and arrived at a helpful course of action. While decoding such messages it is important to remember that a message indicating something isn't right does not necessarily imply that the adults in charge are doing something wrong. Neither Tommy's disrespect nor Mary's escapes reflected on the actions of the adults in charge, who were merely the people interested enough in unraveling the triggers for the disruptive actions.

Sometimes the trigger for problem behavior is neurological or physical. Children with attention deficit hyperactivity disorder (ADHD), learning disabilities, autism spectrum disorder, visual or hearing impairments, sensory integration issues, or other organic difficulties frequently act out—in part to call attention to their complex conditions, which usually require more sophisticated treatment, including an intense skill-building regimen. Years ago while counseling a fifth grader who was constantly misbehaving, I taught her self-management skills, modified her work, and enhanced her peer relations, but nothing worked. Then I learned that she wasn't eating breakfast and couldn't afford lunch so was starving throughout the day. To address the physical problem, I quickly arranged to have food supplied, and her behavior improved dramatically.

Temperament, too, can play a role in misbehavior. Many children who are temperamentally mismatched with their parents, such as an active child born to reserved parents, resort to problematic behavior when they are asked to act in ways that do not mesh with their personalities. The message behind this behavior is usually: "Treat me as I am, not as you want me to be." Nancy Rose, author of *Raise the Child You've Got—Not the One You Want*, encourages parents to love and accept the core self of each of their children.[1] To accept the child they have, many parents first need to mourn the loss of the child they fantasized about having.

The same holds true for professionals. For example, a highly active child might be harder to guide for a professional who is more subdued. Therefore, to successfully guide the children and youth they support, professionals must continually assess how their "wiring" correlates with that of the youngsters.

Interestingly, some acting out that occurs is developmentally appropriate. Perfectly adjusted teens, for example, will do things that drive us crazy—that's adolescence. Understanding normal development and the deviations that occur among troubled youngsters can help us identify the roots of problem behavior. (For further insights into developmental factors, see chapter 5).

The bottom line: Every kid is unique, and the causes of problem behavior can have multiple sources. For some kids it is the environment, and their behavior problems diminish dramatically when a new, optimistic, strength-based adult or team enters their lives. Other kids struggle due to physical or neurological issues. Most often the cause of problem behavior is psychological: something has happened in a youth's life that has him stuck, and to move forward the issue needs to be addressed, if not resolved. Dynamics such as peer pressure, sexuality, family dynamics, and trauma can all be the source of misbehavior. This is why kids, particularly those with emotional and behavioral issues, need adults who listen to them and respond to their needs. This is why play, group, duo, or individual psychotherapy can be so helpful for conflicted young people.

Years ago I was asked to work with a challenging nine-year-old whose divorced parents were constantly fighting and placing him in the middle. Rewards, consequences, skill-building, additional attention…no approach was going to help him activate his strengths until his parents worked through their tensions, which, with our help, they did, allowing him to soon shine.

Whether you are decoding a message or trying to understand its origins, it is important to avoid hasty interpretations. For one thing, children hate pat explanations of their actions. For another, you may be wildly off base. In either case, jumping to conclusions can hinder the growth of your relationships with children.

The person who taught me to beware of quick interpretations was Elroy, a thirteen-year-old who was referred to the court clinic for counseling. His mother reported that six months prior an older relative named Gene had been tragically killed. He had lived in the boy's home, and the two had developed a strong attachment. Initially, Elroy had shown little response to Gene's death, but then he began to show signs of depression.

Elroy and I met for weekly therapy sessions to help him through his delayed grief reaction. For the first nine months of our twelve-month program, he felt too uncomfortable to open up. Then he let down his guard and began to cry for his lost buddy. The more he grieved, the more his depression lifted. From time to time, I would end our session by inviting Elroy, with his mother's permission, to join me for an ice cream cone—my treat. Every time I asked, however, he politely declined. "The kid isn't ready for intimacy," I thought to myself. "I'm a nurturing male figure, and being with me reminds him of Gene, so I shouldn't push it. Man, do I have this kid pegged."

In our eleventh month of therapy, after considerable work on his part to deal with Gene's death, I again asked Elroy to join me for a cone. I thought for sure he would agree to celebrate the triumphant culmination of our work together. But again he politely refused. "What gives?" I wondered. "I know this kid. In the past, his refusal was a message: 'I'm not ready to handle the intimacy.' But now he should be ready. Haven't we worked through the grief issue enough?" Perplexed, I began to have self-doubts about Elroy's course of therapy.

During our next-to-last session, no longer able to stand the suspense I asked Elroy why he refused to join me for a cone, although I should not have put my needs before his and should have had more respect for his boundaries.

"You're dressed a lot better than me," he calmly replied. "I'd be embarrassed going out there with you." The following week, I chucked the button-down shirt and tie, and we enjoyed a few scoops of ice cream together.

The moral of this story: Continue to decode the message of behavior until you're sure about what has triggered it. The more sensitive you are to why the child is acting out, the more effective your response will be. In the end, although good and timely symptom management is essential, long-term success in diminishing troubling behaviors is more likely when the underlying issues are properly understood and addressed.

— CHAPTER 3 —

Responding versus Reacting and the Importance of Managing Number One First

THE MOST IMPORTANT PERSON in any interaction between an adult and a child or group is the adult. If the adult doesn't act properly, the kids are in trouble. And adults don't always act in the best interests of kids. At workshops, I ask the following question: "Have any of you ever spent or worked an entire day with kids, particularly those with emotional and behavioral issues, and not made a mistake with one or more of them?" People laugh, and no hand ever goes up.

Making Mistakes When Faced with Challenging Behavior

When we make a mistake with a kid or group, we're using basic tools in nonproductive ways. I believe there are two major reasons parents and professionals have trouble managing their actions in the face of challenging behavior: negative behavior is taken personally and lack of support causes adults to act in punitive ways. Both factors, once acknowledged, can be rectified with hard work and dedication.

Taking It Personally

Over the years, I've heard many professionals proclaim, "I don't take it personally when kids misbehave." I don't believe them. I think we all take it personally. It's called being human. The day I don't take troublesome behavior personally is the day I leave this business because it's probably the first day I won't feel energized if a challenging kid takes a step in the right direction.

At least two major dynamics occur when we personalize a difficult situation with a child or group: our self-image is damaged and our self-esteem is injured, prompting us not to respond to the situation but to react to it and do things that are not in the best interests of the kids.

Self-Image Damage. We all have multiple self-images, such as the image of the good son or daughter, the competent worker, or the good parent, and sometimes troublesome situations negatively affect these self-images.

The most important thing in my life, other than my family, is my self-image as the "good kid guy." I've spent my entire adult life helping at-risk kids and those who guide them. I would rather lose all my money than have evidence come in that I was no longer good with kids. When I'm struggling to turn around a kid, school, or program, I often get down on myself because my image of the good kid guy is being called into question. People who lose their jobs often struggle to function appropriately because their image of being the "good worker and provider" has been eviscerated.

People who have endured unhappy childhoods might go a lifetime trying to be the good son or daughter to gain the love and affection of an estranged or deceased parent. They may copy the behavior of the parent to get psychologically closer to that person, sometimes unconsciously. For example, if a woman's mother was a yeller and the two never saw eye to eye, the woman may become a yeller to be like her, thinking "I'm a good daughter because I'm just like my mother." Or an individual might act in a way that contrasts with a parent. For example, if a man's dad was a tyrant, the man might swear never to raise his voice or be tough with kids and thereby hold on to the self-image of the avenging son.

Sometimes the self-images we harbor get in the way of the work we do. For example, a calm, laid-back foster parent who suffered abuse as a child might become the avenging daughter, promising herself to never treat kids in a similar, dehumanizing manner. However, if her supervisor comments, "Margaret, the kids are walking all over you. You've got to set some limits," she is likely to resist the advice because she has an avenging daughter self-image.

Years ago I was consulting at a children's psychiatric hospital in New York. One of the head nurses got very upset when I suggested that the patients be allowed to call staff members by their first names preceded by "Mr." or "Ms.," believing that such informal communication would be disrespectful. I then conducted a workshop on self-management and brought up the issue of multiple self-images. At lunch, she took me aside and said, "Charlie, that was my father giving you a hard time this morning. I was being the good daughter. He was always a highly formal man. I kind of like the idea of being called Ms. Becky. I think this will help improve our relationships with the kids."

I can only recall one time when I was seriously admonished by my boss while working as an activities director at a large residential center. He got mad at me for using my own money with the kids, and I was defensive. Months later, I had this revelation: "Man, I was being my father. He was always the big spender whether he had money or not." By imitating my father's behavior, I felt closer to him and was being the good son.

People who guide at-risk kids should start every interaction with a clean slate. All personal baggage should be checked at the door if it's going to interfere with the way the work should be done. In *My Grandfather's Blessings,* Rachel Naomi Remen, MD, advises people who work as helpers to feel blessed about being in a position to positively impact those in need rather than being consumed with the end result. Early in her career, she received a gift bracelet from a therapist that had one word engraved on it: *clear.* When she asked her therapist why she had chosen that word, she was told to look it up in a big dictionary and found that it had more than sixty meanings, many of which had to do with freedom, such as being free from obstruction, free from guilt, and free from blame. She states: "And, of course, its ultimate meaning…is 'able to serve perfectly in the passage of light.' Sometimes it takes a lifetime to become clear. No matter. It may be the most worthwhile way to spend the time."[1]

The average residential youth-care worker in America remains in this rewarding but debilitating job around three to six months. People don't quit because of the hours or the pay, both of which they know about before they begin. I sense, and have experienced as a former program director, that many rookie staff members leave because of what the job does to their self-image. They enter the field with an image of themselves as wonderful people, only to leave days or weeks later thinking: "Guess I wasn't cut out for this. I hate two of these kids, and three can't stand me. I'm making a lot of mistakes. I'm not sleeping. I'm experiencing really crazy feelings. Maybe I need a different kind of job?" This scenario breaks my heart.

Kids who demonstrate extreme behaviors, as do many of the kids who reside in residential treatment centers and other similar settings, often evoke difficult feelings in staff members who guide them, particularly inexperienced ones. I tell workshop attendees who guide seriously troubled kids: "Every feeling you experience is okay to harbor. You are still the good, kind person with great potential despite what you might be temporarily feeling toward a child or group. Learn from your feelings—they are diagnostic."

I often list the following feelings and emotions that I'm convinced are normal to experience while working with seriously troubled children and youth: anger, frustration, indifference, disgust, guilt, sexual arousal, worry, fear, and annoyance. I then ask, "Do you believe any of these emotions would be inappropriate to feel toward a youth you are working with?"

I often hear, "Yes, sexual arousal."

Sadly, many kids who have been sexually abused multiple times navigate their lives in constant fear of it happening again yet, in fact, often set up such situations so they will be in control when it might happen. Rick, twenty-two, began working at a group home for adolescent girls who had all experienced sexual abuse. Carla, a very attractive seventeen-year-old resident, was somewhat attracted to Rick but also terrified that he would rape her and anxious because she felt she had no control over when the abuse might occur. So to gain control of this situation, she became flirtatious toward Rick. She unbuttoned the top of her shirt and came on to him in a subtly sexual manner. Rick had no history of abusing children, but he was also human and a sexual being. It would be okay for him to experience a fleeting sexual feeling. But it would not be okay for him to act on it; if he did, he would be prosecuted to the full extent of the law.

In this example, Carla portrayed counterphobic behavior. She was deathly afraid of being raped again, so she set up a scenario in which that very thing could happen to gain control of it. Rick should be trained to expect counterphobic behavior, so that if and when he experiences it he will not regard any fleeting sexual feeling as a sign of deviance or incompetence on his part. He should be advised to normalize his feelings, maintain appropriate boundaries with kids like Carla, and inform his supervisor whenever sexualized behavior is exhibited. In this way such kids can be helped to deal with the sexual confusion they harbor and learn that some men (and women) can be trusted.

Familiar utterances in the youth-serving arena that often reflect counterphobic behavior are: "Go ahead, send me to the office. I don't care!" "Drop to my level, asshole! Do you think I care?" What these individuals are really saying is: "You're such a loose cannon, I just assume you're going to drop to my level. You get really punitive when you get mad at us, and I can see you're getting really ticked, so let's just get it over with." Parents and professionals who raise or work with at-risk kids should become aware of how, as child-guiders, they can trigger counterphobic reactions if they do not consistently and properly control their tone and behavior.

Self-Esteem Injury. Self-image issues invariablyly compromise effective youth-guiding practice. However, when it comes to taking things personally, the number-one culprit is self-esteem injury. Adults often react instead of respond to problem behavior after their self-esteem has been injured.

It's critical to understand that self-esteem is fragile in all of us, even when it's positive. A mother could be having the best day of her life when a friend comments: "Rhonda, what happened to you? You looked so good before. You've gained a lot of weight, eh? And those wrinkles!" Poor Rhonda is toast. She goes home and grounds her kid for six months for blowing his nose loudly.

Given the fact that self-esteem is fragile in all of us, people who raise or work with challenging kids have one of the most difficult tasks in the universe because during a typical day they will suffer multiple hits to their self-esteem: a good talk does nothing to change a problem behavior; a kid or group is rude; a kid runs away; students sleep during class; kids are out of control; a kid who has been doing really well suffers a serious regression; students don't do their homework. And when adults' self-esteem is injured they will too often react to the offending person or situation—by yelling, threatening, punishing, demeaning, pulling way, or using sarcasm—instead of responding to it. Thus parents and professionals who work with challenging kids must develop an observing ego (see figure 3–1) that guides them to use appropriate language and actions. An observing ego, once developed, allows them to view situations from a broader, more objective perspective. That perspective permits them to respond in helpful ways rather than react in a self-defensive manner that can be hurtful, as reflected in the following scenario.

A youth tells a juvenile justice counselor named Reggie to F off. Reggie thinks: "I'm ticked! I can't stand that punk. He just embarrassed me in front of all of the other kids and staff. Man, I'd like to drop his sorry level!"

But Reggie's observing ego advises: "Reggie, stay cool, brother. All feelings are normal. Remember, behavior is a message. He's a good kid. Try to decipher his message later. Right now you're suffering a self-esteem injury. Remember: *It's an injury, and it will heal.* One hour from now you'll barely remember this. *Respond instead of react.*"

Earlier in this chapter, responding instead of reacting was defined as giving an appropriate, measured response. In reality, responding instead of reacting means to use the golden rule. We have a horrible double standard in our society that dictates adults can say or do things to kids that they would never tolerate themselves. Do adults like being yelled at, bossed around, ridiculed, punished, told what to do without a please or thank you or having rules, appointments, rooms, or medications changed on them without their say—things that adults do to kids every day? After any interaction an adult has with a kid or group, he should ask himself, "Would I have wanted someone to say or do that to me?" And if the answer is no he should apologize and vow not to act in this manner again.

Figure 3–1
The Observing Ego

Strategies for keeping your cool:

1. Remember that lack of support leads to punitive actions, and don't go there. Think: "I can do anything for ninety more minutes."

2. Visualize yourself walking to your car (or going to bed) at the end of this brutal day with a big smile on your face, thinking: "I did a good job staying cool throughout the day. I responded instead of reacted most of the time."

3. Think about tomorrow, reminding yourself: "If I respond instead of react to the end of the shift, my relationships will grow stronger and the job will get easier."

4. Think about a MASH unit, telling yourself: "When I'm at my worst, I need to give it my best!"

5. Don't succumb to the dark side. Think: "Use the Force, Luke!"

Remember the Golden Rule: Don't say or do anything to a kid or group that you wouldn't want said or done to you.

I find it helpful to calibrate the healing time of each self-esteem injury. If I'm working with a kid who won't follow a particular direction, I think: "In three minutes, this injury will heal. It's no big deal. Respond instead of react."

If the principal of a school for which I'm providing weekly consultation criticizes me, I think: "This is a big injury. It will take about four days to heal. Respond instead of react."

If my teenage daughter puts me down by saying something like, "Dad, no one says *dungarees* anymore!" I think: "I do, and if that makes me old-fashioned so what. Respond instead of react."

The important thing to remember is that all self-esteem injuries heal in time, though some may take longer than others. Keeping this in mind makes it easier to respond instead of react.

Lack of Support Causes Punitive Actions

Despite the enormity of self-esteem injury influencing adult behavior, I believe the primary reason parents and professionals react instead of respond to children with problem behavior is lack of support. James Whittaker and James Garbarino edited an enlightening book in the 1980s titled *Social Support Networks*, in which they identify how important support is to proper functioning and well-being, and how lack of support can have deleterious repercussions in the child-guiding arena, often leading to punitive actions.[2]

During workshops I often ask the following question: "How many of you believe that you receive the right amount of daily support at home or your workplace, such as breaks, training, praise, money, and feedback?" People shake their heads, and no hand is ever raised.

I continue: "Don't blame your school or agency. They're probably doing the best they can with the funds they're allotted. It's society's fault. We don't value kids enough to appropriately fund the schools and programs that shape kids' lives. Every one of you should receive more pay, training, empowerment, and feedback. You're given enough support to enjoy your jobs and make a difference, but not nearly enough to keep you from displacing your lack of support onto the kids you guide. Therefore, if you believe that lack of support leads to punitive actions every one of you is at risk to be punitive throughout your day—and often is.

"Let me show you how this works. Five hours into a God-awful, brutal day with the kids you guide, what are you leaning toward: (A) If that kid does it one more time, I'm gonna— or (B) What can I do to make sure these kids go home with big smiles on their faces? I love them so much."

People always answer, "A."

Then I ask, "Does the reason you answered A have anything to do with the difficult behavior of the kids you're working with?"

Most answer, "Yes!"

I respond: "No. Their behavior has nothing to do with your behavior. At McDonald's you expect to see hamburgers. When you raise or work with kids who have emotional and behavioral challenges, you should expect to see acting out. Becoming upset with their behavior is analogous to walking into McDonald's and screaming, 'What! You're serving burgers!' When you inappropriately raise your voice toward a kid or group near the end of a hard shift, you're pretty much yelling at burgers. Are there any behaviors your kids present that aren't expected? No. The primary reason you are more likely to react instead of respond as a rough day progresses is lack of support. If starting tomorrow you were assigned an assistant—a warm, gifted person who did nothing but follow you around all day giving you training tips, breaks, praise, encouragement, and snacks—the odds that you would act out toward the kids as a day wound down would be very low. So here's the sixty-four-thousand-dollar question: 'Is it your kids' fault that you don't receive enough support?' No. Yet you take it out on them every day."

Comments typically heard in most child- and youth-guiding schools or programs as a day winds down are the following: "I'm tired and don't want to hear it," "I've been on my feet all day—not now," and "It's been a long day, so this isn't the time to push my buttons!" Such comments are like those of people getting mad at burgers in McDonald's.

I suggest the following five self-talk strategies to help undersupported parents and professionals avoid reacting instead of responding as a rough day winds down.

1. **Think about the principle "lack of support leads to punitive actions," and resist reacting.**

   Think: "I can do anything for four more hours. It's not the kids' fault that I don't get enough support, and it's really not the fault of my employer. This is the job I chose." Think: "I have the audacity to compare my life to the lives of kids I'm working with? Some of them don't know where they're going to live next month, some haven't seen a parent in years, some are impoverished and I'm feeling bad for myself because I was up all night with my own kid and am exhausted? Stop it. I can do anything for—Hey, just two more hours."

2. **Think about your drive home or when you go to bed.**

   Think: "I always play my day over in my head as I drive home and when I go to sleep. Am I going to feel guilty as I review my day because I shortchanged some of the kids today, lost my cool too often, blew off a kid who needed my help? Or am I going to feel incredibly content knowing that despite my fatigue I gave every kid my best shot. I did it pretty good—not perfect, perhaps, but good enough to make a difference."

3. **Think about the future—tomorrow, next week, next month.**

   Think: "This job is never about today. It's always about the future. The better I respond today, the higher the probability that my kids will do better tomorrow and in the future. And I always want the job to get easier. If I yell, threaten, blow some kids off, react too frequently, the job will probably be more difficult tomorrow and in the future since kids tend to retaliate against those who misuse power."

4. Think of a MASH unit (a mobile, surgical, mini-hospital to attend to the wounded that used to be situated near the front lines of a war).

Think: "If the two lead surgeons, Hawkeye and BJ, operated twenty straight hours and began to trudge back to their tent when unexpectedly a helicopter came flying over the mountains with a wounded soldier who would require six hours of surgery to save his leg, would they claim to be too tired to do the surgery? No, they would wheel that brave young man into the operating room and save his leg. That's what separates a great child-guider from a mediocre one. Professionals and parents should garner tremendous pride from being able to give kids their best when they are at their worst."

5. Think about the Force, Luke!

Think: "Lack of support can cause me to act punitively toward the kids. It's like I have Darth Vader following me around all day, saying, 'Go ahead. Yell at that kid, ground him, keep him after school. You can do it.' It's like I'm being sucked to the dark side as every minute passes. But instead, when I feel the urge to react instead of respond, I need to listen to the voice of Obi-Wan Kanobe saying: 'Use the Force, Luke. The Force is always with you. Respond instead of react.'"

Enhancing Support

Although most parents and professionals who guide at-risk kids do not receive adequate support (training, breaks, praise and encouragement, proper pay, and so forth), the status quo should never be accepted. Child-guiding adults must continually search for ways to change their work environments and home situations to garner more support.

Shawn Achor writes that the key to happiness is meaningful support and strong social support networks. Change occurs on two levels, micro and macro. Micro-level changes are smaller-scale changes that can often be easily enacted. Macro-level interventions relate to systemic change. Adults should always be attempting to enhance support on both levels.

Examples

Micro-level change: Greet kids with a big smile every day.

Macro-level change: Start a mentor program at your school or agency.

The change process can be slow and frustrating, but the kids we serve need our best every day. Stressed child-guiders might think: "Why work so hard? This place doesn't care about its employees! We haven't had a raise in three years!" The answer to this question is: "It's not the kids' fault that a raise hasn't come. Besides, they're counting on us." As a former program director of a midsize residential setting, I felt my number-one job was to make my staff happy. I believed that if I enhanced their support they would be much more likely to function better as professionals, and the approach worked.

An Eco Map for Rating One's Own Level of Support

The following eco map (similar to the version that appears on page 45) is a valuable tool to help parents and professionals assess their level of support in various areas of their lives (see figure 3–2). Just as child-guiders were asked to rate the levels of support for the kids and families in their care, they should rate their own levels of support using the same scoring system. For example, if a child-guider has a bunch of good friends but is not seeing them very often due to work and family responsibilities, she might rate the friends' area 1. If she is going bankrupt, she would rate the finances area -3.

Rate each area, creating additional relevant ones and deleting irrelevant ones, as needed, then tabulate the results. Add the minuses together, add the plusses, and then subtract the minus total from the plus total. For instance, if your totals are -7 and +24, the support quotient to enter would be 18. If in six months you rate the areas on your eco map again and the total is 9, it means you lost 50 percent of your support, placing you at much greater risk of reacting instead of responding to the kids and families you guide. Lack of support causes child-guiders to act more punitively; therefore, parents and professionals must continually look for ways to improve their support numbers. If your job becomes increasingly stressful, begin

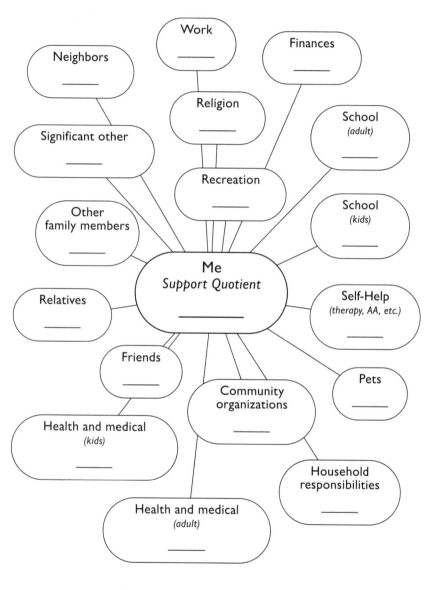

Figure 3–2
Eco Map for Rating One's Own Level of Support

Work
_____

Finances
_____

Neighbors
_____

Religion
_____

Significant other
_____

School
(adult)
_____

Recreation
_____

Other
family members
_____

School
(kids)
_____

Me
Support Quotient
_____

Relatives
_____

Self-Help
(therapy, AA, etc.)
_____

Friends
_____

Pets
_____

Community
organizations
_____

Health and medical
(kids)
_____

Household
responsibilities
_____

Health and medical
(adult)
_____

SUPPORT CONTINUUM

-3   0   +3
Serious lack of support   *Strong support*

adding support in other areas, such as engaging more with neighbors, relatives, and friends; exercising; or taking up a hobby.

It's easy to blame a parent who abuses a child, and indeed such parents should be held accountable for their actions. But instead of blaming, consider how many good decisions you would make if you were being evicted from your apartment, had serious medical problems, a substance abuse issue, a history of trauma, fractured family relationships, and no friends. Increase support for these folks and you can transform lives.

First, however, when working in settings that do not provide you with sufficient support, you must enhance your own support networks so you can respond rather than react to situations. Only by taking care of number one first can you effectively guide others.

The Motivation to Stay the Course

We've seen how typical child-guiders, on a daily basis, experience very difficult feelings, personalize interactions, and lack sufficient support, which can lead to punitive actions. So where's the motivation to stay the course? The image of the house shown in figure 3–3 is what motivates me and many others to maintain enthusiasm for guiding children, particularly those with ongoing emotional and behavioral issues.

The first three years of life, including the prenatal period, are the most important years of existence. If they don't go well enough—if kids don't bond with their parents and receive appropriate developmental care—they are at risk the rest of their lives for serious neurological and psychological challenges. The first three years of an individual's life are like the foundation of a house. If a large house was constructed on a weak foundation, many problems would occur, such as windows popping out and beams cracking, all symptoms of the more serious problem of a foundation with missing bricks.

Feelings of frustration and uselessness often arise when we fool ourselves into thinking that positive interactions, such as a good heart-to-heart talk, will significantly alter a troubled child's life, only to find the child acting out the very next day. The reality is that a good talk or other positive interaction is critically important, for it helps strengthen the child's sense of

Figure 3–3
Enhancing Foundations

A well-fortified
foundation

self and places a brick in her foundation. However, a child who has a weak foundation, resulting in rocky attachments and little sense of trust, is not about to change overnight. Stabilizing a shaky foundation is often a long, laborious process involving positive interactions that occur repeatedly. There are no quick fixes for children who have experienced inadequate care in their first three years of life.

Shifting our perspective from symptom management to bricklaying can go a long way toward reducing our frustration level and preventing feelings of failure, and it can help us feel wonderful about each caring intervention we provide, large or small, knowing it is making a difference. For instance, imagine a new kid entering your classroom, group home, or juvenile justice center—a sad, angry, oppositional child having only 1,243 of the necessary 3,000 bricks because, for a myriad of reasons, she did not receive the good enough care she required. Your job will be to provide what she still longs for by making her feel special, helping her form meaningful attachments, giving her lots of attention, guiding her as she works through her issues, teaching her self-management skills, greeting her with a big smile every day, slapping her five, setting reasonable limits, and responding instead of reacting to her—that is, using positive, strength-based approaches to help strengthen her foundation. As a result, she may leave your care with 1,789 bricks in place, a lot stronger and in a much better position to be all she can be in the world.

Although we may not see the immediate effects of our labor—children tend to continue acting out until their brains fully mature—we can know in our hearts that the bricks we have set in place will never be dislodged and that the more bricks we have furnished, the more we have increased the child's chances of having a better life. Many of my longtime colleagues and I receive calls and emails from people we knew more than thirty years ago when they were severely traumatized kids living at the residential center where we worked. Although they had major behavioral issues at the time, we nevertheless loved and nurtured them. Every time I hear from one thanking me profusely for the love and guidance we provided, I hang up the phone or turn off the computer, look at my wife, and say, "Guess we put in a few more bricks than I thought." At such moments, I think to myself, "Why would anyone have a job that doesn't give them the opportunity to pick up a phone and hear, 'If it weren't for you, I wouldn't be the person I have become. Thank you.'"

Bricklaying is a hard job when it's freezing cold or unbearably hot and humid. But how does it feel six months after agonizing over a difficult-to-install foundation? Doesn't the bricklayer return with his family, gaze upon the house, and comment, "See that beautiful house? It wouldn't be there if it wasn't for me." All the pain and tedious actions that were required to set the foundation will be forgotten, replaced by a feeling of pride and satisfaction for a job well done.

At the end of every night when I play the day over in my head, I never judge my day based on the behavior of the kids I was working with. Sure, I like it when they behave well. Heck, I'd probably lose my job as a behavioral consultant if their behavior didn't improve. But that's not how I judge myself. I ask myself every night: "Did I behave well? Did I make every kid whose life I touched today feel special? Did I use the strength-based strategies in a pretty good way? If I screwed up, did I apologize?" And if the answers are yes I go to bed a happy guy, knowing I put in some bricks that will be with these kids forever.

— CHAPTER 4 —

Relating Empathically

EMPATHY HELPS US SEE PAST NEGATIVE BEHAVIORS and feel for the kids. Would we be upset with a disruptive child if we knew he had observed domestic violence the night before, was being bullied unmercifully, or had an undetected learning disability that made it impossible to do his work without modifications? Probably not. We would most likely respond *empathically* to his situation. As important as it is to be in touch with our own emotions, to be effective at child-guiding we need to empathize with the kids we guide and, if only for a moment, walk in their shoes. In effect, any time a child begins to raise our blood pressure, we should think about the messages he is sending and the factors contributing to his behavior, then see how that makes us feel.

During workshops, I often have professionals reflect on the child who ticks them off the most. "What's the first word that comes to mind when you think about this kid?" I ask. The answers range from the words *frustrating* and *provocative* to *exhausting, manipulative, jerk,* and *ruination.* I then present the following scenario: "Say that tomorrow morning when you arrive at work you go directly to the office to watch a video of the worst ten minutes of that child's life. You see him being horrifically abused and crying out for help. After viewing this tape, how do you think you would respond to the kid that day and forever?"

Some will say, "With a lot more compassion" or "I don't think I'd be as tough with him" or "I probably wouldn't be able to yell at him." While working with children who have had rough lives, it's advantageous to "view the tapes"—that is, review their history—before you act. Not every child who acts out does so because of how she was raised; sometimes the origins of troubling behavior are neurological or physical. But every kid who chronically struggles has at least a ten-minute gut-wrenching tape.

The tapes of Jody were vivid. She was a rambunctious, auburn-haired seven-year-old—one of a group of twelve girls with histories of abuse and neglect residing at a large residential treatment center who required physical restraint two to four times a day to prevent her from hurting herself and others. Entering the unit for the first time as the new supervisor, I quickly spotted her standing in front of a full-length mirror, staring intently at her reflection. She eyed me with a look of impending doom. I mentally reviewed her history. Jody was reportedly a victim of gross neglect who had been sexually abused by her stepfather. She had been kicked out of three foster homes before coming to the center. I tried to imagine what life must be like for her and, given her history of sexual abuse, how she might react to a new male on the unit.

Five minutes after my arrival, the child-care worker on duty gave Jody a time-out for making a rude comment. Jody immediately began to yell and throw objects around the room. Because she was not responding to verbal interventions and her aggressive behavior was escalating dangerously, I knew she would need help to regain control. Using physical management techniques designed to keep kids safe, I escorted her to a part of the building where she would be out of range of the other residents. Once there she screamed and thrashed with intensity, requiring ongoing physical restraint, and repeatedly screamed at the top of her lungs, "Leave me alone!"

I thought to myself, "Oh boy, you've got some heavy work ahead of you with *this* gal." I tried to imagine how badly she must have been treated, the rage she harbored, the pain she carried. Wave upon wave of empathy helped me stay in control as she called me every name in the book and attempted to bite me.

After about ten minutes with no appreciable drop in the decibel levels or intensity of her behavior, I decided to try an experiment. The next time she screamed, "Leave me alone!" I reached in my pocket, retrieved a ten-dollar bill, and placed it in her view. I waited for a break in her wailing and then told her, "You said to *leave you a loan*. All I have is a ten. Is that enough of a loan?" Jody's wailing stopped abruptly, and she slowly turned to look at me. I was smiling. Soon she was, too. Hardly ever did any of us staff members need to restrain her again.

Six months later several of us were at the beach. I was standing about five feet out in the ocean watching the children swim. Jody glided over and looked at me with an innocence only a kid can muster and said, "You know, I thought you were going to yell at me like everyone else. But you made me laugh."

I knew instantly what she was referring to. "Was it better that way?" I asked.

"Yeah," she replied, giggling.

I picked her up and threw her into the water. She laughed as she splashed. It was good to hear.

No kid likes acting out. Always try to walk their walk before taking action that fails to consider their history.

Steering Clear of Negative Labels

Relating empathically also requires us to refrain from attaching negative labels to children because when we do, it adversely affects how we view them and, most importantly, how they view themselves.

To illustrate how negative labeling of children affects how child-guiders view them, I often present the following hypothetical scenario to child-guiders in workshops. "Suppose you have an opening in your class or program and are asked to make an immediate decision regarding two kids who have been referred. You are told that the first child has lived in four foster homes and has horrific burn marks on her arms, which have been traced to abuses by her stepfather; she is portrayed as a sad, angry, and lonely girl who has never had a friend and does not trust adults. She has, however, recently entered into psychotherapy for the first time and is finally talking about the horrible abuse she endured. The second youngster is described as big, smelly, self-absorbed, rude, manipulative, obnoxious, defiant, in constant need of attention and willing to do anything to get it. Which child would you choose?"

Most people I ask select kid number one. When I ask why, they give a variety of reasons:

"We feel pity and sympathy for her."

"She'll be easier to work with."

"She's quieter."

"The other kid stinks!"

"She's more motivated to help herself. She's engaged in therapy."

"She won't get the other kids going as much."

Then I respond: "Well, I just described the same kid."

Relay a child's painful history and people want to reach out to her; label her using pejorative terms and no one wants to work with the child. I recently watched acclaimed psychologist Dr. Wayne Dyer make a comment on public television that sounded like this: "When you change the way you look at a troubled kid, the kid changes."[1]

In the strength-based world, the following adage is etched in stone: *Life isn't what you see, it's what you perceive.* Child- and youth-guiders must perceive all children in a positive light. And, most importantly, the children themselves must be encouraged to do the same. Kids who are at the receiving end of repeated negative labeling will, at times, identify with these labels and stop trying. The pejorative labels often produce deeply entrenched negative self-perceptions. We use the term "stereotype myth" to describe this phenomenon.

According to the daughter of Red Pollard, the jockey of Seabiscuit, one of the great racehorses of all time, a distraught teacher whom he really admired one day angrily retorted: "Pollard, you're a loser, and you'll always be a loser." She said in a PBS interview that those words "haunted my father for the rest of his life."[2]

Years ago I was conducting a workshop at a charter school in western Massachusetts. At the break, a teacher approached me with a somber expression and said, "You're right about the stereotype myth. I have an identical twin, and when I was a young boy a teacher I really liked took me aside and said, 'I guess your brother got the brains and you got the brawn.' I still think about what he said." I would bet a week's pay that this gentleman didn't want to go into teaching but felt compelled to prove to himself and the world that he wasn't a dummy.

The well-known saying "Sticks and stones may break my bones but names will never hurt me" is really a crock. Someone can throw a stick at a kid, break his arm, and it will heal in a month or two. But if you're a teacher, juvenile justice counselor, child-care worker, or foster parent that kid has formed a strong bond with and you call him lazy, rude, or a loser one time too many it could stick. Consider the case of seven-year-old Teddy, a warmhearted child full of spunk and humor. The product of a chaotic upbringing, Teddy possessed negligible self-esteem and had trouble trusting adults. He also lied a lot. Any time he was caught in a lie and confronted with the L word, he would go ballistic. "I'm not a liar!" he would scream. Teddy equated the L word with being a bad kid. He simply could not tolerate being labeled a liar; he was too fragile. The third time Teddy was caught telling an obvious lie his residential counselor tried a new approach.

COUNSELOR: Teddy, what's going on?

TEDDY: I didn't lie! I'm not a liar!

COUNSELOR: Hey, I didn't call you a liar. I just want us to have a little talk.

TEDDY: I didn't lie!

COUNSELOR: I hear what you're saying, and I know what I saw. Let me ask you something: Do you think it's very slightly possible that what you are saying happened is [putting thumb and forefinger together so that they were almost touching] a little less correct than what really happened?

TEDDY [PONDERING THE QUESTION, THEN SMILING]: It's possible that I was a little less correct.

COUNSELOR: Well, thank you for admitting this to me. I know it wasn't easy.

The next day the entire staff began to use the phrase "a little less correct" with Teddy. As a result, his lying soon diminished, and they were able to talk with him in greater depth each time a deep-seated issue surfaced. Teddy's case, as well as an overwhelming body of empirical evidence and wisdom, speaks to the necessity of helping at-risk kids change their negative self-perceptions, something that is at the root of strength-based practice.

In *Cinderella Man* starring Russell Crowe, the true story of James Braddock, a down-and-out Depression-era boxer who, against insurmountable odds, won the Heavyweight Championship of the World, heard these words from his loyal and gifted trainer between rounds of a big fight: "Jim, you've got to beat this guy from the inside out. From the inside out, Jim!"[3] This is what child-guiders do. They use words and passion to change kids from the inside out, getting them to experience and value their strengths and weaknesses, alter self-defeating thinking, and cultivate a new, more hopeful mindset that energizes them to be all they can be.

Interestingly, Carol Dweck writes in her book *Mindset: The New Psychology of Success*: "For twenty years, my research has shown that the view you adopt for yourself profoundly affects the way you lead your life." Dweck contrasts kids and adults who have what she calls fixed versus growth mindsets, as exemplified by the following. Growth mindset: "We all have strengths and weakness. If I fail at something, it's a *great* opportunity to learn something new through hard work and practice." Fixed mindset: "I'm an awesome player, a smart kid, the best at what I do. This is how I perceive myself. The end result is all important."

Kids with fixed mindsets are more apt to get frustrated, blame others, and shut down when their expectations aren't met ("I'm a smart kid—how can I get this problem wrong? This subject sucks! I quit!"). People with growth mindsets embrace their strengths and weaknesses and eagerly accept the challenges and vicissitudes of life ("I don't understand how to do this. No big deal. Once I learn, I'll be even better at it.").

"The passion for stretching yourself and sticking to it, even (especially) when it's not going well, is the hallmark of the growth mindset," explains Dweck. She therefore cautions child-guiders and others to be careful about labeling kids smart, great, the best, and so forth, instead suggesting that adults forgo such labeling and encourage kids to appreciate their fortitude to meet new challenges and forge ahead.[4]

After reading *Mindset*, I created a metaphor I call "the eagle." I stood in front of an endearing fourth-grade class at a low-socioeconomic elementary school and asked the kids: "If I'm an eagle on the ground and begin to flap my wings v-e-r-y slowly, will I get very high?" (I mimicked an eagle slowly moving its wings.)

"No," they answered.

"But what if I start to huff and puff and move my wings with tremendous effort?" (I huffed and puffed, ached and groaned, and flapped my arms as fast as I could.)

"You're gonna get a lot higher!" they yelled.

"Correct! Now repeat after me: 'The harder I try, the higher I'll fly!'" The kids repeated the phrase.

I continued, "Does anyone ever notice which is the highest eagle in the sky?"

"No!" the kids responded.

"You're right. No one cares. It's all about the effort to get up there. Once the eagle is high in the sky, it has lots of choices, like which tree to land on and which food to swoop down on and devour. It leads a good life because it worked hard to get there. Life isn't about being the best or the smartest; it's about working hard. Say it: 'Be the…eagle.'"

"Be the eagle," the kids repeated.

"One more thing. When we try hard, we sometimes make mistakes. That's normal. It's a big part of becoming successful. No one gets it right all the time. But we learn from our mistakes. So what's a mistake? A chance to learn something new."

"What's a mistake? A chance to learn something new," the kids said.

Then I told them: "Alexander Graham Bell invented the telephone but failed many times before getting it right. What if he had said to himself, 'Man, I'm a brilliant scientist. I should have invented this by now. Screw it. Who needs a phone?' Edison failed many times as well. What if he had said, 'Screw it, there's nothing wrong with candles?'"

An attendee at a workshop I recently conducted came up to me afterward and related: "My daughter has been struggling with piano practice. Ever since I gave her the aphorism 'The harder I try, the higher I fly," her approach to practicing has improved dramatically. She loves it." She's become the eagle!

Although I wholeheartedly support Dweck's findings, I've recently altered my stance regarding calling kids smart. Prior to reading her book, I would often use this rhythmic chant with kids: "I'm smart; it's in my heart. Believing in myself is where I start." But after reading *Mindset*, I felt guilt about using it so frequently. I then read an article by Alfie Kohn that criticized Dweck's work, wondering if by constantly focusing on effort we might be sending kids the message that they're not smart. Kohn says: "If you're complimenting me for just trying hard, I must really be a loser."[5] I think Kohn is correct, especially when it comes to kids who have horrible self-images. I work with so many kids who feel dumb and inferior it pained me not to occasionally invoke the word *smart*. So after reading Kohn's article, I put the word *smart* back in my tool bag, such as in the following exchange.

ME: I'm smart

KIDS: It's in my heart

ME: Believing in myself . . .

KIDS: Is where I start.

ME: Now does being smart mean that you're smart enough to know that mistakes are normal and a chance to learn something new?

KIDS: Yes!

ME: Does smart mean if you don't know something it's okay to ask for help?

KIDS: Yes!

ME: Does smart mean if you're not sure how to do something it's okay to check out how others are doing it?

KIDS: Yes!

At-risk kids who question their intelligence seem to benefit from hearing they're smart as long as the word is defined using growth-mindset terminology.

One final note: Although it's good to encourage effort, doing so will cause frustration and despair if the children don't have the skills to accomplish the task at hand. Encouraging a student to "try harder" when her obstacle is a hidden learning disability will intensify her struggle. Encourage effort when you are reasonably sure it will produce the desired outcome.

Decoding Negative Labels

Any time we are about to apply a negative label to a child we should stop, mentally decode the term, and try to uncover the painful emotions and unmet needs it refers to. Listed below are negative labels commonly applied to kids with challenging behaviors. Following each one are points to ponder while seeking to uncover the underlying realities.

Babyish—Is the child developmentally behind? Has he perhaps missed out on the nurturing and attention he should have received years ago?

Dishonest—Is the child afraid to tell the truth for fear of suffering serious consequences? Is he lying to win approval from his peers?

Egocentric—Does the child have to put extra time into looking out for himself because he does not trust that others will do the job? Is egocentrism his way of ensuring that his needs will be met?

Just looking for attention—Has the child failed to receive the attention he needed earlier in life? Does he still lack it? Is it reasonable to think he could be happy with a little bit of attention when what he craves is a mountain of it? Many kids who act out for attention are in fact attention deprived. As a result, they are rarely satisfied with even our best efforts at attentiveness and are apt to lash out at them, when in actuality we should be upset not with them but with the fact that resources have been unavailable to them. The time to be distressed is when they stop seeking extra attention, for then they may have given up.

Lazy—Is the child withdrawn or depressed? Does he have a learning difficulty or a history of failure? If not, perhaps he has previously invested in someone or something and "gone broke." Or maybe he simply has no reason to be ambitious.

Manipulative—Does the child act this way for control purposes? Has he experienced a chaotic and unpredictable life and believe his needs will be met only if he manipulates the environment to get them met?

Obnoxious—Is the child drawing a boundary around himself so that adults will keep their distance from him? Children who have been hurt by adults and are therefore unable to tolerate intimacy with them often use obnoxious behaviors to push grownups away from them.

Provocative—Does he expect to be rejected, and is he attempting to control when and where it happens, thereby eliminating his anxiety (counterphobic behavior)? Has he been mistreated by adults, and is he trying to displace his anger toward those individuals by behaving provocatively toward any adult who stands in his way? Is he perhaps sending the message "Feel how angry I am—and help me." A youth who provokes adults is in many ways helping them experience the feelings the youth is enduring.

Avoiding the Misuse of Power and Control

Many retaliatory behaviors are due to feelings that are aroused when adult power is misused. "Power corrupts, and absolute power corrupts absolutely" wrote British politician Lord Acton. Poet Percy Bysshe Shelley penned, "Power, like a desolating pestilence, pollutes whate'er it touches." Edmund Burke, an eighteenth-century Irish statesman, maintained, "The greater the power, the more dangerous the abuse."[6] Because of the deleterious consequences of misuse of power, parents and professionals must be acutely aware of how they exert power over children—in routine ways as well as reactively.

Psychologist Thomas Gordon's cautionary thoughts about the insidious effects of power and control are as relevant today as they were when he recorded them in his best-selling book *P.E.T.: Parent Effectiveness Training*, published in 1975: "My own conviction is that as more people begin to understand power and authority more completely and accept its use as unethical, more parents will apply these understandings to adult-child relationships; and then will be forced to search for creative new nonpower methods that all adults can use with children and youth."[7]

Following are some of the more egregious ways in which power is misused against children and youth, along with examples.

• Abusing authority

When people in positions of authority abuse their power with children, they shut down conversations, define who is in charge, and send the message "I don't value your input, hence I don't value *you*," which is anathema to the principles of strength-based practice and compromises healthy development. Many young children who have had the power of authority repeatedly misused against them go on to have a stormy, retaliatory adolescence. Gordon points out: "In those families where the parents have relied principally on power to control and direct their children throughout their early years, the parents inevitably come in for a rude shock when their power runs out and they are left with little or no influence."[8]

The following scenario illustrates various ways in which adults abuse their authority when interacting with children. Emotional intensity was already evident in a fourth-grade class that was nearing the end of a year-long conflict resolution program. A fight had broken out on the playground, after which the beleaguered teacher asked, "How can you kids talk about these skills so well in class but not use them outside?"

A few students offered feeble responses. Then Alex said: "Maybe it's hard to use this stuff because we don't see much of it at home. My family is into joking about power. My grandmother laughs and says, 'We've got all the power.' Why can't adults just tell us that they are older and need to take care of us instead of saying that they've got the power? Why can't they give us reasons for things? My mother is using this new program. She says, 'One, two, three,' and then I'm grounded. Most of the time I don't even know what I've done wrong!"

At this point, one child after another started describing authoritative powers that had been used against them. "My ballet teacher tells us we can't wear shirts over our leotards, but she does. When we ask her why she gets to wear one, she says, 'Because I'm the teacher!'"

"My parents never explain why I'm not allowed to do things they do. It's always, 'Because I'm the parent!'"

"My coach says it's his way or the highway!"

It is evident from the children's reactions in this scenario that they can perceive how debilitating the abuse of authority is to them.

• Yelling

When someone yells angrily at us, we usually feel belittled, disrespected, intimidated, and angry and may want to get even with the person. Children feel the same way. Yelling not only reinforces a child's negative self-image but can send a frightening message: "This adult is losing control of his emotions." A child who discovers that the adults in her world have trouble controlling their emotions comes to view her interactions with them as precarious.

There is a distinction between yelling and raising one's voice. Yelling serves the adult's need to discharge anger, whereas raising one's voice in a controlled manner may serve the child's need to understand how his actions make others feel. Some children, however, have a hard time distinguishing between the two. Kids with trauma histories and others with elevated sensitivity to intense affect often react forcefully when they perceive power is being misused against them. Child-guiders must therefore be in tune with the kids they serve and control volume levels and emotions accordingly. For example, a counselor at a residential treatment center working with severely traumatized youth needs to worry a lot more about her tone and affect than a history teacher at an affluent high school, but both should be respectful at all times.

When yelling is reduced, children's behavior improves. In one residential program in Massachusetts where the staff significantly reduced their yelling, the frequency of acting out reportedly decreased by more than 50 percent. In other group situations in which yelling has been reduced, adults say they are relieved to spend their time listening to the children rather than forcing the children to listen to them. A short request to take a break, they note, has more impact when it is announced in a calm, supportive tone of voice than when it is ordered in an angry manner.

If you sometimes yell, do not feel guilty about it. Instead, think about how it feels to be on the receiving end, strive to decrease the yelling over the next few months, and notice how the children respond to your quieter approach. You will certainly be rewarded for your efforts.

• Physical punishment

Physical punishment of children, including spanking, swatting, hitting, and tapping, is a maneuver in power and intimidation. Physically, it hurts. Emotionally, it makes kids feel angry and demeaned. The reason we get away with it is that the children we spank are small, powerless, and unable to strike us back. No adult would tolerate such a demeaning and disrespectful act. The following excerpt, by journalist Brendan L. Smith for the American Psychological Association (APA), describes the potential impact of physical punishment:

> Many studies have shown that physical punishment—including spanking, hitting and other means of causing pain—can lead to increased aggression, antisocial behavior, physical injury and mental health problems for children. Americans' acceptance of physical punishment has declined since the 1960s, yet surveys show that two-thirds of Americans still approve of parents spanking their kids.
>
> But spanking doesn't work, says Alan Kazdin, PhD, a Yale University psychology professor and director of the Yale Parenting Center and Child Conduct Clinic. "You cannot punish out these behaviors

that you do not want," says Kazdin, who served as APA president in 2008. "There is no need for corporal punishment based on the research. We are not giving up an effective technique. We are saying this is a horrible thing that does not work."[9]

Not only do we save spanking for the young and defenseless but we often fail to see how counterproductive this angry act usually is. Spanking informs children that *physical violence is an appropriate response to frustration.* And it invariably teaches children to think: "When I want to control someone, I should misuse power!" If in a moment of anger you strike a child, remember that the good care you have been offering him will far outweigh the ramifications of one spanking. Even so, to help repair the relationship and model appropriate behavior you should recognize what you have done, search for more effective responses, and apologize for having lost control.

• Making decisions without consulting the child

Adults frequently make decisions that impact children's lives without engaging them in prior discussion. Teachers alter seating arrangements; group-home counselors switch residents' roommates; foster parents amend house rules; juvenile justice programs use discipline without seeking the youths' input. Although any one of these unilateral actions may be in the children's best interests, if the kids are not consulted, especially for big changes and decisions, they may feel disenfranchised, angry, and devalued.

Imagine that at work tomorrow your boss unexpectedly orders you to stay late to finish a report. Extending your workday will interfere with your evening plans, which is annoying and might lead to some passive-aggressive behavior on your part. Kids feel the same way when we arbitrarily change expectations and rules on them. To help kids with emotional and behavioral challenges, we should keep them well informed and, whenever possible, value their input on important issues that affect their lives. Although people in authority need to follow through with decisions, and kids need to understand this, the process should be fair and empowering.

If it is necessary to suddenly alter a plan, explain your reasoning and empathize with the child's or the group's reaction. An occasional change in plans without involving the children will not have a disastrous effect; to the contrary, although children require predictability to enhance their sense of control, they also need to learn that unforeseen developments do arise in life. And, most importantly, they should be counseled to expect unforeseen developments from time to time.

Any time you are about to abuse your authority, yell, spank, or make a unilateral decision, catch yourself before you begin, take a deep breath, reflect on the ramifications of your action, and determine if there is a more effective way to exercise your power and control. In general, use the golden rule: Interact with children the way you want people to interact with you.

The Downsides of Punishment

While the role of discipline in guiding at-risk children and youth is a hotly debated topic, holding kids accountable by punishing them is a misuse of power and an unacceptable way to guide children. Punishment is generally not related to the behavior in question but is meant to be painful and serve as a strong deterrent to acting in a certain way again. Yet sadly, many popular books on parenting still recommend punishment, as do numerous textbooks written by brilliant professionals. On TV I heard a parent ask a best-selling author what she should do when her child misbehaves. His response: "Find the thing your child is most passionate about and take it away. Take it away and then give it back."

Consider how you would feel if you were driving home from work and a policeman pulled you over for speeding and asked, "What's your favorite TV show?" and you reply, "*Law and Order,*" then the policeman responds, "Well, you can't watch it for a year because you were speeding." You'd go ballistic.

Elementary schoolteachers often take recess away from students who misbehave, but losing recess has nothing to do with a student making a rude comment at 8:43 a.m. When I conducted trainings in Utah a few years ago, I was told by my contact person that some of their more troubling students hadn't been to recess in five months. This news broke my heart. I immediately wrote a letter to the superintendent of schools. I haven't been invited back.

Consequences instead of Punishment

For discipline to be effective, child-guiders should use consequences instead of punishment since consequences are related to the behaviors in question. When we get pulled over for speeding and are issued a ticket, this outcome makes sense and does not become a source of consternation (We are not upset that we have consequences for speeding; it is the ticket itself that drives us nuts). However, if the police took our favorite possessions or activities away for speeding, we'd have a very angry society. In chapter 18 we'll discuss the efficacy of consequences and how, when, and why to apply them.

The Role of Past Abuses

Relating effectively and empathically requires child-guiders to remember that many children who chronically misbehave have histories replete with serious abuses of power and control. Those who have been sexually, physically, or emotionally abused often harbor tremendous anger; those who have been repeatedly yelled at, spanked, or responded to inconsistently also tend to be angry toward the world, particularly authority figures.

Jody, who came to the residential treatment center with a tragic history of sexual and physical abuse, arrived expecting to be treated unfairly because that was all she had known. On some level, she also wanted power to be used against her, so she tried to provoke staff members to yell at her or physically restrain her. With each provocation, a little voice inside her said: "See I *am* a bad kid. My parents had good reason to abuse and abandon me. I drove them crazy. I drive *everyone* crazy." Even though Jody's parents treated her unfairly, she loved them—they were all she had. She therefore believed that she deserved their mistreatment, that the abuse she experienced was her fault. In provoking adults to misuse their power against her, she was both protecting her parents and affirming her negative self-image. In addition, she was taking control of the situation by setting up the abuse so she would know when and where it would transpire.

As mentioned in chapter 3, the clinical term used to describe the actions of people who, like Jody, bring on the situations they most fear is "counterphobic behavior." It is readily exhibited by students who provoke their teachers into kicking them out of class. They do not want to be sent out; they simply cannot stand not knowing when it will occur.

Over the years, kids have screamed at me and my colleagues, "Go ahead, hit me!" They, too, were attempting to control the situation. They wanted me to prove that they were bad kids who deserved to be hit. They were testing me as well, to see if I would be like the other adults who had mistreated them.

Setting the Record Straight

Our job with children who exhibit counterphobic behavior to keep their parents on a pedestal is to set the record straight, to get them to believe that they are good kids. Our first task toward this end is to help them understand why their parents mistreated them. We might explain, for example, that their parents are good people who made some terrible mistakes, probably due to a combination of bad luck and problems of their own. This explanation gives tormented kids a way of loving their parents while simultaneously harboring feelings of anger and sadness toward them, which, in turn, helps them stop blaming themselves for the abusive actions they experienced. Our second task is to comfort the children as they deal with the resulting sadness and anger that inevitably arises and to encourage them to work through these feelings either in therapy or with trusted child-guiders.

A few years ago I picked up *USA Today* and read the headline story about a twenty-year-old young man who murdered three people on the same day and in the same manner as his father had when he was a child, leading to his father's execution by the state. This young man probably grew up with very mixed feelings toward his father, most likely loving and missing him but also enraged that he had committed such brutal acts and had been put to death. As a troubled teen, he probably heard over and over again, "Keep it up and you'll end up like your dad." Terribly conflicted, he chose to commit the same heinous crime probably thinking, "See, I'm just like my dad." This horrible act likely drew him closer to the dad he missed. I'd like to believe that if this young man had heard something like the following many lives would have been saved: "Your dad was a good guy who made a terrible choice one day and paid for it with his life. But let's focus on the good aspects of his life. Let's talk about the moments you cherished with him."

Another example of setting the record straight for children is the following scenario. Mike was restraining Jonas, a two-hundred-pound adolescent with arms like tree trunks who had just blown up over a minor incident. Although he hardly knew Jonas, he quickly surmised that he was a very troubled young man. After the restraint, when Jonas had cooled down, Mike attempted to process the event with him. At this point, Jonas began to direct rage toward his mother. He talked about how she had repeatedly looked the other way as one of his uncles had sexually abused him. After letting Jonas vent for a while, Mike commented, "I'll bet your mother loves you, and I'll bet she's had a tough life, too."

Jonas looked up at Mike with a how-did-you-know kind of look and revealed, "She was sexually abused as a kid." Then he related some of the details, including information about his own abuse. Suddenly, he began to sob. Mike put his arm on Jonas's shoulder, and they sat in silence for a while.

When we misuse our adult power, even in subtle ways, we risk reinforcing a trauma survivor's negative self-image by fueling his belief that he is a bad kid who deserves to be mistreated. By calmly dealing with the child in a respectful manner, we can help him see that he and perhaps his family members are inherently good people who sometimes make bad decisions.

— CHAPTER 5 —

Developmental Considerations

DEVELOPMENTAL PSYCHOLOGY OFFERS an especially helpful lens for viewing challenging behavior. One reason is that it fosters realistic expectations. Many children and youth who struggle with ongoing social and behavioral challenges are functioning years behind their chronological ages; therefore, adults who respond to their misbehavior on the basis of age alone tend to harbor unreasonable expectations, leading to miscommunication and conflict. By contrast, adults who recognize a child's developmental level are able to realign their assumptions and avoid needless strife.

A second, related reason for a developmental perspective is that some kids with chronic behavioral issues are at times displaying basic unmet developmental needs. The message behind their misbehavior is: "I'm stuck at an earlier stage of life and need help moving through it. Give me *now* what I should have received *then*." The better able we are to recognize the message behind misconduct, the more effective our response will be.

This chapter focuses on some of the key tasks of the earliest years of life, ways in which children function later in life if these tasks have not been accomplished, and what we can do to help.

The Foundation Years and Beyond

The beginning of a child's life, like the earliest phases of house building, sets the stage for all that is to come. To withstand the elements over time, a house needs a strong foundation. Children whose needs are met in a "good enough"[1] fashion during the first five years, including the prenatal period—and in particular the first three years—will have beneath them a sound foundation and will experience comfort and security in knowing that the world is an okay place in which to live. David Winnicott described the first three years of life as a "holding environment," a setting in which kids are literally held and nurtured in ways that produce healthy, life-sustaining attachments and maturation.[2, 3, 4, 5] Every home, school, or agency that guides children should also be a positive holding environment for them.

A child who successfully navigates the initial years of life achieves a crucial developmental milestone: object constancy. She knows that adults are there to love and protect her even if they are not in sight. Knowing that they are loved by people who unconditionally meet their needs creates in children a *cohesive sense of self,* another critical necessity during the foundation years. Children who experience inconsistency and sub-par nurturance during their initial years often struggle with object constancy and a cohesive sense of self, growing up doubting their self-worth and viewing all relationships as tenuous, which becomes a source of anxiety, conflict, and often, acting out.

In the following section we'll examine the prenatal period and the subsequent five years to explore how events experienced during these formative years have everlasting repercussions.

Prenatal Period

If a mother abuses drugs, smokes, or drinks during her gestation period, her child is at much greater risk for being born with serious neurological impairments. Advances in medicine keep more premature babies alive but also increase the odds for neurological problems. More and more children are being born on the autism spectrum, a serious and everlasting neurological condition. For reasons that remain unknown, and certainly not the fault of their parents, children born with neurological impairment will have strengths to help them function, but will be required to build their lives on shakier foundations. Early detection of neurological issues and appropriate treatment can dramatically improve the quality of life for these vulnerable children. In chapter 6, we will explore strategies for guiding kids with neurological challenges.

The First Year

In the first year of life, children are entirely dependent on their parents. To survive, they need food, clothing, shelter, bathing, cuddling, rocking, conversation, sensory and tactile stimulation, protection, and above all, unconditional love.[6, 7] As they begin to navigate their surroundings, they also require guidance and limits. When parents meet these early needs, children form attachments, and critical bonding ensues.

Bonding is the ultimate handshake. When kids bond with their parents, they receive a life-enabling message: "Welcome to the human race. You are not alone. We've got your back. Your needs will be met; you are safe, and we love you." When attachment needs of the first year are not met—if, for example, parents are chronically unresponsive, uncaring, or too punitive—children come to view the world as a cold and unwelcoming place. In time, their personalities become molded by this perspective. They experience encounters with adults as nongratifying and unsafe; and, having learned that depending on others is unreliable, they are convinced that they must take care of themselves. The message they project is: "It's me against the world. I must fend for myself."

Because they have never fully attached to a significant adult, such children often view adults more as objects than as human beings. As a result, they tend to feel isolated in a world they regard as treacherous. Such kids are often at risk for reactive attachment disorder or antisocial personality disorder. These are the kinds of kids who can hurt others without remorse. It makes sense. From their perspective, they are the only people in the world. Everyone else is like an object. We don't feel bad for a chair when its leg breaks; they don't feel bad when they hurt other people.

During workshops, I ask participants, "Have you ever worked with a kid who was highly self-absorbed, hard to relate to, and had no remorse for hurting others?" Sadly, many hands usually go up.

"Okay. Tell me the age at which this child probably got stuck."

"Age one," they invariably reply.

Personality disorders are generally believed to be chronic conditions.

Several types of personality disorders exist—among them, borderline, nar-cissistic, and antisocial—each of which is distinguished by a particular set of criteria. Although the diagnosis of "personality disorder" is not utilized with young children since their personalities are still forming, the behaviors they exhibit are often considered *precursors* to a personality disorder. Personality is a mix of genetics and environment and is pretty well set during the earliest years of life, including any tendencies toward a personality disorder.

Professionals who work with seriously troubled kids and adults need to understand the origin of personality disorders, how to detect them, and what to expect from affected individuals, expecially in terms of their ability to change their core selves. Since personalities are molded by environmen-tal factors, kids who grow up in homes where their basic emotional and physical needs aren't met are at great risk for developing some kind of per-sonality disorder. Most people with a personality disorder are self-absorbed, wary of relationships, and hypersensitive to family interactions because family relations have tended to be inconsistent, often harsh, and unfulfill-ing. Personality disorders are actually healthy adaptations to dysfunctional settings. Once professionals understand the origins and chronic nature of these conditions, they will be able to form better expectations and provide more empathic and effective care for such individuals.

There are no cures for a personality disorder, but great effort is being made to search for approaches that will help these children. Tragically, Russian orphanages are notorious for warehousing babies and not meeting their bonding needs. As a result, many loving adoptive parents have had their lives ruined because all the love in the world would not produce a happy, well-functioning, connected child.

The term *critical period* is used to describe the time during which a child must have her developmental needs met at a particular stage of maturation. Theory dictates that if a child passes through one of these critical periods without having her developmental needs met further intervention will be too late. Thus if a child doesn't bond during his first year of life the prognosis for that child is generally poor.

Any time you are working with a child who has antisocial tendencies—such as a disregard for rules, extreme self-centeredness, hostility, lack of connectedness, or a propensity for abusing animals or hurting peers without feeling remorse—understand that her behavior is most likely a way of saying: "I didn't get what I needed during my first year of life," "I'm unable to be kind to you, because no one in my immediate family has been kind to me," or "I am an unconnected kid. It's me against the world!"

What can be done for a child who is "stuck" at the one-year-old stage of life? We can try to replicate what she missed; address her unmet needs; give her unconditional love and support; offer large doses of physical affection if she'll allow it; make sure her nourishment and basic hygiene needs are amply met; keep her environment safe, neat, colorful, and organized; set reasonable limits; provide firm structure; and, above all, strive to build and sustain a trusting relationship that will allow her to attach to us as a significant adult.

Despite theoretical conclusions to the contrary regarding critical periods, even if a young person has antisocial tendencies and a history of neglect, we can never know for sure whether it is too late for that child. Some children can possess all the characteristics of a certain diagnosis, such as reactive-attachment disorder, yet remain amenable to change. The first child to teach me this was Jay.

Jay was eleven years old when he was referred to our residential setting. He was one of fourteen children born to a very depressed, lethargic mother. His father was in and out of the home. He was referred to our program after vandalizing houses near his home and stealing from stores without remorse. He was also struggling in school. During our first encounter, Jay wouldn't make eye contact with me and appeared odd and disconnected. He responded to most of my questions with one-word answers. Jay had all the symptoms of reactive-attachment disorder. We accepted him into our program.

The day before he arrived, I told the staff members on Jay's unit not to put him on our level system (although we were in the process of doing away with it). I explained that Jay appeared to be a boy whose early needs weren't met and that we would try to replicate what he had missed. When a few of the staff questioned me about this, I explained that we often devise individual plans for kids and that his peers would understand. I then asked the staff members to touch him as much as he'd allow—give him hugs, slap him five, pat him on the back, give him fist bumps, and offer other interactions he had missed as a child and needed now. After the meeting, I went into the attic, found a bunch of toys, and placed them in his room. When some of the staff members questioned why he was getting these things without earning them, I replied: "If you go into the home of a toddler, what do you see? Toys. And did the kid have to earn them? No. They were unconditionally given. Jay needs that same kind of unconditional care that he missed."

For the first few months, Jay's behavior wasn't noteworthy. The staff did as I had suggested, and although he seemed a bit odd he was acclimating to the program. During his third month, I was in my office one morning when suddenly there was a loud knock on my door. Two staff members from Jay's unit who were opposed to the way we were dealing with him entered.

"You know that stuff you've had us try with Jay? Well, it's not working anymore," one said.

"What do you mean?" I asked.

"We went to get him up this morning, and he yelled, 'No.' We told him he has to go to school, and he said, 'No!' He's become defiant," another explained.

I almost fell out of my chair in excitement, realizing Jay had turned two! For about six weeks, he said no to every request. He then turned three. Within the span of eleven months, Jay successfully navigated each stage of development. He left our program functioning at his chronological age level—a happy, connected, warm, and funny kid.

I'd like to report that the developmental-friendly approach we used with Jay has helped many kids over the years, but unfortunately it hasn't. I can think of only a handful of kids, in thirty-eight years of work, at serious risk for reactive-attachment disorder, who evidenced the kind of long-term transformation we saw in Jay. But I do think the developmental-friendly approach has helped numerous kids displaying antisocial, age-one-type symptoms, who probably barely got it "good enough" during their formative years and clearly needed additional bricks. Nonetheless, Jay's story reminds us to never give up on a child.

The Second Year

The second year is a time of unbridled self-expression. Around the beginning of the second year, many well cared for children start to walk, talk, and make better sense of their surroundings as their mobility, articulation, and cognition improve—an exciting but also scary development. Young toddlers overwhelmed by the feelings and impulses age two brings on cannot contain them all within their little bodies.

At this time, the well-behaved "Queen of the Universe," who was previously the center of her parents' world, is now flinging her cereal bowl across the room with cunning adeptness, smacking an innocent playmate on the head, dissembling a cherished family heirloom, and deftly stowing away the TV clicker. Navigating an ever-expanding and increasingly uncertain domain delivers nothing like the ease, joy, and surety of the first year.

This stage is called *separation-individuation* in the developmental world.[8, 9] The child is separating from parental figures and becoming her own little person. Mounting frustration over this state of affairs, as well as the child's need to establish herself as a viable, separate entity, leads to use of a vocal utterance that soon becomes the bane of some parents' existence: "No!"

"No" is the two-year-old's vehicle for obtaining control over an ever-changing environment that no longer feels as safe and reliable as before. Each time a toddler says no she is staking her claim as a separate individual who wants recognition and validation. It is the child's way of letting others know: "I am somebody, and I've got a voice."

In the child's eyes, the individuals responsible for her increased anxiety are Mom and Dad. These tenderhearted people seduced her (during year one) into thinking that life was a warm, fuzzy joyride; but no, life is not so hunky-dory anymore. Sure it's exciting, but it's also filled with uncertainty and restrictions, and the culprits must pay!

The toddler, of course, is not the only one to use the dreaded N word at this time. A fascinating psychological process plays out during this critical phase of life. It begins when the toddler first hears from her parents that restrictive, mind-blowing word, which enters her consciousness as an utter shock: "*No*, Amanda."

"Whoa, Mom. Do you know who you're talking to? This is your little Amanda, your pride and joy. You can't say no to me."

"No, Amanda."

"I think my ears are clogged. Remember, little tykes like me have terrible ear problems. Let's go see that ear doctor."

"No, Amanda."

"Are you blind? This is me, Amanda, Queen of the Universe, ruler of her parents. You can't say no to me. Off with your heads!"

"No, Amanda."

The child wonders, "How can these people love me and still say no to me?" To cope with this stressful quandary, she "splits" both her mother and her father into "good" and "bad" parent figures. In developmental work, the good and bad images are called introjects.[10] The split helps her handle what feels like contradictory perceptions: the accepting parent (good introject) and the rejecting parent (bad introject). "There must be two people inside my mommy and daddy," she says to herself. "When Mommy is being nice to me and saying yes, she is the *good* mommy; when she is being mean and saying no, that's the *bad* mommy."

Toddlers also split themselves. "When I'm behaving well," they think, "it's the *good* me. When I act devilish, it's the *bad* me." Splitting, whether it is directed outward toward their parents or inward toward themselves, helps two-year-olds adapt to the stress of parental limit-setting and to their own battles with impulses, all of which invariably interfere with their pursuit of pleasure—a simple way of making sense of a stressful environment.

At this critical stage of development, a parent's job is to demonstrate balance by complementing firm and predictable limits with ongoing nurturance, encouragement, and affection. The successful resolution of the terrible twos is for the child to emerge from this period with an understanding that she can act well and is capable of misbehaving (as is true of her parents), but she's one cohesive person (as is true of her parents). They can make her upset or happy (act both bad and good) but are not split figures. With balanced parenting, the good and bad figures (introjects) merge, producing a child with a cohesive sense of self, a grounded, secure child who understands and can tolerate the ups and downs of human relations.

A serious imbalance between limit setting and nurturance, however, can negatively affect the child's behavior and compromise healthy maturation. Children raised by loving parents who do not set firm and predictable limits may continue to split themselves into "good" and "bad" parts, never integrating them into a cohesive self. As they mature, they may have difficulty tolerating feelings of frustration and may become disorganized and angry in response to discomfort and stress, given their exaggerated sense of self ("I'm an all-powerful being"). Children raised by parents who draw boundaries but do not provide appropriate affection are likewise unable to feel whole ("I'm not as good as others"). Neither emerges from their childhood with a strong foundation for navigating the vicissitudes of life.

Parents who neither set proper limits nor provide the necessary amounts of love and affection—or worse, subject their children to any form of ongoing abuse—risk arresting them at this primitive level of development. Such kids will emerge from their childhood viewing adults and themselves in primitive, black-and-white terms. If someone treats them right, they're good; if not, they're bad. Not attaining a cohesive sense of self keeps these children perpetually anxious about creating and maintaining meaningful relationships and prone to splitting ("She's good, he's bad!"). Kids arrested at this age are at risk for developing borderline personality disorder, a condition discussed in chapter 7.

The Third and Fourth Years

Youngsters entering their third year of life are remarkably inquisitive, often displaying an insatiable thirst for knowledge. They want to touch, smell, taste, and, in general, interface with everything they see. In addition, they yearn to explore new territory whenever possible. New experiences of this sort can elicit considerable anxiety. Sensory overload, combined with the lack of experience and expertise, often prompts feelings of uncertainty, fear, and confusion. To mitigate these uncomfortable feelings, many three- to four-year-olds develop imaginary friends who can be summoned at will to offer companionship, comfort, and support.

Children of this age seem to know that to surmount obstacles and become capable of functioning competently in their surroundings they must practice. While building with blocks, stirring cookie dough, hammering, painting, planting seeds, playing with dolls or action figures, or dressing up like adults, they devise effective ways to interact with the many facets of their environment and rehearse prospective roles. In effect, youngsters between the ages of three and four are attempting to master the complexities of life by engaging in activities they can control and succeed at. This pursuit of mastery is the child's link with her future.

Three- and four-year-olds who are hindered in this quest or who fail to experience proficiency in an area of personal interest tend to carry a deep sense of inadequacy and insecurity into their later years. Indeed, many kids who evidence behavioral issues or who exhibit insecurity and anxiety about the road ahead never had the opportunity to acquire mastery in early childhood. Some were discouraged from exploring their surroundings; others were dissuaded from playing with an imaginary friend; and still others were never permitted to bring their "play" to fruition.

During parent workshops, I always advise mothers and fathers of children this age to say yes a little more than no. I ask parents: "What message are you sending to your kids when you say no? Sometimes no relays the message 'I don't think you can handle this.' Such a message can dim the spark of creativity and initiative in children. So your kid spills the milk three times trying to pour it. Just clean it up and continue to have her practice the technique. Remind her that we learn from mistakes—they're good! And when she successfully pours it the fourth time get excited, give her a hug, and suggest, 'Let's call Grandma and give her the big news! You poured the milk!'" This advice applies to anyone who guides children, particularly those who struggle with feeling good about themselves.

Whenever child-guiders suspect that children in their care may have missed out on these developmental immersions, it is advantageous to let them achieve mastery in one or multiple areas as practice for the future. This might entail helping them find projects, sports, hobbies, games, or work endeavors that will give them a sense of proficiency; encouraging them to build or fix things; requesting their help in the kitchen, classroom, or office; asking them to organize cans and bottles for recycling or participate in a car wash; or, in the teenage years, asking if they would like to tutor elementary school kids or younger children in their school or home setting.

At-risk kids should have multiple opportunities for success from the moment they wake up to the moment they go to bed. Success and proficiency in one area will, especially when trumpeted by child-guiders, often generalize to all other parts of a child's life. (See chapter 9 for more information on maximizing success opportunities.)

The Fifth Year

Between ages four and five, most children begin formal education and more complex interactions with their peers and the world at large. A child who has attached well to her parents will have the confidence needed to navigate beyond the family cocoon. It is exciting to play with other children and share special moments with them. Soon after entering the social arena, a developmentally on-course child makes a remarkable discovery: "No one is going to play with me if I always insist on getting my way." To be accepted by her peers, she quickly begins to *accommodate* to their desires and *subordinate* her own impulses.[11] Establishing friendships thus becomes a landmark event that diminishes egocentrism, enhances self-esteem, and launches children into enriched social relations.

Children who enter school developmentally delayed, coming from dysfunctional homes, are often unable to make friends because they cannot surrender their egocentrism. They feel a need to be in control at all times, having learned that it is unsafe to depend on others. Their self-esteem, already compromised by the psychologically impoverished environments of their earlier years, suffers yet another blow due to their inability to make friends. The lack of friends and the damage this does to their self-esteem follows these children into maturity and negatively informs their actions.

A Worldwide Epidemic of Friendless School-Aged Kids

A major ramification of struggles with inadequate bonding in the foundational years is today's hidden epidemic of school-aged children without friends. I've asked more than 500,000 workshop participants over the past twenty-five years: "Have you ever worked with a challenging kid who had a best friend or a meaningful, reciprocal relationship with another kid?" Rarely has a hand been raised. The vast majority of kids with challenging behaviors have no one their age to laugh with, explore with, share feelings with, be supported by, or keep company with—a problem possibly worse than bullying.

For children with diminished self-esteem making a real friend is an exhilarating landmark experience and an entrance into a rewarding life. The greatest services child-guiders can offer at-risk kids who have become imprisoned in loneliness is to help them link up with friends—or better yet, make a best friend. When two kids are arguing, override the impulse to dash in and separate them, and instead help them resolve the problem. Be a chauffeur, driving children to visit prospective friends. Refrain from limiting their time with friends or classmates as a consequence for misconduct unless a child's safety is at stake. When observing troubled children at play, help them improve their social skills.

I remember conducting duo therapy—a relatively new treatment method involving the pairing of two children with one adult—with Buster and Elliot, eleven-year-olds who met with me once a week to improve their social skills and, specifically, learn how to make friends. Buster, who was rambunctious and impulsive, had a history of physical abuse, teased his peers, was continually getting into fights, and frequently required physical restraint. Like many kids who have suffered trauma, he was unpopular and quite egocentric. Elliot appeared quiet and easygoing, a façade that masked his inner turmoil. Like Buster, he had a history of abuse, but he chose to respond to the world in a more masochistic manner. He would welcome misuses of power until he could take no more of it, then he would act. Twice he set serious fires. Also like Buster, he was self-centered and had never had a best friend.

During our first two sessions together, Buster frequently teased Elliot—a defense mechanism he employed to keep Elliot at a distance. He'd say, "Elliot, you suck! Eli smelly, Eli smelly!"

"Is it okay if he teases you like that?" I would ask.

"Yeah, I like it," Elliot would cheerily reply. (He was probably planning to burn Buster's locker down later that day.)

Although Buster teased Elliot a lot during the first two sessions, still they had fun together.

The third session was different. This time when I asked Elliot if he liked being teased by Buster he replied, "No, I don't." I advised him to let Buster know the truth. At first, he refused; then he asked Buster to stop the teasing. Buster paused for a few seconds, looked at Elliot, and never teased him again. After three successful play encounters, he was finally ready to take a risk, cease his antagonistic behaviors, and make a friend. Elliot, for his part, had begun standing up for himself, no longer allowing himself to be treated unfairly.

By their twelfth session, the boys had become good friends. Months later they asked to be roommates at their residential center. As the months unfolded, each boy modified more and more of his problematic ways of relating and learned to become more social. For Buster and Elliot, making a friend opened the floodgates to improved social functioning and more positive self-perceptions.

Tips for promoting friendships

1. Have "buddy time" once or twice a week. Pair kids off randomly and have them engage in tasks together. Teach and practice friendship skills. Hang a poster on the wall listing age-appropriate tips, such as:

- If you disagree about what to do, make a deal or compromise.

- Praise your friends when they accomplish something good.

- Think about what your friends like to do, and make sure to split your time together between each of your favorite activities.

- Show an interest in your friends, what's happening in their lives. What are their favorite foods, music, sports, hobbies?

- If you get upset with a friend, use words to express yourself and reach a solution.

After hearing about my training, staff members from a residential program for female adolescents in Iowa created a "buddy wheel." It looked similar to a roulette wheel and contained all the girls' names. Once a week each girl spun the wheel, and whoever's name came up was her buddy for the week. Other schools and programs have also created buddy wheels.

2. Match kids with social deficits in duos and, led by an adult, have them practice friendship-building skills on a weekly basis. As a former program director at a residential setting, I trained my entire staff to lead duos, telling them that duo leaders are like play-by-play announcers, simply letting the play occur, and only offer direction when limits around safety need to be set.

3. Facilitate friendship opportunities. Help arrange play-dates and social get-togethers, making sure none of the children you guide goes very long deprived of having fun with a buddy.

4. Invite friends for lunch or play as part of an individualized incentive plan, in addition to providing unconditional access to friendship development.

Adolescence

Just as the foundation years mark the first phase of separation-individuation, adolescence marks the second phase. It's the terrible twos all over again. The two-year-old is now walking and talking; becoming his own person (individuating); and, as the world opens up exponentially, being bombarded with conflicted feelings. The young adolescent is experiencing the same kind of transformation. He's excited and stressed about the thrills and challenges adolescence brings on, thinking, "Who am I? What's my peer group? Do I fit in? Where am I headed? What's going on with my body? Drugs? Alcohol? Sexuality? Why are my parents so dorky?"

As adolescents begin to think about leaving home and being individuated people, they often feel stressed. And who do they blame for these feelings of insecurity, doubt, and anxiety? Mom and Dad, just as they did when they were two. ("They are the people who are supposed to make my life safe and enjoyable. What the hell is going on?")

Parents and those who guide adolescents must, like the parents of a two-year-old, practice balance. They should accept that this is a glorious time of experimentation, excitement, sexuality, and self-discovery and allow their teens to navigate this stage without being overly restrictive. The key is balance, setting good enough limits while also having a healthy respect for what this stage entails.

Researchers at the National Institute of Mental Health express the significance of balance in these terms: "Research findings on the brain may…serve to help adults understand the importance of creating an environment in which teens explore and experiment while helping them avoid behavior that is destructive to themselves and others."[12]

Bullying, a major problem today, can perhaps be best understood from a developmental perspective. The typical teen is deathly afraid of not being accepted by his peers, of being on the outside looking in. So when confronted by a kid who acts and looks different, such as being heavy, small, gay, transgender, or geeky, the teen often senses, "It could be me. I could be different." This awakens fear and anger in the adolescent about being different, feelings that at times lead to bullying. ("How dare you worry me about being like you! You're gonna pay!") Of course, other kids bully in response to the power that has been misused against them in their lives.

A number of successful programs on the market address bullying. I believe, however, that bullying could be further reduced if schools, parents, and youth-guiders provided more education and support to their adolescents. Teens should have an opportunity to talk and learn more about the stage of life they've entered from both a neurological (how their brains are changing) and developmental perspective, and how and why they respond to kids who appear different from themselves. I've suggested this approach to numerous middle and high school staff members and teens over the years, and most agree. One teen responded: "Man, I didn't know any of this!" Change their thinking and you change their lives. Education and support can go a long way toward stopping problem behavior in its tracks.

The adolescent brain is undergoing lots of changes, and the brain itself doesn't fully mature until around one's mid-twenties. This is why there has long been considerable debate about how to hold preteens and teens who commit serious felonies accountable for their actions. Following is another excerpt from the article written on the adolescent brain by the National Institute of Mental Health: "One interpretation of all these findings is that in teens, the parts of the brain involved in emotional responses are fully online, or even more active than in adults, while parts of the brain involved in keeping emotional, impulsive responses in check are still reaching maturity. Such a changing balance might provide clues to a youthful appetite for novelty, and a tendency to act on impulse—without regard to risk."[13]

Far too often parents and professionals who guide at-risk teenagers grow disheartened when all their efforts to assist a young person appear to fail and the kid ends up in a juvenile detention center, flunks out of school, gets involved with drugs and alcohol, and so forth. They think, "All this work for nothing?" Such discouraging thoughts can negatively influence their efforts to help others or stay in the field. I tell disheartened people that they can't judge whether or not they made a difference with a teenager until the brain fully matures, explaining, "Some of the kids you worked with, who seemed to disregard your words of advice and support, will come back in their mid-twenties successful and thank you profusely for the help you gave them."

Many years ago I was asked to give a motivational talk at a year-end celebration for a large social service agency to which I provided training. Prior to my talk, a young woman in her mid-twenties, who worked at the program and had lived in one of their group homes for a few years, delivered an impassioned talk to the attendees, concluding with these words: "This program planted a seed of hope in my soul that allowed me to become the person I now am. Thank you. I love you."

During a break in the festivities, I approached her and said, "Could I ask you a question?"

"Sure," she replied.

"How long did it take after you left the program for that seed to germinate and for you to become the person you now are?" I asked.

"Five years," she replied.

Clearly, we must judge our success not by how well our kids are doing but by how well we are doing.

— CHAPTER 6 —

Developmentally Informed Interventions

FOR MANY KIDS, A COMPROMISED ABILITY to tap personal strengths and function appropriately stems from problems incurred during their initial three years of life, including the prenatal period. As a result, child-guiders who deal with such kids should employ developmentally informed interventions to cultivate the kids' unrealized strengths, some of which were presented in chapter 5. Following are a few more approaches.

Helping Cognitively Inflexible Kids

Increasing numbers of children entering schools and other child- and youth-serving agencies, such as foster-care programs, residential treatment centers, and juvenile justice programs, suffer from serious neurological impairment. These kids, cognitively inflexible and prone to serious behavior problems, in most cases do not respond to the standard behavior management measures of rewards and consequences. They are often very challenging kids to work with, given their inflexibility, volatility, inadequate communication skills, and underdeveloped social skills.

Although this book can help parents and professionals who are guiding such children, they themselves require a level of treatment that extends beyond the scope of these chapters. Michelle Garcia Winner has written a number of books, including *Inside Out,* that help parents and professionals better understand and respond to kids with Asperger syndrome and other neurocognitive challenges. Some years ago I attended a two-day workshop conducted by Winner and found her insights and techniques invaluable.[1]

Around the turn of the century, as a behavior consultant to a large school system in Massachusetts and a midsize residential treatment center in New York, I was occasionally asked to work with or provide staff consultation for kids with serious neurocognitive deficits, some of whom were at risk for serious mental health issues. These children displayed explosive behavioral tendencies, serious communication difficulties, inflexibility, highly oppositional behavior, and reacted indifferently to the traditional behavioral interventions of rewards and consequences. I employed my strength-based approaches and creative limit-setting and incentive strategies to no avail. So I did what too many professionals do when faced with kids who don't respond to our interventions: I blamed the kids.

At the residential program I was consulting for, there was one child in particular, eleven-year-old Randolph, who was in and out of crises. On numerous occasions his explosive, oppositional, and inflexible behavior necessitated psychiatric hospitalization. He was on multiple psychotropic medications, but, despite a slew of creative behavioral plans, nothing worked and he got worse. We didn't know how to help him. Then I read *The Explosive Child* by Ross Greene, PhD, which changed everything. Greene states that kids like Randolph with serious neurological challenges have a disability of the brain that's every bit as serious as a physical disability. He offers a profound analogy implying that if a child in a wheelchair entered a school or program and all her classes were on the second floor, we wouldn't offer her incentives to climb the stairs or punish her if she didn't; instead, we'd let her take the elevator, build a ramp, or move her classes to the first floor. In short, we would adjust the setting to meet her needs. Yet adults do not always adjust to the needs of kids with hidden disabilities, such as a nonverbal learning disorder, Asperger syndrome, or ADHD; instead, such kids often trigger anger within us and consternation.[2]

For years I've heard remarks such as "I know he can do it if he wants to. He did it perfectly yesterday!" In fact, the first time I mentioned *The Explosive Child*, in a workshop in Kansas City, a woman said, "That's true. When it's a hidden disability people want to believe it's not there. Last year my best friend and I got into serious car accidents on the very same day in different parts of town. She broke four bones; I hit my head on the steering wheel and incurred memory loss. Within seconds, everyone we knew was reaching out to help her, whereas people were getting mad at me, insisting that I was making up the memory loss for attention."

I tell kids with hidden conditions and those who guide them, "It's not a disability—it's a roadblock." I ask workshop participants: "What if tomorrow there were fifteen roadblocks on your way to work and you didn't know where they were? You'll probably be wasted by the time you arrive. That is what a hidden learning disability often feels like."

Creating User-Friendly Environments

Greene opines that adults who guide cognitively inflexible kids with serious neurological conditions provide accommodations for these children in the same way they would for kids with physical disabilities—that is, create user-friendly environments for them. In the original version of his book, he suggests that when dealing with cognitively inflexible, often explosive kids, adults should place their expectations for each of them in one of three baskets: the A basket (This needs to be done), B basket (Let's see if we can compromise about this), or C basket (You don't need to do this—let it go). Placing our expectations for a child into one of these baskets takes the pressure off her, allowing her to relax and learn new skills that will help her function better.

On my next visit to the program I found Randolph in the Quiet Room of the residential school because he had just punched a kid. After I greeted him, we had the following dialogue:

ME: Why did you punch Billy?

RANDOLPH: He wanted to be first to art class, and so did I, so I punched him.

ME [OPTING FOR THE B BASKET]: Maybe you could have made a deal with your teacher. You could have been first to art and maybe fifth coming back.

RANDOLPH: My teacher doesn't make deals.

I realized she had probably learned that from me, since at that stage in my career I was warning parents and professionals not to make deals with kids or they'd walk all over you—that instead you need to be consistent. Now I tell teachers and other professionals, "You can have ten different deals with ten different kids and still be consistent."

Recognizing that Randolph required a more user-friendly environment, I approached his teacher and explained what I had learned from *The Explosive Child*. She reluctantly agreed that, given his complex wiring, he needed a different approach. He had never responded well to motivational approaches of rewards and consequences. So we went one by one through Randolph's trouble spots using the basket analogy.

I said, "When it comes to lining up to go anywhere in the building, there's A (He lines up where you tell him), B (You make a deal with him each time he lines up, such as 'Randolph, how about fifth going down and first coming back?'), or C (He can line up where he wants each time). I think B might be the best response. What do you think?"

"B," she agreed.

"Randolph doesn't like to sit for appreciable periods of time listening to you teach. A (He sits or else), B (You negotiate what he does if he gets up), or C (He can wander around the room all day)?"

"B. He likes video games," she volunteered. "I can get a few educational games from the library and give him a choice of which to play when he gets up. We also have two computers in the classroom, I'll let him choose the game and the computer," she responded.

"Excellent!" I exclaimed. "With inflexible kids, we always offer choices. Now what if Randolph hits someone?"

"A," she shot back.

"Yes. He can't be allowed to hit," I replied.

"He hates cursive writing. Flips out when I ask him to write," she added.

"What do you think?" I asked.

"C," she replied. "He doesn't need to cursive write. Let's take the pressure off."

Shortly after his teacher had created a user-friendly environment for Randolph, he was a happier and more productive student.

Enhancing Inclusiveness

Professionals who work with groups of children or youth in inclusive settings are increasingly likely to have kids in their care who struggle with physical, psychological, or neurological challenges. As a result, it is essential to clarify from the start that every child in the group will be treated in a way that is best for him. This information could be relayed within the context of a "differences talk" delivered at the beginning of the year and then multiple times afterward so the kids will be continually informed about how you'll be meeting their individual needs and dispel any concerns they may have about "unfairness."

Your "differences talk" could go something like this: "We are consistent here, but being consistent doesn't mean we treat you the same as one another. If one of you has asthma, that person gets to use an inhaler; you don't need one. If one of you breaks a leg, we get that person crutches; you don't need them. If one of you has a learning disability—a road-block—in math, we break the math concept down differently than we do for you. We treat each of you for what you need. You will see kids here who don't have to do what you do and who get rewarded for doing things you don't get rewarded for. It's not about favoritism but rather what they need at the time. And in most cases it would be great if you reach out to a kid who needs a little help to get to where you are.

"Every person is wired differently. Some very successful adults, like kids, have ADD, bipolar disorder, Asperger's, or some other different kind of wiring. And they became successful, probably because the people around them knew that they needed to be treated in a certain way, a little differently from the others.

"That said, we are pretty consistent: we don't yell; we have great activities; we keep the place clean and neat; we have pretty good food; we tell corny jokes. Being consistent is different from treating you all the same."

Another way to explain the practice of inclusion is a metaphor I use of a fifty-yard dash. I tell children: "You might see a kid getting rewarded for something you don't get rewarded for, or notice a kid who doesn't receive a consequence for a behavior that you would. If it were a race, you'd be thinking, 'Why is he getting a head start—that's not fair! You're playing favorites!'" I then show them a picture of three kids at the starting line of a race and a fourth five feet in front of them. "But now let me tell you what's really going on. If you see a kid who gets rewarded for something you don't or gets away with a behavior that you wouldn't, it's not favoritism." I then show a picture of three kids at the starting line and a fourth five feet behind them. "If you see that, it's because we figured out this kid is behind you in many areas, and by giving him some breaks and adjusting our expectations we're hoping to get him to where you're at. In fact, I'll be real happy if you guys would go back and help him from time to time."

Kids get this. They know that some of their peers have wiring issues. They just need the explanation for why those kids will be treated somewhat differently.

Seeing Is Believing versus Believing Is Seeing

If we walk into a home where a toddler resides, we see toys everywhere. Did they have to earn them? No. They were unconditionally bestowed. A parent doesn't say, "You know, if you'll just poop a little less I'll get you that binky you've been craving at Toys"R"Us." No, the toddler gets it un-conditionally—she doesn't have to earn it. The same should hold true for a sixteen-year-old.

Unconditional love and support is a major requisite of healthy devel-opment. Sadly, some kids, particularly those with emotional and behav-ioral challenges, didn't get the unconditional love and support they needed during their formative years and still seek it. Therefore, child-guiders should strive to replicate what these kids have missed by providing uncon-ditional love and support whenever possible.

Unfortunately, this isn't always easy because almost every school and youth-guiding home or program uses standard behavior management—

that is, rewards and consequences—to manage their kids. The underlying message of standard behavior management is: "If you behave well, we treat you great. If you don't, it won't be much fun here. Our affection for you is thus contingent on your behavior." I call this approach *believing is seeing*. It's as if we said, "Kid, we like and believe in you *when we see* that you're doing well. If you misbehave, we're not too thrilled that you're here."

I have nothing against the respectful use of rewards and consequences in the grand matrix of child-guiding. However, from a developmental perspective such an approach at times goes against the grain. With kids who have struggled in their formative years, it's critical to more often use a *seeing is believing* approach, whose underlying message is: "It doesn't matter how you act. We care about you unconditionally and will treat you well no matter how you behave." This approach replicates what many of these kids have missed and greatly desire.

My first supervisor in residential treatment, and one of my best friends to this day, Ellen, understood the need for unconditional affection. Ellen and I worked every Friday from 2:00 p.m. until midnight with thirteen girls aged six to fifteen. Each of these kids struggled with serious behavioral issues, and they had all suffered from the horrors of abuse. On some Friday mornings Ellen would call to say, "Bring your suit in." I knew what this meant. Ellen was going to cook a gourmet meal for the kids, which would be served on her fancy tablecloth with china and silverware. On those days, the new kids would return to the unit taken aback by what they saw and smelled: Ellen and I dressed to the hilt; the fancy tablecloth and china adorning the two long, rectangular tables; a tantalizing aroma.

"Who's coming for dinner?" they'd immediately ask.

"You are!" Ellen would reply.

"Why are you treating us so special?" the kid would insist on knowing.

"Because you *are*," Ellen would answer.

It didn't matter if Friday morning was a zoo on the unit or if three kids had been physically restrained the night before—the meal was unconditionally bestowed. I would bet that every one of those kids went to bed on those nights thinking, "This is the best place I've ever been. These people don't care how we act; they love us no matter what." And those meals will be remembered by the kids long after any rewards or consequences fade from their memories.

Seeing Is Believing: A Counterintuitive Intervention

Seeing is believing, labeled "noncontingent reinforcement" by behaviorists, is a counterintuitive intervention. Child-guiders are trained from day one to give rewards for good behavior and matter-of-factly dole out consequences for unacceptable behavior. The seeing is believing approach is the exact opposite.

A savvy child-guider must decide when to selectively use seeing is believing because, if overused, the technique can reinforce undesirable behavior. But when used appropriately every now and then, it can be transformative. To use this approach effectively:

- Have a special lunch with a student who has been misbehaving.
- Cook a favorite snack or meal for a foster child who has been under your skin.
- Take a group that has been ornery out for a good time.
- Throw a football or shoot a basketball with a student you've had a hard time engaging with.

Deliberate Acts of Kindness

Responding every now and then to a child or group at rock bottom with a deliberate act of kindness can lead to valuable moments of insight and transformation. Years ago I was consulting and providing training to a large inner-city residential program in Canada that operated a number of adolescent group homes in its metropolitan area. The director asked if I would visit its most troublesome home. She said, "We don't know what to do. The situation is dire. We have three sixteen-year-old girls living there who run away every night, prostitute themselves downtown, and then return in the morning. And there's a thirteen-year-old girl living in the house who is terrified of the older girls and wants to be moved. The staff members are all very young and intimidated by these kids."

Days later when I approached the house, I saw sitting on the lawn the three older girls, who ignored me. Upon entering the house, I was met by the staff member on duty, named Susan, and Clarissa, the thirteen-year-old. They both appeared on the verge of tears. After a few minutes, Susan remarked, "Why don't we take a walk to the local convenience store. It beats sitting around here. I don't know if the other girls will come, but let's go."

We headed to the store with the three older girls following fifty feet behind us. When we arrived, Susan, Clarissa, and I entered the store. The other three girls stayed outside flirting with boys. At one point, one of the older girls entered the store and stood in front of a potato chip stand. I quickly went over and asked, "Would you like a bag of chips?"

"Yeah, but I got no money," she replied.

"I've got lots of money. I would love to buy you a bag of chips," I told her.

"You don't need to do that," she replied.

"Ah, c'mon. I've got all this Canadian money on me, and I'm heading back to the States in a few hours. Let me spend it. It's no good where I'm going. In fact, get your friends. I'll buy them chips as well," I insisted.

"Really?" she asked. She summoned her friends, who each got a big bag of chips.

"Okay. You've got the chips. So you'll need to wash them down with something. There's a Slurpy machine over there. Go buy the biggest drink you can," I instructed.

"Really?" she asked again.

"Yeah. Take advantage of the old guy from the States. It's my pleasure, and I need to get rid of the money," I repeated.

The six of us walked back to the group home laughing and joking like best friends. When we arrived at the house, we all sat in the living room and had one of the most poignant talks I've ever experienced.

The three older girls cried as they bemoaned the lifestyle they had been sucked into. They hated what their lives had become and reached out for help. Susan and I supported and comforted the kids, and she promised to assist them in getting the help that would turn their lives around. I returned home a little light on cash but with a swelled heart, having added a new technique to my child-guider repertoire that I labeled "a deliberate act of kindness," one that has proved beneficial many times over the years.

— *CHAPTER 7* —

Interpersonal Splitting

A MAJOR CAUSE OF INTERPERSONAL SPLITTING is stress. Splitting, as noted in chapter 5, is a natural way to deal with stress; it begins the moment humans encounter stress and becomes a lifelong dynamic. People split when intense stress produces difficult emotions, such as anxiety, anger, or fear, causing them to mentally assign people or groups to "good" and "bad" boxes. When America suffered its terrible financial crisis in 2008, assigning people to good and bad boxes assuaged the unbearable stress experienced by much of the population.

Because schools and other child-serving agencies rarely receive the funding they need and the lack of support causes stress, most schools and agencies periodically struggle with interpersonal disharmony: teacher against parent, first shift against second, clinical department versus line staff, principal versus teachers, and so forth. During workshops, I often ask, "Do any of you work for a school or agency that doesn't have problematic staff splitting?" Participants laugh, and no hand is ever raised. Stress causes a staff to split and take sides, and such interpersonal splitting keeps the staff from utilizing their human assets to full potential. In fact, many schools and child-guiding agencies seem to be stuck developmentally at the level of a two-year-old, for whom splitting is normal—a dynamic too many leaders are unaware of.

Further, in any setting that deals with kids and adults who have, or are at risk for, borderline personality disorder, which entails just about every setting that guides children and youth, there exist two major reasons for the interpersonal splitting that exists: first, stress gets people to take sides; and second, individuals with this disorder try to engender division between people.

Kids who don't receive good enough care during the second year of life and who have been subjected to some form of trauma early on generally do not merge the good and bad introjects into one—and are therefore at risk for developing borderline personality disorder, as discussed in chapter 5. Such kids, usually teens and adults, present as unstable in their relationships, decisions, moods, and self-perceptions; are often impulsive (cutting oneself is a borderline trait) and insecure; and tend to pit individuals against each other as this brings them back to where they are stuck developmentally and feel most comfortable. It's important to note that a new approach has emerged with amazing results in treating individuals with borderline personality disorder—dialectal behavior therapy (DBT, developed by Marsha Linehan).[1]

School and agency personnel should be taught about splitting and how it originates, then instructed in ways to avoid, reduce, or eliminate it. Specifically, professionals should be taught not to say or do anything to a kid, parent, or co-worker that is likely to reinforce a split and thereby prevent a youth, a school, or a program from progressing. Enhanced communication, education, and developmentally sound treatment keeps teams cohesive, and often results in kids and families making noteworthy behavioral gains, by allowing schools and programs to use their human resources more effectively.

Avoiding, Reducing, or Eliminating Interpersonal Splitting

Here are three viable ways to deal with interpersonal splitting in a home, school, or out-of-home placement setting.

1. Never say or do anything that reinforces a split.

> YOUTH: My mother said you guys are too punitive.

Productive response

> TEACHER: I like your mother. I'll give her a call to make sure we're on the same page.

Counterproductive response

> TEACHER: Your mother hasn't returned my calls in two weeks. She really doesn't know what's going on.

The second response, which pits the youth's mother against his teacher, causes undue stress, keeps the situation stuck, and rarely produces a resolution.

2. Employ split-reducing self-talk.

When stress intensifies and splitting seems an easy way to assuage it, tell yourself: "I'm not as good as I think, and they're not as bad. Stress and a number of other factors is causing me to take sides (see things in black-and-white terms). Stop it! Find the middle ground. Communicate more. Don't be played like a puppet. Stay professional." I say these lines to myself five times a week.

3. Hang a "No splitting zone" sign.

Agencies and schools could post a sign in their staff room that shows a big red circle with a line through it and the words "No splitting zone" underneath.

Helping Those Who Split

It is helpful to respond remedially to individuals who tend to split, particularly those with or at risk for borderline personality disorder. The successful resolution of the terrible twos occurs when the child merges the good and bad introjects into one, thus developing a cohesive sense of self that allows him to successfully march forward in life. The child reaches this point because of his parents' generally balanced approach to child-rearing—setting good enough limits while being nurturing and supportive. Professionals can be enormously helpful when responding to borderline behavior in the same manner. If a youth, parent, or staff member demonstrates a pattern of emotional outpouring and perhaps has a history of trying to play one staff or department against another, the adults in control should maintain balance, remaining nurturing to this person but also setting limits when his behavior crosses the line. By doing this, the recipient is getting what he needs and may have missed in life and, in theory, should be able to move forward.

Years ago I became the family therapist for a mother, Mrs. G, with borderline personality disorder. She was a very scary and intense woman with a documented trauma history who loved her three children. During our initial face-to-face and phone conversations, she swore profusely.

> MRS. G: This fuckin' agency sucks! You have no fuckin' right to restrict my kid!
>
> ME: Mrs. G, I love your passion. You really care about your daughter, and so do we. But I'm uncomfortable with your language, particularly the swearing. If you keep it up, we'll need to continue this talk tomorrow.
>
> MRS. G: Fuck you, asshole!
>
> ME: I'll give you a call tomorrow, Mrs. G.

After five to ten more exchanges, her swearing stopped and she gradually became more effective as a parent. Mrs. G didn't realize how offensive her ranting and swearing were and how they made people feel. In the clinical world, we call this egosyntonic behavior, words and actions that people don't realize are inappropriate. The goal with individuals like Mrs. G is to make this kind of behavior egodystonic—viewed as inappropriate—since you can't expect people to act appropriately if they don't know that what they're doing is outside established norms.

A friend of mine, Rick, a talented psychologist at a large middle school, recently sent me a disturbing email. He's been working individually with a student for about a year. The student presents with a plethora of behavioral and learning challenges. Rick developed a strong relationship with both the student and his mother, and during this past year the student made significant progress. At an end-of-year meeting, the mother was told by the special ed director that services to her son would be curtailed next year. According to Rick, she went ballistic and started denigrating Rick in a horrible way. In an instant, he went from being the great savior of her son (the good father) to an evil man (the bad father) trying to ruin them. It was classic borderline-like behavior. Rick was humiliated and livid that the director allowed this woman to continue ranting. In fact, it was not in the parent's best interest either to rage at Rick in this way. After it became clear to the director that efforts to verbally support Mrs. Jones were failing as she continued to denigrate Rick, he should have informed her that her behavior was inappropriate and nonproductive, then set limits on the conversation as follows.

SPECIAL ED DIRECTOR: Mrs. Jones, I hear what you're saying. You've got a lot of passion and love for your kid, and that's great. Again, let me explain why we needed to make this decision.

MRS. JONES: Rick's an asshole.

SPECIAL ED DIRECTOR: I understand your concerns, I really do, but it's not helping anyone to talk to Rick in the manner you're choosing. He didn't make this decision. Let's get back to talking about what we can do for your son next year.

MRS. JONES: I thought I could trust him. He's a goddamn liar!

SPECIAL ED DIRECTOR: Mrs. Jones, if you keep directing your anger this way at Rick, I think we'll need to adjourn the meeting and try again at a later time. Again, I know this hasn't been easy to hear, and I feel bad about that. But it will be in everyone's best interest if we could move this meeting forward.

MRS. JONES: You're just sticking up for the jerk!

SPECIAL ED DIRECTOR: Okay, I think we're done. We'll get together again when we're all in a better place. Thank you both for coming. Mrs. Jones, could I talk with you privately? Thanks.

Splitting is a cancer that invades too many schools and child- and youth-guiding programs. However, with proper education and practice it can be greatly reduced and human potentials maximized.

— CHAPTER 8 —

Collaborating with Parents

PARENTS DON'T GET A GUIDEBOOK when their children are born, and many people raising kids do so under inordinate stress, some having been raised in homes where good enough parenting skills weren't properly modeled. Given these factors, among others, parenting can be an arduous undertaking for a lot of people. Every time I conduct a workshop for teachers I hear the words: "You should be training the parents." But when I conduct a parent training, the ones who need information on strength-based child-rearing and behavior management don't come and those who are doing okay show up in droves.

Many parents who struggle with raising their kids are self-conscious about the problems they've encountered trying to guide and control them. Ellen, my first supervisor, told me once, "Remember, Charlie, when a parent with a history of mistreating her children pulls into our parking lot they don't see a sign that reads: 'St. Ann's Residential Center.' What they see is: 'Welcome, You Failure.'" Parents often feel sad, angry, and depressed about their family situation and blame themselves and question their parenting skills when their kids get off track. And unfortunately, the overwhelming self-doubts about child-rearing that many parents experience—often manifested through defensiveness—inhibit the learning and practicing of more effective parenting approaches. Yet despite these realities most parents love their kids and want the best for them.

Reaching Out to Parents

It's an irrefutable fact that kids who struggle with emotional and behavioral challenges will often improve their level of functioning if their parents are properly supported and given the help they need to employ more effective parenting skills. Therefore, it is essential for child-guiders to reach out to the parents of the children they serve, and to do so in a sensitive way that first supports the parents and then explores their thoughts and feelings related to their child-rearing, aiming to change some of the self-defeating thinking that many employ. Every strength-based theory and technique in this book can be used to help support them, as well as any other adult.

Following is a powerful observation from *Beyond the Bake Sale* by Anne T. Henderson: "The more the relationship between families and the school is a real partnership, the more student achievement increases. When schools engage families in ways that are linked to improving learning, students make greater gains. When families are engaged in positive ways, rather than labeled as problems, schools can be transformed from places where only certain students prosper to ones where all children do well."[1]

Years ago I read an enlightening article by William Martone, Gerald Kemp, and Susan Pearson titled "The Continuum of Parental Involvement in Residential Treatment," in which they outlined a four-stage continuum for working with families in residential treatment. This article has been instrumental in helping me and many others guide families, particularly those with problematic dynamics.[2] In recent years, I have modified the stage theory, making it applicable to all settings that guide kids and their families, including schools and juvenile justice programs.

The four stages, as described in the following pages, are engagement, participation, empowerment, and discharge. For school personnel, the fourth stage would be considered graduation, and for those who work in out-of-home placement settings I've added a fifth stage—aftercare.

Engagement

When we reach out to parents, particularly those whose kids are struggling with behavioral issues, it's critical to first engage the parents to build a relationship, as it's much easier to solve problems when the parties involved have a positive relationship. This is often done by focusing on what the parents are doing right, exploring their interests and strengths, and sharing some not-too-personal information about ourselves. I also advise schools and other child-guiding programs to have fun nights and activities that parents and staff members can attend to establish positive connections, especially early in the year. When teachers complain to me about parents refusing to cooperate with them, I always ask, "Did you reach out to them first?" or "Was the first time she heard from you when her kid experienced a problem?" In most cases, there was no attempt at engagement.

Any method of engagement that shows empathy for parents or kids can help in forming relationships. I recall my first home therapy visit with Mrs. G, the parent with borderline personality disorder mentioned in chapter 7. I knocked on the big, paint-chipped front door of her dilapidated house, and it slowly creaked open to reveal a short, heavy-set woman with long black hair who glared at me with a menacing expression, then invited me into her living room. We sat facing each other for an awkward moment, and then I said, "Mrs. G, before we get going I've got to tell you something. Your daughter Jennifer [age thirteen] has the best ethics of any kid at our program. She really knows the difference between right and wrong, and I assume some of that comes from you."

Mrs. G lowered her head and started to cry.

"What's the matter, Mrs. G?" I asked.

"That's the first time anyone has said anything nice about my parenting," she replied.

As it turned out, I loved working with Mrs. G and learned a lot from her. Although loud, vitriolic, and very intimidating, she loved her three kids and became a better parent to them.

During the period I worked with Mrs. G, we accepted a resident to our boys unit, Bruce, who was one scary kid and difficult to engage. He would hurt others without remorse and was clearly at risk for reactive-attachment disorder. His mother was incarcerated, and he was allowed to visit his grandparents once a week for four hours. His grandmother didn't trust "professionals" and refused to work with us. After three months of no contact, Bruce returned from one of his visits holding a tin of brownies that his grandmother had baked.

"Could I have one?" I asked.

"No friggin' way! They're mine," he replied.

"I'll give you five bucks for one of those brownies," I offered. This was in 1989, when five bucks could buy a lot of stuff.

"Five bucks! Okay," he agreed, giving me one.

I ate it in front of him. It was disgusting, but I said, "Hmm, this is delicious. I want another one."

"Five bucks," he said.

"Okay," I agreed, giving him another five bucks and accepting another brownie.

"Oh man! These are unbelievable!" I said, actually about to puke! I ended up giving him twenty dollars total and eating each brownie.

The next day when I arrived, I headed straight to Bruce's unit and told him, "Bruce, I didn't sleep a wink last night thinking about your grandma's awesome brownies. You've got to tell her that she's ruined me. I can't focus on my work. All I think about is her delicious brownies!"

Three days later I walked into the office and sitting in my mailbox was a big tin of brownies with a yellow ribbon and a nice note from Bruce's grandmother. I phoned her right away, and she accepted the call. For the next thirty minutes all we did was talk brownies: "Glass, metal, or plastic pan?" "Brown or white eggs?" "Gas or electric stove?" "375, 400, or 425 degrees?" "Thickness of the batter?" "What's that white stuff on the top that looks like sugar but seems lighter?" "What about nuts? Can you mix walnuts, pecans, and almonds? And how do you crush them? I tried, and they went flying all over the kitchen."

"You gotta put them in a bag and beat 'em good, Charlie," she replied.

"Thanks, Mrs. B," I responded.

After a half hour of brownie talk, I asked her if she would like to come in and talk about her grandson.

"Sure, Charlie," she replied.

"And would it be okay if his family therapist, Beth, calls and sets up the appointment?" I asked.

"Sure, Charlie," she agreed again.

When I spoke to Beth, I instructed her in the virtues of brownie talk to start the conversation with Mrs. B, who ultimately became highly supportive of our work with families.

Inventive ways to engage parents can prove invaluable. Many of the verbal interventions introduced in chapter 17, including reframing and solution-focused communication, can often be used for this purpose.

Equally important during the engagement phase is assisting with support. Lack of support causes parents to make bad decisions, such as mistreating their kids. During workshops, to increase parents' awareness of the necessity of support I ask them, "How easy would it be to parent three children if you were a poor, unemployed single parent on the verge of being evicted, physically impaired with a back problem, struggling with a drug problem, estranged from your family, disliked by your school system (your kids rack up special ed costs), and without friends?" While parents should be held accountable for their actions, since we're in the business of helping people we must understand that good people often make bad decisions and, when they lack support, find ways to assist them.

A good device for helping parents build support networks is the ecological map for rating kids' and families' levels of support (figure 1–2). If we help raise a parent's eco map support quotient 10 points, we also increase the odds that family stress will be reduced and all family members will be able to use their strengths more effectively, which will enhance family cohesion and happiness. For example, Mrs. G had a serious back problem, her house was in disrepair, she was poor, had few friends and no family to rely on, and, together with her two children at home, was often hungry. Realizing immediately that her eco map quotient would have been a negative number, a day after my first visit to her home I called her up and said, "Mrs. G, I'm in charge of the food ordering. Every month we have leftovers here that I don't know what to do with. Could you help me out by taking some juices, butter, cereals, and other items?"

"I guess I could do that," she replied.

"I noticed that there's a video store two blocks from your house. I know you have a VHS player, but Jennifer told me you can't rent videos when she visits on the weekends because you don't have a credit card, so I went down and gave them my card. Jennifer said she'll do some jobs around the program to pay me back. Is that okay?" I then asked.

"Sure, thanks," answered Mrs. G.

With continued assists, over a period of months Mrs. G's support was significantly increased. Within months she and her kids were happier and more capable of addressing long-standing communication and parenting issues, and ultimately Jennifer ended up in the navy.

Participation

Once parents have been engaged by professionals—with their support enhanced, strengths emphasized, and negative thinking reframed—and formed positive relationships with them, the next stage of the continuum occurs: participation. Now parents are asked to take a more active role in promoting the welfare of their children and themselves. In out-of-home placement settings, parents are invited to spend time with their children at their placements. Family-friendly residential programs have long been inviting parents to spend time on their children's living units to see and practice good child-care dynamics. Other forms of participation include attending parent workshops; school and program meetings; special activities; and various forms of therapy, if needed. During the participation stage, parents' communication with the key professionals in their children's lives, such as teachers, counselors, and therapists, becomes more regular and productive, and parents and professionals work more as a team.

Empowerment

The third stage of the continuum is empowerment. At this point more control is shifted to the parents. For instance, a teacher or counselor is apt to remark to a child or youth, "I'm not sure what we're going to do about this. Let's call your parents to see what *they* think we should do." Such a statement signals to the youth that the professional trusts his parents and wants their advice—an energizing message to a youth who wants to believe his parents have improved their ability to guide him.

Discharge/Graduation

If the family work has progressed in a positive way, the culmination of a team's (the parents' and professionals') collective efforts is discharge or, in school settings, graduation.

Aftercare

Children and youth who live in out-of-home placements should ideally remain connected to their treatment staff members after they are discharged. Kids who leave out-of-home placement settings generally return home or go to settings that offer less support, a change that is often difficult. At this critical period, kids and families especially need the support and guidance of staff members who have become integral to their lives. Toward this end, more and more residential programs are including aftercare services.

Understanding the Message of Difficult Parents

Parents should be viewed through the same strength-based lens as their children. After all, parents are just big kids. As a parent, I know this to be true. Whether age seven or thirty-seven, people all want happiness for themselves and their loved ones.

It's also important to remember that no one of any age likes to act out. Behavior is a message, and a difficult parent is sending the message "I need help. My family needs help." We should all listen and respond.

PART II

Preventing

Challenging Behavior

— CHAPTER 9 —

Enhancing Self-Esteem

MOST CHILDREN AND YOUTH who struggle with emotional and behavioral challenges suffer from low self-esteem. They want to feel better about themselves, and as soon as they begin to their behavior generally improves. In chapter 1, compelling neurological evidence was cited that connects enhanced functioning to positive feelings, including findings from Shawn Achor indicating that the human brain is designed to perform at its best when it is positive.[1] Study after study shows that when at-risk kids feel better about themselves they are more likely to learn social skills, handle frustration more effectively, feel less anxious, talk about personal issues, make friends, work harder at school, and take more appropriate risks.

Unfortunately, due to fear of failure and the specter of further emotional pain and embarrassment many at-risk children with low self-esteem are reluctant to engage in new activities or relationships, including those that could stimulate positive, energizing feelings. "Why play softball if I'm gonna strike out and be embarrassed?" a child may wonder, or "Why try hard in science? I'm stupid—I'll never get it right!" or "I don't like to draw; I'm no good at it," or "Why talk to that kid? He'll just brush me off. He knows I'm a loser. I don't need to be reminded of that *again*."

Recall the library metaphor: kids who have suffered trauma overuse their survival brains and are afraid 24/7 of being hurt and humiliated. These kids have wings of shame, wings of humiliation, and don't want to risk adding any more books. Also recall the elephant metaphor: elephants circle together when sensing danger. Kids who have suffered trauma, as well as kids with low self-esteem, often overuse their survival brains and don't venture outside its protective boundary to try new experiences or cultivate existing strengths. Instead, most at-risk children and youth, having suffered enough, prefer to play it safe by engaging in activities they are "good" at or that present little emotional risk, such as computer games, TV viewing, or social media.

The task of child-guiders is to help these children build self-esteem by stretching the boundaries of their comfort zones and utilize their inherent strengths to enjoy multiple successes in numerous domains, including academic, recreational, familial, and social. To do this, parents and professionals should provide multiple opportunities for personal success, cultivate kids' existing strengths and interests, uplift their spirits, and offer praise accordingly.

Providing Multiple Opportunities for Personal Success

Providing a multitude of success opportunities for at-risk kids is a sure-fire strategy for transforming lives. When at-risk kids enjoy more success, they became happier, which both neurologically and psychologically primes them for success across every region of their lives. Thus from the instant an at-risk child wakes up in the morning to the moment she retires, she should be offered many opportunities for personal achievement.

Two pioneers in the strength-based world, Robert Brooks, PhD, and Sam Goldstein, PhD, wrote in *Nurturing Resilience in Our Children*:

> If children do not believe they are competent in any area they are likely to feel insecure and vulnerable. . . . We must remember that an important feature of the resilient mindset is the belief that we all have strengths. *Success breeds success* (emphasis added). Identifying and reinforcing one island of competence can serve as a catalyst to attempt other challenges.[2]

The Power of Play

There are myriad ways to build success opportunities for at-risk kids through creative play. For example, in my part-time work as a behavioral consultant to two large school systems in Massachusetts, I see twelve to fifteen kids a week with serious behavior problems. I don't provide "therapy," although what I do is therapeutic; rather, my job is to get them functioning better in school. During sessions, if we're not outside throwing a tennis ball or football, I play age-appropriate board or card games with them, such as Uno, chess, checkers, war, or gin rummy, while pumping them up with inspirational metaphors, other strength-based interventions, and a host of customized self-management strategies that we practice together.

Prior to playing our first game, I tell them: "I've never lost a game of _____. If we play, I want to make sure you won't get too upset if I win every game." (For teens, I say that I rarely lose). Most agree to play. If it's my first time with a kid, I'll usually win the first game and on purpose lose the second, third, and fourth ones. I'll then feign anger: "Don't you tell anyone that you beat me!" Most of the kids I work with get orgasmic when they see me because they know how angry I get when I lose, but what they don't see is me smiling inside.

When I play cards with kids, I use two decks and set up two piles of cards to draw from. Periodically I reach out to straighten the piles, and while doing so I drop an ace or wild card on top to help them win. As they grow emotionally healthier, I begin to win a little more often, after which a dialogue such as the following may ensue.

> KID: Did you practice Uno with your daughter last night?
>
> ME: Yeah, I was up all night playing. I won ten, she won seven. You're going down today, kid! I'm ready for you! I brought a box of tissues in case you cry when I win. Let's do this!

After thirty minutes with me, kids have enjoyed multiple successes and generally return to their classes happy, with skills enforced and ready to learn.

Some folks question whether it's right to lose on purpose. "Don't kids need to learn how to lose?" they ask. No, they have PhDs in losing. They hunger for more winning. If he were alive, Charles Howard, rookie owner of the racehorse Seabiscuit, would agree.

Seabiscuit: An American Legend by Laura Hillenbrand tells the story of how the winless racehorse Seabiscuit, purchased by Howard in August 1936 despite being labeled unmotivated and lethargic, went on to become one of the greatest thoroughbreds in equine history because Howard hired Tom Smith, a down-on-his-luck, laid-back racing veteran with superior wisdom, experience, and instincts, as a trainer. Smith immediately reviewed the stallion's history and realized that Seabiscuit had never won a race and needed to experience the sensation of winning. So he hired a bunch of jockeys, secured a half-dozen horses, and staged a number of simulated races. Prior to each race, Smith told the jockeys to pull up near the finish line and let Seabiscuit win. In race after race Seabiscuit galloped to victory. When they eventually entered him in a real race, Seabiscuit continued to gallop to victory.[3] I'd like to believe every kid is a Seabiscuit, a champion waiting to win.

I also often hear, "But don't they know if you're faking? Isn't that worse?" Yes, it's not good if they know you're faking. That's why parents and professionals need to be great actors.

Another way to build success opportunities is by implementing the strength-based principle *focus on doing versus understanding*. Sure, it's important to explore why kids misbehave since behavior is a message. But what kind of message do we send a child who is scheduled for psychotherapy three times a week—that he's one hurting kid? I would prefer the child go to a good therapist once a week and fill the rest of his free time with guitar lessons, soccer, after-school sports, a job, or other activities that can offer him multiple opportunities for success. The more kids do things they succeed at, the better they do in life. As it is said in racing terms, "Success breeds success."

A good example of the benefits of increasing success opportunities by focusing more on doing are the changes I saw in a student named Cyrus. Years ago I was asked to provide two days of training to a school district in Utah. After conducting the training, the mentoring directors, Dick and Emily, asked if, prior to departing, I would visit with Cyrus, their most challenging student. A fifth grader who had repeated first grade, he resided in a trailer park on the outskirts of town with his mother, who was emotionally limited and sold rocks for a living. His father and two older brothers had abandoned them a few years back and were now residing in another state. "Cyrus is an overweight, depressed kid who doesn't come to school very often," Emily informed me. "He has poor self-esteem and few friends. If he's here tomorrow and you visit with him, he'll come across as a happy-go-lucky kid, but that's just the mask he wears when he meets new people."

The next day, Cyrus arrived on time, and the following exchange took place.

MR. A: Hi, Cyrus, I'm Mr. A.

CYRUS: Hi.

MR. A: So what are you good at, Cyrus?

CYRUS: I'm really good at chess.

MR. A: Wow! What a coincidence. I'm a great chess player. I teach people chess. I never lose. Do you want to play?

CYRUS: Okay.

Cyrus and I played. He was awful, unaware of where to place the pieces or how they moved. Yet he somehow beat me three times in a row.

MR. A: I can't believe it! You beat me three times in a row. No kid beats Mr. A three times in a row. Dick, Emily, get me his records! I need to check this kid out. He's not an eleven-year-old boy (I pointed at him). He's a forty-seven-year-old chess master from Russia hiding out in Utah. I think his real name is Boris Patuchkin. I want DNA testing, now! I can't believe I came all the way from New England to lose to a kid!

Cyrus was giddy with delight. I then took out two dice that I had in my pocket (carrying dice is a strength-based standard operating procedure), and the following exchange took place.

> MR. A: Okay, Cyrus, let's see how good you are with the dice. [I placed them in his hand.] How many times can you roll the dice without getting doubles?

He rolled for five to ten minutes. The best he could do was ten in a row without doubles.

> MR. A: That's amazing! You rolled ten in a row without getting doubles. You are now the Utah State Elementary-Age Dice-Rolling Champion. No elementary student in all of Utah has made as many consecutive rolls as you without getting doubles. Dick, could you please write this accomplishment down on a banner and hang it on the hall?"

Within minutes it was hanging on the wall. Cyrus couldn't stop looking at it.

> MR. A: Cyrus, you and I are out of shape. We need to start exercising more, right?
>
> CYRUS: Yeah.

I then went to the three-foot by four-foot flip chart that was in the room and began making a chart. I drew a huge rectangular box with lots of rows and columns. I wrote our names on a left-hand column, which was about five inches wide, and to the right I drew multiple quarter-inch columns and then four horizontal lines to create multiple quarter-inch boxes. I then drew a diagonal line through each box. At the top I wrote, "Cyrus's Lap Chart," and under that I wrote, "One lap equals one time around the gym—walking or running." We later pasted in pictures of runners on the perimeter.

Mr. A: You and I are going to get into shape. I'd like you to start filling up this lap chart. Every week have Dick or Emily send me an email with your total. I'll do the same. Let's see who can run or walk the most laps.

A lap chart provides a wonderful opportunity for recording personal success and subsequently building more success opportunities. I've used such a chart in residential programs and in regular and special ed schools all over the world in many ways. If, for example, Emily and Cyrus take a ten-minute walk outside, she comes back and writes down ten laps and places her initials under the ten in the top half of the next box, and below the ten she calculates his new total. I also recall using a lap chart with a very obese fifth grader named Juanita, who was being bused from the inner city to an affluent suburban school. She was quiet, depressed, and did little work. After we created the chart for her, all the staff members in the school were encouraged to take her for a walk. As a result, she started losing weight and feeling good about herself. Soon her mood and academic output improved significantly. At times, it helps to offer Jogging Superstar T-shirts, entrance into a one-mile fun run, or some other incentive for completing a set number of laps.

After making Cyrus's lap chart, I said good-bye to him, Dick, and Emily and headed back to New England. Soon the emails started coming: "Hey, Mr. A, I ran twenty laps today!" "Hey Mr. A, I rolled seventeen in a row today!" I dutifully wrote Cyrus back: "Oh, man. I rolled sixteen—thought I could beat you. Keep up the great work, dude!"

Three months later I received the best message yet: "Hey, Mr. A. Guess who was voted student of the month in my school? Me! Cyrus Smith!"

"You the man," I replied. "I knew you could do it!"

Cyrus rarely missed a day of school after I left. Dick and Emily took the baton and kept on running. They not only immediately built on his initial successes with me but helped transform this wonderful young man into a happy and productive student.

Six months later I returned to Utah, and we celebrated Cyrus's success. I treated the three of them to dinner at the fanciest restaurant in town. We invited Cyrus's mom, but she failed to come. A few months later Cyrus was placed in foster care. Despite aggressive efforts to engage his mom, she couldn't step up to the plate. Yet, although his family situation did not change, the caatalyst of multiple successes had helped Cyrus transform himself.

An important point to remember when we play games with at-risk kids is that it's analogous to play therapy. They're relaying to us, through their play, personal feelings and information; and if we respond in a therapeutically sensitive manner, a great deal can be accomplished. In play therapy, if a young child has suffered trauma in her life she might replicate the violence that still torments her, by having two or three dolls play out what she experienced.

Similarly, while playing games with a child-guider she might cheat. Many kids with emotional and behavioral challenges cheat when playing board games, and how we as child-guiders respond can impact them in significant ways. When kids cheat, they're telling us about their lives. Many kids with serious emotional and behavioral challenges got cheated out of a good life—or at least feel that way. This upsets them, and, if given the opportunity, they will tell you about it through their play; they are already telling you about it through their behavior.

During workshops, I ask participants what they would do if a challenging kid cheated during a game. Some answer, "I would tell them that they're cheating." Others say, "I'd ignore it." And still others remark, "I would say, 'Man, it seems like it's really important for you to win.'"

I then suggest a fourth option: "Wow, this is confusing. I thought the rule was you go, then I go, then you go. But it seems like you're going three times in a row before my turn. It's really hard when you think one thing is going to happen but something else does." I also say this to a kid who is cheating: "It's okay if you bend the rules with me. I'm here to pump you up and work on making better choices. But if other kids join us, I don't think they'd be too happy if you did that."

From time to time, I will also say to a child who is cheating, "Man, isn't it great to have total control of something? It's hard when you expect one thing and something else happens." In saying this, I'm mirroring her life. Months later I might add, "I'm kind of curious, has that ever happened to you? Have you expected something and it didn't happen?" Then a kid might reveal something like, "Yeah! I didn't think my parents would get a divorce!"

I once worked with a young boy with a brain tumor who loved to cheat. A bright, fun, and sensitive kid, Billy didn't have emotional or behavioral challenges but simply lacked the physical and emotional energy to get all his work done given his chemotherapy treatments, so I offered to help— just to pump him up. Any time I was close to winning a board game, such as chess, he'd brush his hand across the board and wipe out all of my pieces, yelling with a big smile, "It's Billy time!" I'd comment, "It's really great to have total control of this, isn't it?" "Yeah!" he'd reply.

Another child, Ella, a fifth grader with oppositional defiant disorder, made her cheating very blatant, but I responded with sensitivity because I felt she needed more success, more control in her life. Every week when we played Fish, I'd ask, "Do you have any fours?" "No, fish," she'd reply. "Do you have any fours?" I'm a competitive guy, but I'd still respond (somewhat reluctantly), "Yes, here you go." Her behavior improved dramatically over the course of six months. She responded especially well to using creative self-talk. Near the end of the year, I said: "Ella, I want to tell you something. I know you bend the rules when we play fish. I'll ask you for a six, and you'll say, 'Fish,' and then you'll ask me for a six. And do you know what? It's okay. I don't want you to ever feel bad about how you played. We had a lot of fun, and you had an amazing year. Everyone, including me, is proud of you. I'm here to help you feel better about yourself and get you back on track. And it's happened. You're doing it, kid." When I approached her class the next week, she was unusually eager to see me. "Hi," I remarked. "Let's go, c'mon!" she replied, and rushed me to the room we used for our sessions. "Let's play Fish," she insisted as soon as we sat down. I gave this kid my heart, and in the end she gave me her fours.

Kids with emotional and behavioral challenges really do transform when parents and professionals offer them a wide range of success opportunities.

Tip: Given the cautiousness many at-risk kids harbor regarding new endeavors, it's often helpful to use incentives or some other hook to get them to try something new. But once they try something new and succeed at it they'll do it forever—and they'll be much happier and more productive kids. In the strength-based world there is a great principle: Little changes can ripple into big solutions. If we can motivate kids to take one baby step toward a desired outcome, it could change their lives.

Success-Enabling Endeavors

Numerous endeavors are field-tested success enablers. Here are some of them.

1. Playing card games (Uno, Blink, Fish) and board games (chess, checkers, Connect Four)

Playing card games or board games can be like play therapy for kids and provides multiple success opportunities.

Tip: Be a good actor. Practice your losing techniques.

2. Following professional and amateur sports teams

People live vicariously through their beloved sports teams. I'm from the Boston area, and when the Patriots win I feel like a winner. Being a sports fan has significant social and psychological benefits. For many people, the next game on the schedule helps them navigate through a stressful week. Sadly, many kids with behavioral issues didn't grow up in homes where a parent introduced them to a love for professional or amateur sports.

Tip: Hang pictures of your favorite sports teams. Talk about the team and its players. Encourage the kids to learn about a particular sport. Take them to a game. Watch games on TV or clips on YouTube. Post the sports page with team scores. Wear your team's logo.

In the late 1970s, I was the unit director of a latency-aged boys unit at a large residential center thirty minutes from Boston. None of my thirteen boys knew anything about professional baseball or liked the Red Sox. One day I put all the Red Sox players' names in a hat and had each kid pick a name. I told the boys if their player hit a home run they would get an ice cream sundae. And if the Red Sox pitcher struck out a player, they would get a chocolate chip cookie. Within a few weeks, I had most of the kids hooked on baseball. I hung the box scores in our living room, and we went to a few games that summer. I'd like to believe that some of those kids, who are now in their forties, play catch with their kids and argue, cry, laugh, and cheer about the Red Sox.

3. Participating in special events

Participating in special events provides purpose and encourages collaboration.

Tip: Start or join food drives, car washes, bottle-collecting missions, walk-a-thons, and other community events.

4. Playing music

Playing music makes kids feel good, helps them make friends, and encourages their self-expression.

Tip: Buy old violin cases and put kazoos inside them. For birthdays and other celebrations, pick four or five kids to be the Kazoo Band and belt out "Happy Birthday." Any kid can play a kazoo. Do karaoke. If they can read, they can sing a song. Drum with your kids. More and more schools and youth programs have African drumming groups. I bring bongos to every session I have with kids. We often create helpful self-talk and then give it a beat. Playing soothing music during various times of the school day makes kids feel good; letting them choose from the music of various artists or sing, rap, or dance along promotes their self-expression.

Encouraging kids to play an instrument can also help them gain self-confidence. One of the best days of my daughter's life was her first day of band practice at high school, when she made friends instantly. If you're an educator, you can sing some of the academic work, creating musical mnemonics. If you're a principal, you can play music during morning announcements.

5. Volunteering

In *Reclaiming Our Prodigal Sons and Daughters*, by Scott Larson and Larry Brendtro, generosity is cited as one of the four essential qualities for healthy youth development.[4] Putting at-risk kids in a position where they can help others promotes this important value, can boost self-esteem, and may fuel impressive growth.

Years ago, as the program director of a midsize residential center, I encouraged a number of our kids to volunteer at an old age home near our facility. The kids also visited some homes of families in our program and did odd jobs to help out, such as mowing lawns, painting fences, and changing lightbulbs that were too high for the homeowners to reach. The psychological benefits of volunteering proved to be immeasurable.

I recently heard a lecture by Dr. Robert Brooks in which he mentioned an informal study he conducted in the late 1980s during which he asked a number of adults, many of whom worked in schools, to fill out an anonymous questionnaire. One of the questions involved describing their best memories of their school days. The most common positive memory was of being asked to help out.[5] The results of the study appear in Brooks's book *The Self-Esteem Teacher*.[6]

After my first visit to the dilapidated home of Mrs. G, I got permission slips signed by all the parents or guardians of the ten boys living on our adolescent boys unit to go to her house and paint, mow the lawn, fix her picket fence, clean, change lightbulbs, vacuum, and rearrange furniture. The boys were glowing when they returned to the program, knowing they had made a difference. Mrs. G gave them all hugs. The staff and I would periodically remind some of the kids about this act of kindness when they began questioning their self-worth.

Tip: Have kids volunteer to help younger ones, the elderly, disabled, or various professionals in your setting, such as secretaries, maintenance staff, or librarians.

6. Having hobbies

Every kid needs a go-to endeavor that fuels them for the journey ahead.

Tip: Encourage kids to find a hobby that engages them, such as art, music, theater, drawing, technology, collecting, reading, dance, gardening, pottery, graphic arts, debating, creating and producing videos, photography, or carpentry. Have kids plant and tend to indoor or outdoor gardens, or grow plants or vegetables in their classroom, home, or program. Hold debates, which are great for kids who like to argue. Public libraries often organize interesting groups focused on specific activities. I used to take one of my residential teens to a comic book drawing class at the local library every Wednesday night.

7. Interacting with animals

Animals can be unconditional friends for at-risk kids. Viewing marine life in fish tanks reportedly lowers blood pressure.

Tips: Get your school or program involved in therapeutic horseback riding. Boo McDaniel, creator of the therapeutic horseback riding program Horse Power in Temple, New Hampshire, was one of the first to offer horseback riding for kids with emotional and behavioral challenges.[7] A friend, the late Marge Kittredge from the Windrush Farm in North Andover, Massachusetts, was also a pioneer in this field.[8] I watched many kids, particularly those who appeared with-drawn and had suffered intense trauma, come out of their shells in response to the riding experience.

Have kids volunteer at an animal shelter. Buy a rabbit, guinea pig, or turtles for your class or program, and have kids contribute to their care.

Bring your dogs to work. Dennis, an engaging New England high school principal, brings his black-haired, cuddly dog Jake to school with him each day. Agitated students frequently ask for "Jake time." The low-key pooch wanders the hallways providing a calming presence and friendship to all.

When I took my teenage daughter on a tour of the University of Maine, at the library our guide stated, "We bring in therapy dogs during exam weeks to calm our students." Bingo.

8. Focusing on fitness, sports, and the great outdoors

Kids function better when they are fit and exposed to nature.

Tip: Create lap, sit-up, push-up, or jumping jack charts and track the kids' improvement. Introduce yoga into your class or program. Take your kids for walks, hikes, or bike trips. Many kids love the serenity of fishing. Lakes and oceans provide wonderful places to hang with kids. The benefits of being outdoors, particularly in a scenic setting, are convincingly documented in one of my favorite books, *Last Child in the Woods* by Richard Louv. He writes: "Although countless children who suffer from mental illness and attention disorders do benefit from medication, the use of nature as an alternative, additional, or preventative therapy is being overlooked. In fact, new evidence suggests that the need for such medications is intensified by children's disconnection from nature."[9]

If kids know there is regular time scheduled outdoors in a scenic natural setting, it creates positive anticipatory feelings that lead to higher functioning. This works for adults, too. However, sometimes the full benefits of outdoor excursions are not apparent until long after the events.

The worst activity trip in my residential career, I thought, occurred when I took four twelve-year-old girls from my program on a hike up Mount Monadnock, in Jaffrey, New Hampshire. The most popular trail to the top takes three to four hours to climb, and it is strenuous at times. The girls complained the entire way up. I had to carry one of them, Lisa, for the last quarter mile. The ringleader, Sandra, was particularly vocal. When we finally reached the top and opened our sandwiches, a fly landed on her tuna sub, and she refused to eat it. The entire trip seemed horrible.

But three months later we were all sitting in the kitchen, and for some reason the Monadnock trip was mentioned. "That was the best thing I ever did in my life," Sandra commented. The other three girls echoed her sentiment. I was floored—and have never forgotten. On my second date with my future wife, Cheryl, I hiked with her to the top of Mount Monadnock. On the way up, I regaled her with my hiking stories. Fog encompassed the entire summit. We got lost hiking down and ended up fifteen miles from where we parked. She has never forgotten!

Sports can be a wonderful outlet for high-motor kids. Encourage them to get involved in sports that provide clear opportunities for success, such as martial arts, soccer, bowling, and roller- and skate-boarding. I read a story about an angry teen who took up boxing, which changed his life for the better.

9. Doing chores, maintenance, repair work

Doing chores or being involved in maintenance or repair work can quickly build self-esteem.

Tip: Have kids work with the office or maintenance staff. Get them involved in such activities as landscaping, painting, clerical work, moving furniture, and rearranging rooms. Nothing provides more satisfaction than a job well done.

10. Holding a part-time job

Part-time jobs in the community can be life-changers for at-risk adolescents, giving them self-confidence and experience for future jobs.

Tip: Cultivate relationships with fast-food restaurants and other businesses near your program or school. Have the managers speak with your kids. "Greasing the wheel" significantly increases the likelihood of an at-risk teen getting and holding a part-time job. Also, provide part-time jobs within your class, school, or program.

11. Challenging world, school, or program records

Competitions hold kids' attention, help them develop skills, and provide opportunities to succeed.

Tip: Hold contests for kids or teams to see who can roll the dice the most consecutive times without getting doubles; construct the longest domino chain; stack playing cards the highest; or excel at other competitive endeavors. Post the winning names, dates, and scores. Periodically give kids a chance to break the record.

Modifying Activities to Enhance Success

A lot can be accomplished when existing activities are modified. Great effort should be devoted to ensuring that the activities you provide offer an opportunity for universal individual success. Ask yourself, "Can every kid partake in this endeavor and be successful?" If the answer is no, then consider some modification that will ensure everyone of an opportunity to succeed.

At my first big job, as activity director at a seventy-bed residential treatment facility, I decided to start an intramural softball league. I got the director to fund a new backstop. But only eight of the seventy kids who were eligible to play signed up. I then realized I had made a big mistake, so I told the kids, "Hey, I forgot to tell you, I'll be pitching every game, and there's no striking out—it's spring training." As a result of this modification of the sport that made it seem less intimidating, almost all the kids signed up, and some shined. Six weeks later it was still spring training.

The importance of offering an opportunity for universal individual success became clear when I took on the most challenging job I've ever had, at a short-term detention center an hour from my home. The place was out of control. It was overcrowded and often in lockdown. Half of the mid-management team had been fired for using improper restraint methods. The tension between the staff members and juveniles was palpable. I agreed to take on a leadership role. (I was scared but needed the money.) On my second day, I learned they would be playing bingo that night. I quickly drove to the nearby convenience store and purchased forty Babe Ruth candy bars—the biggest, gooiest, chocolate bars I could find. That night I asked the staff member in charge if I could call the first game. He said sure. I stepped in front of the forty kids in the center's tense, over-crowded cafeteria and stated, "Okay, whoever gets up-and-down wins a candy bar, and the kid on his left also wins." I showed them a candy bar. "Thanks, bro!" I kept hearing the kid on the left say. Halfway through the night I made this announcement: "Okay, the next kid who gets full-card wins a candy bar, and the kid closest to him who hasn't won also wins." Those kids learned that if they showed up for bingo they were going to be winners. Based on the results, we started playing bingo three or four times a week—with candy bars. It was an opportunity for guaranteed success and something fun to look forward to.

Further, I soon noticed that of the forty kids on the unit only seven regularly went to play basketball, the only sport offered at the center. The others didn't feel they were good enough to join in the activity. At the following staff meeting, I made this announcement: "I watched you guys play basketball with the kids. I want you to play even more, but we're making a new rule: no ball can be shot unless it's passed three times." The only way we were going to change this unit was if all forty kids woke up with multiple opportunities for success. Soon, most of the kids were playing basketball, and some were pretty good.

We also taught each kid how to play chess, made some other modifications and a few rule adjustments, and within a month the center had calmed down significantly.

Sometimes it's also helpful to modify scoring procedures. Justin, age seven, acted more like a two-year-old. He had limited impulse control, negligible tolerance for frustration, and extremely low self-esteem. It was felt that he might have pervasive developmental disorder. These characteristics were all evident the day I decided to take him bowling along with two other boys. They were fairly good bowlers, but Justin was not; he could not roll the ball down the lane without falling over. When I tried to teach him how to release the ball, he brushed me off, preferring to figure it out himself. Midway through the first game, I could see that Justin was in agony. While the other boys were playing well, he was getting zeros, ones, and twos. To make matters worse, the alley had recently installed an overhead scoring display. Upset about this public display of his poor bowling skills, Justin began cursing under his breath, putting himself down, and acting rudely toward me as well.

Clearly, something had to be done. After the fifth frame, I said, "Justin, from now on score yourself. He stared at me incredulously, then bowled his sixth frame. This time he did not fall down; in fact, he scored a four, his highest score of the day. Slowly returning to the scorer's table, he looked around and then gave himself a strike. The huge X appeared overhead, whereupon he laughed uproariously. The other kids complained, but when I explained that we were just having fun they stopped.

Justin then bowled his seventh and eighth frames, each time knocking down five pins. He returned to the scorer's table and marked two more strikes. He was in ecstasy—his score was rocketing and his bowling was significantly better. His success was breeding better results.

His excitement continued throughout the second game. Each time someone walked past our lane, Justin would point gleefully at the overhead score sheet and yell, "Hey, look at my score!" At the end of the tenth frame, he had bowled a three hundred—a perfect score!

He brought his "perfect game" score sheet back to the treatment center, and we hung it on our Good News Board where he'd see it every day. The staff agreed to use this unique score-keeping approach on future bowling trips. Within three months Justin, liberated from his fear of failing, had become a pretty good bowler and was slowly transitioning back to traditional scoring procedures. Soon afterward, we signed him up in a Saturday morning bowling league. He bowled okay and started making friends among the kids from the community. He left our program months before his anticipated discharge date.

Cultivating Existing Strengths and Interests

The second approach to enhancing self-esteem in at-risk kids is to cultivate existing strengths and interests. All kids have strengths, but sometimes they are submerged below the heavy weight of turmoil, sadness, self-doubt, and despair. With at-risk kids, child-guiders should go the distance to identify, encourage, and amplify the children's strengths and interests.

Following is an excerpt from the book *Helping Traumatized Kids Learn* that echoes this point:

> Every child has an area of strength in which he or she excels, whether it is in academics, art, music, or sports. When educators can identify and focus on a child's strength, they afford the child the opportunity to experience success, with all the emotional implications of doing something well. This is an important starting point in mastering academic content and social relations, which in turn serve as a basis for success...[10]

Robert Brooks, PhD, is a brilliant child-guiding authority, prolific author, expert in fostering resilience in children and enhancing their self-esteem, and my go-to person any time I have a field-related question. Once midway through a lecture he talked about a depressed young girl, Lisa, with learning disabilities, poor peer relationships, and a growth hormone deficiency, who had been referred to his practice for weekly psychotherapy. During one of their initial sessions, her mother joined them. Brooks, wishing to initiate a strength-based approach, asked Lisa, "What do you think you do well?" She responded, "Nothing." He asked her again and got the same response. After a third attempt failed, she replied: "Dr. Brooks, do you know what it feels like every day in school to be chosen last when the other kids choose up teams? I don't even know why the other team cheers when they beat my team—look who they've beaten." Saddened by her situation, Brooks struggled to formulate a response. Suddenly, Lisa began to smile and said, "I just thought about something I do better than the whole school. I take shots better than anyone!"

Lisa's mother poignantly reinforced her daughter's observation by commenting, "Dr. Brooks, you will find as you work with my daughter that she is one of the most courageous children you have ever worked with."

With Lisa and her mother's permission, Brooks shared with Lisa's teacher her belief about taking shots better than anyone in the school. The teacher creatively encouraged this strength by telling Lisa that many children have to take shots but often don't know what to expect because there wasn't one book in the school library about preparing to take a shot, and she encouraged Lisa to write such a book. With the teacher's assistance, Lisa wrote the book, which was then placed in the school library.

As a result, Lisa's life was transformed. A simple question—"What do you do well?"—was the catalyst that changed this girl's life. The full account of her remarkable story is told in Brooks's book *Raising Resilient Children*.[11]

Steve Baron, PsY, a gifted psychologist in New York and clinical consultant for this edition of *No Such Thing as a Bad Kid*, contributed a chapter to the book *Play Therapy Interventions to Enhance Resilience* that demonstrates the importance of identifying and cultivating strengths.[12] In it, he discusses the plight of Mary, a struggling student. Mary was a third grader who arrived late to school every morning; she told her mother every day that she hated school. She did not participate in lessons and often kept her head on her desk and stayed away from her peers. She was floundering.

Baron learned that Mary enjoyed being in charge of activities and was quite skilled in organization. He spoke to her teacher, and it was decided that she would be given the job of attendance monitor. Within days of accepting this position, Mary became, according to Baron, "increasingly animated and happy, and she began interacting more frequently with peers." Mary was struggling at home, as well. Baron suggested she start a "Good Behavior" book, writing down all her daily accomplishments. Each night at bedtime she and her parents reviewed her accomplishments—her successes. This intervention, similar to her job at school, brought about a positive change in her home behavior and relations.[13]

I had a memorable experience identifying and cultivating a student's strength when, around the turn of the century, I was consulting at the Martin Luther King Elementary School in Cambridge, Massachusetts, where I encountered Ricardo, an energetic and expressive second grader who made noises all day long. During my first meeting with him, I brought up his noise-making and asked if he would perform all of them for me. "Really?" he replied. He proceeded to serenade the office with a wildly creative assortment of squeaks, guttural sounds, belches, fart noises, whimpers, and animal expressions. "Wow!" I proclaimed. "Those were absolutely fabulous noises! What range! What timbre! Was that staccato at the end? You are an incredibly talented and creative performer." As he beamed, I continued, "The only problem is if you make these entertaining noises while Mr. Rodriguez is trying to teach the kids a lesson, they sometimes don't hear what he's saying. And you don't want that to happen, do you?" "No, I like the other kids," he responded. "Okay then, Mr. Rodriguez and I have come up with a plan: If you can control your noises better each day, he'll allow you to perform a concert for the class at 2:45 p.m. every Friday. Would you like that?" I asked. "Cool!" he said. I also talked with him about his hyperactivity and a new break system that Mr. Rodriguez and I had designed, and he helped craft some new interventions. The plans worked. By the end of the year, Ricardo was performing in the auditorium every Friday. The kids called him "Mr. Noise." When parents and professionals identify, encourage, and amplify the existing strengths and interests of the children they guide, particularly those with emotional and behavioral challenges, some of the challenges become less of a problem.

At times, it's helpful to show kids a list of strengths and have them identify their talents. Robert Dousa, a gifted drug and alcohol recovery and intervention coach on the West Coast, works with inner-city high school kids to help them find ways to resist doing drugs and alcohol. He gives each kid a strengths assessment, which helps them identify what they're good at and how this information can shape their lives, providing them with hope. Since instituting this approach, Dousa reports a significant reduction in marijuana use among his students and the cultivation of great adult-student relationships.

Uplifting the Kids' Spirits

Using tried-and-true methods of uplifting the spirits of at-risk children is another way boost their self-esteem. There are endless ways to offer upliftment.

1. Trumpet and memorialize success.

Show enthusiasm for work well done. Display successful school papers on classroom and hallway walls—or on the trusty refrigerator. Mount artwork. Keep a scrapbook of noteworthy accomplishments. At my last residential program, on a child's first day a staff member was assigned to create a memory book for him and, throughout his stay, to maintain it by adding such items as pictures from fun activities; notes to the child from staff members who were quitting; ribbons, certificates, and diplomas; successful school assignments and projects; and, prior to his discharge, good-bye notes and pictures from all the other kids and workers. Kids will look at such memory books for the rest of their lives. They become what we call transitional objects, items that remind us of being loved. The classic transitional object is the teddy bear the young co-ed brings to college to remind her of being loved by her family when she's missing home. Sadly, too many at-risk kids don't have transitional objects, which can be instrumental in helping them navigate difficult passages in their lives. For example, kids who suffer separation anxiety, such as new preschool children who have tantrums when their mothers drop them off at school, can be helped by being given transitional objects that remind them of their parents.

My wife doesn't understand why I have an old frying pan in my office, but it is because it's the pan we used to cook our Sunday pancakes when my daughter was young, an object that brings back cherished memories.

Robert Brooks's parents kept a scrapbook containing birthday cards, school report cards, childhood drawings, photos, and objects related to some of his accomplishments. His father maintained the scrapbook (or "file," as it was called) after his mother died. Years later when Brooks visited his father in Florida, his father said, "When you get back to Boston, if there is anything you can send me for the file, please do. I always enjoy receiving things from you. I love you very much." Just a couple of days after returning to Boston he received word that his father had suddenly become seriously ill. By the time he flew back to Florida, his father was in a coma in hospice, and he passed away the following day. Brooks has often emphasized how his father's last words to him were very positive and powerful, creating a memory that he cherishes.

When the parent of a challenging student hears the phone ring and sees "Baker Middle School" on the caller ID, she may think, "Oh, jeesh, what did he do now?" Some won't even pick up the phone due to PTSD (Parent Telephone Stress Disorder).

To mitigate such reactions, teachers and school personnel, as well as any professionals who guide kids should more frequently contact the parents of at-risk kids when there's good news to report.

Tip: If you're a teacher, buy a lot of postcards. The online company

Vistaprint sells high-quality postcards at cheap prices. Tell your students: "At some point, you're all going to do great work in my class. I like to send postcards to your parents or caretakers to let them know about your amazing efforts and wonderful results. So when I give you a few postcards, please write on each one the name and address of the person I should send it to. Thanks!"

Teachers and others who guide students with emotional and behavioral challenges should have such postcards ready to be sent at the beginning of every year. When the postcards arrive at each kid's home, they inevitably go on the refrigerators! Then every time Mom or Dad, as well as the student, opens its door to retrieve some food a little more dopamine and serotonin gets released into the brain. After seeing the postcards, a challenging kid might be more apt to do her homework that night and not argue with her parents.

I recently conducted a four-day workshop for educators in Vermont. I ordered one thousand postcards online from Vistaprint, gave each teacher ten free cards, and explained what to do with them. I then asked each of the fifty participants to write a postcard, such as the following, to their parents about a successful activity they were engaged in.

Dear Mr. and Mrs._____,

Your son (daughter)_____ recently attended a four-day training I conducted in Killington, Vermont. The training topic was How to Use a Positive, Strength-Based Approach with At-Risk Students. (Your name)_____ was a fabulous attendee. He (she) was very invested in the topic and an active participant. (Your name) _____'s strong passion for reaching out to struggling students was evident throughout. I was honored to work with him (her).

Warm regards,
Charlie Appelstein, MSW

I signed each one. At the end of the week, the organizers informed me that "the postcard thing really resonated with the teachers." A teacher in Vermont recently told me that her mother still proudly shows the postcard on her fridge to all her friends.

Months ago, I received this email message from Dawn, a teacher in Massachusetts:

> *I thought about your idea for a few days and decided, "Who doesn't like mail that says something positive?" So I ordered postcards that I designed from Vistaprint, bought stamps, and started writing.*
>
> *I have to say that the feedback I've received has been fantastic. Parents have been emailing me, kids are coming up to me beaming, and thank-you cards are being sent. One student, who had been struggling, now comes in early every morning to catch up on his work.*

One simple act of kindness can have immeasurable impact, especially with a child.

2. Spend time together.

Showing kids that you like being in their company will help them feel good about themselves. If you are a biological or foster parent, play video and board games with your kids, take walks, hang out together in the kitchen, go bike riding, or work side by side in the yard. If you are a teacher, eat lunch with a student or group every now and then. During free periods, play sports, music, or games with them. Kids living in out-of-home placements should have guaranteed one-on-one time with an adult on multiple occasions throughout each week. Child-guiders should attend their kids' sporting events, art shows, and musical performances. Being there counts.

3. Compliment children on their appearance.

Occasionally complimenting children on their appearance can go a long way in helping to bolster their self-esteem. For instance, at two low socioeconomic elementary schools where I work part time, many kids come from single-parent homes or have parents who are incarcerated, and consequently long for more attention. So every time I walk into a school, in addition to giving enthusiastic greetings I give compliments: "Sarafina, you look marvelous today. Who did your hair, dear?" "My, you are handsome today. Look at the buttons on that top!" "Hey, that's one heck of a vest, dude! Where do I get one?" Such compliments make the children feel good and encourage them to succeed. And when we praise appearance we're careful to honor kids from the inside out, focusing more on their effort to look good and our happiness to see them looking good than on any expensive new clothing they may be wearing.

4. Let children take responsibility for chores.

Chores teach children about being accountable, the importance of helping others, and working as a team. They also foster a sense of mastery, which enhances self-worth. Schools and child-guiding programs should, and usually do, engage kids in these tasks.

Tip: Occasionally do a kid's chore! "Why are you doing my chore?" he will ask. "Because I'm a nice guy, and thought we could have a good talk while I work," might be a good response. Or help a kid with his chore. It's not the military. Small acts of kindness can go a long way.

During my first week as a program director at a midsize residential setting, I entered the bedroom of the program's most challenging kid, Carla. She was cleaning her room, which was a mess. I told her to sit and relax, adding, "I'll clean your room."

We had a great time getting to know each other. An hour later her unit director stormed into my office and said, "You cleaned Carla's room! Why did you do that?"

"Because I'm a nice guy, and I thought it would be a good way to build our relationship," I replied.

"I don't think so," she shot back. "She's going to expect the entire staff to do this now."

"No she won't," I insisted.

"I told her that from now on I'll be asking staff members to occasionally do the kids' chores. Kids need a break now and then. And it's a nice thing to do," I explained. She left in a huff.

Brooks, who isn't fond of the term "chores," suggests substituting "helping out" or something similar since doing a chore often carries a connotation kids don't like without conveying a sense of contribution or purpose. He makes a good point. A sense of contributing to a positive difference is a basic component of resilience.

5. Write complimentary notes.

A complimentary note can lift the spirits of a kid who's feeling down. A number of classrooms, schools, and programs hang Shout-Out Boards, and any time kids or staff members perform a positive act, they can write it up and post it on the board for all to see.

6. Be physically affectionate with the kids you guide.

Showing affection through physical touch can reinforce a child's sense of self-worth and facilitate relationship building. Hugs, fist bumps, slapping fives, or a pat on the back can all forge meaningful connections and warm chilly souls. Dachar Keltner, in his article "Hands On Research," states, "From the frontier of touch research, we know thanks to neuroscientist Edmund Rolls that touch activates the brain's orbitofrontal cortex, which is linked to feelings of reward and compassion."[14]

A word of caution: In our litigious society, child-guiders need to be careful about engaging in physical contact with children. Those who work in a school or other child-guiding setting need to find out what is acceptable and, within the limits, offer as much age-appropriate physical outreach as possible. At the same time, because most children with trauma histories are anxious about being touched by an adult, be sure to respect their boundaries; ask them first if it's okay, and avoid touching children who are not comfortable being touched.

7. Ask children for their advice.

Give kids choices, and request their advice whenever possible to let them see that you value their opinions. Empowering children in this way helps them feel respected and trusted. A study done in Japan many years ago found that workers in automobile plants preferred having more say at work than more money.

8. Initiate the honoring of traditions.

Established traditions bind families and groups together, often giving them a sense of identity. Best of all, traditions inspire at-risk kids to look forward to predictable occasions when they will play a familiar part in the events.

Examples of possible traditions that can be established are the following:

- For those who work in out-of-home placement settings, let kids select the dinner menu on their birthdays and have a kazoo band belt out the birthday song.

- On Thanksgiving, ask the oldest kid in the class, group, or home to offer a few words of thanks before the meal.

- On the Fourth of July, take the kids swimming or out for ice cream, then to the park to watch fireworks.

- On the Friday before the Super Bowl, bring in a six-foot sub and have a party.

- On Halloween, let the kids wear costumes.

- On St. Patrick's Day, make sure all the kids wear green.

- On Martin Luther King Day, have the kids read one of his speeches aloud.

- On April 1, April Fool's Day, let the kids pull harmless pranks.

9. Honor hellos and good-byes.

Life is a series of hellos and good-byes, and lots of kids with emotional and behavioral baggage struggle with their experience of one or the other. For some, it is like a ball and chain tied to them, making it difficult or impossible to move forward until the weight is released.

In the clinical world, it has been observed that you can't say hello to anything or anyone until you have first said good-bye. For instance, if a mother drops her kid off at school in the morning and her last words are threatening, like "Wait till I'll see you after school," the child will not be in a good position to say hello to school since she will be fussing over the missing good-bye all morning.

Kids who act out, many with trauma histories, are often removed from foster homes, schools, or residential programs due to serious behavioral issues and never hear from the discharging family or program again, an egregious scenario that occurs too often in the child welfare arena and makes it hard for kids to move forward. Families, schools, or programs that discharge children under difficult circumstances should, within a month, be required to write them a letter saying good-bye, such as the following:

Dear Billy,

We're sorry you needed to leave our home (school, program). You were going through a rough time, and we didn't have enough tools to help you out. You're a great kid who will do wonderful things in this world. Not a day goes by that we don't think of you with love and fondness. Good luck, Billy.

Warm regards,
Eugene and Susan Flood

If a kid doesn't receive such a letter, he can't be expected to say hello to the next placement, instead beginning every day under a cloud of worry and fear, wondering, "How long until these people kick me out like the last family (or place) did? No one likes me."

Three days before Mark, age twelve, was scheduled to leave his residential program and return to live with his adoptive parents, the Clearys, they abruptly abandoned him, telling the center personnel and his social worker, "We can't handle him. Keep him." The professionals were livid. The Clearys had adopted Mark at birth, and he had lived in their home for ten years before being put in a series of out-of-home placements, ultimately ending up in our treatment center. His behavior was often problematic. We eventually reengaged his adoptive family and found out they had been pressured to take him home even though they knew they couldn't manage him. So they panicked and cut the cord, even though their decision had made them emotionally distraught.

After a series of meetings between the Clearys, their family therapist, me, and Mark's therapist, it was decided that Mark would have four family visits a year but wouldn't be able to live with the Clearys at this time. When I broke this news to Mark, he began sobbing uncontrollably. As he regained his composure, he said, "I couldn't move on with my life until I saw my family." Ultimately, he was the valedictorian at his special education's class graduation, with his parents sitting proudly in the audience.

Both kids and adults often need to mourn the loss of someone or something precious before they can move on, just as people grieving the loss of loved ones go through stages of grief—shock and denial, anger, sadness, and acceptance. Child-guiders, at times, need to help kids work through these stages. Professionals who work with older teens in independent living programs often find it difficult to engage their kids in life skills material until they first help them mourn the loss of the childhoods they should have had.

Also, kids with ongoing behavioral issues have a better chance for success and happiness if their child-guiders are open to saying hello to the baggage they transport, as illustrated by the following story. Manny was a quiet, somewhat depressed child from Honduras who rarely followed through with his work. He clearly missed his father, whom he loved but saw only during the summers. His fourth-grade teacher, Judy Devine, was one of my favorites. A bright and passionate educator, she was very concerned about Manny's lack of effort and occasional back-talk. After school one day I said, "Judy, you need to talk to Manny. He needs to hear that you understand why he can't say hello to learning yet—because he's still fussing with his good-bye from his dad—and that he's a good, loyal son."

"You're right," she replied.

Around midnight, Judy emailed me, saying, "Okay, I did what you suggested. After school, we talked in my classroom. I told him that I really do understand that he misses his dad terribly and that he's a wonderful son. And that it's sometimes hard to give your all when you miss someone like that. I then told him that I could relate to what he's going through because my mother died when I was fourteen and I know what it's like to long for a parent. I then choked up and started to cry…and so did he. We hugged and he went home." From that moment on, Manny was able to say hello to school and excelled in it.

When parents and professionals focus on promoting thoughtful, well-managed hellos and good-byes, kids feel better about themselves and their surroundings. However, parents and professionals need to remember that when kids say good-bye to a person, group, or thing that is special to them, they should focus not only on the negative aspect of the good-bye but also on the positive side of the pending loss. To encourage this important practice, you could tell them something like this: "Guys, we're all upset that Mr. Parcel, who's been a wonderful assistant, is leaving next week. I'm even angry at him for taking a new job, although we all move on at some point. Are some of you angry at him? Well, go ahead and tell him. He's a big boy. But I got to say something else, as well. I'm feeling pretty lucky that we had Mr. Parcel with us for almost the entire year. He helped make this a very special year. We could have had anyone start the year with us, but we got Mr. Parcel, and I feel blessed that he was part of my life for eight months. Do any of you feel lucky that you got to work with Mr. Parcel this long? Well, go ahead and tell him."

Many at-risk kids have experienced horrible good-byes in their lives and thus need proper hellos and good-byes modeled for them. One way to model a proper good-bye is to have a ceremony such as a "good-bye circle" at special times, such as during a kid's final week at a school or facility in which staff members and children form a ring and express words of appreciation, recall funny anecdotes, share sentiments, or simply let the child know how valued he is. At the end, the child himself can say a few words. The good-bye circle may be followed by a farewell party, at which the child is given his cherished memory book.

10. Respect the children's need for autonomy.

Exercise acceptable means of nurturing children's growing sense of independence. Children as well as teens like to experiment with self-reliance, often wondering, "How much can I do without assistance?" The more supported they are in this quest, the more self-confident they will feel, and the better they will function.

11. Respect and honor cultural diversity.

Some kids, particularly those with trauma histories, have trouble identifying with their biological parents, which deflates a kid's sense of self and feelings of connectedness. But all kids should be able to identify with their cultures, which can be a source of great pride.

Tip: Actively promote cultural strengths and diversity. Talk about famous historical figures from the cultures of the kids, and hang their pictures and bios on the wall. Learn to recite words and sentences in their native languages: "Shalom, my friends!" "*Ni hao!*" "*Bonjour!*" "*¡Hola!*" Bring in foods famous in their cultures, honor the traditions, and play the music. The message you send is: "This person really respects my culture and me. And people like me have excelled. So can I." Hope is humanity's fuel.

12. Have friends, family members, teachers, and other child-guiders call or write to celebrate the children's birthdays and noteworthy accomplishments.

The staff at one residential center had ten kids call a lonely resident on her birthday, and as a result she was ecstatic. It does indeed take a village to raise a child. Encourage all the villagers in your setting to reach kids who would benefit from feeling special.

The Praise Connection

Praising at-risk children who struggle with low self- esteem can help elevate their self-worth and engage them as long as it's specific. When I first started working with children at risk, I praised them continuously to bolster their self-esteem, no matter what they did. When Sally drew a picture in twenty seconds, I expressed admiration, as if Pablo Picasso himself had drawn it. When Albert sharpened his pencil, I praised his technique. I was convinced that these children needed enormous amounts of positive feedback to make up for the lack of encouragement they had no doubt experienced. I wanted them to know that someone believed they were important.

However, after a while, I realized that my excessive unconditional praise began to appear less meaningful to the children and seemed to keep some of them from working harder. Rather than feeling good about themselves, they were learning that very little effort could bring a round of applause, which was not a helpful message to convey. I also began to read books and articles that echoed this same point.

I then decided to let the children know that praise had to be earned. The next time Sally presented me with a quickly executed sketch, I politely thanked her and asked her how much time she had spent on it. When she told me, I suggested that devoting more time to her artwork might earn her a great deal of praise. Responses such as this conveyed a valuable lesson: With effort comes results. At that point, my compliments began promoting self-esteem and competency.

Eventually, I expanded my understanding of "effort" from the time and care invested in a project to the gesture made with it. One afternoon a child who had never extended himself to me suddenly drew me a picture. I praised him enthusiastically, explaining how meaningful it was that he would create such a beautiful image for me. His history of faulty attachments to adults had impressed upon me the importance of complimenting not only his artwork but, perhaps more importantly, his effort to connect.

It has become clear to me that our first job in elevating the self-worth of at-risk kids who have learned to keep their distance from adults is *to honor the links they make with us.* In such moments of reaching out, we need to think more about their inability to appropriately relate to adults than about the laziness that unconditional praise may spawn. Only after engaging such a child is it wise to become more discriminating in the praise we bestow.

Our second job in elevating the self-esteem of children who chronically act out is to celebrate improvements in their behavior. Sometimes this means praising a child whose actions still fall short of our expectations. A second grader who was sent out of the classroom ten times last week, for example, should be complimented for being sent out only seven times this week. The strength-based world champions the powerful principle

"Little changes can ripple into large solutions." When we acknowledge a child's efforts to improve, we support his earliest strivings, affirming him for where he is, not where he should be. In response, the child will feel better about himself and be more motivated to take responsibility for his actions.

Even though my views on praising at-risk children were basically formed early in my career, more recent research overwhelming supports what I and many others knew then and still know: praise is important but should be specific. Examples include "By and large the literature on praise shows it can be effective—a positive motivating force" and "Praise is important, but not vacuous praise. It has to be based on a real thing—some skill or talent."[15] Still, for those working with kids who lack trust in adults or receive little praise and attention in their lives, we should worry less about the long-term implications of unspecific praise and more about the importance of creating a link to these kids and lifting their spirits.

✱✱✱ Reality Check ✱✱✱

Currently, the pendulum has probably swung too far in the direction of boosting kids' self-esteem (every kid gets a trophy) and emphasizing the importance of a desired outcome (winning, being the best). If kids are happy in their domains but are underachieving, what good is that? If they feel great about themselves but get easily upset when they fail or struggle, what good is that?

Po Bronson wrote an insightful article for *New York Magazine* in 2007 titled "How Not to Talk to Your Kids," in which she examined the effects of praise and self-esteem building on children and noted research concluding that high self-esteem is not the key requisite for a good life. She pointed out the work of author Carol Dweck, whose research indicates that we need to be cautious about telling kids they are smart, the best, awesome, and so forth because doing so can create *a fixed mindset* about who they are—smart and all-powerful beings—which leads to frustration and avoidance when they struggle or fail. "I am smart. I don't need to put out effort," these kids think. Expending effort becomes stigmatized—public proof that you can't cut it on your own.[16] As mentioned, Dweck encourages child-guiders instead to help kids develop a growth mindset by emphasizing and praising effort not end results, helping kids understand that mistakes, failures, and disappointments can be opportunities for learning and growth, and that success comes when we keep going despite obstacles.

Mantras such as the following reinforce these ideas and are fun to use with kids:

"The harder I try, the higher I fly!"

"Be the eagle!"

"What's a mistake? A chance to learn something new."

"What's a mistake? An opportunity to take!"

Paul Tough writes about "grit" being a positive indicator for future success. Grit is about accepting and responding enthusiastically to adversity. He cites the work of Angela Duckworth, who developed a test to measure grit that she called the grit scale. It asks individuals to respond to twelve statements such as "Setbacks don't discourage me," "I am a hard worker," and "I finish what I begin." Respondents rate themselves on a scale of 1 to 5, with 5 being "I totally agree with this statement." Her results showed that kids with higher grit scores invariably are more likely to succeed in any chosen endeavor. Specifically, Duckworth found that children at a National Spelling Bee with high grit scores were more likely to survive into the later rounds.[17]

Caring child-guiders can only benefit from the research presented by Dweck and others with similar philosophies. However, when it comes to kids with emotional and behavioral issues, Robert Brooks gave some good advice when he told me, while discussing the pros and cons of various child-rearing techniques, "We have to do what's best at the moment for a child." Examples of this principle are the following actions:

- If a languishing student can be pulled out of his intense malaise with a creative incentive system, we'll do it, even though numerous studies disparage incentive systems.

- If I walk into a school in a low socioeconomic area with hundreds of needy kids, I'll shower them with unspecific shots of praise all day. It's what they need at 8:13 a.m., 8:42 a.m., 9:11 a.m., despite research findings to the contrary.

- And If I'm working with an inner-city, insecure boy who feels stupid and inferior to his classmates I'll let him know he's smart and can do great things in this world. We'll be chanting these words as he beats me in Connect Four: "I'm smart; it's in my heart. Believing in myself is where I start." But he'll also hear: "Being smart doesn't mean you always have the right answers. Being smart means you're smart enough to know that everyone makes mistakes and that they provide important chances to learn something new. You are smart and capable of being very successful in school and in life." He'll get both from me because it's what he needs at the moment.

For years I had been quoting a statement Brooks reportedly made regarding using praise with kids, then I recently decided to make sure he actually said it. I told Brooks that even though I support the new thinking on praise—that it's got to be specific—it saddens me that some parents and professionals might be more hesitant to praise kids who desperately need to hear more affirming words, according to this new wisdom. I informed Brooks that in workshops I often tell people that Dr. Brooks says too many kids "suffer from praise deficit."

"No, Charlie. It was someone else who wrote it in a draft of an article that was sent to me many years ago. Unfortunately, I can't remember the author's name," he said.

I was disappointed but again stressed my concerns about challenging kids not getting enough praise, and he agreed. "You know what, Charlie, even though I didn't introduce the term 'praise deficit,' I agree with the basic message that many challenging kids are deprived of praise and positive feedback. So keep making that point in your work and writings." Bingo.

—— *CHAPTER 10* ——

The Role of Consequences

KIDS AND ADULTS ALIKE cannot adequately function in settings that lack rules, laws, and accountability. In general, kids with emotional and behavioral challenges behave better when they are guided by competent adults whom they like and respect, and when they live in homes and centers, and attend schools, that keep them safe, challenged, and responsible for their actions. They seriously act out when placed with people or in settings that are unsafe, unpredictable, punitive, and inattentive.

For at-risk kids to feel safe and maximize their potential, child-guiding settings must therefore apply discipline with the utmost respect for the purpose of reinforcing values and accountability. Interestingly, the role of consequences for misbehavior, when viewed from this perspective, departs from the traditional role of consequences, which has been to teach kids right from wrong by establishing limits and deterring unwanted behaviors.

The Controversy over Consequences

I've always advocated for the use of consequences rather than punishment in response to problem behavior because consequences can be logically related to the misbehavior in question while punishment is about inflicting pain as a deterrent—not an effective or exemplary way to teach children how to shape behavior. However, there has long been a group of child-guiding experts who do not value holding kids accountable for their actions. Early in my career I attended a seminar led by one of the most prominent child-guiders in the field who, I had heard, opposed logical consequences. After his seminar, I had this dialogue with him.

ME: Is it true that you don't believe in using logical consequences for serious behaviors?

EXPERT: Yes.

ME: Well, I'm currently consulting at a juvenile detention
center. What would you do if a kid broke a window?

EXPERT: I'd say, "You broke the window? You *broke* the window."

I was troubled by his response. While I understood why he'd reach out
empathically to the youth, I couldn't grasp the lack of accountability he
seemed to favor.

Years later I had a discussion with another prominent child-guiding
expert whom I knew eschewed traditional discipline. The conversation
I had with this expert was equally troubling, but it led to a "eureka moment" that has helped me shape a cogent view of the role of consequences.

ME: Is it true that you don't value logical consequences for
kids?

EXPERT: Yes.

ME: Well, I give my young daughter time-outs. Do you
think that is wrong?

EXPERT: What is she doing that warrants the time-outs?

ME: She's being rude, defiant, or throwing things.

EXPERT: Does she know what she's doing is wrong before you
give her a time-out?

ME: Absolutely. She knows the difference between right and
wrong.

EXPERT: Well, then, you're not teaching her anything by giving
her the time-out. You're simply imposing your will on her.

My immediate thought was, "No, I'm imposing my love for her."

> ME: I'll be driving home in a few minutes. I know there are speeding limits and consequences for going too fast. I'd probably be dead if there weren't. I know the speeding laws exist before I drive. I don't learn anything when I get a ticket, but they are still helpful to me. Do you think most folks would drive safely without speeding limits?

> EXPERT: Probably, because people value their safety.

The conversation left me wondering if I could be wrong about the role of consequences in teaching right from wrong.

A few months later while thinking about all this, I had my eureka moment. "He's right," I thought. "Consequences don't really teach kids how to behave better. The kids usually know beforehand what's right and what's wrong. Consequences don't teach—*adults do*. But consequences are important because they reinforce the values of a setting."

I then flashed on the importance of having the intervention itself model those values. I thought: "If a high school student is rude to a teacher, and the teacher gets mad and screams, 'Go to the office. I'm sick of the way you're talking to me!' he cannot possibly reinforce the value of being respectful by acting disrespectful. You can't teach kids about values through words alone; the values need to be modeled."

By contrast, if a foster child hits another child, which he knows is wrong, and the logical consequence he receives reinforces the values of kindness, safety, and respect that normally exist in this home, he might not like the consequence but he will feel more secure and happier living in an environment that is kind, safe, and respectful. Children want to live in a home that honors these types of values.

Emphasizing this concept, Michael Eric Dyson, a professor of sociology at Georgetown University, in a stimulating article published in the *New York Times* titled "Punishment or Child Abuse?" states that the point of discipline is to transmit values to children. We teach kids that everyone makes mistakes and mistakes are learning opportunities. So when a child acts out (makes a mistake) then receives and completes a consequence (takes responsibility), we could argue that it builds character and resilience.[1]

Robert Brooks and Sam Goldstein, in *Raising Resilient Children*, speak eloquently about the need for kids to develop resilience, the capacity to bounce back after experiencing adversity, and to develop more positive outlooks on life.[2] In an online article titled "Continuing Thoughts about Resilience and Caring,"[3] Brooks presents an invaluable insight from the book *Resilience* by Navy Seal Eric Grietens: "The first step to building resilience is to take responsibility for who you are and for your life. The essence of responsibility is the acceptance of consequences—good and bad—of your actions. You are not responsible for everything that happens to you. You are responsible for how you deal with what happens to you."[4]

To further confirm my eureka discovery, I investigated behavior management programs widely used in school and home settings. Positive Behavior Interventions and Supports (PBIS)—a systemic, schoolwide, proactive approach to "establishing the behavioral supports and social culture that is needed for all students in a school to achieve social, emotional and academic success"[5]—is utilized, with impressive success, in thousands of schools and child-guiding settings throughout the world. At the heart of PBIS is the understanding that for students to achieve success across multiple domains, schools must teach, model, practice, and reward appropriate behavior and have clear consequences for targeted behaviors. Every element of the PBIS program has been thoroughly researched and scientifically validated. Recently, I spoke with its codirector, prominent behavioral expert George Sugai, PhD, and shared the story about imposing my will on my daughter and how this led to my new understanding that consequences don't teach but rather they reinforce values. When I asked Sugai if he agreed with me, he replied, "Absolutely!"

Parents throughout the world successfully raise their kids using the Love and Logic[6] and 1-2-3-Magic[7] child-guiding programs, each of which advocates introducing logical consequences as part of a comprehensive, positive, and proactive approach to guiding children. Here, too, it appears that while consequences are an integral part of the child-guiding matrix, when the focus of child-guiding is on what kids do right, on changing negative self-perceptions and building from the inside, and on teaching, modeling, practicing, and reinforcing appropriate behavior, the actual *need for* discipline drops dramatically.

After forty years in the field, I believe limit setting in guiding children is overrated. After all, consequences don't teach: *adults do*. Modeling and teaching positive behavior should occur throughout a child's life, and for kids with emotional and behavioral challenges it should happen with greater frequency and sophistication. And of course, after a child misbehaves the incident should be processed with the child in such a way that it serves as a learning opportunity.

When Consequences Can Be Counterproductive

Kids who are currently being referred to residential treatment centers and certain special education schools are often acutely disturbed young people who come with a plethora of mental health issues, including one or more disorders—among them, borderline personality, autism spectrum conditions, post-traumatic stress, attention-deficit/hyperactivity, obsessive-compulsive behavior, anxiety, and oppositional defiance, as well as severe learning disabilities, character disorders, psychosis, depression, or sensory integration issues. Many of these kids are taking multiple psychotropic medications to help them regulate their lives since they generally have negligible self-management skills and are prone to bouts of serious acting out. Watching at-risk kids in these settings, I often observe a very counter-intuitive approach to helping them. They will hit, kick, bite, knock over furniture, destroy property, swear, and, at times, receive only minimal consequences, if any. The focus is instead on what they're doing right and teaching them to decode their body's signals and develop self-management skills.

A friend who works at a residential treatment center once lamented,

"The kids can do whatever they want and there are no consequences! It's ridiculous!" I thought a lot about her comment and questioned how the different approach to traditional limit setting I and others advocate jibes with what is occurring in many of these settings. But then I figured out that her statement is incorrect. The approach is not ridiculous, because the kids currently being referred to intensive settings are suffering from extreme mental impairments, and to issue consequences for their *expected* misbehavior is, in many cases, analogous to disciplining a child in a wheelchair who refuses to climb the stairs. They all *want* to do what's right but can't—yet. And my friend who was upset because the kids were not receiving consequences for their actions needs to understand that living in a residential center *is* a huge consequence since the kids there lose their individual freedoms and are often removed from their friends and families.

These kids, like the ones we initially lose games to on purpose, are at the beginning of a very specialized treatment program. As they progress and become healthier, they will hopefully return home or move to less restrictive environments where they will attend schools and live in a world that respects values and employs a fair and logical approach to discipline.

Contextual Considerations

When arriving at the best possible response to a challenging situation or behavior, context should always be considered. Child-guiders should generally know the ideal way to respond but, based on circumstances, be ready to offer an alternative response. For example, my friend, John, who runs a mental health clinic in New York, relayed a powerful story about a new principal who took over the reins of a failing inner-city school where the student-to-teacher ratio was thirty-five to one, morale was low, and the students acted out a great deal. The principal informed the students that if they uttered any disrespectful words to a teacher they would be required to stay after school for a considerable length of time. Within weeks, the school was transformed as his tough stance on disrespect worked. While in most cases, students shouldn't stay after school for making disrespectful comments, context drove his decision, which turned out to be a best possible response.

The first step in responding to problematic behavior is to assess the circumstances. The second step is to formulate an intervention that fits the *context* of the situation. In general, the more serious the problem the more prompt and direct the response should be. A child who punches someone, for example, requires immediate attention and support, as do his peers and victim. A school or program that is out of control needs immediate intervention.

The most serious forms of misconduct are those that threaten safety and stability. As a rule, the more out of control a misbehaving child or group appears, the more *appropriately* controlling a child-guider will need to be to help restore security and safety. In settings such as classrooms and treatment facilities, where one child's escalating behavior can negatively affect an entire group, consequences, such as having the child or the other kids leave the room so the child can calm down, often need to be immediate and direct.

Ten Key Questions to Consider

When formulating a context-sensitive response to a situation, consider the following ten questions.

1. Are safety issues at stake?

If anyone's safety has been compromised, firm limits need to be set. Strive for less talk and more action. In a group setting, prompt action is a must. At home, if no other children are around the response need not be as immediate.

2. Is this really a problem?

Kids sometimes do things that set us off yet fall within the parameters of acceptable behavior, such as teens using crude language, wearing garish clothing, or covering their walls with offensive posters. In such instances, consequences are not always needed—and, in fact, can be counterproductive. Be sure to assess whether the child's actions are acceptable in terms of current norms, rules, and values so that you will not react solely out of personal discomfort.

3. Why is this behavior occurring?

Remember that acting out is a signal of distress, and discovering the underlying reasons for it will likely lead to the solution. Often a child will act out big time and, just before a consequence is issued, share some tragic news, such as a death in the family, abuse, or impending eviction, dramatically changing the child-guider's response.

4. How much responsibility should I assume for this incident?

If a child-guider has contributed to the problem—through poor planning, an inappropriate comment or action, or an oversight of some sort—it is best to quickly admit to the mistake, apologize, and work hard to avoid repeating it. A consequence may or may not be appropriate in such an instance. The more accountable child-guiders are for their actions, the more responsibility the children or group will assume.

Sometimes an adult's inappropriate action prompts a child to act out. For example, a juvenile justice worker angrily yells at a youth, and the young man swears—a clear rules violation. The worker should not have yelled; he provoked the youth. If, however, the worker does not impose a consequence because he set the youth up, then the message he sends is: "It's okay to break rules if you are unjustly wronged." A best possible decision needs to be made during these times. Often a minor consequence will suffice, such as: "Reggie, I was wrong to have yelled at you. It's been a long day, and

I overreacted. I'm sorry. But I still can't allow you to swear without a consequence. What message would that send? It's okay to break rules if you've got a good reason to do so. How about we both do a little cleaning in the day room? We took away some of the good vibes in this place by how we acted. Let's give something back." (I call this consequence *reparation*. It's like community service and is explained in chapter 18.)

5. Who else is available to help?

Outreach is often the intervention of choice. Sometimes bringing in a neutral party reduces tension. Fewer limits will need to be set if the kids know that their child-guiders work as a team and will bring in other people to assist them in times of agitation.

Child-guiders often get angry at kids who incessantly act out. Sometimes the anger seriously crosses the line. At the juvenile justice center I guided, I noticed right away that certain staff members who openly disliked particular kids were keeping those kids on lower levels by manipulating the point system. Within a week, I changed the system so that every night all the staff were responsible for level assignments, a decision that had a very positive effect on the behavior of the residents.

Child-guiders are prone to overdo discipline when they are deprived of meaningful support and adequate teamwork. In residential settings, I often suggest to leaders that no care worker be allowed to issue a consequence that extends beyond his or her shift, a safeguard that protects all concerned.

6. Has this behavior occurred before, and does it follow a pattern?

If the behavior is recurrent and adhering to a pattern—occurring, for example, at the same time of the day, week, or month—look for possible precipitating factors (see chapter 12). Great effort should be devoted to detecting patterns and addressing the triggers.

7. How strong is my relationship with this child or group?

The stronger child-guiders' relationships with children or a group are, the more flexibility they will have in formulating an effective response. A very experienced child-guider with great relationships can let a kid or group act out more than a new guider should, because he has their trust and the skills to rein in their actions. Because children at risk tend to test adults to see who can keep them safe, any time relationships with children are not well established, child-guiders need to set strict limits to prove they can be trusted; softening limits over time is easier than firming them up. But they should not overdo it. New teachers often approach me in August, asking, "Do you know what the old teachers are telling me?" I respond, "Yup. Don't smile until Christmas!" The advice implies that if we start out warm, funny, and friendly with our students they'll walk all over us, which is not necessarily true. Be warm, funny, and friendly but have high expectations and set good-enough limits.

8. What do I know about this child's developmental, social, medical, neurological, and psychological histories and current issues?

The better informed child-guiders are about children's backgrounds, the more beneficial their responses will be. Each hour spent exploring a child's history can reveal important information and eliminate untold hours of strategizing. Kids with serious cognitive-developmental issues need an entirely different response approach.

9. Which approaches have worked in the past and which have not?

To avoid relying solely on trial and error, child-guiders should reflect on previous responses to children's misconduct and, after eliminating those that did not lead to behavioral changes, repeat those that did. Some kids will be okay with doing an extra job as a consequence but will not take a time-out or a break if asked to. Child-guiders who have no history of the children should begin collecting data for the future.

10. **What personal characteristics—such as age, height, weight, family customs, physical appearance, hygiene, coordination— could be influencing the child's behavior, as well as my understanding of it?**

Personal factors such as these are often linked with low self-esteem, hence it is important to be empathetic. A boy who acts out in gym class, for example, may require additional sensitivity if he is over-weight and uncoordinated. Also child-guiders should be mindful of their own prejudices, and refuse to let these influence their responses.

Is it possible to reflect on all ten of these questions in the few seconds that pass before you must act? Yes, it is; the human brain is capable of factoring in copious amounts of information and responding appropriately in a brief period of time. Child-guiders will soon find that the more experienced they are at assessing such issues, the more helpful their interventions will be.

Case Examples

The following examples illustrate how and why context determines the best possible response regardless of the behavior at hand. In each case, although behavior is the culprit circumstances provide the corrective insight.

Carol, while driving her troubled seven-year-old foster child Mark to his dentist appointment, noticed that he was growing increasingly anxious and restless. When they were about five blocks from the dentist's office, he swore at her. She knew that Mark was terrified of the dentist and that his fear, combined with his heightened state of agitation, might cause him to physically overreact to any kind of consequence. To avoid compromising their safety while on the road, she decided to ignore the swearing until after his appointment.

When they returned home, Carol discussed the swearing incident with Mark, empathizing with his anxiety. She helped him see that he had hurt her feelings and that even in times of great anxiety there are better ways to respond. Mark apologized for swearing, whereupon Carol explained that there would be no consequence, given how nervous he was; that in the future she would expect a little more from him; and that swearing would warrant a five-minute time-out. She also apologized to him. She said she could have done a better job preparing him for this visit.

Four hours later Mark became upset when Carol reminded him to complete his assigned chore of clearing the dinner table. Again he swore at her. Carol calmly asked him to take a two-minute time-out and to think about better ways of expressing his anger, strategies they had been working on. This time the same behavior (swearing) elicited a different response. Because their safety was not at stake, Carol was free to act in a therapeutically ideal manner.

Another example of a context-driven intervention is the following story. A staff member named George was left alone to cover a group home for at-risk adolescents while his co-worker, Stan, went to pick up a video. Manny, one of the largest and strongest residents, suddenly lost control and, swinging his fists in horizontal arcs, began moving toward George. No amount of verbal redirection halted his advance. George, acutely aware of the risk to his personal safety, headed for a nearby office, shut the door, and called the police. The arrival of the squad car prompted Manny to cease his aggression. When the officer left, George and Manny processed the event and jointly determined the consequence: due to the seriousness of the incident, Manny was grounded to the house for two weeks.

Later a resident named Larry began shouting obscenities and advancing in a threatening way toward George. This time Stan was available to intervene. Together, they physically restrained Larry and led him to a quiet room. After helping him regain control, they reviewed the incident and set the consequences: Larry was to be separated from the other residents until bedtime and grounded to the house for three days; he was also asked to write about the episode, identifying better choices he could have made. In this story, two similar forms of aggression elicited different responses, each of which was needed to preserve safety. In the first incident, the kids needed to know that extremely stiff consequences would be levied for violent behavior during times of inadequate staffing; when understaffing was not an issue, the consequences were less severe and more therapeutically ideal.

A third example of how context should impact response involves Mr. Nickerson, a sixth-grade teacher with thirty students and, due to budget cutbacks, no full-time aide. One day Samuel hurled a spitball across the room. In response, Mr. Nickerson calmly asked Samuel to report to the principal's office. Mr. Nickerson knew he could not afford to devote too much attention to one student at the expense of the other thirty-four. Yet he also knew that ignoring the behavior would identify him as a weak limit-setter who ignored inappropriate behavior, opening the door to more misconduct. Considering the lack of human resources available, Mr. Nickerson provided the best possible intervention. Even so, he felt frustrated. He told one of his colleagues that if he had had a full-time aide and only twenty students he would have sat with Samuel at the back of the room and quietly talked with him to discover what had precipitated his behavior. Then he might have found out that the boy was being scapegoated by other students, and devised a plan incorporating a special signal, changed seating, and regular check-ins, as well as a consequence for throwing spitballs.

A Best Possible Response versus the Therapeutic Ideal

Because of the diminishing availability of support systems and resources, as well as safety concerns, foster parents, teachers, child-care workers, social workers, and detention counselors are often forced to respond to situations in ways that are not therapeutically ideal and to intervene instead with measures that fall within a range of best possible responses. Chuck discovered this reality while counseling Fred and Shannon Cartright, a couple about to adopt two foster sisters—Ashley, age nine, and Brandy, age five—who had been living with them for six months. Things were not going smoothly: the sisters, having come from a highly dysfunctional biological family and then an abusive foster family, spoke rudely to others, stayed up into the early-morning hours, refused to accept limits, and were at times physically aggressive toward each other, as well as the Cartrights. By the time Chuck was asked to intervene, Fred and Shannon were about ready to give up on their adoption plans.

It was clear to Chuck that the Cartrights loved these girls and that, despite the turmoil, meaningful bonding had taken place. To help restore order and buy time until more resources could be put in place—namely, individual therapy and self-management lessons for the girls, family counseling, and respite opportunities—he recommended behavioral incentive charts for Ashley and Brandy. Improved conduct would be indicated on the charts and would earn the girls stickers that they could trade in for material rewards. He also instructed the Cartrights to enhance their interactions with the girls in other behavioral strategies.

Ashley and Brandy responded well to the structure the sticker charts provided. Before long, more and more outside supports were set in place, during which time the home climate continued to improve. Two months after the first sticker charts were hung, the girls did not need them anymore. Incentives are often a means to an end. (The use of incentives is examined in greater detail in chapter 19.)

Chuck, however, had second thoughts about the intervention. Aware that certain schools of thought disparage forms of behavior modification based on "bribing" children, he hoped the girls would modify their behavior not in exchange for material rewards but to improve their relationship with the Cartrights and thereby "earn" their foster parents' ongoing nurturing. After reviewing the situation from a context perspective—the girls had been close to being removed from the home, no one had been happy, and something had to be done—he concluded that the incentive charts had been a catalyst for more harmonious family relations and had been the best possible solution to the situation until more therapeutic measures could be set in place.

Any time that we, like Chuck, begin to doubt the value of an intervention we have recommended, we should remember the following guidelines. Our first obligation is to provide the best possible context-sensitive response to challenging behavior; our second obligation is to advocate for better resources so that in the future our best possible response can more closely approximate the therapeutic ideal. In effect, good behavior management occurs on two levels: micro and macro. While performing micro-level work, we must do the best we can with the resources at hand. While performing macro-level work, we need to look at the broader picture of behavioral change and advocate for additional support. At the end of each day, we can think about our interactions with the children and ask ourselves, "Did I respond in the best possible manner?" If the answer is yes, rather than worry that we may have failed to give the kids enough we can look in the mirror and say, "I did the best I could today with what I had… and I must fight for more!"

— CHAPTER 11 —

Asking the Right Questions

THE BEST WAY TO DEAL WITH PROBLEM BEHAVIOR is to prevent it through proactive thinking. Proactive thinkers prepare for the future by reflecting on the past and present. Any time a child acts out, for example, a proactive thinker will ask, "What could I have done to avert this situation?" She will then pose a series of questions to arrive at a productive answer.

Proactive Thinking in Action

At the conclusion of a behavior management workshop for elementary school parents, a visibly worn-out foster mother named Stephanie stated: "Weekday mornings are awful at our house. We start off each one tense and argumentative, then the kids fight in the car on the way to school. If it's not about who sits in the front seat or which radio station we listen to, they'll find something else to bicker over. I spend the entire trip yelling at them. What can I do?"

What Stephanie could do, I reasoned, depended on the particular triggers for the children's misbehavior. Consequently, over the next fifteen minutes I asked her a series of questions to help her view the problem proactively:

- What do the kids eat in the morning? Is it hot or cold? Do they make it themselves, or is it made for them? Do they sometimes skip breakfast?

- What does the interior of the car look like—messy? neat? What about the interior of the house, such as common areas and bedrooms?

- Are the children physically and emotionally prepared for school?

Does anyone make sure they are properly dressed, clean, well groomed, and carrying their homework as well as other school essentials?

- Are there established routines and chores in the morning—set wake-up and shower times, table setting, clean up, and so forth?

- What do the children do before getting into the car? Do they enjoy a somewhat relaxed breakfast or do they quickly gulp it down? Do they do something interesting before entering the car or do they sit around bored? Do they fight over the TV, computer, or use of the bathroom? Is there a schedule in place that lists individual responsibilities?

- Does anyone give each child a hug or warm words of farewell before they leave for school?

- Do the kids run to the car or do they walk calmly? Is there a seating assignment for the car? Who decides which radio station to listen to?

- How do the children act at school? Do they get along with classmates? Do they have one or two good friends? How would you describe their relationships with teachers and their academic performance? In other words, are there factors at school that could be causing anticipatory anxiety?

- How well do the adults in the children's lives communicate with one another and the kids? Are the kids well informed about events that comprise their lives?

- Are there social, physical, psychological, or neurological issues at play that could be interfering with group dynamics and individual functioning?

- What kind of self-management skills are the kids practicing?

After contemplating Stephanie's answers to these questions, I helped her see the value in better structuring the children's morning routine and their transition to school by jointly preparing a weekly car-seating chart and radio preference schedule. I also suggested she start having weekly family meetings with her kids, during which they could properly schedule each morning's routines (shower times, chores, TV preference) and be empowered to bring up and resolve any ongoing issues like the ones she presented, and during which she could praise the kids' positive accomplishments. Further, I suggested she put more effort into teaching and practicing new self-management skills with her kids, especially skills that had been presented in the workshop.

A few weeks later I received a note from her explaining that our proactive plans had significantly defused the morning chaos, and the family meetings had enhanced their communication and family cohesion. Similarly, daily or weekly class or group meetings can help teachers and youth-care professionals better connect with the students and enhance group cohesion.

Key Areas of Inquiry and Prevention Techniques

When we play detective and ask the right questions, the answers often inspire a remedial course of action. Following are key areas of inquiry along with techniques that can help prevent many of the problem behaviors child-guiders grapple with in every setting.

Are Basic Needs Being Met?

Kids with emotional and behavioral issues have at times missed out on having basic needs met in their earliest years of life; therefore, they yearn desperately to have them met as they mature. Under basic needs are two major aspects of healthy development—nutrition and safety, each of which must be addressed independently to help prevent troublesome behavior.

Are Nutritional Needs Being Met? The need for food should be met unconditionally. Withholding food should never be used as a consequence for misbehavior; if it is, it will most likely interfere with learning and spark more serious transgressions. Youngsters who head off to school hungry or who skip lunch are less apt to learn and more likely to act out, as are children who live with uncertainty about their next meal. A good breakfast in the morning increases the likelihood of a successful start to the day, especially if it is prepared by a significant adult because then it is both physically and emotionally nurturing. With teenagers who prefer to skip breakfast or make it themselves, the importance of eating a solid meal at the start of the day can still be stressed, thereby conveying the message that you care. Try to meet teens halfway. If they prefer an oatmeal bar to a sit-down meal, go for it. In addition to breakfast, kids need ample snacks, sufficient portions of food, and regular mealtimes, requirements that enable them to function at their highest potential socially, emotionally, behaviorally, and cognitively. More and more is being written about the benefits of the family dinner, a time when families can reconnect and recharge without electronic gizmos. Further, teachers should keep a stash of snacks in their room for kids who are hungry. And when a teacher has an occasional lunch with an at-risk student it can significantly enhance their relationship. Needless to say, the families of kids with ongoing food deprivation issues should be contacted, and assistance offered.

Be aware that many kids who reside in out-of-home placements and have histories of neglect and deprivation secretly steal food from the kitchen to hoard in their bedrooms because they do not trust that adults will offer enough. Showing such kids the pantry may help eradicate this behavior by assuring them that food is in plentiful supply. For example, at a residential center where I once worked, I would give newly arrived kids a tour, making sure to take them to the basement to view the storage closets well stocked with food.

Is the Physical Environment Organized? For at-risk kids who require a high degree of structure, predictability, and safety, messy, disordered environments are a behavioral hazard, sending the message "This setting is unpredictable and possibly unsafe. We don't take pride in this place or care about you."

I recall how three hours into my first shift as senior counselor at a residential treatment center for abused and neglected children, the place was in chaos. Twelve girls, ranging in age from seven to fourteen, were misbehaving big time, and my requests for quiet were falling on deaf ears.

I dialed the home number of our unit director, Ellen, and explained: "You've gotta get in here. The girls are wild. They're not listening to anything I'm saying."

"I'll be right in," she promised.

I could hardly wait for Ellen's arrival. I pictured her, brilliant and directive, charging through the doors and immediately putting the kids in their place. Finally, Ellen walked into the fray and, with eyes like lasers, scanned the large living room, then said, "Cathy and Joan, get the mop and head into the bathroom. I want to see that floor shinin'! Ellie, Rhonda, Becky, take the laundry into the dorm and start folding. Mavis, get a cloth and some Windex, and hit the mirrors; I'll help you out in a minute. Lisa, Jill—get the two vacuum cleaners. Jill, you do the hallway; Lisa, the living room and dorm." Within two minutes the unit was serene. These girls, all of whom had come from chaotic environments, relied on order and consistency; I, however, inexperienced and naïve, had let the state of the unit deteriorate by prioritizing talking over doing. Now whenever I enter a school or other facility that serves children, particularly those at risk, I remove papers from the floor, return chairs to their proper places, and straighten the pictures on the walls because I have learned that kids with underdeveloped internal structures require external structure to experience a sense of organization and safety. Even kids with no remarkable baggage do better when an environment is ordered and attractive.

During workshops, I ask participants, "How would you feel if you returned home tonight and your home or apartment was neat?" People say, "Great!" "That would be fantastic!" "Awesome!"

"Yes, you'd feel energized!" I comment. "But how would you feel if you entered your home and it was a mess?"

"Terrible," "Unmotivated," "Drained," they say.

I then suggest, "Multiply how you'd feel times ten, and that's how at-risk kids feel. If a setting looks bad, kids feel and often act bad!"

If you work with kids who smash holes in walls or doors, write on walls, knock over or break furniture, or throw objects around a room, think twice about letting them work or live amid the devastation; the disorder of the setting will exacerbate the internal disorder they already harbor, leaving them even more prone to act out. Although an appropriate consequence is to let them restore their settings to their original state or repair any damage, if this can't be done in a reasonable period of time find another way to hold them responsible for their actions and consider restoring the environment yourself. Think of it as adding bricks to their foundations.

I recall taking over as the program director of an adolescent girls' program that was experiencing serious behavioral issues. All I did for the first few weeks was paint, organize, and clean. Some of the girls would ask, "Why are you so into how this place looks?" "Because how this place looks is a reflection of how much we care!" I'd respond. Within a month or so, the level of functioning among the residents had improved dramatically. Kids are happier, and their brains are primed for enhanced success, in environments that are clean, neat, and attractive.

In addition to cleanliness and order, a focus on warmth, color, and stimulation makes kids feel good and increases the probability that they will function well. Too many classrooms and programs for at-risk kids have drab walls and an uninspiring appearance. If your setting is anything like these, think about a fresh coat of paint, as well as vibrant artwork, festive curtains, captivating posters, and perhaps a plant or two. A spruced-up environment energizes and engages, as well as sending a message of safety and caring.

In addition, well-placed furniture offers protection by creating clear boundaries, which decreases anxiety levels. When designing the layout for a classroom or common area, use chairs, tables, and couches to partition areas for different purposes. By creating small, semiprivate gathering places, child-guiders divide and conquer, an invaluable approach.

When deciding on the placement of furniture and equipment, be sure to allow for unobstructed supervision sight-lines that offer direct visual access to the children. If you are a foster parent, make sure your outdoor play area is visible from the kitchen window, front or back porch, or living room. If you are a teacher, make sure all the children's desks are within view when you are seated at your desk. Two or three rows of desks arranged in a semicircle facing the board a teacher uses most frequently, provide better sight-lines than a linear arrangement of six rows of desks. The easier it is for child-guiders to see the children, and the closer child-guiders are to the kids they serve, the better they will be at preventing potential difficulties and quickly responding to problems that arise.

Another feature essential to a safe environment is break areas. Kids with behavioral issues often require places they can retreat to when they need to chill out and regain composure. To avoid needless disruptions, kids should have multiple places for retreat; they are more likely to use these areas if they can choose where to go. Break areas will vary according to the setting. In general, they should be in sight of the child-guiders and comfortable. In some schools, teachers will ask an agitated or disruptive student to chill out in another teacher's room in lieu of the office—a place far less conducive to reflection—whereas in other schools a behavior inclusion specialist will escort the child to a quiet setting to work through the incident. Programs that deal effectively with seriously disturbed youngsters create safe time-out rooms where children who are having difficulty can regain self-control. Mats are available in case a child needs to be physically restrained, and light fixtures as well as other potentially harmful objects are safely out of reach.

Regardless of the setting, a chill-out space should have a nonpunitive atmosphere, since its purpose is to assist children in regaining control, talking about their actions and alternative ways to express their feelings, and exploring possible underlying issues. Toward that end, chairs need to be comfortable and facing the center of the room rather than a corner. Lighting should be pleasant, reading materials or schoolwork readily available, and, at times, soothing background music can be beneficial. For kids whose behavior is influenced by organic issues, such as those associated with sensory-integration conditions, weighted vests, a swing, clay, and a host of other calming tools and apparatus should be available.

Sadly, I have visited special education schools and residential programs that make quiet rooms unpleasant for their kids. At one program, they kept the temperature abnormally cold. Quiets rooms should never be designed to be aversive. Interestingly, it appears that when residential and special education schools minimize or get rid of their quiet rooms behavior improves.

Are the Children Physically and Emotionally Prepared for Each Endeavor?

Kids who are prepared for each segment of the day fare better than those who are not. One of the most critical facets of readiness is appearance. Because a child who looks dirty and disheveled on the outside is apt to feel the same way on the inside, it is important to emphasize the value of dress, personal grooming, and hygiene. A youngster who is expected to look neat and well-groomed will feel loved and cared for, and think, "I'm worth fussing over. I'm a pretty important person." Even kids who cringe at such proclamations as "Time for a shower" or "Please wash your hands" are likely to feel better about themselves once the "ordeal" is over. Students who enter school improperly groomed and clothed are far more likely than others to struggle with behavioral issues. Teachers should gently reach out to students who need help in this regard, making sure at all times not to undermine their dignity.

Years ago I was the unit director of a group of seven- to twelve-year-old boys at a large residential treatment center, all of whom had histories of abuse and neglect. Every morning as they lined up to go to school I scrutinized each one to make sure his belt was on, his hair was combed, his fingernails were clean, his clothes were free of holes and dirt, his shoes were tied, and his face was scrubbed. At times, the kids gave me trouble, saying, "I don't *care* how I look!" or "I don't *like* combing my hair!" In response to their complaints, I would reply, "Let me get this straight—you're mad at me because I care about you and want you to look handsome for school?" I also constructed a pegboard to hold twelve hairbrushes, and any time a kid messed up his hair at the last minute, I would have his brush ready to restore neatness. I wanted these kids to go off to school with the knowledge that someone valued them and thought they were good-looking dudes!

But what about clashes with kids over colored hair, "fashionably" ripped clothing, or shorts in winter—where do we draw the line? Distinguishing between acceptable and unacceptable clothing for school is not always easy in today's society, but if we want kids to know that school is a place for behaving respectfully and learning, we need to inform them that the clothes they wear to the mall may not be appropriate for class, drawing a line somewhere. If you are a biological or foster parent or a milieu counselor, check out "appearance norms" and allow your kids to be in style without going to extremes. Then discuss the matter with them, listening to their point of view, and negotiate mutually agreeable terms, such as it's okay to wear one earring, a small spike in their hair, and ripped jeans once a week—but no earring through the nose.

Some kids overdo their appearance to assert their individuality or to broadcast their unhappiness about their lives. In such instances, you might try to address this issue in a gentle, empathic manner such as the following: "Sometimes kids come to us with extreme appearances, such as piercings, rings in multiple places, multicolored hair, intense clothing. Sometimes kids do this to assert their individuality. And sometimes they look the way they do to send the message 'I'm one unhappy kid. Help me.' I'd like you to think about this. Maybe it's time to tone it down. If how you appear is in any way a message, we got it and we're going to help you get back on track. And one other thing to think about: people—future employers, teachers, and others—sometimes get turned off by kids with extreme appearances. We want to help you eliminate roadblocks on your way to a successful life."

Some schools and programs require their kids to wear uniforms or the same kind of clothing each day, which can reduce interpersonal tensions among kids for numerous reasons. The choice to enact such rules should be based on the needs of the group. However, the practice some residential and detention programs have of requiring kids to wear colored T-shirts based on their behavioral level stigmatizes the lower-level kids and is at odds with strength-based practice.

In addition to hygiene and grooming, being prepared refers to gathering all the essentials needed for each upcoming event. For example, a child who has not completed his homework, has forgotten to have a note signed, or is missing the right materials, such as writing instruments, books, or papers, is likely to start off the school day in a state of anxiety, which may only intensify as the hours unfold and lead to behavioral issues. With kids who are organizationally challenged, establishing a regular "check-in time" the night before to ensure that all necessities have been taken care of, then in the morning quickly making sure everything the child will need is in his book bag, can enhance readiness.

Educators can reduce behavioral issues by helping kids with their organizational challenges and talents. A plethora of strategies exist that help organizationally challenged kids function better, such as assignment books, lists, and Post-it notes for reminders. Homework is often a trouble spot for kids. Failure to complete an assignment may hinge on any number of factors—among them, the work is too difficult or not properly broken down, the home environment is too chaotic, the child is preoccupied with personal issues, or the child has forgotten to bring it home. The child-guider's task is to discover the causes of the problem and come up with reasonable solutions. Tackling homework as part of a structured routine— at the same time every day, for example—is a time-tested way of helping to ensure its completion. It is also wise to have the child do his homework in the same place, preferably one that is quiet and free of distractions. Strong school-to-home communication can also greatly enhance homework output. Ultimately, the child-guider's goal is to encourage kids to develop systems for making sure everything is in place before embarking on any new task or endeavor.

Are There Established Schedules and Routines?

Daily schedules and set routines provide structure, predictability, and a sense of safety in the sometimes scary world of an at-risk kid. In fact, the more anxious and out of control a child feels, the more critical the need is for predictable schedules and routines. Parents of a healthy eight-year-old can afford to be more relaxed about daily schedules than foster parents of an eight-year-old who has grown up the hard way. The same holds true for special education teachers and workers at a juvenile detention center or other out-of-home placement settings. Although middle and high school teachers don't post and review the daily schedule each morning the way an elementary school teacher would do, it's often helpful for them to preview the class in advance, saying, "Okay, we'll be doing independent work for the first fifteen minutes, followed by…"

Routines also delineate segments of the day, helping a child feel comfortable about stopping one activity and beginning another. Given a schedule, he can anticipate the end of playtime, for example, assured that it is time for another activity and that he can play again the next day.

"Okay," Frankie's foster father might say, "in ten minutes it will be time for dinner. Why don't you start putting away some of your trucks." If Frankie understands that dinner is usually served at the same time each evening, chances are that he will start cleaning up and come to the dinner table on time. However, if dinner is served at a different time each evening and if he is not given ample warning, he is more likely to procrastinate, be late for dinner, and misbehave during the meal.

A lack of structure to the day often precipitates power struggles. This phenomenon becomes highly visible among many at-risk kids just before a school vacation. Rather than being excited about their upcoming free time, they become increasingly anxious about its ill-defined structure and begin acting out more intensely. Instead of being excited about summer vacation, many kids seem upset and depressed about the months ahead, feeling that they are losing the predictability and warmth that school provides.

One way to help at-risk kids feel more at ease about impending transitions is to post daily schedules. Foster parents can display upcoming events at the start of each morning so that all family members will know the plan for the day; home-to-school and school-to-home shifts, traditionally hectic interludes, can be calmed with a five-minute preview or catch-up meeting, setting the stage for the next segment of the day. Similarly, elementary school teachers can post a class schedule on the bulletin board and review it aloud at the beginning of each day, whereas junior and high school teachers can inform students about the content of each class, explaining, for example, "We'll do independent work for the first twenty minutes, then we'll have the review quiz." Residential care workers can post a daily "What's Happening" sheet listing the staff members on duty, appointments, activities, medications, visits, chores, and even menus, and review this information at the daily transition meeting after school.

Are the Kids Kept Informed about Upcoming Transitions?

If a child is rambunctious during a transition, his agitation will carry over to the next activity. To avoid such situations, inform children of significant transitions well before they occur. Your announcement can be as simple as, "Kids, we'll be leaving for school in ten minutes. Please turn off the music, put the cards away, and sit quietly in the living room with your book bags. Thanks." Similar notification can be given before the next class, a meal, or bedtime.

Remember, kids with emotional and behavioral challenges often have difficulty delaying gratification. If they are having fun, they are reluctant to stop for fear that more fun may be a long time coming. Because they live for the moment, they must often be eased out of pleasurable activities.

Many variables can be manipulated to reduce stimulation for a child about to transition to a new activity. Consider decreasing physical exertion levels, for example, as well as dimming the lights, lowering the volume on the TV or radio, and redirecting evocative conversations. The point is to be mindful of *how the current activity will impact the next one.* If bedtime is rapidly approaching, do not plan on sending a child off to bed in the middle of a gripping movie but rather choose a TV show that will end before bedtime—or better yet, read a story or involve him in quiet, pleasing activities. In a group-home setting, do not allow phone conversations immediately before bedtime, for they may be overly stimulating.

Robert, the new director of a twelve-bed young boys' residential unit, worked with another variable to ease the transition to bedtime. The routine in place before his arrival proved to be a dismal failure: from 7:30 p.m. until "lights out," the boys were required to sit quietly and watch TV in the common area. Because some of the boys had ADHD and short attention spans and many others had poor social skills, the quiet-time routine lasted about fifteen minutes before dissolving into tantrums, boisterous acting out, and unfriendly staff-child interactions.

During his second day on the job, Robert purchased four wall lamps and hung them in different areas of the large living space. That night he told the boys that instead of watching TV they could choose to spend their quiet time drawing, having fun with action figures, or playing games in any one of the newly designated areas. He also made the kitchen available, a room that had previously been off-limits after dinner. Robert's "divide and conquer" strategy worked wonders. The kids loved having choices and adapted well to their new level of personal responsibility. Evenings soon became mellow—the frequency of misbehavior dropping dramatically—and, in turn, the adult-child relationships improved.

How Are Transitions Managed?

Because poorly managed transitions can cause acting out, it is important to conduct them effectively. The key to orderly conduct during transitions is to ensure that children understand how they are to behave when moving from one point to another and are given the opportunity to practice good transitions. Just as importantly, child-guiders must provide proper supervision during these times, such as being present in hallways between classes in middle and high schools. The following scenario reflects the results of poorly managed transitions.

Emily, a new unit director at a residential treatment setting for abused and neglected children, was placed in charge of a rowdy group of seven-to twelve-year-old boys. The boys frequently misbehaved during meals and other group events. Emily reasoned that the high level of acting out was fueled by the poorly managed transitions that were taking place. As a result, Emily decided to tighten them. For the next two weeks, any time the boys strayed from the group, fooled around, became too loud, skipped stairs, or ran while en route to a new activity, she took them back to their starting points and had them try again. As she walked them back, she respectfully let them know why it was important to proceed in a calm and orderly fashion. Once, on the way to dinner she had the boys return to their living unit four times to "try it again" because they were not walking properly. Within a few weeks, Emily was conducting excellent transitions, and her group was far better behaved during the subsequent activities.

Is it also possible to line up teenagers—kids who do not like to conform, because they are carving out niches for themselves as separate individuals? The answer is yes and no. While it is important to keep teens feeling safe and secure, control measures must be tempered with respect for their autonomy. The level of structure to employ in transitions, therefore, needs to rise and fall in relation to the degree of acting out. In other words, the more frequently problem behaviors occur, the more tightly monitored the youths must be.

To ensure their safety, incarcerated teens at a juvenile detention center are expected to line up and walk quietly from one activity to the next. Those who do not are held accountable for their actions, often losing key privileges. At the other end of the spectrum are junior and senior high school students whose teachers report problem behaviors in the hallways. Increased adult supervision between classes has been shown to reduce such tumult. In all teenage settings, the challenge for adults in charge is to maintain a safe environment without misusing power.

Are There Significant Problem Areas?

Many children misbehave in anticipation of a stressful situation, such as an appointment with a therapist, a difficult class in school, a confrontation with an antagonistic peer, or a visit from a biological parent. The better a child-guider is at identifying the source of anxiety, the more effective her proactive interventions will be.

Children who misbehave before and during school, for example, may be asking for academic assistance, saying, "School isn't much fun for me. Figure out why it's so difficult. Help me succeed." For children chronically struggling with academics, a thorough evaluation is often imperative to determine if there are neurological, psychological, or physical issues compromising their academic progress.

Another way to prepare children for anxiety-producing events is by letting them know what to expect. One foster mother uses this approach: "Doug, you have an appointment with Dr. Sullivan after lunch. Remember the testing we talked about at your last conference? Well, Dr. Sullivan is going to give you three reading tests today, none of which will involve right or wrong answers. The results will help your teachers know how to teach you better. You should be finished by three o'clock, then we'll go to the arcade." A camp counselor employs a similar approach: "Sarah, we will be going to the infirmary after lunch. Dr. Harvey is just going to make sure your ear infection has cleared up. She'll probably look in your ears and throat." A simple explanation of a dreaded encounter can help dissolve most negative fantasies about it, especially among kids who often fear the worst. Knowing that things are under control gives them courage to face their fears without sending out more behavioral flares for help.

Are Hellos and Good-Byes Conducted Meaningfully?

Hellos and good-byes, as noted earlier, highly influence human behavior. Children who are greeted warmly by child-guiders are neurologically and psychologically primed for better functioning. Good-byes are equally important. A child who receives a big hug and smile from his foster dad as he is dropped off at school walks into his classroom more apt to say hello to learning. By contrast, a child whose parting message from his dad is "Wait till I see you after school—this kind of nonsense is unacceptable!" enters his classroom burdened by a lingering negative good-bye. No matter how strained a situation early in the day may have been, a child-guider's last encounter with a child calls for warmth, understanding, and at times, affection, such as "Craig, it's been a rough morning, but you're still my main man.

Have a great day!" or "You were a bit off track today, Joel. All trains get off track from time to time. But no matter what you do, remember I'm thrilled to be working with you."

In his book *Before Happiness*, Shawn Achor writes about a major health-care operator that wanted to improve the quality of care in its hospitals. To do so, they implemented the 5/10 rule: If any of their employees (doctors, nurses, maintenance) came within ten feet of a non–hospital employee, they were asked to make eye contact and smile; if they came within five feet, they were to stop and say hello. Not surprisingly, the new protocol significantly enhanced morale and quality of care in these settings.[1]

When I told a friend, Ann, director of a psychiatric unit for adolescents in Virginia, about Achor's 5/10 protocol, she immediately responded: "We do that. But we call it 'four and eight.' An employee who comes within eight feet of a non–hospital employee has to stop and greet them; one who comes within four feet must approach the patient and offer to take her to her appointment." Ann believes the four and eight rule has had a very positive effect on their level of care.

In my forty-year career, I have visited hundreds of schools and child-guiding programs. I can usually tell within thirty minutes how well a setting is functioning just by the "feel" I get when I arrive. Right away I observe how visitors are greeted upon entering. I look to see if people acknowledge each other or mind their own business. With schools, I arrive very early to observe who is greeting students when they exit their buses and enter the building and if the principal is enthusiastically greeting kids and staff. I also look to see if the setting is neat and attractive and if displays of staff and child recognition are visible.

When homes, schools, and programs create safe and engaging cultures, they help reduce the occurrence of major problems. George Kelling and James Wilson coined the term "broken window theory" in 1982, which maintains that when small issues are addressed, such as repairing broken windows in vacant or occupied apartments, bigger problems decrease, such as violent crimes.[2] People tend to act and feel better when they live in settings that look good, provide positive human interaction, and feel safe, while settings devoid of positive human interaction and in a state of disrepair breed greater problematic behavior. During the 1980s, Rudy Giuliani, the new mayor of New York, along with his police captain, William Bratton, dramatically lowered the frequency of serious crime in New York using elements of the broken window theory.

My favorite restaurant is Moe's Southwest Grill because whenever a customer walks through its doors all the employees yell, "Welcome to Moe's!" The greeting makes customers feel good, enhancing happiness and positive functioning. Based on the psychological and neurological effects of a warm greeting and how such actions contribute to positive relationships and cultures, it behooves child-guiders to make their hellos and good-byes warm and meaningful.

During workshops, I ask participants to walk around the room and greet as many people as they can. When asked, "How are you doing?" they are told to choose one of five responses: "Fantastic!" "I'm living the dream!" "Unbelievable!" "Awesome!" "All the better for seeing you!" People smile and laugh during this exercise. I then ask them, "How are you feeling?" They say, "Great!" "Pumped!" "Happy." And I say, "Okay, make sure you greet the kids you work with like this every day."

I also encourage the kids I work with to use a memorable greeting. I tell adolescents: "Imagine you're one of four kids waiting to be interviewed at McDonald's, and the assistant manager comes out and says, 'Hi, I'm Albert Smith, the assistant manager. I'll be interviewing you all in about ten minutes.' Then he approaches the first kid and asks, 'How are you?' 'Okay,' he responds. 'And how are you?' he says to the second. 'I'm good.' 'And you, sir?' he says to the third. 'I'm fine, thanks.' Now he approaches you, the last in line, and asks, "How are you doing, young man?' 'I'm living the dream, sir. How about yourself?' you respond. Who do you think made the best impression and will get hired?"

Depending on the circumstances, it's often beneficial to accompany these salutations with a gesture. Based on the age of the kids, your relationship with them, and a setting's protocols, hugs, a slap five, or a fist bump are wonderful ways to enhance hellos and good-byes and foster strong connections. Michelangelo, who celebrated the value of touch, put it this way: "To touch is to give life." And research conducted by neuroscientist Edmund Rolls reveals that touch "activates the brain's orbitofrontal cortex, which is linked to feelings of reward and compassion."[3]

A guidance counselor, Susan, at an alternative high school in Indiana sent me a note that read: "Charlie, I attended fourteen hours of your training. But the best thing you taught was to give kids fist bumps and slap them five. Ever since I've added touch to my repertoire, my relationships have improved significantly."

Some child-guiding schools and programs do not allow any kind of touching between staff members and kids, employing a no-touch policy. Although it's understandable why such a policy has been established, in most cases it's detrimental to children and child-guiders alike.

Are Communication Systems in Place?

Child-guiders who communicate well among themselves prevent and de-escalate challenging behavior far more effectively than those who do not. Why? Because ongoing communication within a child's inner network of providers—including foster parents, teachers, counselors, coaches, and clergy—keeps everyone informed each step of the way and reduces splitting.

Following are five proactive guidelines that can be used in developing a top-notch communication system. First, keep all important telephone numbers, email, and other addresses on hand. Record the telephone numbers and addresses of key players in an easily accessible Rolodex, address book, tablet, or smartphone, and update this data as needed. For foster or adoptive parents and out-of-home placements, prominently post telephone numbers for critical local contacts, such as the fire department, police department, poison control center, and, for immediate refreshment, your favorite pizzeria.

Second, identify roles, boundaries, and expectations. Agree on whose job it should be to relay information; how frequently it should be transmitted; the sort of information that needs to be conveyed; the best medium for communicating, such as telephone, fax, mail, email, text, or face-to-face conversations; and the factors that constitute an emergency situation.

Third, establish crisis response procedures. Whenever safety appears compromised and reactions are slow, confused, or nonexistent, uncertainty takes hold and tension levels rise in subtle yet destructive ways. Having a plan for such eventualities can instill child-guiders with the confidence needed to set proper limits. The best team approach is to devise your own 911 communication system for securing behavioral help fast.

Years ago an elementary school in Massachusetts created a new position for a behavior inclusion specialist and hired Sean for the job. Before the school year began, however, the faculty realized that since each classroom was equipped with only an antiquated intercom, teachers would be unable to reach Sean quickly if one of their students was in serious trouble. To solve the problem, the school bought four walkie-talkies: one for Sean, one for the front-desk secretary, and one for each of the two teachers with the most challenging students.

When school opened in September, the faculty was delighted with the crisis response system they had created. Sean kept his walkie-talkie clipped to his belt and arrived promptly on the scene whenever he was called. The teachers who had not been furnished with a device buzzed the office, whereupon the secretary would dispatch Sean to the proper class. In many instances, he was able to help a struggling student stay in class and work through the difficulty rather than take a time-out in the office and perhaps never examine the situation. At the end of the year, one of the teachers told him, "What a difference emergency backup has made. We were more relaxed, more positive, able to give the kids more attention, and could set more effective limits."

A fourth recommendation for enhancing core-group contact is to utilize written forms of communication. Verbally conveyed information is often rushed, sketchy, easily distorted, and unlikely to reach the appropriate person. Writing down the facts, on the other hand, ensures that they will be properly relayed. Written communication can take several forms. Child welfare agencies could post important information on walls and bulletin boards. Residential centers could require staff members to read key logs and initial the documents before starting a shift; such logs might be used to track behavior patterns, note important events, and store data for treatment planning. Some foster parents keep a daily journal of their children's progress, in which they record the frequency of misbehavior, times of day in which it occurred, precipitating factors, and duration of the episodes. Such entries are often personally enlightening as well as informative to counselors and teachers.

Lastly, meet regularly—with group members and the children in your care. Weekly core-group meetings can provide a forum for reviewing each child's progress, addressing logistics, and keeping your vision unified. Weekly meetings with the children in class, on the unit, or at home can keep your communication lines open regarding recent happenings, changes in rules, current issues, and upcoming events. Daily meetings, when needed, can release tension and enhance relationships. Children who are empowered to participate in such discussions, and are respected for doing so, tend to exhibit improved behavior because regularly scheduled meetings of this sort foster connections.

In addition to meeting formally with the children, plan on more casual encounters with them. In fact, it is a good idea to check in with each child on a daily basis to see how things are going. A ritual of this sort, conducted at the same time of day, is sure to comfort many youngsters.

When communicating with a group of children, envision yourself as a pie with an equal slice of your best communication going to each one. Focusing on this image, you will be less tempted to veer away from kids whose behavior pushes you away, the ones likely to need you the most.

Are There Social, Physical, Psychological, or Neurological Issues at Play That Could Be Interfering with Group Dynamics and Individual Functioning?

Some kids struggle due to psychological factors, while others misbehave as a result of neurological stressors because their wiring compromises their ability to function appropriately. Many kids who struggle behaviorally have attention deficit hyperactivity disorder (ADHD); are on the autism spectrum, such as kids with Asperger's syndrome; or have been neurologically impaired by trauma. Sadly, growing numbers of children appear out of sync with their bodies and have sensory-integration issues. For child-guiders who raise or work with kids with emotional and behavioral challenges, it is imperative to know the kids from the inside out—their diagnosis and how to respond accordingly. This book provides a foundation for dealing with any kid who struggles with emotional and behavioral challenges, regardless of diagnosis. However, child-guiders should take extra steps to learn more specifically about the various diagnoses their kids have and develop diagnosis-appropriate approaches for guiding them.

For many kids, regardless of diagnosis, behavior problems are often related to underdeveloped self-management and social skills. A good understanding of at-risk kids clearly involves analyses of their self-management and social skill levels. It's not the diagnosis of ADHD that causes kids to misbehave; kids with ADHD have amazing strengths and potentials. The acting out is, at times, due to their lack of understanding and skills to properly manage their impulses and tendencies. Chapter 14 presents some innovative ways to help kids learn these important skills.

For some kids, especially those with neurological challenges, skill development is absolutely critical for improved functioning. But kids with the self-management skills to function better may lack the motivation to do so, and for them a powerful, strength-based environment can play a life-transforming role. Garbarino's research showed that if a troubled teen with a history of aggression enters high school and connects with an adult whom he believes views him as terrific, the odds of that kid committing further acts of aggression drop to around zero—results stemming from motivation rather than a new set of skills. For years I've watched unruly classes and groups change, almost overnight, when a new, strength-based child-guider assumes command. Skill development *and* a positive, strength-based environment lead to maximized potential.

Are There Any Underlying Psychological and Systems Issues?

An important consideration in developing a proactive viewpoint is understanding the psychological origins of misbehavior from a systems perspective. Clinical theory suggests that every family, school, or group-care setting is a system, and that members of a system will act out any time its leaders need help. Thus a child will sometimes misbehave to call attention to the problematic conduct of one or more of his caregivers, such as his parents, foster parents, a child-care provider, a teacher, or the staff at a residential facility. His acting out forces the adults into public view, exposing their issues and child-care practices, thereby increasing the likelihood that these adults will receive the help they need, and consequently, so will the child.

To apply a systems approach, take a long, hard look at what a child's actions are attempting to tell you. Who is he trying to help—parents experiencing marital discord, a stressed single parent making poor decisions, a burned-out teacher, or residential staff members who are punitive or not communicating well? When a child-guider takes the time to find answers to these questions, problem behaviors often dissipate.

Are the Kids Engaged?

People often ask, "What are the best residential programs you have visited?" I usually respond, "The best programs are the ones with the best activities that keep the kids engaged and active." If kids aren't stimulated by their environment, particularly those with emotional and behavioral challenges, they tend to act out.

Randall Sprick, an expert in classroom management, states two major reasons for student misbehavior: they don't believe they can do the work and the topics being taught are not relevant to their lives. A history teacher might be lecturing on Spain, while three of her students are worrying about Main, as in Main Street, a place they might be evicted from next week.[4] At-risk students will function remarkably better if the content is interesting, relevant, and engaging.

Following are two illuminating excerpts in this regard from *The Mo-*

tivational Breakthrough by Richard Lavoie, one of the foremost experts in student motivation.

> As teachers, let us commit to learning why "unmotivated" kids are able to find their drive and inspiration on playing fields, on skateboard courses, in poolrooms, in video arcades, on mall concourses . . . or at nine thousand feet. What do these settings provide that we do not provide in the classroom? We constantly search for ways that we can "change the child." Perhaps the first significant change should come from us. Perhaps we should first analyze and change our policies, procedures, and practices when dealing with hard-to-reach kids.[5]

> Most teachers and parents recognize that motivation is the key to learning. Reflect for a moment on your favorite teacher in high school. The chances are that he was an effective motivator. He inspired you. He was not merely a teacher, he was also a leader. He did not necessarily make learning fun, but he made learning attainable and purposeful. Whether you serve children as a teacher, parent, coach, or instructor, you will multiply your effectiveness immeasurably if you learn how to motivate your charges and maintain that motivation throughout the learning process.[6]

Years ago while consulting at a large high school in Colorado in a low socioeconomic area, I was asked to observe a problematic art class in which many students lacked motivation, had tuned out the instructor, and were chatting with their buddies or sleeping at their desks. To give the teacher a better idea of how to motivate the students, I approached him during a break and, playing the role of tough teen, engaged him in the following dialogue.

ME [IN TOUGH TEEN'S VOICE]: So why do I need to learn art?

INSTRUCTOR: Well, what are you going to be after you graduate?

ME: A mechanic. I'm good with cars.

INSTRUCTOR: Well, are you going to paint any of those cars?

ME: Of course I'll paint them.

INSTRUCTOR: Well, then, you're going to need to learn how to mix colors.

ME: Okay. I guess I should learn a little about art. Now how about telling the students what you just told me.

My college buddy Bob recently retired as head of the history department at a large high school in Maryland. Bob had taught for thirty-five years and never presented his material in a didactic manner. Instead, his students debated historical events, did exercises, and role-played. He understood that engaging teaching methods often turned underachievers into stars! Bob's implicit message was: "You will all succeed if I do my job right. I believe in all of you."

Kids clearly function much better if child-guiders make their environments more fun, hands-on, relevant, and interesting. Providing engaging activities will reduce behavior problems far more than rewards and consequences ever will.

— CHAPTER 12 —

Troubleshooting Misbehavior in Advance

THE GOOD NEWS ABOUT MISBEHAVIOR is that it is often predictable because it tends to be triggered by certain precipitating factors that, once detected, can be strategically addressed to eradicate or minimize it. A child-guider's task is therefore to cultivate a preventive mindset in order to forecast problematic behavior using the four following techniques.

Pattern Identification

One reliable technique to use in forecasting problematic behavior is pattern identification, or looking for misbehavior recurring at similar times or places and tracking it to its source. To develop expertise in pattern identification, each time you encounter a troublesome behavior ask yourself: "Do I see a pattern here? Is this behavior noticeable at the same time each day, week, or month? If so, what might be triggering it?" You may find, for instance, that a child in foster or residential care repeatedly acts out before visits with her biological parents; a student with a stressful family life frequently misbehaves prior to school vacations; a student continually becomes disruptive when a certain subject is taught; or a child who has been sexually abused loses control at bedtime.

Once you have identified a problematic behavior pattern, the first step is to look within and ask: "What am I (we) doing that is causing the pattern of behavior? What could I (we) change? What more do I (we) need to learn about this child or group?" As a former program director and current behavior consultant, I am always looking for patterns and then brainstorming with child-guiders about changes we might make, as reflected in the following scenario.

Dennis, an eight-year-old trauma victim, developed a pattern of hitting kids, particularly the ones he liked, whenever they did anything better than him. If someone was better, this meant he was awful and potentially unloved. We decided that he needed to practice friendship building, so I began seeing him and one of his friends every week for thirty-minute sessions. During the sessions, we talked about the nature of friendships and how it's normal for one kid to be better at something than the other. I also emphasized that it's the doing more than the winning—or being the best —that makes playing fun. We then played a lot of games and sports, and I helped Dennis practice these new lessons. I gave him lots of praise for keeping his cool when his buddy beat him in a race or threw a ball farther than he did. After four or five sessions in which he practiced the desired behavior, Dennis rarely hit again.

The second step after identifying a problematic behavior pattern is to talk to the child about the pattern. Begin by choosing a calm moment in which to talk gently about the pattern you have observed and see if she is able to recognize it. Empathize with her and encourage her to generate some possible solutions; together devise a plan, based on your ideas and her input. Such a plan might call for more adult support, additional counseling, journaling, more breaks, an incentive, a new activity, or the introduction of select self-management techniques.

The process is the same if you're working with a group. For example, Cathy, an eleven-year-old resident of a group home, acted out frantically on Thursday nights just before her Friday visits with her biological mother. The Thursday after I identified this pattern I asked Cathy, "What time should I take out the boxing gloves tonight?"

"What are you talking about?" she queried, with a puzzled look.

"Every Thursday night we go round after round," I replied, pretending to spar with an imaginary figure. "You're given a short time-out for misconduct; you scream and yell; and after an hour or two of 'boxing,' you quiet down. So I want to know what time the bout will start so I can have my gloves ready," I insisted.

"Get out of here," she scoffed.

Around 7:15 p.m., Cathy was given a time-out for rudeness, where-upon she began to argue, gradually increasing the volume of her protests. Hearing her loud cry, I jumped in, saying, "Wait a second, Cathy. I think it's time to get the gloves from the staff room. Please hold your cool for two minutes until I get back, and then you can start screaming again." She laughed.

With the tension broken, Cathy was able to look at why Thursday nights were so difficult; then together we created a plan to help her work through her pre-visit anxieties. She suggested doing a voluntary chore on Thursday nights, and we advised her to stay in close proximity to staff members and record her thoughts and feelings in a journal. She also consented to having staff members gently talk to her about the feelings she experienced prior to the visits and said she would do the same with her therapist. At last able to understand the reason for her pre-visit jitters, she began managing them more appropriately.

A child-guider named Victor used pattern identification to solve a behav-ioral problem in a group situation. While conducting an activity/therapy group consisting of nine seventh graders who were having behavior prob-lems in school, he noticed that about ten minutes before the end of each session the kids became restless and started teasing one another, rough-housing, and throwing pens and pencils. Then, during a calm period early in a session, he told the students that although some of the problem was his fault, as he tended not to prepare for the final moments of their session, they were nevertheless responsible for their behavior. He asked for sugges-tions on how to keep the last ten minutes of their time together running smoothly. One of the boys proposed a game of Uno, which is precisely what solved the problem. Toward the end of their next session, Victor dis-tributed three decks of Uno cards, and much to everyone's delight the kids played well together with no disruptions. It's absolutely critical to empower kids to be part of their own solution. When we do this, they take more ownership of the interventions.

Tip: Often it's helpful for child-guiders to create a plan for addressing a patterned behavior but then lead the child or group to it, such as in the following scenario. Dennis was getting upset and hitting other kids when his friends did something better than him. I had already decided to place Dennis and his friend Billy in a peer-to-peer group so Dennis could practice friendship, but in advance I had the following conversation with Dennis.

> ME: Dennis, we've noticed that when your friends do something better than you you get upset and sometimes hit them. It's good that you want to do things well. But when you express your feelings by hitting, kids get hurt. And you don't feel good about what you are doing, do you?

> DENNIS: No.

> ME: So we've been thinking maybe you could use more one-on-one playtime with your friends to help you practice friendship stuff, like not getting too mad when a kid does something better than you. What do you think?

> DENNIS: Yeah, that would be good. I really like Billy. Could I play more with him?

> ME: Let me look into that. I think it sounds like a great idea.

This empowering approach elicited a better response from Dennis.

Proactive Exploration

A second reliable technique to use in forecasting and preventing problematic behavior is proactive exploration. To troubleshoot a kid's challenging behavior occurring at a particular time, try Proactive Exploration Exercise 1 (see figure 12–1). Begin by writing across the top of a sheet of paper: "Factors that may be leading to behavioral difficulties at _____ (the troubling time)." Then list every precipitating factor you can think of, no matter how trivial it may seem. (It is also possible to make a mental list.)

For example, imagine that you work at a residential treatment facility where dinnertime is consistently loud and hectic, and you complete this exercise by listing the twenty-five precipitating factors shown in figure 12–1. With practice, it is possible to be on top of all these factors, depending on how well trained and dedicated your child-care staff is and on the resources at your disposal.

After completing Proactive Exploration Exercise 1, bring your findings to a staff meeting and ensure that before every dinner members do their best to have each factor under control. Whenever a thunderstorm is forecast, for instance, you could talk about thunder and lightning before dinner and have the most frightened kids sit beside a staff member.

Sometimes only a few simple changes can dramatically affect children's behavior. I remember spending huge chunks of time at staff meetings debating the most minuscule details, such as how a kid's pants should be folded or whether we should use bar or liquid soap. I would think, "This is why I went to graduate school, to spend fifteen minutes arguing about soap?" Then invariably I would remind myself, "Yes, this is exactly why I went to graduate school, because the soap is an integral part of the larger dynamic inspiring behavioral change." A child-guiding setting is, after all, much like the inside of a clock, where numerous mechanisms work in sync to keep the proper time, and whenever one mechanism is not running well the entire timepiece can malfunction.

Use of the Proactive Exploration Exercise is not limited to behaviors associated with time patterns. In Proactive Exploration Exercise 2 (see figure 12–2), Ms. Padilla, a third-grade teacher, wrote out every reason she could think of for recent class disruptions provoked by John, a student struggling to control his behavior. After looking over her list, she decided to address each factor, beginning with those she could tackle right away. She immediately gave John step-by-step assignments, tidied up the classroom, moved his seat, initiated meaningful contact with his parents, then augmented additional changes as time went on. The more John's learning environment fulfilled his personal needs, the more self-control he asserted.

Figure 12–1
Proactive Exploration Exercise 1

Factors that may be leading to behavioral difficulties at dinnertime:

1. The transition to dinnertime is mismanaged.

2. The dining room is unpleasant, due to its dim lighting, cold temperature, and drab decor.

3. The dining room is not cleaned before the kids arrive, nor is the table properly set.

4. The dining room is too small; the kids are eating elbow-to-elbow.

5. The time-out area is so poorly situated that each misbehaving child who is asked to leave the table disrupts others on his way out.

6. Dinner is served at a different time each day.

7. Dinner is poorly prepared: the food is cold, unappealing, and in short supply.

8. The seating arrangement fails to place a staff member between the most disruptive kids.

9. The group does not take a moment for silent gratitude at the start of the meal.

10. Rules and procedures for mealtime are unclear, and no "chore chart" is posted.

11. Staff members provide inadequate supervision.

12. Staff members fail to facilitate conversation or use humor.

13. The kitchen phone is answered during the meal, and is out of the diners' range of vision.

14. Because of a staff illness, an unfamiliar substitute is often present.

<cont.>

15. There is too much shuffling around during the meal, with kids getting up to refill their glasses, find their favorite salad dressings, and so forth.

16. Kids who experience conflict or disappointment prior to dinner receive inadequate attention.

17. The staff members on duty are inexperienced.

18. Some staff members on duty are not coping well with personal issues.

19. The staff members supervising dinner are not working as a team.

20. Staff members sometimes wear provocative clothing.

21. Unfamiliar visitors walk through the dining room during dinner.

22. Thunderstorms are common at dinnertime.

23. The kids are not properly warned about dinner coming to an end; some still have food on their plates when it is time to clear the table.

24. Staff members do not help the kids with mealtime cleanup.

25. The kids have no fun activities to look forward to after dinner.

Figure 12–2
Proactive Exploration Exercise 2

Factors that may be causing John to misbehave in class:

1. John is having trouble understanding the subject matter, which embarrasses him in front of his peers.

2. I have stopped breaking down his class assignments into sequential tasks. Because he has attention deficit hyperactivity disorder, he does not respond well when I simply say, "Do the worksheet."

3. He has been sitting between two students who often tease him and who may be egging him on.

4. He has been having a rough time at home and appears to have a lot on his mind.

5. I have been tired lately, which has decreased my tolerance for fooling around. Perhaps my tone, affect, and language are a bit too strong.

6. He forgets his assignments and is not prepared for class.

7. Because he has been acting out a lot, I am presently not fond of the kid. Actually, I don't like having him in my class! Perhaps I have been conveying that message to him.

8. He appears hungry as soon as he comes in the door.

9. The classroom has been in a state of disarray.

10. Lately, I have been changing the class routine without much warning.

11. John sometimes seems nervous about his lack of after-school plans.

12. He seems to enter the classroom on the verge of erupting. Perhaps he is having a hard time on the playground before the bell rings.

13. End-of-the-morning announcements over the loudspeaker have been interrupting our class discussions.

Any time you are confronted with difficult behaviors it is a good idea to explore possible precipitating factors then implement needed changes. The extra energy invested in preventing future problematic behaviors is minor compared with the energy expended grappling with them. When responding to the behavior of challenging kids, always remember the axiom "Pay now or pay more later."

Resource Evaluation

A third reliable technique for troubleshooting problematic behavior in advance is an evaluation of available human and physical resources. Here the operative law is: A setting with many demands and limited resources is at increased risk for ongoing and episodic behavioral difficulties. With resource evaluation, as with pattern identification, strategic interventions can play a preventive role. Never underestimate the importance of securing the human and physical resources you need. For example, you can bet that a new parent aide in a second-grade classroom with thirty-two students will have a more positive impact than an increase in rewards or disciplinary measures. Similarly, a donated air conditioner is apt to improve summertime behavior at a group home for at-risk adolescents far more than a new behavioral approach will.

Finding Human Resources

When it comes to dealing with children at risk, often adults underutilize other human resources, failing to see that by not taking care of themselves they are less able to take care of the kids. The greatest untapped human resource for supporting children in schools and residential facilities is parents. Many employers now offer flextime, enabling mothers and fathers to participate in their children's school life. With appropriate training and support, parent helpers in schools can be asked to tutor students, monitor lunch and recess, and assist teachers in meeting curriculum needs. Participating parents who are clear about classroom rules, procedures, expectations, and responsibilities can enrich the school community by lending not only extra hands but also a multitude of talents.

Residential facilities also benefit from parental involvement in day-to-day operations. Increasingly, treatment providers are realizing that the advantages of family-centered care extend well beyond therapy sessions. Many residential centers are now inviting parents to spend large segments of time with their children, doing such things as taking them clothes shopping, tutoring them, chauffeuring them to medical appointments, or simply hanging out with them in their living quarters. In some centers, parents are encouraged to interact with other residents as well, by cooking a favorite dish or organizing an activity. Such cooperative, empowering approaches give rise to win-win-win situations for the center, the parents, and most importantly, the children.

Another underutilized human resource for helping support children in schools and residential facilities is mentors. Numerous studies attest to the power that one significant adult can have in changing a child's life; moreover, an adult who serves simultaneously as coach, ally, and confidant can spell the difference between an at-risk child "making it" or failing miserably. Too often, lonely kids at risk are placed on a long waiting list for "big brothers" or "big sisters," never to be matched with a mentor. Some public schools are taking up the slack by asking teachers to mentor their most worrisome students. Caring volunteers electing to spend time each week in this capacity have inspired dramatic improvements in the children's behavior.

Out-of-home settings, too, are starting mentoring programs. For example, a residential setting in Nashua, New Hampshire, upon learning that the local "big brother" agency had too many other children to match, found adult mentors for nearly 75 percent of its residents. Staff members conducted the interviews, screening, and reference checks; paid for the criminal records check; made the matches; and provided training as well as ongoing supervision. The center's success in attracting mentors was due, in part, to its relaxed visiting schedule: mentors were allowed to visit every other week in lieu of the standard weekly commitment. The staff's belief was that the benefits of securing special relationships for as many kids as possible outweighed the benefits of providing more frequent visits. And interestingly, most mentors who committed to biweekly visits ended up coming more often. The mentoring program also worked out quite well for the residential director. A year after he started it he married the last mentor he recruited (and we're still married twenty-one years later)!

Many foster parents who are unable to engage the services of "big brothers" or "big sisters," and even some who do, develop a network of caring adults to support them in decreasing problem behaviors at home.

Friends, relatives, or neighbors come to watch the kids for an afternoon, or agencies such as boys and girls clubs provide them with more structured activities—all of which give foster parents an opportunity to run errands or simply take a break when they need one.

Some foster parents, by contrast, are reluctant to let others care for their children. "I'm the only adult this kid trusts. I could never leave her with someone else," they will say. Such a mindset can lead to unbearable stress, exhaustion, yelling, and overly severe consequences. The reason for the fallout is that being a foster parent to at-risk kids is similar to running a marathon: by the time you experience great thirst, you are already dehydrated and in serious trouble. Just as a marathon runner must drink plenty of water *before* the marathon, so must a foster parent avail herself of replenishment *before* the need arises. If you are a foster parent, do not let yourself reach the point at which you cannot stand another second of child-rearing. Instead, seek relief each step of the way. Call a friend for encouragement or advice. Visit a neighbor or family member who can validate your feelings of guilt, shame, or isolation—feelings that each of us has at times experienced. Plan a weekly dinner with good friends. Look for support groups through your agency, local schools, or nearby clinics. In short, develop a support network that can sustain you in times to come. This advice applies to all child-guiders who sometimes give more than they receive.

Volunteers and student interns willing to work with child-guiding program administrators, teachers, and foster parents are also great human resources for helping at-risk children. Volunteers who can be located through local newspapers, religious organizations, word of mouth, radio, and television may include woodworkers, artists, musicians, landscapers, and tutors, as well as other individuals with special talents. For at-risk kids, contacts of this sort can open doors to creativity and competence.

Student interns are also becoming increasingly visible now that more high schools are encouraging, if not requiring, their students to volunteer in the community. Undergraduate and graduate schools, too, are often in need of field placements for their students. Taking on a student intern will necessitate training and supervision—a small time investment reaping enormous returns. Although it may take "a village to raise a child," a few volunteers from the village can make a world of difference.

In addition to securing human resources, it is a good idea to creatively reutilize those already on hand. Some public schools solicit teacher volunteers to provide one-on-one attention on a daily or weekly basis to children with learning or emotional difficulties. Others divert funding for teacher aides to a clinical behaviorist who both works with the students and presents training sessions to teachers, parents, and support staff. Such effective reutilization of on-site human resources can prevent students from slipping through the cracks and teachers from throwing up their hands in despair.

Many child welfare settings are reutilizing their resources as well. Several residential centers for at-risk kids are training their support staff, including maintenance workers, secretaries, cooks, and nurses, to take more active roles with the children and parents. Others are teaching their childcare workers to conduct duo and group therapy with their kids, thereby freeing up program therapists to work with the families, perform collateral tasks, and, in some instances, provide aftercare. Such institutions, spurred on by the current climate of dwindling resources, are reexamining every staff position in an effort to do the best they can with what they've got.

Increasing Physical Resources

Children need many physical resources that may not be readily available in some low socioeconomic settings. Tony Brown, a distinguished African American author and advocate for minority families, once said on his television show *Tony Brown's Journal* that every family, rich or poor, should have a computer at home, and that poverty should never be used as an excuse not to have one. "Find a way," he urged his viewers, convinced that a personal computer could help young children learn and thereby give them a more advantageous start in school.[1] In addition to computers, children need books, bicycles, book bags, school supplies, recreational items, as well as many other physical resources, and our job as caregivers is to "find a way" to ensure that they have them.

Although finding ways to increase physical resources is often grueling, it can ultimately help avert problematic behavior. One way to replenish depleted coffers is by seeking donations and gift certificates, especially between November 1 and December 25, when people are inclined to help needy children. If you work in residential or foster care, and your facility or home is not in need of toys, you can always ask instead for gift certificates to fast-food establishments or a local bowling alley, movie theater, theme park, or clothing store. A large supply of certificates can be used year round to augment an inadequate budget.

Another way to increase physical resources is through fund-raising. This can be as simple as sending pledge cards to twenty corporations or making ten solicitation calls.

A third promising way to increase physical resources is by enlisting help from local businesses. Bowling alleys, miniature golf courses, martial arts academies, music schools, health clubs, hair salons, fast-food restaurants, outdoor adventure firms, video stores, and wilderness supply shops are often willing to offer services, products, or space at reduced rates, if not free of charge. In addition, some office supply stores give teachers substantial discounts on classroom supplies.

Because at-risk kids tend to experience heightened anxiety in anticipation of summer vacation—a long period of unstructured time—a fourth avenue to explore is affordable summertime activities. Camps frequently offer discounts or scholarships; low-cost or no-cost structured opportunities may also be available through swimming facilities, country clubs, youth clubs, libraries, activity groups, and municipal park and recreation departments. An imaginative search for enjoyable scheduled activities can lead to less acting out during May and June and a more enjoyable summer for everyone.

Relief is also available by creating transportation options. At-risk kids often lose their desire to go places when they have no way of getting there. To overcome such deficits, make sure the kids you care for know how to use public transportation (let them earn bus passes or have the passes donated); buy used bicycles at garage sales; form carpools; or seek out volunteers to provide rides at prearranged times of the week. Agencies that work with families having limited access to transportation can consider providing them with rides, bus schedules, or gas money. Such efforts are often rewarded by improved relationships with the families and more optimally functioning children.

Preparing for Change

A fourth reliable technique for troubleshooting problematic behavior in advance is to devise strategies for anticipating change and difficulties that might arise in its wake. Altering aspects of life can be extremely unsettling not only to kids but also to adults. Schools and other child-guiding programs are continually transforming to improve or for other less positive reasons. Significant change produces a myriad of feelings that can interfere with a smooth transition. Those who guide at-risk kids and their families should always anticipate change and be ready to manage personal feelings and injuries when they occur (It's an injury, and it will heal. Respond instead of react). Managing change is helped by acknowledging change as a recurring part of life and creating the right story: "These changes aren't occurring because I or my group has been performing badly; no, they are being implemented to make good workers even better."

Kids and adults often struggle with change because it takes them out of their comfort zones—even if change is for the better. My cousin Gil, a retired substance-abuse counselor, told me that it's not uncommon for an alcoholic to become sober only to have his spouse try to get him drinking again. "The wives tell me, 'I don't like his drinking, but at least I know where he is every Friday night. I know he's not going to leave me.'"

When kids with histories of chronic behavior problems begin behaving well, it often produces intense feelings that lead to a regression in their behavior that is actually healthy. We call them "positive regressions."

For children, change may be even more difficult than for adults. Kids who frequently misbehave have often become comfortable in this style of relating, making life predictable. For example, the monologue running through eleven-year-old Andrew's head two weeks after Mr. Johnson, his unit director, created a new incentive program, gave him a special job at the program, and taught him a series of self-management techniques probably went something like this: "Hey, it feels pretty good acting better and getting along with people. I like what they're saying about me. Mr. Johnson has really gone out of his way to help me. But this isn't going to last. Adults are always turning on me. At some point, they're going to abandon the chart, take the job away, and start getting on my case again. Why don't I get the waiting over with and act out—go back to how things were." By the third week, Andrew may have been growing increasingly anxious, perhaps thinking: "It feels weird being polite and getting all this positive attention. I'm not used to it. Plus they're now expecting more from me. I've got to work a lot harder—it's not easy! No, this dude was more comfortable before. Hey, Mr. Johnson, you're an asshole!" Andrew subsequently reverted to some of his earlier behaviors, but finding that Mr. Johnson was not one to wilt under pressure, he soon stopped fighting the changes in his environment, accepted a more positive self-image, and resumed behaving better. The child-guiding process toward sustained, internalized, positive change is generally a "two steps forward, one step back" journey, as illustrated in figure 12–3. In fact, rarely does a child change for the better without positive regressions along the way.

To sustain children's long-term behavioral gains during positive regressions, child-guiders need to resist the temptation to overreact or vent their disappointment, to avoid saying something like, "Bobby, you were doing so well. I thought you learned to stop acting that way!" or "This new program isn't working anymore. The kids are worse than before!" Instead, it is far better to anticipate positive regressions and know that with ongoing support the children will eventually get back to improved functioning.

Such a mindset, however, is not always easy to maintain. In a co-ed juvenile detention center that had recently instituted new rules pertaining to violence and aggression, male-female relationships, and the earning of privileges, I encountered a momentary calm followed by serious acting out requiring the need for a number of physical restraints. When on several occasions the residents were close to rioting, I began to wonder if we would ever improve the functioning of the unit. Yet throughout the tumult the direct-care workers did not overreact to the positive regressions by abandoning or sabotaging the new approaches; and, as a result, we did indeed produce sustainable change. That, for me, reaffirmed lesson number one in how to become a successful agent of change: If you truly believe there is no such thing as a bad kid, and if you appreciate how people react to change, then you empower folks to be part of the solution, formulate and enact the changes, and stay the course, aware that positive regressions are a normal part of the process.

Figure 12–3
The Road to Better Functioning

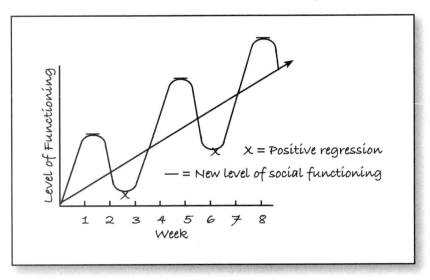

There's another reason kids, particularly those who have suffered trauma, are prone to positive regressions. Some kids who have been abused by their parents still, on some level, love their parents and, as a result, blame themselves for the abuse: "I'm a bad kid, and I deserved to be hurt." If they can get child-guiders to react instead of respond to them, it keeps their parents on a pedestal. "See, even these people treat me poorly. I'm a bad kid."

With such kids, the job of child-guiders is to make it clear, through words and actions they understand, that there are no bad kids or bad parents, just bad luck and bad choices. This added factor makes it even more essential not to overreact to positive regressions.

One good way to stay the course through these typical up-and-down periods is to think two to three months into the future, telling yourself, "I can take all the acting out this child may throw at me for the next two and a half months. It will be worth it if in ten weeks he is functioning far better, with relatively few relapses."

Lesson number two in how to become a successful agent of change—to radiate confidence—came while reading Robert Crichton's *The Great Imposter*, a biographical account of Frederick Demara, a genius who roamed the world taking on other people's identities—from forging the credentials of a prison administrator and subsequently reforming a southern penitentiary to posing as a navy doctor during the Korean War and performing surgery on several Koreans, saving their lives.[2] The mindset he adopted upon entering each situation in which he'd had no prior experience was this: he would walk in with a supreme sense of initiative and purpose. This man who seemed to will himself into pulling off miracles inspired people to believe in him by exuding confidence and hope no matter how insecure he felt. This is the attitude I strive for in my work with at-risk kids. When I hear that there is a crisis in Room 211, I sprint over as fast as I can, but just before reaching the room I take a deep breath, slow my pace, and enter with a nonchalant, relaxed air, as if to say, "I'm not worried. I'm in control, so don't panic. Things will be okay!"

Whether beset by a momentary crisis, a child or group that seriously—but temporarily—regresses, or a school or program in dire need of restructuring, the secret to being a successful agent of change is to stay the course and adopt a positive, strength-based attitude and approach; radiate confidence; and smile a lot despite the apprehension you may feel inside. In other words, be an actor. And remember, you get better with practice and success—and the kids do, as well.

PART III

Responding to
Challenging Behavior

— CHAPTER 13 —

The Power of Humor

HUMOR—A LONG-OVERLOOKED component of child-guiding—
needs to be taken more seriously. In the all-too-sobering business of child-
guiding, lightheartedness can play a unique role in encouraging bonding
and de-escalating problematic behavior. Indeed, studies of endorphins suggest that suffering subsides with laughter, and with the suffering the inclination to act out. Years ago I heard an ex-nun report that a research team
from Stanford University conducted a study on the effects of humor in
the classroom and found that students learn 700 percent more if humor
is an integral part of the teaching. "But I'm not that funny," many child-
guiders lament when the topic is broached. The truth is that *anyone* can
be funny, and whether you are humorous by nature or by intent, you can
help children smile their way into a better place.

Many forms of humor do not require a predisposition toward the
lighter side. For instance, you do not have to be a bona fide comedian to
read puns from a joke book after the completion of a difficult quiz or
noonday meal. And if you're not that funny, you can make a commitment
to take a few baby steps in this direction. After all, someone who isn't funny
but tries to be—now that's funny!

The Preventive and Curative Actions of Mirth

Among its many special behind-the-scenes effects, humor has many
remedial effects. Here are some of them.

• Humor sheds light on darkened lives.

The energizing and uplifting power of humor's light brightens the dark-
ened lives of kids who lead hard lives and are at risk. Humor, like sunshine,

radiates warmth and vitality, hope for the future, and endearing links with others. Those who guide children at risk are grappling not only with troubling behaviors but with overcast minds, and their task is to shed lots of sunshine.

• Humor memorializes meaningful uplifting moments.

Each time we fill at-risk children's memory banks with laughter rather than fear or humiliation, we offer an enduring gift that memorializes meaningful uplifting moments. When I recall my teenage years, I immediately think of my cousin Jon. Five of us were playing poker one afternoon before heading over to the local ice cream parlor, where Jon ordered a chocolate milkshake so thick that he kept tilting the glass for a sip until its entire contents splashed onto his face! We all laughed uncontrollably, and I will never forget the spectacle of his eyelids, nose, and chin engulfed in chocolate. Every time I reflect on this uproarious image, now frozen in time, I remember the intoxicating camaraderie we felt as we made our way through adolescence. This milkshake incident is far more than a memory; it forms the gateway to a reservoir of meaningful uplifting moments that buoy me through tough times.

At-risk kids, however, have few memories of meaningful uplifting moments. For kids returning to visit a residential center that once served as their home, disgrace and defiance often color their memories. For instance, in reminiscing with a staff member, they might ask, "Remember the time you restrained me on the playground?" or say "Remember when I broke the chapel window?"

Filling at-risk children's memories with humor also relays the message that we like them and want them to feel good—so much so that we are willing to look foolish in front of them, which helps restore their faith in adults as well as themselves. Love fortified by such faith is the best deterrent there is to misbehavior.

• Humor engages resistant children.

Humor is a helpful way to engage resistant children. Every Wednesday during my first clinical social work internship, fellow intern Jane and I conducted group therapy at the Boston Juvenile Court Clinic, working with eight teenagers mandated by the court to attend. Midway through the year, fourteen-year-old Wesley was ordered to join the group. Week after week, despite our many attempts to help him open up, Wesley sat there in stone silence, appearing angry and sullen. Not until his seventh session did he speak up. Partway into the session he raised his head and asked, "What are those metal gates for on top of the building?"

I had no idea why the gray, archaic, five-story stone building that housed the clinic had metal gates on its roof but was not about to pass up an opportunity for humor. "That's where we lock up kids who don't talk during group therapy," I calmly replied. Although Jane turned white and nearly choked on the pretzel she was eating, I broke out in a big smile. Then Wesley grinned. Engaged at last, he went on to become an active participant in the group.

• Humor demystifies the power of authority figures.

Because of their difficult histories, many at-risk kids are wary of authority figures. A good chuckle can clear the air of past associations and create a friendlier, more balanced setting by suggesting, "It's not me against you; it's us together. If we can share a laugh, we can work as a team."

Upon meeting a new group of children, you will have barriers crumbling if you begin on a humorous note. Use of jokes and self-deprecating humor as icebreakers help kids see you as a caring adult rather than a commander in chief. Remember, initial impressions set the tone for future communications.

• Humor enhances relationship building.

Humor can enhance the relationship building that is so important to the effective guidance of at-risk kids, as reflected in my own experience as a student. My eighth-grade math teacher, Mr. Burns, was the classiest man I had ever met. Six feet three inches tall, always dressed impeccably in a black pin-striped three-piece suit, Mr. Burns spoke perfect English with a slight British accent. He had a dry wit and frequently replied in axioms, such as

"A rolling stone gathers no moss," "A penny saved is a penny earned," and "A stitch in time saves nine." When he asked me for the answer to a trick question one Friday afternoon, I fell for the bait—hook, line, and sinker, as he would have said. Mr. Burns smiled, cast his gaze down to where I was sitting, looked me right in the eyes, and declared, "Mr. Appelstein, there is a sucker born every minute."

I stared right back at him and replied in my best British brogue, "Mr. Burns, it takes one to know one." The class erupted in laughter, then fell into a quiet hush, wondering how Mr. Burns would respond.

He immediately closed the book in his hands and solemnly strode to the front of the room, where he picked up a piece of chalk and etched a small vertical line on the upper right corner of the blackboard. "That is one for you, Mr. Appelstein," he said in proper English. It was a moment I will never forget. Although Mr. Burns did not spend extra time with me, the humor ingrained in his teaching inspired me to make it through math and to deepen my relationship with him.

I believe that every time a child-guider asks a kid to do something he doesn't want to do, like walk away from a volatile situation, in the millisecond before he responds he thinks, "Who just told me what to do?" And if the child-guider is an engaging and dependable person who properly uses humor with him, the kid is more apt to comply, thinking, "Man, I don't want to walk away—this jerk is really pissing me off. But Raoul is a cool guy. Goofs with me a lot. I'll go because Raoul asked me to."

• Humor fosters identity formation.

Kids who exhibit chronic behavior problems often struggle with identity issues, and humor can help them improve their perception of who they are. Better yet, it can improve their perception of who they can become, as reflected in the following story.

Will and Artie Bender were brothers, though you would not know it by looking at them: eight-year-old Will wanted nothing to do with five-year-old Artie. They had been brought to the residential center after being abandoned in an automobile by their mother and left to eat out of trash bins. Although Will had done his best to take care of Artie, the burden of caregiving had taken its toll. By the time he arrived at the center, Will was filled with rage—at Artie and at the world. Artie, too, was angry; moreover, he was deeply hurt by Will's rejection of him.

The staff went to work restoring the brothers' relationship by administering large doses of physical nurturing, which the boys craved. Hugs soon turned to wrestling matches. Stan, the unit director, let them win each match with him, and then one day he had a brainstorm: he would agree to wrestle with Will only if Artie was around, and this time he would not let him win. When Will and Stan began their next bout, Stan took the lead, and Will's frustration was evident. After a few minutes, Stan said, "It's a good thing your brother isn't helping you. I wouldn't want to take on the two of you!" As if on cue, Artie jumped in, whereupon Stan yelled, "Oh no, it's the Bender brothers. Put 'em together and you have Bender power!"

"Bender power!" they cried out with each new maneuver. Delighted that they had joined forces, Stan let them destroy him.

In time, Will and Artie moved into the same bedroom. At bedtime, Stan would often tell them a science fiction story. It always had the same theme: aliens taking over the world until out of the sky bursts the Bender brothers! "Bender power!" they extolled as they destroyed the aliens and saved the world.

"When you guys work together, anything is possible!" Stan would comment.

A month later Will, who had previously referred to Artie by name, was calling him "my brother." Having reclaimed their identity as siblings, the two deepened their relationship, and before long the agency found them a home together with a caring adoptive family. (*Note:* These incidents took place in the early 1980s, when a staff member at a residential program could wrestle with a kid in front of other staff members, a controlled form of roughhousing that, sadly, is generally no longer allowed at these programs.)

• Humor reduces tension.

Tension often permeates the atmosphere of child-guiding settings. Teachers addressing restless classes experience it. Foster parents confronting their potential runaway teens feel it. Juvenile justice counselors trying to maintain composure as their groups veer out of control could write a book about it. Amid mounting tension, adrenaline starts to flow and the risk for reacting instead of responding increases. When our actions do not reflect our best efforts, however, it may be time to turn to levity. The following approaches can be used to evoke laughter and diffuse stress.

Mission accomplished. When a group or child's behavior disturbs you, one good retort is: "You seem to be trying very hard to upset me. And do you know what? You're doing a fabulous (said humorously) job. I am upset." Use of this tension reducer can model good control while giving you a few seconds to regain composure before addressing the issue.

In the same vein, when I'm getting angry with a first grader I often like to quip, "You know, you're acting just like a six-year-old!"

"But I *am* six," the kid will respond.

"Oh yeah, I forgot," I will reply.

You're my bodyguards. When two children are squabbling, tension is rising, and you are unable to help them resolve the conflict, consider inviting them to be your bodyguards. This approach can serve as a promising alternative to the "divide and conquer" option of separating them, especially if you have a good relationship with each child.

Imagine that Ellie and Judy are not getting along and have been unable to resolve their differences. You can bring them together and say something like this: "Okay, Ellie, I know you and Judy have refused to make up. I also know you have hated Judy all your life. You even hate the name *Judy*. In fact, you hate words that start with the letter *J*. When we go outside, we ask you to play on the 'ungle gym' so you won't get mad. And Judy, I know you've hated Ellie all your life. Every time it rains, you blame her for the downpour. Each time you break a fingernail, it's Ellie's fault!" At this point,

Ellie and Judy may burst out laughing and willingly resolve their conflict. If tensions persist, however, it is a good idea to inform them that they will both need to be by your side like bodyguards until they work through the problems. It is best to utilize this technique only when you sense that a quarrel is due to a minor misunderstanding and that intervening in this way is not likely to exacerbate the situation.

Mirroring the mimic. As long as child-guiders are careful not to denigrate a child, mimicking can at times be fruitful, as reflected in the following example.

One afternoon Luther, a bright, angry thirteen-year-old who lived at a residential center, was in a particularly foul mood as he, five other kids, and I hung out in the unit's large living room. All my attempts to get him out of his funk had failed, so when he spoke disrespectfully to another kid I asked Luther to please take a five-minute time-out.

"I didn't do anything!" he quipped.

"I know you're upset. Please take the time-out, and after that we'll talk," I replied.

"Go to hell," Luther shot back.

"If you don't start the time-out within a minute or so, you'll need to take a ten-minute time-out," I politely informed him.

Luther's defiance continued to escalate, whereupon he received a ten-minute time-out, refused to take it, and was asked to cool off in the hallway. I followed him out of the room. He began pacing back and forth, cursing under his breath. To break the tension, and simultaneously appear calm, I called out to three kids playing at the far end of the hallway, "John, Chuck, and Joey, you've got twenty minutes before we go outside."

Luther snidely mimicked me, calling out, "John, Chuckie, and Joey, you've got twenty minutes before we go outside."

I ignored his remark and a few minutes later tried another diversionary ploy. "Hey, Ethan, make sure to pick up your Matchbox cars before dinner. You can't leave them out like that." Again Luther echoed my words.

He was starting to get under my skin. My observing ego kicked in, and I began coaching myself to stay calm. Desperately attempting a third maneuver, I called out, "You guys in the bathroom, you need to be out of there soon," well aware that no one was in the bathroom. Luther repeated the sentence before the last word had left my mouth.

I was almost at the end of my rope and knew I had to try something new. Although looking eye-to-eye with a kid whose rebellion is escalating would not be recommended, I took a step toward Luther, then, looking him straight in the eyes, said, "Okay, I'm ready to do my time now."

Without blinking, Luther shot back, "Okay, I'm ready to do my time now."

A slight grin eased onto my face. "Well, go ahead," I replied.

Luther stood silent, pondering the volley that had just taken place. He then shuffled into the living room for his time-out.

As I walked past him, we smiled at each other. Drawing an imaginary vertical line in the air, similar to Mr. Burns's etching on the blackboard twenty years earlier, I remarked, "That's one for me, Mr. Boswell." From then on, Luther and I enjoyed a special relationship.

Nike called. Stacy Willet, a very talented and humorous child-guider from Iowa, shared the following humor technique with me, which I have since included in my repertoire.

A girl named Kayla with whom I was working in a group residential home struggled with a fear of failing at almost anything. One day the group was out at the swimming pool, and she was scared to venture out into the deep end for fear of going underwater. Being a certified lifeguard, I made a mental note to keep an eye on her. Then, since I'm always making corny jokes with the girls, I called out, "Hey, Kayla! Someone called me yesterday." She just looked at me funny, as if to say, "All right, where are you going with this?" I said, "It was Nike. They told me to tell you something." She said, "Nike told you to tell me something?" I said, "Yes, they wanted me to tell you to just do it." The girls all laughed. Needless to say, Kayla was not only underwater by the end of pool time but also opening her eyes underwater. This then became a joke amongst the group. They would say, "Hey, Nike called me, and guess what they told me to tell you."

I overheard another use of this technique when a child-guider said to a kid who would benefit from a break, "Hey, Ronald McDonald left a message for you."

"What?" the kid asked.

"He said you could use a break today," the child-guider replied.

Nonsensical imagery. I was working with a young man on the autism spectrum who was often anxious and easily agitated. I told him one day, "Next time you start to feel upset, think about a pig in a mink coat." He came back the next week laughing, telling me that he couldn't get the pig in the mink coat out of his head.

Distraction. Most behavioral experts recommend distraction as a major tool for de-escalation. When dealing with a kid whose behavior is escalating, I see him on a treadmill going faster and faster to a point of danger. And I see an effective child-guider using distraction to keep the kid safe by knocking him off the apparatus.

A creative ditzy distraction can save the day. For instance, I like to use color cards to distract kids. I go to paint stores and grab a bunch of the color cards. Then, when a kid's problematic behavior starts to escalate I hold them up and blurt out, "Hey, what color would you paint your bathroom—the mauve or the fuchsia? I mean, who paints their bathroom mauve or fuchsia? I can't even say 'em. Mawaaave . . . fewsha. It's ridiculous! What is my wife thinking? Help me out here, brother!"

Another ditzy distraction came to the rescue at my first job in residential treatment as a child-care worker on a girls unit with thirteen girls aged six to fourteen. The girls knew I loved to eat (a lot). One night at dinner the fire alarm sounded, scaring many of them. It was midwinter, and we all quickly huddled on the screened-in porch outside the unit. Some of the girls were crying, many were afraid, and tensions were rising. "Look, I know this is upsetting to a lot of you," I called out. "You'll be okay. But you do need to think about one important thing right now—how I'm feeling knowing that my pork chops and mashed potatoes are getting colder every minute we're out here." After a momentary pause, most girls laughed and beat me over the head!

An equally effective distraction is the interjection of superheroes' or famous people's names into a situation, like: "Hey, this is not easy, but what would Luke Skywalker do if he was in your shoes. He'd use the Force, my young Jedi, and make a good choice." (Humming the *Star Wars* theme can set the mood.)

Kids on the autism spectrum tend to respond especially well when heroes are invoked. Years ago I was working with a cognitively impaired, low-IQ, unattractive young girl on a residential unit who wasn't very popular. I tried hard to make her feel pretty and good about herself. When her misbehavior escalated, I'd often say, "Lisa, what would a beautiful movie star do right now?" It often helped her. Late one night it helped me. I was trying to get her to go to bed, and she wouldn't stop fooling around. I finally looked at her and moaned, "Lisa why are you doing this? It's late—you need to go to bed." She responded, "I just can't help myself because you're so handsome." Stunned at first, I then laughed and replied, "Where does it say, 'Kid uses my line'?" She was asleep in a few minutes.

Six Rules for Using Humor

Following are six rules for making humor an indispensable tool in child-guiding.

1. Give up attempts at humor quickly if unsuccessful.

Any time a child does not respond positively to an attempt at humor, it is wise to abandon the approach. Prolonging the intervention may only convince the child that you are making fun of her or that you are not taking the situation seriously. As you get to know the kids in your care, you will learn who responds well to levity, who does not, and who can be gently nudged into a chuckle.

2. Avoid using sarcasm and nicknames.

Sarcasm, no matter how funny it may seem, is usually perceived as a put-down. Edward Hallowell, a prominent child-guider, leading expert on ADHD, and author, stated that sarcasm makes kids afraid of adults.[1] I heard another expert refer to sarcasm as veiled hostility. Most at-risk kids have experienced copious amounts of humiliation in their lives, and another pernicious blow to their self-esteem does nothing more than reaffirm an already poor self-image. Any time child-guiders think about using sarcasm with a kid or group, they should ask themselves: "Whose need is being met here?" Sarcasm is rarely what kids need.

Nicknames, too, are belittling. Scott, a fifteen-year-old detention center resident with severe cognitive and emotional impairments, picked up the nickname Dog. Almost all the residents and staff members called him by this name, unaware that he consequently saw himself as having animal-like impulses, further devaluing his sense of self-worth. Only after his nickname was dropped did Scott begin to feel better about himself and behave more appropriately. The moral of this cautionary tale is that child-guiders should use humor at their own expense, not a child's.

3. Establish familiarity before using humor.

Before using humor in situations involving heightened tension, it is best to establish a trusting relationship with the youngsters because at-risk kids need to see that they can count on the adults in their lives. Once the kids are confident that you care for them and will not intentionally hurt them, it is safe to begin clowning around.

4. Integrate levity into everyday interactions.

There is no need to reserve levity for special occasions. On the contrary, it should be woven into the fabric of everyday interactions. Periodically creating moments of levity throughout a shift can be a powerful teaching device. As mentioned, Rick Miller, founder of Kids at Hope, asked, in *Youth Development,* why schools can't be happier places,[2] and the answer is, they can and should be.

I was asked to counsel a young fourth-grade teacher who was assigned a class with kids who had struggled behaviorally the year before. We decided to lighten the atmosphere. On the first day of school, she went over the rules and then listed the daily chores the kids would take turns doing. The one that raised eyebrows was "class comedian." Every day one of the kids had to stand on the piano bench, wear a jester's collar, and tell a few jokes. They had a wonderful year. I'm not joking!

5. Be versatile.

The humor that works today is not likely to have the same impact tomorrow. So to activate infectious laughter, it is necessary to be aware of societal changes, employ creativity, and follow your intuition.

6. Don't worry (too much) about overstimulation.

A popular decree in almost every child-guiding setting is, "Don't get the kids going! If you do, they'll never settle down!" This warning is one my greatest pet peeves. Every time I hear it, I think, "Get them going? Where the hell are they going to go?" Radio Alert/All Points Bulletin: "We joked with a group of Milwaukee preschoolers this afternoon. Got them going. They just crossed the New Mexico border! We can't stop them from going!"

While humor can cause children to break out of patterns of obedience, the task of child-guiders is not to ensure compliance but rather to build character. The secret to generating jovial moments is to develop skills that will assist the children in regaining control. In other words, instead of worrying about the possibility of overstimulation *give structure to the chaos.*

Moments of fun can be structured in any number of ways. One way is to plan ahead for a wind-down period. For example, lower your voice, preview the next activity, or dim the lights before proceeding to the next activity. A second way to structure fun is by letting the kids know that funny times will come again—and again—provided that they are capable of settling down afterward. In these ways, the structuring of fun transforms the stimulation of humor into a lesson in self-discipline.

Developing a Repertoire of Humor

To create a jovial atmosphere at the drop of a hat, it is best to develop a repertoire of humor ranging from revered puns to jokes and riddles to unexpected attire. Having a repertoire of humor offers limitless possibilities and should include the following staples, all of which can be modified to suit any age group, setting, and particular relationship the child-guider has with the kids.

Self-Deprecating Humor

Demonstrate humility by allowing kids to laugh at us is a powerful relationship enhancer. Exposing a few funny foibles of a child-guider can endear us to kids. For example, I advise teachers to start the year by reviewing these class rules with the students:

1. Come prepared.

2. Treat people the way you want to be treated.

3. Raise your hand when you want to contribute.

4. Most importantly, if the [name of the teacher's favorite sport's team] loses and you bring it up the next day, you'll be suspended.

I also advise child-guiders to hang posters of their favorite teams on the wall. And I emphasize the importance of losing games on purpose to at-risk kids and then warning them not to tell anyone—and if they do, to feign anger.

Jokes and Riddles

Kids love jokes and riddles. Child-guiders do not need to come up with new material all the time; instead, they can memorize a few one-liners to say as the need arises. Or they can write them on numbered slips of paper and give one or two to each child in their group. They can have the children clap five times, then have the child holding joke number one stand and read it aloud; have the kids clap five times and request joke number two; and so on. They can also buy a few corny joke books and let the kids take turns reading the entries out loud.

When Alex, an extremely challenging student, joined Susan Flood's fourth-grade class, she knew it was time to lighten up. At the beginning of his second day of class, she marched up to his desk and asked him to say the word *stock* five times fast.

He looked confused, then said, "Stock, stock, stock, stock, stock."

Susan immediately asked him, "What do you do at a green light?"

"Stop," Alex replied.

"So, Alex, you stop at green lights. That's a funny way to drive!"

Everyone laughed, including Alex.

I like to ask kids, "So will you remember me, the Great Mr. A, after this year?"

"Yeah," they insist.

"Knock, knock," I continue.

"Who's there?" they reply.

"Ah, you forgot me already!" I say.

Nonsense Sayings

To reduce tension, child-guiders can be quick to intersperse nonsense sayings such as the following.

- "Okay, Mary, you have a choice. You can do your room now or you can take the curtain, or spin again, Vanna."

  "Son of a gun, we're gonna have fun on the bayou."

- "People aren't making good choices, and I feel . . . like dancing, dancing, dance the night away. Okay, let's focus."

- "Why? Is that what you're asking? Because . . . you know . . . I'm all about that bass, 'bout that bass, no treble. I'm all 'bout that bass, 'bout that bass, no treble. I'm all 'bout that bass . . . you asked!"[3]

The Translator

To break the tension, pretend a kid is from a country no one has heard of and speaks a language no one can understand. Pick another kid to translate what the foreign kid says. Have other kids and staff interview the foreign kid. Have the foreign kid speak in gibberish, and if the foreign kid gives a short answer, have the translator give a long reply, and vice versa, such as the following.

INTERVIEWER: What is your favorite food?

FOREIGN KID: Yip-ca-be-dokee.

TRANSLATOR: She says that in her country there is a wide variety of foods and that it is outlawed to have a favorite food because it might disrespect the other foods. If, on the other hand, you were to have asked her what food she likes, she would have most gladly replied, "Why, the devil dog, of course."

Planting Words

When dealing with a kid who doesn't want to talk, a child-guider can talk for her, but this technique is only advised if the two share a special relationship.

CHILD-GUIDER: What's that? You want to know how I'm feeling today? Hey, thanks for asking. I'm actually feeling pretty good. What was that? You want to know if I received my Foster Parent (Teacher)_____of the Year award? It's on the way. Again, thanks for asking.

Slapstick and Physical Humor

Slapstick and physical humor can be downright hysterical. Following are some motifs that are sure to arouse laughter.

Costumes and Sight Gags. A goofy costume can set a happy tone for the day. Young kids, especially, love to wear costumes and will be thrilled to see that the child-guider does, too. For example, a teacher can dress in period garb to illustrate a history lesson, or don an outlandish hat, a strange tie, a plastic nose, and huge black sunglasses just for fun. Or before the kids arrive for help with their homework, the teacher can put on the glasses. When they enter, they'll ask, "Why are you wearing those glasses?" And then the teacher can pick up some of their reports or test results, and declare, "Because you're getting so bright I have to wear these glasses!" Similarly, a teacher checking a kid's chore can don a Sherlock Holmes hat and use a large magnifying glass.

Water or Shaving Cream Fights. Indoors or out, water fights can provide hours of joyous abandon, assuming that they are governed by ground rules such as "Aim only for grown-ups" and "Steer clear of electronic equipment." Shaving cream requires a bit more cleanup but is well worth the effort.

Props and Gizmos

Wind-up toys extract instant chuckles. Sending a plastic squirrel across the table during a serious talk with a child is apt to immediately eradicate gloom. Card and magic tricks, available at most toy stores, also add a frivolous touch, as do plastic eyeglasses with motorized windshield wipers.

Amusing Games

The more innovative a game is, the more likely it is to captivate a tough group of children. For unequivocal enticement, try embellishing on an old favorite or, calling upon the kids' inspiration, invent a new one.

Bonkers Bingo. This game lends itself to at least three different renditions. One, Ognib—*Bingo* spelled backward—is a perfect option for kids with poor self-esteem who moan, "I never win" every time one of their peers yells, "Bingo!" In Ognib, the children each play with only one card, which they turn over once it is filled; the winner is the last child to do so. For added amusement the contestants, while turning over their cards, can moan, "I've got Bingo."

A second variation entails the ringing of a bell midway through the game to signal "ESP time," an interlude in which each child tries to guess the next number to be called. Those who guess correctly win a prize.

In a third variation of Bonkers Bingo, designed especially to hold the attention of children who are easily distracted, the caller announces the numbers in a variety of tones and inflections.

To further assist kids who hate to lose, more than one winner can receive a prize. Tell the kids, for example, "Whoever gets up-and-down Bingo wins a prize, and so does the kid to the left of her."

Simon Says…with a twist. Simon Says can be as zany as you wish, and the more descriptive you can be the more laughter you will evoke. A child-guider could announce, "Simon says to walk like the Hunchback of Notre Dame," for instance, or "Simon says to jump like Lebron James," or perhaps, "Simon says to jump like Lebron James and hang in the air. Okay, come on down. . . . Hey, Simon didn't say to come down!" Replacing Simon is another possibility, as in "Shaq says, 'Walk big like me.'"

Personalized Mad Libs. A collection of prewritten silly stories known as Mad Libs, which allows participants to fill in the blanks, can be purchased at most gift shops. Many troubled children, however, quickly lose interest in prefabricated stories and prefer to contribute to more customized tales that ask for their own names as well as those of familiar adults, thereby enhancing their sense of relationships. A teacher can design Mad Libs stories related to class material. A foster parent or youth worker may want to create a crazy Mad Libs adventure in which they and the kids band together to save the day (see figure 13–1). Whatever the decision, you could include a blank for the name of every child in the group, place the adults in hilarious self-deprecating situations, and prepare to make a copy of the completed story for each participant.

The Memory Game. This comical game will delight kids between the ages of five and thirteen. The instructions are as follows: One child sits comfortably in a chair without moving, while another child is asked to study him and, after a few minutes, leave the room. The seated child then changes five aspects of his appearance; he may decide, for example, to untuck his shirt, switch his left and right shoes, untie one lace or both, roll up one sleeve, cross his legs, comb his hair in the opposite direction, take off or put on glasses, or take off or put on a watch. The child who has left the room then returns and tries to guess the five changes.

When playing the memory game, have the children take turns as changers and guessers. Be sure that you rotate in as well.

A Modified TV Game. Teachers can play Who Wants to Be a Millionaire? or other popular TV game shows with their students, interspersing straightforward academic questions with silly ones. A special education teacher in Wyoming was having trouble engaging her teen students in an important skills training. She remembered playing Who Wants to Be a Millionaire? at my training and tried it out with her students. They immediately hooked in to the material. Making games more engaging is often an excellent way to draw out strengths. And that's my final answer.

Loony Tunes

The universal language of music is an unsurpassed medium for self-expression. Indeed, an amazing mood shift can take place when troubled children gather together with simple "instruments" and a shared desire to "ham it up." Following are three of the dozens of possibilities.

Kazoo Band. Child-guiders can start their own kazoo bands for amusing entertainment. One fourth-grade class in New England boasted a five-

Figure 13–1
An Invented Mad Lib

The (Adjective) _____ Trip to Yankee Stadium

(Adjective) _____ (name of adult) _____ decided to take six kids
to a New York Yankees baseball game. Before going, the kids
made (adjective) _____ (deli meat) _____ sandwiches on slices of
(number) _____ -day-old bread. (Name of kid) _____ wanted
(condiment) _____ and fried (insect, plural) _____ on her/his
sandwich, even though the (same insect, plural) _____ sometimes
got caught between her/his teeth! (Name of kid) _____ liked
her/his sandwich with a touch of (liquid) _____. (Name of same
adult) _____ rented a (adjective) _____ (color) _____ (unusual
mode of transportation) _____ to get the children to the game.
(Name of kid) _____ wanted to drive, but (name of same adult)
_____ reminded her/him that she/he only had a license to drive
(adjective) _____ (color) _____ (same mode of transportation,
plural) _____. On the way to the game, a (adjective) _____ (noun)
_____-shaped object suddenly dropped from the sky and landed
in front of the group. "It's a UFO!" cried (name of kid) _____. Instantly, a door opened and (number between 5 and 50) _____
(adjective) _____ (color) _____ aliens emerged from the ship. Incredibly, they all looked like (funny cartoon character) _____.
(Name of kid) _____ called to them, "Aliens who look like (same
cartoon character) _____, do you come in peace?" "We come to
see Yankee game. Where is Yankee game?" "Follow us," yelled
(name of kid) _____. Together, the aliens and the kids from (foster
home address or name of facility) _____ saw a great game. The
aliens caught all the foul balls with their (adjective) _____ (noun,
plural) _____ and gave the balls to the kids in return for a bite of

> (first kid's name, possessive) _____ sandwich. Aliens, it turns out, love fried _____ (previous insect, plural)!

member kazoo band that played in talent shows and for birthday celebrations, dressing up and entering the room with their kazoos packed in violin or guitar cases. For effect, the band leader would announce a guest soloist, who generally stepped forward and played one note, usually the last one of a song.

Pots and Pans Rhythm Band. Child-guiders can form a pots and pans band in which each cooking vessel has a distinct sound when drummed with a large utensil, such as a wooden spoon. Such "metal drums," together with two large pot covers for cymbals, and barrel-shaped or tapered pots for bongos and congas, can make for a rib-tickling ensemble. Show tunes, such as the theme songs from *Hello, Dolly!* and *Auntie Mame*, are highly conducive to pots and pans band jamming.

One-Line Raps. It's often fun to listen to or sing raps—especially funny ones—with at-risk kids.

Whimsical Poems

When writing poems to kids, a little self-disparagement can add a pleasing touch. More importantly, be sure to end with a line of appreciation since gratitude cannot be expressed often enough to at-risk kids.

Howard, a therapist assigned to a unit at a large residential center, never missed a child's birthday dinner. After the meal, he would read a funny poem he had written in the child's honor. Perhaps what the kids enjoyed most was the fact that he had taken time to do something special for them. See figure 13–2 for a birthday poem he wrote for thirteen-year-old Mike, a resident known for his unkempt room and remarkable artwork.

Figure 13–2
Mike's Birthday Poem

Today you hear my poem, and it will be very good.

Tomorrow we will eat pizza—and watch *Robin Hood*.

On Sunday you will definitely need time to rest

But the staff won't let you . . .

'Cause your room will be messed!

Face it, Mike, you and I aren't very neat

But at least we're both handsome and sweet.

And we both love spicy chicken wings, and we're both
incredibly smart

And we both love stoppin' at Dunkin Donuts

After Art!

Hey, all kidding aside, I think of you with

Tremendous pride!

You're bright, strong, and witty—

And if we eat too much pizza

It won't be a pity!

Happy Birthday

Grandiose Praise

When challenging kids do something noteworthy, the door separating them from the world begins to open. If we stick a foot in that opening with grandiose praise, indelibly imprinting a moment of victory on the child's mind, the door is less likely to shut again. Following are some examples.

- "Sarah, that is a *wonderful* picture! I'm calling the art museum right away, and that painting's going in. Picasso, Rembrandt, Sarah—the names fit together like salt and pepper!"

- "Ezra, I really like the way you solved that problem. Are you trying to take over my job? Aren't you satisfied with being a kid for a few more years?"

- "Sam, you got a 90 on the math quiz. I've got to scream that out the window. [Opening the window and yelling] 'Sam got a 90 on his math quiz!'"

- "This is a great class. I'd like to thank you all for being such outstanding students!" Then, pointing at the kids one by one, "Thank you, thank you, thank you . . ."

I once suggested yelling praise out the window to a group of elementary school teachers from Belmont, Massachusetts. A week later they returned to the second training and proclaimed, "We did what you said, and it worked! The kids loved that we did it. In fact, they started working harder so we'd keep on yelling. And then they asked if they could be assistant yellers. It's been fabulous, and they're working so hard!"

Frivolous Standbys

Here are two all-time favorite frivolous standbys to hold at the tip of your tongue for use in emergency situations.

The Escaping Smile. In many circumstances, this intervention is a reliable way to turn a solemn face into a cheerful one.

Twelve-year-old Abby was looking dejected and refused to talk. Larry, her foster father, said: "It's in there, I can see it. There's a smile at the bottom of your throat, and it's trying to get out! Ah, it's climbing up your windpipe, slowly but surely making its way to the top. Oh, it's jumped onto your tonsils and has begun swinging back and forth. Now I can see it better—it's a big smile. Hey, it just flew onto the back of your tongue.

Do you feel a little tickle there? Whatever you do, don't swallow or burp because now it's taking out a hammer and chisel and chipping away at your front teeth. Now it's come through your teeth and is pushing against your lips; they're starting to quiver. You can't hold it back any longer. It's coming. *There it is.* What a smile!"

The Gorilla Story. This tale can be told in five to twenty-five minutes, depending on the needs of the situation and your willingness to embellish the basic premise.

A downtrodden janitor, after spending his last dollar on a lottery ticket, wins the largest payoff in lottery history. With his winnings he buys a gigantic mansion. After living there a few days, he realizes he needs a maid, but every housekeeping agency he visits has booked all its service personnel. Calling on the last agency in town, the man pleads with the owner to send him some help. Although this agency, too, is fully booked, the owner reluctantly offers him an "experimental" maid, who turns out to be an 800-pound gorilla. Upon seeing a demonstration of the gorilla's extraordinary cleaning skills, the man agrees to engage its services, whereupon the owner sternly cautions him not to touch the gorilla. The man, promising to heed this advice, takes the gorilla home and assigns it thousands of difficult cleaning tasks around the mansion.

After three months the man, who can no longer resist touching his new maid, taps the giant creature on the shoulder. The gorilla immediately goes berserk and begins chasing the man—by skateboard, sports car, and private jet—at last trapping him in a cave at the Grand Canyon. Unable to escape, the man crouches against the wall of the cave and stares at the creature's silhouette as it passes back and forth beyond the entrance. From the dark interior of the cave, the gorilla appears to weigh 1,600 pounds! Terrified, the man's heart begins beating out of control. As if this weren't bad enough, the gorilla slowly advances toward him, its mouth and huge protruding fangs dripping saliva, and its powerful forearms raised in the air. Paralyzed by fear, the man can only watch as the gorilla's huge forearms extend even further, then swing violently downward to crush the man's scalp. Within one-half inch of his head, the gorilla's hands freeze. The gorilla smiles, gently pats the man's head, and says, "Tag—you're it."

Humor needs to be taken more seriously as an intervention tool when problematic behavior escalates. Its many varieties makes humor one of the most flexible and accessible tools available to child-guiders.

── CHAPTER 14 ──

Teaching Kids Self-Management

CHILD-GUIDERS OFTEN DISAGREE about the approaches and techniques that should be used to assist kids with emotional and behavioral challenges. Most interventions have a time and place where they can be used effectively, but no intervention can be applied universally. There is, however, one approach in which all child-guiders fervently believe: kids with emotional and behavioral challenges should practice the desired behaviors.

Malcolm Gladwell, in his bestselling book *Outliers*, writes that many of the world's icons, such as the Beatles and Bill Gates, didn't ascend to their lofty levels because of genetics; no, they attributed their success to the hours and hours of practice they put in.[1] In fact, Gladwell has surmised that ten thousand hours of practice seems to be the magic number needed to multiply the odds for becoming exponentially exceptional.

To practice the desired behaviors, kids often first need to be taught them. Child-guiders must therefore weave customized skills training into their daily regimen. There are countless books, CDs, and DVDs that help child-guiders teach kids social skills and strategies for self-management. This chapter augments existing self-management programs with a host of fun, innovative, and helpful methods. But first let's explore the mechanism of self-management.

The Power of Self-Talk

Effective self-management is all about good self-talk. Strength-based practice is essentially about getting at-risk kids to change their negative thoughts and perceptions, enhance their strengths, and practice appropriate behavior, all tasks that require improving their self-talk.

Self-talk has many forms, including corrective and inspirational. What stops people from misbehaving or acting in ways that will increase stress and unhappiness is self-talk such as the following:

If I hit this kid, I could get suspended!

If I swear at this dude, I'll lose my privileges.

If I wait till the last minute, I won't have enough time to do it properly.

If I eat that this donut, I'll get fat. If I eat three, it will be even worse. Go! Run from the bakery!

If I don't bring home all my assignments, I'll fall behind and get in trouble.

If I call out without raising my hand, the teacher will get mad and ignore me.

In his book *Youth Development*, Rick Miller writes the following about the power of self-talk:

The prestigious Mayo Clinic published the following article on self-talk. "Positive thinking often starts with self-talk. Self-talk is the endless stream of unspoken thoughts that run through your head every day. These automatic thoughts can be positive or negative. Some of your self-talk comes from logic and reason. Other self-talk may rise from misconceptions that you create because of lack of information."[2]

Examples of positive self-talk are the following:

- It's okay to get some problems wrong. I'm not stupid; I've just got to keep at it. Mistakes are opportunities for learning something new. The harder I try, the higher I fly. I've got to be the eagle!

- I don't have a learning disability; I've got a few roadblocks. Every major city has roadblocks, yet people get to work on time because they find a way around them. That's all I have to do.

- I'm really good at volunteering. I love going down to the first-grade class and helping kids read. I've got math coming up. I generally suck at math, but my teacher says it's all about the effort. I think I'll give math some extra effort today.

- My father didn't leave us because we were bad kids. No, he made a bad choice because of other reasons. He loved us.

- This teacher is giving me a hard time. I'm pissed, but I've got to deal with it using problem-solving skills.

When kids actively practice positive, corrective self-talk, their functioning improves, often dramatically. After shooting the ball ten thousand times with his opposite hand, Boston Celtic Star Larry Bird didn't need to use self-talk ("Grip it at the seams, cock the wrist, tuck in and bend the elbow"). No, he'd just dribble the ball and let it fly—that's the power of practice. Neurobiologist Bruce Perry writes, "The brain is designed to change in response to patterned, repetitive stimulation."[3] This is the neurological explanation for why saying or thinking lines and thoughts over and over, or practicing the right moves until you drop, produces transformative results. Some call it muscle memory.

Sometimes it's the inspirational self-talk of kids who believe in themselves—"I can do this. I believe!"—perhaps with a child-guider's help, that encourages them to perform and aspire to greater accomplishments. Sometimes it's a simple line that can produce the desired effect, such as "Let it go, Joe."

Rick Miller, through his work in the schools, has thousands of students around the world reciting these lines every morning:

I am a Kid at Hope.
I am talented, smart, and capable of success.
I have dreams for the future, and I will climb to reach those
goals and dreams every day.[4]

After a while they believe it and think it. First it's new, and then it's you.

Rewiring the Brain

Many kids with emotional and behavioral challenges have atypical brain development or neurological wiring that compromises their brains' ability to function efficiently, as noted in chapter 11. As a result, they may struggle with executive functioning issues, attention deficit disorder (ADD) or attention deficit hyperactivity disorder (ADHD), learning disabilities, or anxiety. Following are simplified descriptions of each condition.

Executive Functioning: Executive functioning, controlled by the brain's frontal lobe, involves a set of mental skills that help people get things done. It helps individuals manage time, pay attention, switch focus, plan and organize, remember details, avoid saying or doing the wrong thing, and perform actions based on experience.

ADD or ADHD: Attention deficit disorder or attention deficit hyperactivity disorder is a chronic disorder whose core symptoms include inattentiveness, occasional hyperactivity, and impulsivity.

Learning Disabilities: Learning disabilities are neurological disorders that interfere with the brain's ability to receive, process, analyze, or store information. Kids with learning disabilities are as smart or smarter than their peers, but they may have difficulty reading, writing, spelling, reasoning, recalling, or organizing information by themselves, especially if taught in conventional ways.

Anxiety: Anxiety generally results from the brain misperceiving and exaggerating the risk in a situation, prompting an impulse to avoid it in order to survive. Child-guiders help kids with anxiety issues by having them challenge their anxious thoughts and understanding of situations. Teaching these kids breathing and relaxation techniques is also important.

Kids who struggle with one or more of these conditions demonstrate their capacity to excel in and out of school when given sustained support in navigating the ups and downs of life. The section that follows offers creative and inspiring self-management tools, including an innovative self-talk technique, to help them do just that, all the while improving their self-perceptions and functioning as well. In terms of supporting kids with executive functioning issues in particular, Sarah Ward, a renowned authority on executive functioning, has descrived the importance of helping these kids work through tasks by actually seeing the steps they need to take. Helping kids positively visualize their futures, short- or long-term, has become a key component of strength-based treatment.

Cueing: One-Line Raps or Coping Self-Talk

Cueing, through one-line raps or coping self-talk, involves rhythmic coping-lines that usually rhyme and are frequently repeated, such as "If you got to do it, just hop to it." Cues are often created with a set rhythm: "If you got to do it (BUM ba bah ba bah-da), just hop to it (BUM ba ba-da)." I bring bongo drums when introducing kids to cueing. We create a rap and an accompanying rhythm and then practice. After a while, the rhythm can take the place of the words. For instance, when the teacher taps, "BUM ba bah ba bah-da . . . BUM ba ba-da," the kids hear, "If you got to do it, just hop to it," and they hop to it.

Many years ago I conducted a training at an adolescent psychiatric hospital in Virginia on a Monday. On Thursday, I received the following uplifting message from the director, Ann Graham: "Charlie, thanks for coming. It's already working! We have a sixteen-year-old girl on our unit who hadn't taken a shower in three months. We tried everything. We offered her rewards, issued consequences, changed her meds, and even brought in a consultant. Nothing worked. This morning, three of my staff stood in front of her room and chanted, 'Don't be sour, take a shower. Don't be sour, take a shower!' The girl laughed and jumped in the shower. Thank you!"

A year later I returned to the hospital to conduct a follow-up training. Before we began, I asked Ann, "Did that really happen? I've been telling people all over the world this story."

"Not only did it happen," she replied. "We forgot to tell you that *she* came up with the rap the night before, and another one, too: 'Don't be a dope, use the soap.'"

After this experience, I ramped up my usage of cueing. I then had a watershed experience that crystallized its effectiveness. I was asked to work with a middle school student, Josh, who was terrorizing the two special educators who manned the school's learning center. He didn't want to visit their room every day and vented his displeasure by being incredibly disrespectful. Josh struggled with learning disabilities and seemed to be carrying some emotional baggage as well. Upon visiting his home, I learned that he came from a very well-to-do family. Prior to our first session, I asked the assistant principal for the names of the two specialists he was targeting. She said, "They're Mrs. Mumford and Mrs. Lucci, and Mrs. Lucci dislikes him so much she's thinking of quitting."

When I met Josh the next day, after a strength-based introduction I asked him to repeat the following line: "Mumford and Lucci, treat like Gucci! Mumford and Lucci, treat like Gucci!" He laughed but went along for the ride.

> ME: Mumford and Lucci...
>
> JOSH: Treat like Gucci!
>
> ME: Mumford and Luccia...
>
> JOSH: Treat like Guccia!

We sometimes played cards and chess, and whenever I'd recite the first half of the line at such times, he'd finish the rap and I'd slap him five.

We also talked about why he didn't like going to the learning center, which I empathized with and reframed into a better story. Trying to help him see things from the specialists' perspective, I'd explain, "They're just doing their job." As we finished up, I told him to write down the line, say it to himself over and over, and think about it every time he went to the learning center.

A week later I got an ecstatic email from the assistant principal, asking: "What did you do to this kid? He's had a super week. He's been very respectful to Mrs. Mumford and Mrs. Lucci. How did this happen?"

Josh continued to be respectful and hardworking, then after a month of vastly improved behavior I felt compelled to do some probing.

> ME: Can I ask you something?
>
> JOSH: Sure.
>
> ME: When you walk into the learning center, are you thinking, "Mumford and Lucci, treat like Gucci"?
>
> JOSH: No. It's already in there, Mr. A (pointing his index finger to his temple).

From that moment on, cueing has been a staple child-guiding technique for me and countless other parents and professionals. When I was asked to assist a student who was a chronic liar, I got him to practice the line "Say what's true. Fibs are through!" As a result, his lying decreased.

I used to give biweekly parenting advice on a major cable TV channel along the East Coast. One month after I conducted a segment on cueing, one of the on-air personalities took me aside and said: "Thanks for the advice on cueing. As I drove home after the show, I kept saying to myself, 'If you talk in an angry tone, you'll live alone.' I've been a much better dad and husband since the show."

We can understand why one-line rapping is a highly effective tool for helping kids with or without wiring issues if we consider what happens when we play a favorite CD from our past and notice how after the first song ends we are singing the next one because, like Josh proclaimed, "It's already in there." Similarly, consider what we do when we hear the question "What's 7 × 7?" We all know the answer is 49 because it was drilled into our heads. We could be on our deathbeds—ninety-two years old, with no minds left, incontinent, gasping for breath—and upon hearing a child in the waiting room doing her homework, saying "Seven times seven?" we would utter, "Forty-nine," and then die.

Following is a comprehensive listing of raps, or cues, that help kids internalize needed coping skills. The child-guider generally begins implementing this technique by reciting the first half, and the child completes the rap. We call this skill-building approach "pre-correction" since it is used to address a problem behavior *before* it occurs—before the child becomes agitated. Most behaviorists postulate that if we warn a kid about a behavior while it's happening, we are probably too late. It should also be noted that from a neurological perspective there is evidence that a rap starting with a negative word, such as *never*, is tuned out by the brain. Therefore, if a rap can be framed in a positive way it's probably wise to do so. For example, "Here's some advice, talk real nice" might be better than "Don't talk rude 'cause I'm the dude." (*Note:* I generally start raps with *Don't* when I can't come up with a better-sounding positive opening.)

Raps

Anger Control

Let it go, Joe. Let it go, Joe. Just stay cool, no need to blow.

I can, I will, I gotta chill. And if I do, it's quite a thrill.

NBD (no big deal) easier than one, two, three.

If I get mad, don't do bad—just talk or walk. Talk or walk.

Walk, talk, or squawk!

Don't cuss, it will cause a fuss. And get you kicked off that yellow bus.

Don't swear, choose to care.

When you're heading toward red, take a walk instead.

When you feel yourself overheat, move your feet!

Just count to five and give no jive.

Count to ten and then do it again.

Don't hit, it will cause a fit.

Don't bite, it just isn't right.

Use my words and fly with the birds. Soar to success!

Social Skills

Take turns when I talk. If I don't, the kids might walk.

Give kids their space; it's their place.

If you act like a boss, kids give you the toss.

Stay arm's length away today.

Think about them thinking about me. It's as easy as one, two, three.

If the other kids choose, I won't lose.

Treat kids with respect. It will have the right effect.

Here's some advice: treat kids nice.

Here's some advice: talk real nice.

Don't make the noise if it annoys.

Say what's true, fibs are through.

Use an indoor voice cause it's a very good choice.

Be nice to your mother. You've got no other.

Hey, hey, hey, just think what I say.

Life's hard enough, don't text bad stuff.

Line up quiet, don't cause a riot.

If the other kids go first, my bubble won't burst.

If you lose, don't sing the blues. They're just games, James.

Here's the deal: think about how others feel.

Understand it fully: it's sad to bully!

Public Masturbation

Don't touch as much.

Impulsivity

Don't call out, share the air.

Think before I act, that's the fact.

Staying in control, that is the goal.

Just reach (raise hand) and say, "I need a little help, Teach."

Following Through/Getting Things Done/Learning/Paying Attention

Inch by inch, life's a cinch.

Take step after step, that's the prep.

If I can take it, I can make it. (From the movie *Unbreakable*)

Do it little by little and play the fiddle.

Don't quit; take it bit by bit.

Visualize what I've got to do, and see it through.

Hocus, pocus, focus.

Like a king (queen) on a throne, I can start on my own.

Like a king (queen) on a throne, I can do it on my own.

The harder I try, the higher I fly. Be the eagle!

Take it yard by yard, and life's less hard.

A mistake is a chance to learn something new, through and through.

For goodness' sake, it's okay to make a mistake!

Take a deep breath, then do it again; this technique helps in the end.

Following Directions

If you got to do it, just hop to it.

Do what I'm told and win the gold!

High Energy

Sit and relax, and learn to the max.

Don't move all over the place; sit and learn with a happy face.

Sit and learn; it's my turn.

Just ask for a break for goodness' sake.

Anxiety

Don't be in a hurry to worry.

Breathing in, breathing out eases doubt.

Count to ten and then do it again.

Count to five and feel good about bein' alive!

If it's stinkin', change the thinkin'.

Replace what you think before you sink.

Here's the deal: think what's real.

Think about this twice, and it will end up nice.

Worry-wise kids don't hit the skids.

I've done it before and can do it again.

Rethink the situation, and add relaxation.

"I should, I must" causes too much stress and fuss.

Breathing at a slower pace brings about a happy place.

You don't need to be the best to pass a test!

Organization

Make a list, it will assist.

Write things down, Charlie Brown.

Organize and be wise.

Prepare for tomorrow and avoid the sorrow.

Don't wait, write the date.

Before I go, stop and think, bro (Flo).

Putting things in the same place makes for a happier face.

Throw away the clutter before you melt like butter.

Tips on the wall help you stand tall.

It's sometimes great to delegate.

Self-Harm

If you hurt number one, it's never better when you're done.

Encopresis

If you feel the urge to go number two, hit the bathroom and send it through.

Drugs and Alcohol

I can make it if I choose; it's time to quit the drugs and booze.

If you lose hope, don't do dope.

Weed can mess up your brain all the same.

Smoking

Don't smoke, it's a joke.

If you smoke when you're young, you destroy each lung.

Encouragement and Affirmations

I can make it if I choose; only I can make me lose.

If it is to be, it's up to me.

If you take the right road, you'll lighten the load.

Child-Guiding

Don't yell, gently tell.

Say please and thanks, and take it to the bank.

It makes a lot more sense to use a consequence.

As they get louder, you get quiet. C'mon, pal, it's time to try it.

If you talk in an angry tone, you'll live (work) alone.

It's an injury and it will heal—that's the deal.

Try to say yes more than no. Yes instills confidence and helps them grow.

Optimizing the Use of Raps

1. Raps are more likely to be internalized and put to use if presented before the target behavior occurs.

Examples

ADULT: How was your week?

ANGELA: Pretty good.

ADULT: Do you want to play cards?

ANGELA: No. Let's play chess.

ADULT: Okay. The harder I try . . .

ANGELA: The higher I fly.

ADULT: What do you do if the work gets hard?

ANGELA: Ask for help.

ADULT: Just reach and ask for help from the teach. Yeah.

ANGELA: Can I be white?

ADULT: Sure. Be the . . .

ANGELA: Eagle!

ADULT: You're not going to cry if I beat you? Should I get a tissue box?

ANGELA: You're toast.

ADULT: Don't quit . . .

ANGELA: Take it bit by bit.

ADULT: Make your move . . .

In the following example, a milieu counselor is walking with a group of boys to the dining room.

COUNSELOR: Let's keep it single file, please. Remember, we've got basketball after the lunch chores.

YOUTH: Did you bring the whistle?

COUNSELOR: I've got it. If it is to be . . .

YOUTH: It's up to me.

COUNSELOR: Good thoughts will set me free. Think before you act...

YOUTH: That's the fact!

COUNSELOR: I can't hear you.

YOUTH: That's the fact, Jack!

COUNSELOR: Eat up, boys.

2. Raps are most effective when the kids help create them.

I was working with a fifth-grade girl diagnosed with oppositional defiant disorder. She was hypersensitive to criticism and very demanding. During our first session, I empathized with her situation. We agreed that she needed help in not overreacting to situations.

I then suggested this rap: "Let it go, Flo."

"I don't like that," she said.

"Well, what do you like?" I asked.

She suggested, "How about 'Let it go, so.' So I can do better."

"I love it!" I replied. So she went on to have a super year.

Interestingly one day, after a sustained period of social and academic progress, she stated somewhat indignantly, "You know, I don't always think, 'Let it go, so' anymore."

Smiling and pointing to my temple, I said, "Yeah, it's already in there."

Realizing I was right, she immediately gave me what we call a "recognition reflex," acknowledging, at least for this brief moment in time, that she'd accomplished a significant behavioral gain.

3. Avoid putting words that suggest inappropriate behavior into a rap.

For example, it would be counterproductive to use "Don't cut when you're in a rut." It would be better to say, "If you hurt number one, it's never better when you're done."

People sometimes question whether this technique will resonate with tough teens. The answer is simple: it's not whether the technique works since neurology is indisputable; it's whether you can sell it to them.

A few years ago I was asked to provide training at a boot camp for inner-city gang kids, many of whom had been diagnosed with conduct disorder. I trained for three months to do the brutal morning calisthenics. Once on the gym floor with the eighteen kids, I was in agony as the staff members repeatedly got in my face and yelled, "Ten more, Appelstein!" For thirty minutes, we did push-ups, sit-ups, and jumping jacks with no breaks. I ripped my right hamstring muscle and was seeing double. At the thirty-minute mark, the drill sergeant yelled, "Appelstein, front and center!" I quickly marched up to him. "The group is yours, sir," he said. I then yelled, "Hands to the side and repeat after me," as I started to do jumping jacks to the following rap.

> ME: I can make it if I choose.
>
> GROUP: I can make it if I choose.
>
> ME: Only I can make me lose.
>
> GROUP: Only I can make me lose.
>
> ME: I can make it if I choose.
>
> GROUP: I can make it if I choose.
>
> ME: It's time to kick the drugs and booze.
>
> GROUP: It's time to kick the drugs and booze.

ME: If you lose hope, don't do dope!

GROUP: If you lose hope, don't do dope.

ME: If it is to be, it's up to me.

GROUP: If it is to be, it's up to me.

ME: I can make it if I choose.

GROUP: I can make it if I choose.

ME: Only I can make me lose.

GROUP: Only I can make me lose.

A week later I got a message from the drill sergeant, saying, "Some of my toughest kids have been walking around snapping their fingers and chanting, 'If you lose hope, don't do dope.'" Bingo.

On another occasion, Alicia, a professional working with at-risk adolescents in one of our Rocky Mountain states who had heard me present the rap technique, wrote:

> I used a rap with a teenage girl in my program who was having many issues with her self-esteem, which had caused her to cut on herself almost daily. I asked her if she would be willing to try out this technique with me, and she was on board, so I gave her the rap "If you hurt number one, it's never better when you're done." She really liked this, and I started repeating it with her a couple of times an hour until she had it memorized; then I had her say it with me before she went home each night. I asked her each day how she was doing at home and if she was cutting, and after a few days she began reporting that she wasn't cutting at home anymore and she had now gone three weeks without hurting herself!

Music

Cues appear to be even more effective when paired with music since an accompanying melody gives the words more staying power. Music also enhances relationship building, which, as we know, provides the energizing power at the heart of strength-based practice with at-risk kids.

In his book *Musicophilia*, Oliver Sacks addresses the power of music to heal and transform, remarking, "Active participation in music creates a bond between the participants. . . . While music can calm us, animate us, thrill us, or serve to synchronize us at work or play—it may be especially powerful and have great therapeutic potential." He also cites William James, who in 1890 wrote, "Humans have a susceptibility to music."[6]

For these reasons, child-guiders should consider weaving music into their environments. Many teachers, for example, extol the benefits of playing soothing background music in class.

Cueing seems most successful when paired with a melody. Years ago I worked with a fifth grader who was transitioning from a self-contained to a mainstream classroom. Initially, he wasn't confident about succeeding in his new class, so we wrote the following song together and sang it often throughout the year:

> I'm a mainstream guy; this year I'm gonna fly
> I'm a mainstream guy; this year I'm gonna fly!
> Learning is my ticket to a really good life.
> It's going to get me a job and a really cute wife!"

Despite a few bumps along the way, he soared.

To emphasize the power of adding music to cues, I once took cues I had written in collaboration with kids and created a musical CD titled *One-Line Raps for Girls and Chaps*. I've been told that when kids listen to it while beating drums or a mat or desk with both hands, the raps sink in better. Occupational therapists have informed me that the improved outcome is a result of "bilateral stimulation."

Two years after creating my first CD, I conducted a training for foster parents in Maine, where I had presented at the previous year's event, as well. There a mother came up to me at the break and stated, "Remember me?"

"I do. You had a big issue, didn't you?" I replied.

"Yes," she responded, "I was the big yeller!"

"So what did you do about that?" I asked.

She explained, "After your training, I went home, gathered my kids, and we came up with 'Don't yell, gently tell.' And it's worked. If I start to get mad, one of the kids will remind me, 'Mom, don't yell, gently tell.' Then I calm down."

That night I couldn't get the line out of my head. By the time I woke up, it had become a Gregorian chant. I got so excited that I maxed out my credit cards, refinanced my house, and created a second CD, *Parent Rapsody: Songs & Musical Mantras for Successful Parenting*. The eighth song, sung by the choir at my original temple in Newton, Massachusetts, is "Don't Yell, Gently Tell." If you go to YouTube and type in "Don't Yell, Gently Tell," you'll see four monks on a bed singing the song to a mother who is yelling at her daughter. Parents often tell me, "I've stopped yelling due to that song, but I hate the melody!" On the other hand, I was at the Lexington, Kentucky, airport once when a woman grabbed my arm and said, "You're Don't Yell, Gently Tell, aren't you?"

"Yeah, that's me, although I generally answer to Charlie," I replied.

"I play that song all the time. It's been a lifesaver. My son even likes it, and he has a serious neurocognitive disorder," she stated.

Mnemonic devices, especially when coupled with music, can be used to help kids remember important details, whether they're related to a behavioral issue, academics, or general information. I recall helping a young girl at a residential center win her fourth grade spelling bee by figuring out a mnemonic device to help her learn the word *pneumonia*: **P**atrice **N**ever **E**ats **U**nder **M**y **O**range **N**ectarine **I**n **A**ugust.

Some years later, when my daughter was in her eighth grade science class, she was given a difficult taxonomy assignment involving lots of memorization and asked if I would put the facts to music. The following lines were written to the tune of "She'll Be Comin' 'Round the Mountain."

The Classification Song (first half)

There are e-i-g-h-t levels of classification. *Yeah, eight!*
There are e-i-g-h-t LEVels of classification. *Really, eight!*

We classify living t-h-i-n-g-s into groups—so that the organisms are easier to study. We classify…things into groups.

(Faster) Taxonomy is the science of classification. *Classification!*

(Slower) Taxonomy is the S-C-I-E-N-C-E of classification.

(Still slow) And Linnaeus invented a naming system… called binomial nomenCLAture.

(Still slow) And each organism is given a two-part name. *A two-part n-a-m-e!*

(Faster) The genus is the first part, which is capitalized. *HEY, it's capitalized!*

(Faster) The genus is the first part, which is capitalized. *HEY, it's capitalized!*

Species is the second. It's pretty cool, I reckon.

BUT the first and largest level is the domain. The domain.

The song helped my daughter ace the assignment. Then when she got to high school and her freshman science teacher gave the students a lengthy review test she was the only student who remembered every classification.

One of my most memorable experiences of feedback from cueing came after I provided a full-day workshop to some of the surviving spouses from 9/11. One mother frequently mentioned how angry her twelve-year-old daughter remained but was reluctant to open up about her feelings. A few days later I received a touching email from the mother, explaining that she played my CD for her daughter, who at bedtime subsequently commented, "You know, Mom, I can write better ones than that guy." And she promptly recited, "I don't mean to get so mad, it's just that underneath it all, I'm still so sad."

Motivational Metaphors

Motivational metaphors coupled with rhythmic cueing often enhances an at-risk child's self-image, happiness, hope, and self-management. Motivational metaphors provide not only corrective self-talk but positive imagery that can be inspiring. Following are some of the most popular motivational metaphors used by child-guiders.

The Train

I tell every kid that all kids and families are like trains, big and powerful with super engines, yet all trains get off track from time to time. I further explain that my job is to help them get back on the rails. Because I know that it's highly effective to marry a cue to a metaphor, and I want self-doubting kids going to bed at night with trains popping into their Rolodexes, I suggest a cue such as "I'm like a train, and all trains get off track from time to time. Back on track, Jack!"

I used the train metaphor extensively with Steven, age eight, who was often angry, defiant, and prone to explosive outbursts, and whose parents were entangled in a messy divorce. We drew a train track on an incentive chart and called it Steven's Getting Back on Track Chart. If he could go five minutes without a big message (tantrum), we drew a tie in the track. Once he collected six ties, he'd earn extra computer time. We used this chart for a month to stabilize Steven's behavior. He responded enthusiastically to the chart, the train metaphor, and other strength-based interventions we utilized. Every year his behavior and academic functioning improved. When he was fourteen and entering eighth grade, his middle school guidance counselor called and said: "Steven's doing well. A few hiccups now and then. But you don't need to see him anymore. Why don't you come one more time. Maybe take him out for a special good-bye. Thanks for your help." Later that week I took Steven out for a pizza after school. We had an emotional final meeting, reminiscing about the five years we had worked together. When we arrived back at his house, just before exiting the car he looked me in the eyes and said "You know, Mr. A, I've been thinking a lot about that train thing you've been talking to me about all these years."

"Really. What have you been thinking about?" I asked.

"I've been thinking that when you and everyone else started working with me you put a lot of coal in my engine. But when the coal ran out, I'd act out. I've been thinking maybe it's time for me to put the coal in."

"Yeah, Steven, maybe it is," I gave him a hug and said good-bye, and then drove to the hobby shop near my house and bought a Lionel locomotive for $100. Now when I meet a kid for the first time, I cite the train metaphor and then hand them the train, saying, "That's you, dude—a powerful train. But right now you've got some wheels spinning, oil seeping on the floors, smoke bellowing. We've just got to get you back on track. Say it: 'Back on track, Jack!'" I now also include in my bag of tricks a giant wooden train whistle and a conductor's cap, items that should be standard inventory for all child-guiders. If I see a kid I'm working with fifty feet down the hallway, and I know he's been doing well, I put on the cap and yell to him, "Isaac, I heard about the quiz yesterday—9 out of 10! You da man!" I then blow the whistle. It's a hoot!

The Car

Since too many at-risk kids have negative views of themselves as hopeless and incapable of change, I use the metaphor of a car to drive home the message that all kids can improve their ways. I tell kids that they are like cars and that cars improve every year, with new models having sleeker designs, getting better mileage, holding the road better, and being more popular. I then inform the kids that they, too, get better every year, even every day: "Every day you wake up you're a little smarter, sharper, and more mature than the day before. There is no such thing as same old you. 'Hey, hey, hey, you get better every day!'"

Once when working with a very troubled second grader, Antoine, who suffered a serious behavioral regression, I took the car metaphor for self-improvement one step further.

ME: Can I ask you something kind of personal?

ANTOINE: Okay.

ME: Did you poop in your pants a lot when you were a baby?

ANTOINE: I guess I did.

ME: And when you were two did you have big tantrums?

ANTOINE: I probably did.

ME: Well, are you doing this now—pooping in your pants and having wild tantrums?

ANTOINE: No!

ME: Why not?

ANTOINE: Because I'm older and more mature.

ME: You've got that right. Hey, hey, hey—

ANTOINE [SMILING]: We get better every day.

The Melting Snowball

The metaphor of a melting snowball helps counter anxiety about an upcoming change, loss, or event, as reflected in the following story. Seven-year-old Chuckie, who had been abandoned by his mother and had trouble trusting adults, was scheduled to leave his residential center for an adoptive home within a few days when Tom, his unit supervisor, received a call that Chuckie had run from his classroom. Finding him sitting outside on the stairwell, Tom slowly approached and asked what was wrong. Chuckie said he was scared to leave, feeling his new family would probably abandon him as well.

Tom supported his feelings and then proposed, "Chuckie, I want you to pretend that your nervousness about leaving and being abandoned is a big snowball sitting in the middle of your chest. . . . How big is it?"

Extending his arms out to the sides, Chuckie replied, "It's this big!"

"Well, Chuckie, every day you live with your new family that snowball is going to melt a little. In a few years, it will probably be this big," said Tom, using his hand to form a circle about the size of a dime. "Chuckie, that snowball will always be there; it will never go away. But with luck and hard work it should get small enough not to bother you too much. Lots of people who are living very happy lives are walking around with such snowballs."

A year later Chuckie's adoptive family brought him back to the center for a surprise visit. When he saw Tom fifty feet down the hallway, he blurted out, "It's this big, Tom!" His hand then formed a circle about the size of a dime.

JB, a fifth grader I worked with some years ago, finally got back on track midway through his final year in elementary school after years of struggling. But then he suffered a serious regression due to the pressure of a new identity and heightened expectations, as reflected in the following dialogue.

> JB: I'm terrible. None of the kids like me.
>
> ME: Right now doesn't feel very good. I hear you. But who is the kid who had two or three great months recently?
>
> JB: Me. But none of the kids like me.
>
> ME: The kids had trouble liking the old JB, not the new one. The old JB was a great kid but off track. The new and improved JB is much more popular and was beginning to make friends. If you show them the new and improved JB, the old JB will melt like a snowball, like a piece of ice. If you bring back the new JB, the friendships will come. Remember, we get better…
>
> JB: Every day.

JB got back on track. During the final month, he was enjoying meaningful playdates and, for the first time, earning autonomous privileges at home. On the final day of school I asked his parents if I could drive him home. When we got to his house and he was almost out of the car, I said to him, "Hey, dude, I think the *old* JB is like a little speck of ice now. Am I right?"

He paused for a few seconds, smiled, and replied, "It's liquid, Mr. A… Liquid."

The Fork in the Road

The metaphor of a fork in the road is invaluable to use with teenagers who make decisions that get them into trouble since it challenges them to look ahead, think carefully, and choose the right path, as illustrated by the following story. Sixteen-year-old Shawn, who was incarcerated at a juvenile detention center and had a long history of petty crimes, started an intense fight one afternoon with another resident and had to be physically escorted to his room by Greg, the staff member on duty. After venting for a while, Shawn broke down in tears and spoke hopelessly about his life. Greg listened compassionately and then said: "Shawn, you've had a tough life. No one can blame you for being so angry. But now you're at a fork in the road, and you've got to decide which way you're going. The road to the left is easier. Kids who go left keep on acting out their anger and often end up in places like this. Prisons are full of people who've had tough childhoods. The road to the right is a harder journey—it's about controlling your impulses to lash out—but it leads to a wonderful place. Shawn, you've got to decide which road you will take . . ." ("If you take the right road, you'll lighten the load.")

The Poker Game

The metaphor of life as a poker game is useful for encouraging at-risk kids because even if you're dealt a bad hand in poker you can still win the game. I ask kids, generally adolescents, to list their options if dealt a bad hand in poker. They respond, "You can bluff, fold, draw one or more cards, or stand pat."

"And there's one other option," I remind them. "You can blame the dealer: 'Freaking dealer, you never give me any good cards!'" I then tell kids that prison is full of people who blame their parents and others (the dealers) for being incarcerated, but in reality no one made them break the law. Regardless of what has happened in their lives, they must play the cards they were dealt. ("Even if you're dealt a bad hand you can still play in the band!")

The Eagle

The eagle metaphor champions effort over results. If an eagle flaps her wings hard, she ascends to a lofty level. Whether or not she's the highest eagle in the sky is meaningless. What's important is the effort she expended to get to her desired location. I give kids the cues "The harder I try, the higher I fly! Be the eagle!" "What's a mistake? A chance to learn something new." ("An opportunity to take!")

The Ticket

The ticket metaphor can help kids understand the concept of a requirement for an accomplishment. For example, school isn't always easy for kids with emotional and behavioral challenges, but it is their "ticket" to a good life. The dialogue usually goes something like this.

> ME: What do you need to get on a bus?
>
> KID: A ticket.
>
> ME: What do you need to get on a train?
>
> KID: A ticket.
>
> ME: What do you need to get into a movie?
>
> KID: A ticket.
>
> ME: You can't get anywhere without a ticket. When you go for a job, the interviewer will want to see your ticket, which is your education. Learning is your ticket to a great life!

I've advised teachers and other child-guiders to hang on a wall a big three-foot by two-foot collage full of tickets for planes, trains, dry cleaning, and movies that the kids have brought in, then superimpose over it, with colored construction paper, the sentence "Learning is my ticket to a great life." I ask them to periodically point to the sentence for inspiration.

I also suggest that if an additional motivational system is necessary child-guiders can have "tickets" reinforce and celebrate noteworthy academic achievements. Kids can earn physical objects like stickers, fake dollars, or tickets that can later be exchanged for some type of reward.

The Backpack

The backpack metaphor is helpful for getting kids to understand the importance of taking psychotropic medications. When kids are reluctant to begin taking these medications, you can use the metaphor of the backpack, telling them, "Say we're going to climb a mountain today. It's a three-hour, rather strenuous hike to the top. If you don't take the medication that we think will help you, it will be like climbing to the top carrying a twenty-five-pound backpack. You'll still make it. You're strong and tough. But you'll need to stop more, and it will require a lot more effort than it otherwise would. If you take the medication, it will be like climbing without the backpack. You'll still need to do the work, but it won't be as hard. The medication doesn't make you do better; it allows you to better use your talents to get things done." ("Lose the pack and stay on track!")

Rapid-Fire Infusion

Child-guiders can use inspirational metaphors and other uplifting, mind-altering words of hope with the help of a technique I call rapid-fire infusion. If done correctly, it can, as Shawn Achor writes, "spark positive emotional contagion," providing sudden bursts of positivity that send chemicals to the brain, making kids happier and more receptive to learning.[7] It's essentially a means of reinforcement that's fun for all, as illustrated by the following dialogue, which can take less than a minute.

> TEACHER: Okay, I want you to do problems 7 to 14 at your desks. Train on track...
>
> STUDENTS: Jack!
>
> TEACHER: Learning is...
>
> STUDENTS: My ticket to a great life!
>
> TEACHER: You'll have fifteen minutes to get them done. Even if you're dealt a bad hand...
>
> STUDENTS: You can play in the band.

TEACHER: The harder I try…

STUDENTS: The higher I fly!

TEACHER: Be the…

STUDENTS: Eagle!

TEACHER: And tomorrow I want your journals on my desk when you walk in. No excuses. We get better…

STUDENTS: Every day!

TEACHER: Train on track…

STUDENTS: Jack!

TEACHER: I can't hear you! Train on track…

STUDENTS: Jack!

TEACHER: I love teaching you guys. See you tomorrow (doing a few fist bumps and high fives as the kids leave).

It's also fun to invite some of the kids to throw out one of the lines in the middle of a class or group activity. Don't worry about this technique getting them going—where the heck are they going to go?

Externalizing and Naming a Problem Behavior or Habit

It's often easier to address a problem behavior or habit with a young person when the child-guider creates a sense of distance between the problematic action and the child, often accomplished through externalizing and naming the action. For example, if a child tends to experience frequent fits during the day or at specific times, a child-guider might suggest to the child not to let Mr. Fitz bring him down: "Man, you've been doing great. Before your visit tomorrow, don't let Mr. Fitz show up and get you in trouble." After a pause, the child-guider could add, "Oh man, it looks like Mr. Fitz is in the house. Tell him to get lost!"

I once worked with a fifth grader who was a perfectionist. A highly driven and talented student and athlete, he'd often act out when things didn't go his way. Every time I greeted him we engaged in the following exchange.

> ME: Babe Ruth . . .
>
> CHILD: Struck out more than any other player in baseball history.
>
> ME: You don't need to be the best . . .
>
> CHILD: To pass a test.
>
> ME: And who is not allowed in class with you?
>
> CHILD: Mr. Perfecto.
>
> ME: Yeah, he's a bum! He thinks he has to get everything right or he's no good. He's way off base. Lose the dude!

I also used this technique with Jason, an adolescent at my last residential setting. He was often rude to the teachers and support staff at his public high school. One morning I walked him to the bus. Before he boarded, I told him that I'd be picking him up at the bus stop every day that week and asking him one question.

> JASON: What's that?
>
> ME: Did that bum Rudy show up with you today?
>
> JASON: What are you talking about?
>
> ME: Well, you go to school every day, and too often you choose to act rudely to people. It's a bad habit, and we're going to call it Rudy. Rudy's a bum, and you're a great kid. I don't want him getting you in trouble anymore and hurting people's feelings. Don't you agree?
>
> JASON: Yeah.

That afternoon when he stepped off the bus I was waiting. "No Rudy today!" he exclaimed with a smile. I slapped him five and told him he was the man. The technique helped him identify, speak about, and ameliorate the problem habit.

Popular names that can be used to externalize and name a problem behavior or habit include the following.

Issue	Name
Being late or truant	I.B. Late or I.B. Truant ("They're cousins and up to no good!")
Arguing	Mr. R. Gue ("Tell him to argue in a courtroom, not here!")
Tantrumming	Mr. (Mrs.) Fitz ("They're way too dramatic.")
Provoking	I.B. Provokin
Rushing through things	Mr. (Mrs.) Russian
Worrying	Wanda (Wally) the Worrier
Perfectionism	Mr. (Mrs.) Perfecto
Rudeness	Rudy

Here are names that can be used to externalize and name a desired way of relating.

Issue	Name
Inflexibility	Mr. (Mrs.) Flex
Anxiety	I. B. Comma
Anger	Mr. (Mrs.) Cool
Impulsivity	Mr. (Mrs.) Thinkbeforeyeact
Rudeness	Mr. (Mrs.) Nice

"Stretching" or Repetitive Quizzing

Athletes always stretch their muscles before exercising or playing a game. For some kids, a similar kind of preparation is necessary before engaging in an evocative or difficult activity. Children and youth who are socially challenged, inflexible, and prone to explosive outbursts often have trouble participating in physical activities that can be rough and unpredictable, such as touch football and basketball. Asking or requiring these kids to "stretch" prior to one of these activities might prevent injury.

For example, years ago I was referred a fifth grader and outstanding athlete, Zack, who appeared to have high-functioning autism. Up until fourth grade he had demonstrated no symptoms of the disorder. It was felt that his condition might have resulted from a head injury. We created a user-friendly school environment for Zack (modifying our expectations and enhancing his accommodations), and he started off the year well. I then received reports that he was getting into fights during recess. The kids played tag football every day, and it was clear that Zack couldn't differentiate between normal roughhousing and a deliberate hit. If he was bumped, he'd punch the bumper. We could have kept Zack from playing, but instead we tried something else.

I asked him, "What does a good athlete do before he plays a game?"

"He stretches," Zack responded.

"Yes," I said. "Before you play tag football, I think you need to stretch—not your muscles but your brain—by answering some questions." I then gave him the following series of questions along with his hypothetical answer, calling them Zack's Two-Minute Stretch Warm-Up Exercise:

1. Is football a very physical and unpredictable game? Yes.

2. Is there a chance someone is going to hit, grab, pull, step on, or trip me? Yes.

3. If something rough happens to me, what do I think?

   a. "This is typical. Don't get mad." Yes.

b. "I'm upset. Let it go—NBD (no big deal)." Yes.

c. "If I make a bad choice and hit, I could hurt someone or get suspended." Yes.

d. "If I make a bad choice, people (can list names) will be unhappy with me." Yes.

e. "If I do well, they'll be proud." Yes.

4. Am I warmed up and ready to play? Yes.

Every day Zack dutifully answered these questions before playing football, after which his ability to play games improved dramatically.

The brain is designed to change in response to patterned, repetitive stimulation. Teachers quiz students to make sure they learn the material. Child-guiders can repeatedly quiz kids about an important subject or skill, or create scripts to help students prepare for and practice potentially difficult interpersonal interactions.

Distinguishing Wants from Needs

An effective method for helping kids control impulses and make good decisions is dissecting wants and needs. This is done by having kids differentiate what they *want* to do from what they *need* to do in regular discussions.

Example

> ME: Talk to me about wants and needs. Give me some problem situations you were in where you thought about this.
>
> KID: My brother was teasing me at home. I wanted to hit him. But I needed to walk away, and I did.
>
> ME: Excellent! I wanted to get a chocolate donut this morning, but instead I ordered the veggie egg white on flatbread.
>
> KID: Excellent!

The more child-guiders talk about wants and needs, the higher the probability that the kids will use this method of thinking.

Anger-Management Strategies

The best way to stop problem behavior associated with anger is to practice desired behavior. For example, if you want kids to stop hitting, put them into staged situations where they are being provoked (by you or other "actors") and then have them practice the desired behavior instead, such as walking away, counting, asking the instigator to stop, or stating how the instigator's behavior makes them feel and asking an adult to help. Getting excited every time they do the right thing can reinforce good problem-solving abilities.

Following are seven effective anger-management strategies:

1. Stop and count to five or ten (or one hundred).

2. Take a deep breath. Breathe calmly. Take a step back from the scene.

3. Decide what the problem is. Ask yourself, "Who (or what) am I really mad at?"

4. Think rap! ("NBD—no big deal," "Walk, talk, or squawk," or "Let it go, Joe!")

5. Consider alternative options:

   Walk away or ignore.
   Talk it out in a friendly manner.
   Ask for help.
   Give a reason for the person to stop.

6. Think about the consequences of making a good versus bad choice:

   "If I hit him, I could be suspended."
   "If I walk away, I go to the mall tonight free of hassles from home."
   "If I hit him, no electronics for a week."

7. Avoid stinkin' thinkin' by replacing negative thoughts (stinkin' thinkin') with more positive ones.

Initial Thought	Replacement Thought
This teacher doesn't like me.	She's having a rough day.
I'm stupid!	No one gets it right all the time.

Yoga, Mindfulness, and Exercise

Increasingly, schools and child- and youth-guiding programs are incorporating yoga, mindfulness, and daily exercise into their schedules to improve the functioning and experiences of kids from a mind-body perspective.

Social Thinking

Some kids with challenging behaviors, for a myriad of reasons—including cognitive, psychological, or developmental—lack empathy and the proper social thinking to respond appropriately in social situations, which thwarts the fulfillment of their desire to form meaningful relationships. Thus it's not enough to simply teach and practice social skills with these kids. It is also imperative to teach them how their words and actions affect others and, based on context, how and when to use their social skills. For example, yelling encouragement might be okay on the ballfield but not okay during a quiet study period in class. Further, certain kids need to be continually taught age-appropriate social skills as they grow older or they won't be cool!

Speech-language pathologist Michelle Garcia Winner, who writes and trains extensively on this subject, tells us:

Having good social skills means one is able to adapt effectively based on the situation and the people in the situation. It also means that social skills are not behaviors that are simply rehearsed, memorized, and produced based on a singular stimulus or response. Instead our social skills are part of our larger system of Social Thinking and social problem solving. In reality, we use our Social Thinking far more often than we use our social skills.

Our social-emotional learning systems should be nurtured and developed through discussion and instruction across school, home, and community settings. This learning is not restricted to grades K-12 or just within educational environments. Our social learning continues across all ages and throughout our lives, as the social expectations people hold for us change across our lifetime!

To summarize: our social skills are a by-product of our ability to use our Social Thinking to interpret social information and then decide how we want to be perceived by others. The behaviors we exhibit largely affect how people feel about us, which in turn can affect how we feel about ourselves.[8]

Behavior analyst Jessica Minahan offers practical suggestions for teaching self-regulation. In her books *The Behavior Code* and *The Behavior Code Companion*, she discusses the need to help children identify their emotions and states of regulation, develop strategies to calm themselves, and practice those strategies so they are easy to remember when stressed.[9] Minahan was kind enough to contribute the next section of this chapter.

Self-Monitoring and Self-Calming Techniques

Teaching and reinforcing self-monitoring and self-calming skills gives kids the tools they need to regulate their own behavior. When children become agitated—cry, whine, argue, or speak rudely—they will likely hear from a child-guider calming suggestions such as "Go get a drink of water and calm down" or simply "Relax." But such advice is futile for many kids who don't know *how* to calm down, and might even make them more upset.

Kids who display chronic agitation or noncompliance often lack self-regulation skills, and if we don't teach these skills, their behavior is unlikely to change for the better. Here are some useful skills we can teach them.

Helping Kids Learn to Self-Monitor Escalating Emotions. Teaching kids to be aware of how their emotions escalate incrementally from calmness to frustration to anger allows them to realize they need to use a calming strategy before they become too irrational. In a classroom, for instance, the teacher typically observes students becoming dysregulated (wiggling in their chairs or exhibiting frustrated facial expressions) and offers them a solution ("Sit up," "Lower your voice," "Stop wiggling"). While this works in the moment, unless students are taught to be aware of the escalation of their emotions and find solutions, the teacher will have the job of regulating the students all year.

It is therefore helpful to teach them to do a body check. To do a body check, students read clues their bodies give that they are getting upset. The teacher can help students notice and decipher these clues—"Your shoulders are up, your face is scrunched, your fists are clenched, all clues your body is giving you that you are getting frustrated." Older students can also be taught to be aware of internal signs, such as racing thoughts or faster heartbeat.

Once students have learned this technique, instead of telling them to "sit straight," the teacher can cue them by whispering, "Do a body check!" Each body check prompt is a crucial teaching moment where students learn to identify their regulation state and employ self-monitoring skills to move toward independence.

Developing Self-Calming Strategies. When children look agitated, we often offer strategies to calm them down, such as going for a walk, getting a drink of water, or coloring. Many kids who deal with anxiety or depression or who anger quickly can get stuck thinking negatively, ruminating hundreds of times on thoughts like "I hate this program" or "The teacher hates me." Such kids need self-calming strategies that offer cognitive distractions, opportunities to stop the negative thought loops. This is why many of us love movies—they distract us from anxiety-provoking thoughts. Activities that can have the same effect for older kids are reading aloud, Sudoku, or Mad Libs. Activities that can have the same effect for younger kids are hidden picture games, *Where's Waldo?* books, listening to recorded books, or having child-guiders read to them. Such activities can help children calm down more successfully than taking a walk or taking a break in a quiet place.

Biofeedback software is a great way to have kids collect data on their physiological state before and after using a calming strategy to help them know if it worked. Biofeedback is the use of electronic monitoring, usually a sensor on the finger connected to a mobile device or computer, to teach a person how to control his body's responses, such as heart rate. The more the child controls the body's responses, the more visual feedback he will receive, such as seeing black-and-white pictures turn to color.

Once you have helped children discover self-calming strategies that work for them, it is important for them to access those strategies easily when needed. For example, keeping a cognitively distracting object such as a water ring toss game keychain on a child's belt loop will ensure that he has a strategy always at hand. Displaying a visual "menu" of strategies that have worked for students can help them find an appropriate one when needed.

Developing Automaticity. When children are agitated or anxious, their memories, which help them recall their self-calming strategies, are greatly impacted. By teaching skills to reduce such emotions when kids are calm and rehearsing them frequently, the strategies become automatic—accessible even when children are upset and their memories are impaired. Children can often role-play how they behave when frustrated or anxious, and practice their self-calming strategies. Rehearsing such skills in the place where children will go when actually upset can increase the likelihood that their self-calming strategies will become automatic. Too often, I see students go into the guidance counselor's office and scream and cry for thirty minutes or more. The students can thus develop an association with that space of being unhappy and acting out. By practicing self-calming strategies in the place they are likely to be when upset, such as the classroom's quiet corner, their bedroom, a quiet room, or the counselor's office, they can create automaticity of skills, reducing the need to access memory, and the space can evoke the use of calming strategies even when their emotions are escalated.

How quickly children learn self-monitoring and self-calming skills varies. Some children learn in a few days, while others will need support for a while. Child-guiders can learn how to teach identification, strategies, and automaticity of skills without overprompting and while fostering independence. Not only can it prevent challenging behavior in the future, but it is an essential skill for success at school, at home, and in social settings.

Enhanced Self-Regulation

Katherine King, the school jurisdiction principal at Unlimited Potential Community Services in Edmonton, Alberta, shares the following information about the work she is doing with her students to promote enhanced self-regulation.

> I teach a social skills class once a week in all classrooms with students who attend our school due to their emotional and behavioral challenges in community schools. The course is called All about Relationships, as interactions with others is one of the biggest challenges for many of our students. I have found the program described in *Zones of Regulation* by Leah Kuypers to be extremely helpful for students. It helps them foster self-regulation and emotional control. Leah's work is closely tied to the social thinking work of Michelle Garcia Winner. The Zones of Regulation have four colors for students to identify their feelings: blue (low energy), green (good to go), yellow (warning zone requiring caution), and red (out of control).[10] On more than one occasion when teaching the zones, kids have commented, "Man, I don't have a yellow zone! I go right to red!" This insight is the beginning of learning to pay attention to what is going on in the body so they have a chance to do something (skills they have been taught) to move themselves back to feeling better. For staff and students to have a common language to use in the classroom, in the halls, gym, and on outings helps keep things simple and consistent for everyone.[11]

Child-guiders who actively help at-risk children and youth transform problem behaviors into desired behaviors do kids an enormous service. In learning to manage their responses to emotionally volatile situations, they make immeasurable progress toward becoming all that they can be.

— CHAPTER 15 —

The Essence of Communication

NURTURING STRENGTHS, CHANGING MINDSETS, and creating energizing environments are the initial steps in working effectively with kids who struggle with emotional and behavioral challenges; the final step is responding attentively to their behavior and the messages they send. The most successful responses arise from adults who inspire change through the communication dynamics they establish.

In their book *No-Drama Discipline*, Daniel Siegel and Tina Payne Bryson speak eloquently to this point. Although they refer to the parent-child relationship, their words apply to all child-guiders when they write, "The research is really clear on this point. Kids who achieve the best outcomes in life—emotionally, relationally, and even educationally—have parents who raise them with a high degree of connection and nurturing, while also communicating clear limits and high expectations."[1]

To promote healthy communication dynamics, child-guiders need to pay close attention to not only their verbal messages but the many subtleties that underlie them. *What* they say is certainly important; but *when* and *how* they say it often determines whether or not it will make a positive difference.

Their most helpful responses are those accompanied by an affect, tone, word choice, and body language that are empathic and respectful of children's emotional needs and sense of dignity. All four of these communication dynamics are within our realm of control and are compelling influences regardless of the history, biological makeup, or temperament of children.

Affect

The responses most likely to inspire at-risk children to alter their troublesome behaviors are those delivered with an affect, or emotional expression, that meets their needs for safety, support, control, connection, and respect and will vary depending on circumstances. For instance, when a child or group begins to lose control, the adults in charge must demonstrate that they are in control by staying calm and respectful, maintaining an atmosphere of safety. The guiding principle at such times is to establish an inverse relationship between the child's level of agitation and our own expressiveness; simply put, the louder and more out of control a child or group appears, the quieter and more controlled child-guiders need to be.

A good way to gauge the affect most appropriate to a volatile situation is to imagine an affect scale similar to the one shown in figure 15–1. Here, as a child "loses her cool" and the left side of the scale rises, the adult must respond by becoming that much more subdued (lowering the right side of the scale). In other words, the degree to which the child is out of control determines the degree to which the adult must show that she is in control, as illustrated in figure 15–2. As one of my supervisors used to say, "The

Figure 15–1
Affect Scale

professionals most respected in child-care settings are those who don't yell at the kids but stay calm in the face of emotional outbursts."

If both sides of the scale go up—that is, if both child and adult lose control of their emotions—communication becomes seriously threatened, and the child, hypersensitive to misuses of power, will invariably strike back in anger, if not fear. An unfortunate predicament of this sort unfolded for George during an afternoon gym trip at a residential center where he had recently started as a new child-care worker. After he had taken three kids to shoot hoops with him in the gym, one of the boys, ten-year-old Luke, immediately ran to retrieve a ball at the far end of the room. When George ordered him to come back and sit in the bleachers, Luke ignored the request and picked up the ball. George marched over and commanded him to drop the ball and sit on the bleachers, but Luke refused, leading to the following dialogue.

> GEORGE: Take a five-minute time-out for not listening to me.
>
> LUKE: Fuck you!
>
> GEORGE: Now you've got a ten-minute time-out!

Figure 15–2
Affect Scale during Escalation

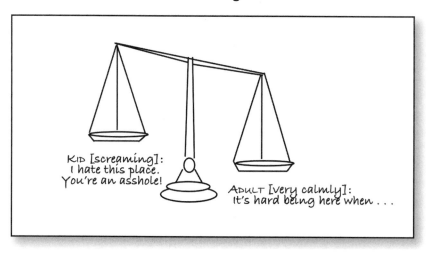

LUKE: Fuck you!

GEORGE: A fifteen-minute time-out.

The verbal volley continued until Luke was on the verge of violence, the time-out was approaching forty minutes, and both sides of the affect scale were rising dangerously. Then Dave, a more experienced staff worker, quietly reminded George that time-outs were usually capped at ten minutes, whereupon George realized that he had been as out of control as Luke.

Considerable self-discipline is required to stay calm and suppress the impulse to yell at, or speak negatively to, a child or group whose behavior is growing more extreme. Suppressing such natural impulses is a major requisite for most child-guiders when fear and anger spike; and it is a skill that can be relatively mastered. The calm demeanor to be maintained comes by using the observing ego to self-manage ("It's an injury and it will heal—respond instead of react") and by using the important communication techniques described in this chapter. It's also helpful to remember that at a later time the troubling situation you are dealing with will most likely be processed and resolved.

When the beam across the top of the affect scale is relatively balanced, both you and the child are in the level zone, where kids with emotional and behavioral challenges are more apt to be receptive to emotional give-and-take. This is a good time to explore and discuss what is transpiring: "Jeb, what's going on? You don't seem to be making very good choices. What can we do to make this a better day?" or "Sarah, what's up? The kids are getting a little upset with how you're choosing to act. Could we please take a walk? Thanks."

As the beam tilts, however, this window of opportunity for emotional give-and-take slowly closes. In the following dialogue between nine-year-old Carl and his teacher, Carl's opening statement suggests that he has exited the level zone and that expressing emotions to him is apt to cause him to feel worse and to retaliate because he is likely in a self-protective mode, thinking only about his own needs and feelings. In such circumstances, it's best for Carl's teacher to first bring him to a better emotional place, as reflected in the following two dialogues.

CARL: I really hate this class. You never help me!

TEACHER [ANIMATEDLY]: Carl, it upsets me when you say that. I do spend a lot of time with you.

CARL [MORE ANGRILY]: I don't care if you're upset. You're a jerk like all the rest!

Better

CARL: I really hate this class. You never help me!

TEACHER: You seem pretty upset, Carl, and I'm worried about you. I feel bad that you believe I've been letting you down. Let's talk after class. Okay?

CARL: Well, okay.

Kids with emotional and behavioral challenges are going to act out—that's what they do. The job of child-guiders is to get them to where they no longer feel the urge to act out. However, child-guiders must be careful, during the early stages of a conversation, about telling at-risk kids how their behavior makes them feel; this dynamic is usually counterproductive because the kids already feel bad about their actions.

If the behavior is upsetting to a child-guider and the kids see this, it's okay from time to time for her to respectfully convey how their actions make her feel—but at the right place and time, such as during a processing session. Kids benefit from honest and respectful communication.

Always keep an image of the affect scale in mind as it is likely to be among the most effective tools in your work with kids. "As they get louder, you get quiet. C'mon, friend, it's time to try it!"

Tone

Even when a statement is expressed with little affect, emotionally fragile children can infer a negative message because, accustomed to having power used against them, they are prewired to pick up on disempowering statements. While talking to highly sensitive kids, it is therefore essential to monitor tone of voice. When this does not occur, hypersensitive children can more easily slip into self-protection: "Am I in trouble here? Am I safe? Let me see if I can pick up where this person is coming from."

While the content of a statement may be the same, the use of different intonations can relay different messages. For example, whereas the statement "The house is pink" informs the listener about the color of the house, accentuating the word *pink*, as in "The house is *pink*," relays the message "Why on earth did you paint the house *pink*?" And while "You look *great* today!" promotes good feelings in the listener, "You look great . . . *today!*" means "Don't eat that Twinkie you stashed away for later."

A nonsupportive tone of voice can lead to any number of problematic reactions. Said angrily to a child at risk, a seemingly nonthreatening statement like "You need to knock it off" may be interpreted as ominous. She may conclude that the speaker is angry at her and will not want to hear her side of the story, is verbally attacking her, and is treating her like all adults do. Her natural reaction will likely be to argue, refuse to accept responsibility for the problem, and fight back. It was not the words but rather how they were delivered that led to such a reaction.

In fact, the tone in which a statement is delivered tends to correlate closely with the tenor of the child's reaction. Imagine that you are a special education teacher and that Eli, one of your most challenging students, has just thrown an eraser at you, hitting you in the forehead and barely missing one of your eyes. You're very upset; yet it's critical to respond in a manner that maintains your image as a trusted professional and does not impinge on the sanctity of your relationship with Eli and the other kids. The message Eli and his classmates hear, as well as their ultimate reaction, will depend on the tone of your response, as illustrated in the following four scenarios.

Scenario #1. "I am really upset with the choice you made, Eli!" delivered in an angry tone of voice.

Possible messages: "The teacher is angry, and I'm in big trouble," "This stinks," "Who the hell is she?" "What's going to happen next?"

Angry messages often evoke angry reactions, especially if your anger is harsh and intimidating. Children who hold in their resulting anger are likely to release it in a later, perhaps unrelated, context. This behavior is known as displacement.

Scenario #2. "Iamreallyupsetwiththe choiceyoumade, Eli!" delivered in a rushed, almost hysterical tone.

Possible messages: "The teacher is very angry and doesn't seem to be in control of her emotions," "This is scary," "I can't trust her—I hope nothing worse happens."

Blurting out irate remarks can shake a child's confidence in your ability to manage him and ultimately provoke an angry reaction and increased acting out. An erratic child-guider who has trouble maintaining her cool often triggers a counterphobic response in kids, prompting them to deliberately bring on the undesired consequences, to avoid more uncertainty and take back control. Such children are apt to think, at least subconsciously: "This counselor is getting really upset. And when she gets upset she starts dropping levels and punishing us. I can't stand the uncertainty of not knowing when she's going to screw us, so let's get it over with. At least I won't have to worry about it anymore. I will have taken back control."

Scenario #3. "*I am really upset* with the choice *you made*, Eli!" delivered in a loud, furious tone with negative emphasis on key words.

Possible message: "The teacher is ticked off and needs to drive her point home."

When a statement starts out loud and furious, it immediately raises the defenses of a sensitive, perhaps trauma-reactive, child, increasing the likelihood that he will overreact and fail to hear the rest of the words. Such insensitive reacting can trigger a "fear, fight, or flight" reaction for a child. If you catch yourself beginning your response in a loud and angry voice, try pausing and altering your tone. Adding humor to the situation can help lower the child's defenses. I sometimes say to a kid: "You seem to be trying very hard to make me angry. And do you know what? You've done it! I'm angry! So what can we do about this?" These words, communicated in a humorous way, serve to de-escalate both the situation and yours truly.

Scenario #4. "I am really upset with the choice you made, Eli," delivered in a firm yet controlled manner.

Possible messages: "The teacher is upset yet calm; I know she likes me but isn't really happy about the choice I just made" and "Man, I could have really hurt her, but this isn't the end of the world."

When you need to respond to problem behavior, at times it's best to say very little or nothing at all. At other times, the best way to communicate is to describe your feelings in a steady, unhurried cadence, using a supportive tone and avoiding the emphasis on power words. In part this works well because the child's reaction is apt to mirror the controlled tone of your statement, and also because in refusing to verbally attack the child you have not activated his defenses, so the message can come through and the other kids can see that you are able to manage them through rough stretches. The more closely you adhere to these guidelines, the better your relationships with the children will be and, as a result, the more behavioral changes you will eventually see.

Word Choice

Because children at risk have trouble tolerating power-laden content without overreacting, careful word choice is critical in our efforts to support them and forge a connection. For example, when giving a child directions it is generally helpful to say "please" and "thanks." For example, "Could you please go to your room—thanks" is far more encouraging and better received than "Go to your room." Similarly, "Hey, John, would you please take out the trash—thanks" is much more likely to yield the desired result than "Take out the trash."

In addition to saying "please" and "thanks," avoid utilizing an overly directive "you," as in "You better knock it off!" "You need to stop that!" and "You come here right now!" The perceived hostility underlying such messages is apt to prompt an adverse reaction, while substituting *you* statements with *I* or *we* statements can lead to increased rapport. This approach was popularized by Thomas Gordon in his book *P.E.T.: Parent Effectiveness Training*.

The following examples illustrate ways to shift to more effective messages by changing just a few words.

Less effective: "You need to stop talking like that, John."

More effective: "John, I'm uncomfortable with that sort of language."

Less effective: "You need to stop running in the hallway."

More effective: "We don't want kids getting hurt, so I'm asking you to please not run in the hallway."

Teachers and child-care workers alike report that adding "please" and "thank you" to their conversations with children, as well as replacing *you* statements with *I* or *we* statements, has led to dramatic improvements in their behavior. Communicating respectfully with kids has the additional advantage of encouraging them to communicate respectfully with us.

Body Language

Body language is as significant as word choice in communicating effectively with children. Because kids with emotional and behavioral challenges are often hypersensitive to nonverbal messages, it is necessary to take extra care in controlling body language.

Facial Expressions

To be effective, facial expressions need to be in tune with a child's emotional state. The more in control a child appears, for example, the more expressive you may safely be. When a student has quietly added an interesting observation to a class discussion, feel free to extend your enthusiasm; "What a marvelous contribution!" you might declare, with a big smile and brightly shining eyes. Kids will cherish exaggerated facial expressions in response to their accomplishments as long as they do not feel you are being insincere or making fun of them.

Conversely, when a child appears distraught, facial expressions should generally become less animated. If an agitated child is approached by a child-guider with a scowl, the entire interaction might be ruined. Of course, there are exceptions. For instance, when we support kids who have received upsetting news, facial and verbal expressions of empathy will be welcomed, as will the message "Oh man, I feel terrible that you're missing your visit!"

Hand Gestures

Improper use of hand gestures tends to exacerbate anxiety. Finger-pointing, for example, which often sends a negative message rippling with power, control, and anger, can dampen a child's motivation to change her behavior. Effective use of hand signals, however, can keep the volume in the room at a reasonable level, facilitate the relaying of information, reduce stress, and help build self-esteem. Following are several examples.

Palms Up at Waist Level. This hand gesture gives the impression of asking for help rather than demanding compliance.

The Okay Sign. This popular universal gesture, formed by holding the palm outward, creating an O shape by touching forefinger to thumb, and pointing the other three fingers upward, is a sign of validation, as if saying, "That was great."

Thumbs Up. The thumbs-up sign, like the okay sign, reinforces positive verbal messages, and in some instances is a perfect substitute. A child who has been having a rough time and is beginning to regain control will most likely benefit from a supportive thumbs-up signal, especially if she is not yet ready to converse with you.

Handshake. Shaking hands makes use of touch to convey the message "I care about you." For a kid who craves physical attention, a handshake may be the best possible way of connecting.

An elementary school teacher I know in Texas makes a point of physically touching each student at least once a day during the school year. Whether it is a tap on the shoulder or a handshake, this physical contact, she is convinced, reinforces her emotional and intellectual ties with her students. Aware that some children may not want to be touched against their will, she starts off the year by asking each one individually for their permission.

The Fist Bump and Slap Five. Even more powerful than a handshake, a fist bump or slap five can truly reinforce the good vibes that exist or are being nurtured between a child-guider and a child.

Nonverbal Cueing

Nonverbal cueing is an art form that invites as much creativity as you wish to give it. These nonverbal cues effectively deliver a message without interrupting an activity or calling attention to a particular child.

Visual cues. Pictures or diagrams can be posted on a wall to remind the children of proper conduct. That way, rather than stopping to address a misbehavior you could point to a poster or simply glance in the direction of a word-card to communicate the needed message. A third-grade teacher I know begins every school year by creating a mural of her students' handprints. Thereafter, whenever a student speaks without raising her hand, the teacher points to the mural. And when the class gets rowdy, she turns off the lights to restore peace and quiet.

Body gestures can be used in much the same way. When Audrey, a group home supervisor, grabs her earlobe, the child she is looking at knows it is time to "stop, think, and act."

Sign language. Some adults who work with at-risk kids create hand signals to relay such messages as "Please be quiet," "That was great," "We're a team," "No, don't do that," "Return to your seats," "I need your attention," "Five minutes until the next activity," "I'm upset," and "Thank you." A sign often used to restore quiet is a hand raised in the air, palm facing outward.

Auditory signals. Sound is an excellent way to capture the attention of a group that has become unfocused or loud. One auditory signal used frequently by elementary school teachers and youth-care workers is rhythmic clapping, or clapping loudly in a particular sequence—such as three slow claps followed by a short pause, two quick claps, another short pause, and four quick claps—which the children then repeat. This method is less intrusive, and far more productive, than shouting, "Pay attention...*now!*" Other auditory possibilities include ringing a small bell or playing music.

Morphing. At times a funny stunt or saying can quickly engage kids' attention, allowing the child-guider time to shift to a more traditional technique. My personal way to restore calm and focus when I enter a kindergarten class that seems a bit uproarious, is to place a chair near the front of the room then stand on it, bend forward a little, with one leg back, and put my outstretched hand to my temple like I'm saluting. Eventually the kids approach me and ask, "What are you doing, Mr. A?" I wait until most of them have drawn near, and then I respond, "I'm looking for some good behavior!" A moment later I morph into either the leader of a Simon Says game or rhythmic clapping.

Positioning Dynamics

Physical proximity often sways the outcome of our interactions with kids at risk. In most cases, an agitated child needs space in order to regain composure; therefore, it is best to avoid stepping too close to her until she has settled down. Staring at her or forcing eye contact with her can also be counterproductive. Because she is not ready for an "invasion" of the space surrounding her, and will therefore guard it with her defenses, it is preferable to respect those defenses and slowly approach only after they have been lowered. In general, it's wise to stay two arm lengths away from an agitated child when attempting to communicate with her.

Regarding body positioning, eye-level contact or below works best, particularly if the child is under stress. Whereas towering over her while she is seated is likely to provoke feelings of powerlessness and intimidation, crouching down so that your eyes are parallel with hers is not. If she is agitated, however, it is often prudent to approach her at a forty-five-degree angle. If she is extremely agitated, an even lower body position may be more helpful. I have had some of my best conversations with kids while stretched out on the floor.

Effective physical positioning also includes circulating among the children rather than standing continuously at the front of the room or sitting behind a large desk. Teachers note that in response to varying their proximity to the students, their attention spans lengthen, and those in the back of the room are pulled into the day's lessons. If a student is tapping a pencil, just walking toward her will usually stop the disruptive behavior. Active teachers are engaging and send the message that they are really invested in their students' well-being.

In milieu settings, it's not uncommon for staff members to sit for long periods of time in their staff rooms rather than circulating among the kids. This lack of physical proximity between the staff and children often initiates preventable problem behavior.

Physical Appearance

Because children are keen observers of adults, a child-guider's physical appearance can evoke strong reactions. Inadequate attention given to hygiene, grooming, or dress may send the message "I don't care much about myself"—a statement that will invariably be interpreted as "If he doesn't care about himself, he certainly won't care about me."

The appropriate clothing for a job depends on the nature of the job. In some instances a suit and tie, or a dress, can indicate that you take your occupation and the kids seriously. In other instances, such attire constitutes overkill. It is hard to play ball, for instance, in a three-piece suit and fancy shoes.

The single most important clothing guideline is: never wear provocative attire. Beer or cigarette insignias, or sexually suggestive clothing, may excessively stimulate at-risk kids. A youngster who has been abused by an alcoholic uncle, for example, might look at an adult wearing a Budweiser shirt and wonder, "Is this guy safe?" The shirt, after all, is likely to imply: "I like Budweiser. I like to drink. And I might hurt you just like your uncle did." In the context of a child-care setting, it may intimate, "The program is now hiring people who are unsafe to be with."

Emotional Appearance

Emotional appearance, like physical appearance, can help make or break a connecting bond with an at-risk child. Although I believe it is essential for child-guiders to be good actors, there are times when it's better to be honest about your emotions, such as when you just can't fake it because you've experienced something truly awful in your life. When you are communicating with at-risk kids, some emotional honesty can help cultivate trusting relationships. If you are in a bad mood and say, "You know what, kids, I'm in a really lousy mood today, but I just know it's going to change," they may even give you a break. Caution is advised, however, for they may take this comment personally or may fear that your mood will negatively affect their day.

Certainly, any time a person's safety is at stake, honesty is unquestionably not the best policy. In fact, such situations require top-notch acting. And admitting to fear or showing alarm will only exacerbate tensions and out-of-control behaviors. The stage directions in times of peril call for taking charge and remaining in control. If a child asks, "Are you scared?" your best reply is, "I'm a little worried, but I know we'll be okay."

One night the teenagers at a detention center in New Hampshire seemed ready to riot. We were short staffed, and the tension was rising dramatically. A few of the residents, having committed acts of violence, were being physically restrained, and, for the first time in twenty years, I feared for my own safety. While I was physically restraining one resident, others walked by hissing, "It's zooey tonight!" and "The place is bonkers!" and "This unit is gonna blow!" Each time I feigned a reassuring reply: "It's loud now, but things will be okay. We've got a few people coming in. We'll be fine." By providing some semblance of composure and control, my coworkers and I managed to quell a near revolt.

Caution: Avoid message discord. Although it will at times be necessary to disguise your feelings, always ensure that your verbal and nonverbal messages are in sync because otherwise the resulting message discord will likely intensify the problematic situation, as reflected in the following anecdote.

In response to rude remarks twelve-year-old Jon had made to classmates, his teacher walked quickly to his desk, peered down at him, and, appearing to be upset, said respectfully, "Jon, please talk to the other kids more kindly."

"Get out of my face!" he barked, triggered by the message discord he had experienced between her verbal statement and her emotional appearance.

Communicating is an art form. Conducted skillfully, it can richly enhance relationships with at-risk kids; ill-used, it is apt to compromise even the hardiest attachments.

A magnificent scene in the movie *The Horse Whisperer* conveys the essence of effective communication and, in particular, de-ecalation, in child-guiding. The movie features Robert Redford as Tom Booker, a legendary horse whisperer who has an extraordinary ability to connect with and transform wounded and often out-of-control horses. In the scene, a New York executive named Annie drives her daughter, Grace, and her wounded, out-of-control horse, Pilgrim, cross-country to Montana to find Tom Booker, who is their last hope for saving Pilgrim's life. Grace and Pilgrim had been involved in a horrific accident that badly injured both, leaving Pilgrim with open wounds and so traumatized that he had not allowed any humans to provide him with the care he so desperately needed.

Early on, Booker and his team gently guide Pilgrim into a stream, and the dirt on him slowly washes away. Just before they are about to bring Pilgrim out of the water, Annie's cell phone rings loudly, startling Pilgrim. Although connected to a myriad of ropes and harnesses, Pilgrim breaks his shackles and runs with abandon toward the valley ahead.

Eventually, Pilgrim stops at a sprawling pasture blanketed with wild grasses and flanked by majestic mountains. The sun is slowly setting. Pilgrim, a solitary wounded soul standing alone, afraid, angry, and confused, has a tenuous will to survive. He glances back toward the stream and sees Booker, a hundred yards away, looking in his direction. After a few minutes, Booker crouches down in a patch of tall grass, keeping his eyes fixed on the horse. For a few hours, neither moves as the sun continues its descent through a resplendent blue-gray sky. After a close-up of Booker, the next frame shows the two staring at each other, but Pilgrim has moved appreciably closer to Booker. Booker never moves but keeps his eyes on Pilgrim. At this point, Annie comes by and starts to talk to Booker, but, out of respect for the horse, he ignores her. The message he is sending to Pilgrim by not addressing Annie is "There is no one more important than you. You're in pain, and I'm with you. You will be okay."

After other close-ups of Booker, Pilgrim is fifty feet away; once the sun has almost set, he is only a few feet away. Then Booker slowly rises, gently strokes the horse, and guides him back to the barn.[2] No words are spoken. I get choked up every time I watch that scene.

Effective communication with at-risk kids, too, depends on empathy, patience, and determination to help them improve their well-being and reach their full potential.

— CHAPTER 16 —

Core Strength-Based
Verbal Interventions

MANY PEOPLE WHO WORK PROFESSIONALLY with children have a natural ability to connect verbally with them. Relying solely on nature's gifts, however, is often inadequate when interacting with more complex and challenging kids, which generally requires a large tool bag of basic and sophisticated communication skills. In the following two chapters we present a plethora of communication tools and theories that can enhance child-guiders' effectiveness. All the techniques presented for communicating with individual kids may be adapted for use in responding to groups.

The Pre-Talk Routine

Just as professional golfers develop pre-shot routines to improve their odds of hitting the ball straight and long, to maximize their potential as effective communicators child-guiders establish pre-talk routines before uttering a word to kids or groups. A productive pre-talk routine consists of components arrived at through reflection on the eight key questions that follow. Included under each one is self-coaching advice that can be personalized while dialoguing with the observing ego, as described in chapter 3.

1. How can I engage this child?

The more committed you are to creating an empathic bridge linking your feelings to the child's, the more receptive he is apt to be. Any time you approach someone who is upset, think: engage.

Self-coaching advice: No matter what he says, support his feelings. Let him see that you empathize with his plight and are able to handle his anger without retaliating. Sit with him a while; don't be so quick to resolve the problem.

2. What is on my mind?

The better you are at putting aside any personal issues or professional pressures that may sabotage the intervention, the greater your chances will be for successful relating.

Self-coaching advice: Although you might be mad because your car broke down and it's going to cost a bundle to get it fixed, or you're worried about falling behind schedule and incurring the wrath of your supervisor, remember that such concerns are peripheral to your relationship with the child. Let go of all pressures while talking to him; you can deal with them later. As Rachel Naomi Remen states so eloquently in *My Grandfather's Blessings*, come in "clear" every day.[1]

3. How do I feel about this kid or group?

It may be more tempting to speak harshly to an angry kid you do not like than to one you are fond of. To be fair, explore your personal feelings toward the child and, if they are negative, counter them with as much objectivity as possible. Think: pie. Every kid deserves an equal slice of your time.

Self-coaching advice: Okay, you don't like this kid. But you have to deal with him in the same way as all the others. And if you do it right you may end up liking him after all. Remember, the kid who is pushing you away the most is probably the one who needs you the most.

4. What is the child's side of the story?

Even when a child has obviously messed up, it is vital to hear his point of view. If you begin your conversation without listening to what he has to say, you are likely to risk shutting him down and tarnishing your relationship.

Self-coaching advice: You saw the kid knock the desk over (fire the spitball across the room, cut a hole in the curtain). You're angry and want to deal with the offense right away. Instead, be patient and listen. Find out what triggered him, then get to the desk (spitball, curtain) situation.

5. What nonverbal messages will I send?

The manner in which you advance toward the child, use your hands and arms, and demonstrate facial expressions will carry more meaning than the words you say.

Self-coaching advice: Walk slowly. When you get to the kid, crouch down instead of hovering over him. Approach at a forty-five-degree angle. Keep your hands out of your pockets or he might worry about what's in them. Look calm, and refrain from pointing at him. Breathe naturally.

6. How will I cope with a defensive reaction?

Defensiveness is often a child's best means of protecting himself, whereas opening up may only increase his sense of vulnerability and fear of rejection. Therefore, as you approach the child anticipate resistance, a provocative word or two, and displacement (when a person places onto you feelings he has for someone else). Start your conversation in a lighthearted manner, and as the protest wanes, shift gradually to more serious topics. If you respond appropriately, he might reveal his issues with others in his life.

Self-coaching advice: He's going to either deny the wrongdoing or blame it on someone else. He may even yell at you and hold you accountable for the incident. Although his accusations may hurt, do not take them personally. It's an injury, and it will heal. Respond instead of react. After he has vented for a while, slowly work through the incident.

7. Are consequences necessary?

If the situation calls for consequences, identify a few ahead of time. Be clear about the discipline options you will offer to the child, then let the child help decide on the most appropriate ones.

Self-coaching advice: Never before has the kid done something like this, so maybe you can cut him a little slack. See what he has to say. Also make sure you let him know about the progressive discipline that is practiced here, that we view repeated offenses as loud calls for help, and that such actions often result in tighter supervision, enhanced support, and, at times, more stringent consequences.

8. **Was I responsible for this incident? If so, what could I have done to prevent it?**

Kids often act out when their calls for help have been ignored, or when they have been placed in precarious or threatening situations. For example, elementary school students who, not properly supervised, act out during recess are set up for misbehavior on a daily basis. Teens in residential settings who act out because of inconsistent disciplinary practices should be held accountable for their actions, but the adults in charge should also own some of the problem.

Refrain from coming down too hard on the child for a situation beyond his control or one that you may have set up. Instead, accept responsibility for the part you have played, openly admit to your error, and make plans to prevent a recurrence of the episode.

Self-coaching advice: Had you been more involved, you might have prevented this incident. As a result, although the kid needs to assume responsibility for his actions he also needs to hear that you let him down a bit. Collaborate on a better approach for the future.

Adults who work on the front lines with children at risk are often strapped for time, and, as a result, good communication practices are frequently compromised. But taking time to go through a pre-talk routine is a useful preventive discipline that can significantly reduce the amount of time later spent reacting to behavioral issues.

Core Verbal Interventions

Although expertise at intervening with at-risk kids comes from experience, anyone can jump-start meaningful conversations by working with the following fourteen interventions, all of which meet the communication needs of challenging children. Two points to keep in mind when using this approach are the following. First, a meaningful conversation with a struggling child ideally consists of a beginning phase, middle phase, and end phase. The beginning phase entails nonevocative dialogue intended to engage the child. Once engagement is evident, it is time to embark on the middle phase, which involves a gentle introduction of more serious topics. The end phase brings closure to the discussion, sheds light on the future, and closes with good-byes. The beginning phase consists of the first six interventions outlined in figure 16–1 at the end of this chapter; the middle phase, the next seven; and the end phase, the final intervention. Second, in practice the sequencing of interventions within the first two phases will vary as needed from conversation to conversation.

By way of illustration, the interventions described below contain a running dialogue between a challenging twelve-year-old named Ned and his sixth-grade teacher, Mr. Neil. Ned is the bright, rambunctious son of a hardworking single mother who loves him but is often unavailable and a father who visits him infrequently, factors that have contributed to Ned's struggle with anger. As the dialogue opens, Mr. Neil is on his way to talk with Ned, who has been kept after school for throwing a pencil at him. Ned is sitting on a bench in the school office.

1. Nonjudgmental Exploration

The number one goal when attempting to converse with upset or agitated kids is to engage them. Starting with a nonjudgmental question or comment often gets your foot in the door.

Examples

> ADULT: What's up?

> KID: I hate Billy! He always has to get his way!

ADULT: What's happening, man?

    KID: You said you were going to take us out this afternoon.

ADULT: What's going on?

    KID: Nothing. I don't want to talk.

2. Supportive Comments

Supportive comments are empathic statements voiced to offer help and comfort in times of emotional unrest. Their purpose is to connect with a child by supporting his feelings and position.

Examples

    KID: I hate this place!

ADULT: Seems like you're pretty upset.

    KID: Get out of here! I don't want to talk. This place is so unfair!

ADULT: Man, you seem mad. I don't blame you for feeling this way. Anything I can do to help?

    KID: My mother is a jerk!

ADULT: It sounds like you're really mad at her. That's too bad.

    KID: John was picking on us!

ADULT: No wonder you're so angry.

    KID: I don't care.

ADULT: Seems like you're pretty discouraged.

TEACHER: Kids, I don't blame you for being upset. It's terrible when it rains and you can't go out. I'd be mad, too.

Mr. Neil and Ned

After approaching Ned, who is sitting on a bench in the school office, Mr. Neil sits on the same bench, about three feet away, and slouches down until he is almost at eye level with Ned.

MR. NEIL: How's it going, Ned? (nonjudgmental exploration)

(No reply)

MR. NEIL: It seems like you're still a bit angry. Who can blame you? It's been a hard day. (supportive comments)

Mr. Neil tried to connect with Ned. By establishing that he is not mad at Ned and by supporting Ned's feelings, he creates an opening for further communication.

Because children who are agitated or angry are bound to say things they do not mean—displacing their feelings onto others—it is important not to take their words too literally. In a classroom or other group setting, a good response to such venting is to provide a private place, such as an office or "think-time corner," for expressing frustration without jeopardizing the safety and stability of others and the dignity of the child.

3. Repeating or Paraphrasing

Repeating back almost word for word what a youth has said or paraphrasing a comment will give him the feeling that he is being listened to. This technique should be used judiciously, however, because kids will often rebel against anyone who uses too much "psychology" on them or who engages in too much parroting.

Examples

> KID: I hate going to bed this early!
>
> ADULT: So you're saying you hate going to bed this early.

> KID: Get out of here—I don't feel like talking.
>
> ADULT: I hear what you're saying: you don't feel like talking. I'll come back in a little while.

> KID: I feel like running away.
>
> ADULT: You feel like running away. Wow, you're really going through a lot right now. That's not good.

> KID: My parents are always making me do things I don't want to do.
>
> ADULT: So you're saying that you're a bit ticked off at your parents.

NED: You never call on me! I know the answers, but you ignore me.

MR. NEIL: Ned, you're saying that I never call on you? No wonder you're upset. No kid wants to be ignored.

Mr. Neil, familiar with Ned's family dynamics, knows that Ned is hypersensitive to being ignored by adults, particularly men, since his father abandoned the family a few years back, so he needs to tread carefully.

4. Feelings Check

Periodically asking how a child is feeling and sharing your feelings can model ways to identify emotions and appropriately express them. Kids who are trauma victims often react explosively to stress and are not in touch with what they are feeling. Such kids need considerable help in identifying their feelings and reacting accordingly. A feelings check needs to be conducted with sensitivity for another reason as well: at-risk children are often resistant to acknowledging how they feel, because doing so might increase their vulnerability, exposing them potentially to more talks and pain. Some kids also think negative feelings are bad. During a feelings check, a child-guider can set the record straight, informing the child that all feelings are okay and that acting them out is what causes trouble.

I often ask kids if anger is a good emotion. Many say no. I then tell them that Martin Luther King was very angry about the way African Americans were being treated and that Mother Teresa was equally angry about the huge numbers of hungry people in the world but that both did something good with their anger: "They made the world better and so can you."

Examples

> KID: Sarah is always making fun of me.
>
> ADULT: That's too bad. (supportive comment) How do you feel when she teases you? (feelings check)
>
> KID: It really makes me angry!
>
> ADULT: Of course it does! I'd be angry, too. (supportive comments). Thank you for letting me know that. Let's see if we can take your anger and turn it into something helpful. Let's meet with Sarah and see what's going on.

> TEACHER: I'm feeling frustrated about our lack of effort today, kids. What will inspire you to try harder?

5. Positive Recognition

It often takes a lot of courage for children who lack trust in adults to own their feelings and actions as this may be unchartered waters for them. Therefore, as soon as they do it's helpful to positively reinforce their admissions.

Examples

> KID: I know, I shouldn't have sworn at the cook.
>
> ADULT: Thanks for admitting this. It's not always easy to own up to things.

> KID: I got so angry I couldn't help myself!
>
> ADULT: Thanks for sharing what you were feeling.

MR. NEIL: How does being ignored make you feel? (feelings check)

NED: It makes me feel terrible. I get really angry.

MR. NEIL: I don't blame you. I'd get angry, too. (supportive comment) Thank you for sharing that. (positive recognition) By the way, Ned, there is nothing wrong with anger. You just have to learn how to express it the right way. Remember what I said about Martin Luther King. Try it. Say, "Mr. Neil, I was angry because you didn't call on me."

NED: Mr. Neil, I was angry because you didn't call on me.

MR. NEIL: Thank you for letting me know this. (positive recognition) I want to talk more about this.

Mr. Neil helped Ned better express his feelings. By quickly praising him for opening up as well as practicing the desired behavior, he increased the likelihood that Ned will enhance his ability to appropriately express his feelings.

6. Praise (General, Animated, Specific)

Current wisdom dictates that for praise to be effective it should be specific. That said, there are times when different kinds of praise, such as general and animated, meet the needs of a child or group.

General praise is praise that positively recognizes a person or accomplishment.

Examples

A youth earns a higher level at a residential center.

> ADULT: Nice going, Alberto! I knew you could do it.

A student gets a good grade on an exam.

> ADULT: Nice job, Sally! Way to go, kid!

A youth at a juvenile justice center sinks a three pointer.

> ADULT: Great shot! You've got the touch, brother!

Animated praise is praise with a little umph.

> KID: I got an A on my history report.

> ADULT: That's *fantastic*, Ellie! I am so proud of you. Slap me ten!

> KID: I let Frankie go first.

> ADULT: What a *nice* thing to do! It's not easy to let someone else go first. I'm proud of you.

> TEACHER: This is the greatest class in the entire world! You kids are working so hard and accomplishing so much that I expect you'll soon be teaching me. I might call the president. He could use some talented assistants.

Specific praise explicitly identifies the behaviors being praised.

FOSTER PARENT: Man, you did a great job cleaning your room. I love the way you organized your drawers, straightened out your desk, and folded your clothes. You the man!

> NED: And I was doing good before I threw the pencil. I got the whole writing assignment done.
>
> MR. NEIL: Yes, you did a great job on the assignment. (general praise) I really liked the way you took your time and used each of the vocabulary words. (specific praise) And you worked extra hard to keep your sentences on the lines. (specific praise) Are you trying to take my job? (humor and animated praise)

Mr. Neil used the opening Ned gave him to expand on some of Ned's accomplishments throughout the day. He knew that when talking to kids about problem issues it's always good to balance the talk by inserting some of the good decisions the child or group have recently made. Here Mr. Neil used all three forms of praise effectively.

7. Apologizing

Apologizing helps diffuse power struggles by balancing the interplay and models honesty, humility, and vulnerability, thereby enhancing relationships. Admitting your errors and apologizing for them early on in a conversation will significantly increase the odds for a more meaningful dialogue and relationship.

Examples

KID: You didn't have to yell at me.

ADULT: You're right—I apologize. I didn't need to talk to you that way.

KID: You said we would go to the movies tonight.

ADULT: I forgot that my mother was coming to visit. I'm really sorry—I know you were looking forward to going. We'll do it tomorrow night.

CHILD-CARE WORKER: I'm sorry, guys. I forgot to defrost the turkey. Dinner is going to be late. I really messed up this time.

When you are feeling defensive, or have been accused of something you did not do, try a nonresponsibility apology.

KID: You didn't have to yell at me.

ADULT: I'm sorry you think I yelled at you. I know you don't like people raising their voices at you. I'll be more careful in the future. Thanks.

NED: I kept raising my hand, but you never called on me.

MR. NEIL: You're right. I apologize.

NED: Why didn't you call on me?

MR. NEIL: Well, Ned, you were raising your hand. But you were also calling out without doing so. So I thought if I didn't call on you it would get you thinking more about raising your hand. I think I could have done a better job reminding you about this.

---

8. Sandwiching

It's often effective to sandwich two positive statements around a more negatively perceived one, such as a consequence being delivered.

Example

TEACHER: Ozzie, I'm glad you wanted to get a good grade on this test. I've got some kids who don't even care. (reframing) But copying off Elsie's paper was a mistake. I would like to see you after school for some make-up work. Oz, you don't need to take shortcuts to success. You are more than smart enough to do well on any of these tests. I believe in you. See you later.

NED: You said you're sorry, but I got sent to the office. Teachers love screwin' kids. Are you going to call my mother? Am I going to get suspended?

MR. NEIL: Ned, you made a serious mistake throwing the pencil—I could have been hurt. But you made a really good decision to walk calmly from the class without making things worse. (specific praise) You've also been sitting here like a gentleman. (general praise)

NED: Yeah, sometimes I don't always leave in a good way.

MR. NEIL: Thanks for owning up to that. (positive recognition) All trains get off track from time to time. I think the Ned train is moving in the right direction. But I will need to call your mom.

NED: She's going to ground me, I know it!

MR. NEIL: If you'd like, I can let her know that overall you've been doing a lot better. You made a big mistake today, but I really believe you're heading in the right direction. I just know you're going to finish up the year strong.

Mr. Neil sandwiched his need to call Ned's mother between two positive statements. He also managed to praise and encourage Ned during the conversation.

9. Humor

Injecting humor into a serious conversation can often diffuse tensions. It can also backfire, so be sure to avoid using sarcasm, which has been called "veiled hostility."

Examples

> KID: You're a fat pig. Get out of here.

> ADULT: Okay. I am trying to eat healthier. My wife is now cooking me tofu instead of fried chicken. It's disgusting! Yecch! You had to bring this up!

> NED: How would you like it if I called your mother?

> MR. NEIL: Do you want her number? Please call her. She says I don't call enough. I think she'd like you.

Ned made a mistake and Mr. Neil will hold him accountable. But what is most important to Mr. Neil is the relationship he has developed with Ned, which supersedes everything else. By interjecting humor into this serious conversation with Ned, Mr. Neil sent a message that all is not lost.

10. Reasoning Responses

Reasoning responses, which provide an explanation to kids for decisions child-guiders will make, reflect respect for the child. ("You are important and have a right to know why we're taking this action.") Giving reasons for decisions makes a child's world feel safer and more predictable and enhances relationships, whereas authoritative statements such as "Because I told you so" devalue the child, increase stress, and undermine relationships. In reasoning responses, the key phrase is "What if."

Once the reason for an action is given, there should be no more discussion about it—no power struggles. ("I gave you the reason, and I'm not going to discuss it any longer. Let's get moving. We need to be out of here in five minutes. Thanks.")

Examples

KID: Why can't I go outside after eight at night?

ADULT: Because it's dark out, and it's hard to see. What if all parents let their seven-year-olds play in the neighborhood after dark? I think we'd have a lot of kids getting hurt, don't you?

KID: But why?

ADULT: I gave you the reason, and we need to move on.

KID: Why am I grounded?

ADULT: Katie, you made a big mistake by taking the car without permission. What if your father or I had an important appointment to get to? We like letting you have the car—you just have to ask before using it. Plus, you had us worried sick. We didn't know where you were.

NED: Why do you have to call her? I promise I won't do it again. I have been doing better. You said so!

MR. NEIL: Throwing a sharp object at a teacher is kind of serious. It can really injure a person. I know you were just mad and didn't want to hurt me.

NED: No. I like you, Mr. Neil.

MR. NEIL: And I like you, Ned. But throwing the pencil wasn't a good way to express your frustration. Parents need to hear when their kids do great things and when they

> make unwise decisions—not so they can punish the kid but so they can help him. You're working on controlling your anger. Your mom needs to hear what happened so she can help you. What if we didn't call parents when kids break safety rules? Those parents would be pretty upset if they heard their kid had a problem and they weren't told about it.
>
> NED: Yeah, but I'm still gonna get screwed. My mom hasn't been doing that well lately.

Mr. Neil wasn't thrilled about having to call Ned's mom. But he understood that when it comes to a safety issue it's usually best to call. Behavior is a message. And if a child is sending big messages—big calls for help—parents need to be informed and on board with solutions. Mr. Neil took the time to explain why he had to call. Statements such as "Because I said so!" or "Because that's the rule!" do little to enhance relationships. It's okay, however, for child-guiders to say, "Because that's the class rule. Remember, we came up with that when kids were getting teased."

11. Connecting Statements

When adult and child are on opposing sides of an issue, connecting statements can bridge the two viewpoints. With the exception of supportive comments, connecting statements are the verbal intervention most capable of dissipating power struggles. The key message of a connecting statement is "It's not me against you; we're on the same side."

Such statements are often used in conjunction with reasoning responses such as "It's not me against you; we're on the same side. But what if…" And they are often followed by an empowering intervention: "So what can you (we) do next time to make sure it doesn't happen again? Let's strategize."

Examples

> KID: I hate being grounded.
>
> ADULT: Hey, it's not like I enjoy grounding you. It's not me against you. We're on the same side. (connecting statements) Heck, I'm president of your fan club. But what if every parent let her kid come in three hours past curfew without a consequence? The message might be: "It's not a big deal." And it is. We were worried about you.

> KID: You like giving me chill-outs!
>
> ADULT: I'm sorry you see it that way (supportive comment) because it's not me against you. We're on the same side. (connecting statements) I didn't wake up this morning thinking, "Sure hope I can give Bobby a lot of chill-outs today." But what if every youth-care worker let the kids swear without doing anything about it? It wouldn't be a very comfortable place, would it? And we certainly wouldn't be teaching you guys how to express your feelings appropriately.

> TEACHER: Kids, I don't like the way this day is going. I'm feeling like a meanie. I'm not the enemy; I'm on your side. (connecting statement) I love this class. What can we do to turn our day around?

> MR. NEIL: Ned, I don't like having to call your mom with bad news. I know she's been under a lot of pressure lately. This isn't me against you. But what if every teacher didn't notify a kid's parent when they broke a major safety rule? We might have a lot of angry parents and kids who aren't getting the help they need.

What was most important to Mr. Neil in this exchange was maintaining, if not strengthening, the positive relationship he was developing with Ned. He did this by using a connecting statement. Mr. Neil, aware that Ned was hurting because his father rarely sees him, knows he has become a critical male figure in Ned's life.

12. Empowering Messages

This intervention shifts power back to a child by asking for her opinion and giving her choices in areas related to her well-being. Empowering messages can gently nudge an insecure child to take more responsibility for her life. At the same time, they entrust her with the decision making, crediting her with competence—a message that a child with little self-confidence needs to hear repeatedly in order to believe it.

Examples

ADULT: I'm not sure what we should. What do you think? Let's play out a few options.

ADULT: What have you done before when you were in such a situation?

ADULT: I'm confident you can make the right choice now. You have before.

At times, it's beneficial to offer a little help.

Examples

ADULT: I'm not sure, but maybe if you did the routines after school you'd have more free time after dinner. What do you think?

KID: Yeah, we should do the routines after school.

ADULT: That's a great idea.

Empowering reflects valuing. In a study done in Japan many years ago, car factory workers stated they would much rather have a say in their company's procedures than more money. Similarly, although it's often easier and more expedient to be direct with a child, in the long run child-guiders experience fewer behavior problems and create more energizing environments when they empower kids in matters that affect them.

Examples

KID: What's going to happen to me?

ADULT: What do you think should happen?

KID: What should I wear?

ADULT: Why don't you decide? You know what looks good.

KID: Bruce is bothering me!

ADULT: What can you do to get him to stop? What are some of the strategies you've been using?

KID: What's my consequence?

ADULT: What do you think it should be?

TEACHER: These are the subjects we need to work on today. Can you kids come up with a schedule showing when each one should be covered?

CHILD-CARE WORKER: We'll go to the movies tonight if you all do your chores and the unit looks spiffy. Tell me your plan for getting everything done.

MR. NEIL: So what can we do to make sure you control your anger better? (empowering) You have been doing pretty well up until today. (positive recognition)

NED: I don't know. I guess I got to do what you told me— think before I act.

MR. NEIL: Because that's the...

NED: Fact!

MR. NEIL: What else can you do? (empowering)

NED: Think what I want to do, like throwing the pencil, but do what I need to do, like not call out without raising my hand, and wait my turn. I wanted to throw the pencil but needed to find a better way to let out my anger.

MR. NEIL: Don't call out...

NED: Share the air! And if I get angry count, or ask for a break, or think, "Let it go, Joe!"

MR. NEIL: Bingo! And what could I have done differently? (empowering)

NED: When you see me calling out without raising my hand, talk to me about it or give me a signal. Don't just ignore me.

MR. NEIL: I can do that. Thanks!

NED: So what about my consequence for the pencil?

MR. NEIL: What do you think we should do? (empowering)

NED: It was the first time I threw something. I don't think I should be kicked out of school for that.

MR. NEIL: I agree. You've generally been doing a good job controlling your behavior.

NED: How about a job? You do that sometimes.

MR. NEIL: Yes, sometimes we see misbehavior as taking away some of the good vibes we have in our class. So when kids act out, we sometimes let them give something back as a consequence.

NED: Can we do that this time?

MR. NEIL: Sure. I've got a lot of cleaning and organizing to do in my class. You can help.

Mr. Neil empowered Ned to think of better ways to handle his frustration. In doing so, he demonstrated confidence in Ned's ability to act on his own behalf. He also balanced the conversation with respect to owning the problem by asking Ned to suggest ways Mr. Neil could have handled the situation better. At the end of the conversation, Mr. Neil empowered Ned to come up with a consequence for throwing the pencil at him. More and more, Mr. Neil had been using the consequence of community service, or reparation, to work through behavioral incidents.

13. Explorative Responses

Explorative responses can be used during any phase of a conversation to glean more information. Following are three kinds of explorative responses that help child-guiders connect better connect with at-risk kids.

An **explorative fact-finding response** is often helpful to help gather missing information needed about the events leading to a troublesome situation. Although at times child-guiders think they know what's going on with a kid or group, they should nevertheless search for the facts as part of a respectful response to a problem incident.

Example

> ADULT: Please tell me exactly what happened. Who was involved, and why do you think it got a little out of control?
>
> YOUTH: It was me, Ruben, and Boris. Boris called Ruben a fag, and I pushed him over.
>
> ADULT: Had anything been going on with you three before this happened?
>
> YOUTH: Yeah. Ruben was dissing Boris about his clothes. He's wearing a lot of old shit. His parents aren't working.

An **explorative reflective response** is used to help kids reflect on their actions and assess whether those behaviors were in their best interests. The most popular explorative reflective question is "Is that working for you?" This question can get kids to look at both the pros and cons of a certain behavior. When giving this response, avoid being judgmental. Let the child reveal her inner thoughts and feelings, then gently guide her toward an acceptable resolution of the issue.

Motivation Interviewing[2] is a tremendously effective communication approach with at-risk kids that encourages child-guiders to explore and resolve a kid's feelings regarding troubling issues. It's about change being generated from the inside out.

Example

> COUNSELOR: Sasha, I notice you've been giving Rhonda a hard time.
>
> SASHA: So.
>
> COUNSELOR: I'm just curious if it's working for you? I mean, what does giving her a hard time accomplish? For instance, is it making you happier? How about we look at both sides of this…reasons for why it makes sense to con-

tinue what you're doing and possible reasons to stop. Can we talk about this?

SASHA: I didn't ask you to get involved.

COUNSELOR: I know. But I care about both of you.

Not all conversations end with a satisfying resolution. At times, child-guiders plant seeds that will hopefully germinate in a child's head, leading to better interactions in the future.

An **explorative psychological response** helps a child talk about difficult underlying issues, including any anger that has been displaced onto the current situation. Signs of displacement include little annoyances turning into major episodes and displays of anger that are disproportionate to the circumstances. Although an explorative psychological response can help identify such problematic underlying issues, care must be taken when using this technique. While encouraging a child to talk about sensitive issues, a trusting relationship usually needs to be already in place, the child's defenses and boundaries must be respected, and overly aggressive questioning should be avoided.

Examples

> ADULT: Heather, it seems like you got pretty worked up about a rather small issue. You don't usually act this way. Could something else be bothering you?

> ADULT: Hector, it seems like you've been upset all day. Is there something on your mind you'd like to talk about?

When a child's defenses are down, it is sometimes a good idea to gently suggest a possible reason for his discontent, or to lead him to a conclusion of his own. For example, eleven-year-old Matt, who becomes increasingly anxious as his weekly Friday dinner with his father approaches but does not understand the source of his anxiety, or is reluctant to talk about it, might benefit from an explorative psychological response such as "Matt, tomorrow is Friday. Is anything happening tomorrow that might be making you a little nervous?"

Kids with emotional and behavioral challenges often traverse their lives with very heavy baggage. Establishing strong, energizing, and trusting relationships with these kids can often lighten the load.

MR. NEIL: Ned, I want to be sure about something. (explorative fact-finding response) You're saying you were mad at me for not calling on you, right?

NED: Yeah.

MR. NEIL: So nothing else was going on in the classroom that was bothering you? (explorative fact-finding response)

NED: Well, every time you called on Ray he looked at me and kind of rubbed it in. He was really tickin' me off.

MR. NEIL: That must have felt terrible. (supportive comment) Thanks for letting me know that. (positive recognition) Thinking back, what could you have done about Ray's smirking? (empowering)

NED: I could have talked to him about it, maybe after class. Or told you what he was doing.

MR. NEIL: Excellent ideas. (animated praise) Or you could have tried harder to ignore him, right? What often happens when you ignore behavior like that?

NED: The kid stops doing it.

MR. NEIL: Bingo!

> NED: So are you still going to call my mother. If
> you do she'll yell at me. She's been in a bad mood
> lately.
>
> MR. NEIL: Are things okay at home? (explorative psychological
> response)
>
> NED: My mom's father is sick. She's spending a lot of
> time at his place helping out. She's tried to get my
> dad to come by more often, but he says he's too
> busy at this time of year. Mom's real tired—I can
> see it. And when she's tired she gets into bad moods
> and yells more.
>
> MR. NEIL: Boy, it seems you and your mother are going
> through a really rough time. (supportive comment)
> That's too bad. I like your mom. It sounds like she's
> under a lot of pressure. (supportive comment)

Mr. Neil, having opened up a channel of honest communication with Ned, gently explored other factors that may have contributed to the incident. When Ned opened up about Ray's smirking and his mother's situation, Mr. Neil provided empathic support and, regarding Ned's mother, tried to build her up in the eyes of her son. He knew Ned was in pain over the way she had been dealing with him recently.

14. Plan Making

Plan making, which marks the end phase of a meaningful conversation, can help a child take more control of his life. Created collaboratively, a plan identifies steps the child agrees to take to eliminate recurrences of the misbehavior. Plan making is also used as a proactive intervention to add more predictability and structure to an environment.

Examples

ADULT: Bob, I'm proud of the way you talked about this. I know it wasn't easy. Do you think we can create a plan to help you avoid making the same mistake next time a similar situation arises?

TEACHER: This class didn't run as smoothly as I had hoped. Can we take a few minutes to come up with a plan for our next class?

NED: Maybe things will get better at home when my grandfather isn't sick anymore.

MR. NEIL: I hope you're right, and I want to thank you again for talking to me about this stuff. (positive recognition and general praise) You really have it rough right now. (supportive comment) Do you think we could make a plan to help you get through the next few weeks? (plan making)

NED: That would be okay.

MR. NEIL: We talked about some of the strategies you can use when you get upset. We talked about counting, ignoring, using a rap like "Let it go, Joe," asking for a break, thinking about wants and needs. All of these can help. Maybe we should write them down.

NED: Okay.

MR. NEIL: Sometimes kids are helped by writing in a journal. They write about their lives and what's going on and then share it with someone they trust. Would you like to try that?

NED: Okay. But I don't like writing.

MR. NEIL: You type pretty well. Maybe you could do it that way?

NED: I'll think about it.

MR. NEIL: Any other ideas? (empowering)

NED: Maybe I could do more chores around the house. And keep my room neater. Mom's awful tired.

MR. NEIL: Those are *terrific* suggestions! (animated praise) Hey, I've got a stack of old *National Geographic* magazines in my storage closet. Didn't you tell me once your grandfather was in the army and stationed overseas?

NED: Yeah.

MR. NEIL: Do you think he might like to look at some of them?

NED: Sure!

MR. NEIL: Okay. I'll bundle some up.

NED: Thanks.

MR. NEIL: One more thing. Given what's going on, I want you to come in every day and, right away, write a number down on this piece of paper I'm now taping to my desk. It's a feelings check. I want to know how you're doing before we begin. Write a one if you're feeling horrible; a ten if you feel great; a five if you are feeling in between. You and your mom have been under a lot of pressure. I want to make sure you're okay and ready to say hello to class. Would that be okay?

NED: Sure.

MR. NEIL: Great.

NED: So are you still going to call my mother?

MR. NEIL: What? You think because we had a good talk and I'm feeling all mushy that I won't call? That's ridiculous. (humor) I'm not going to call this time because you missed when you threw the pencil—your aim stinks (humor)—and you haven't done anything like that before, and I'm impressed with how you've been talking with me, (positive recognition) and I like the plans we developed. (plan making) Now get outta here, kid, before I change my mind.

Mr. Neil ended a productive conversation with some concrete plans for helping Ned navigate a tough period of life. He was ambivalent about the call home. But since this was the first time Ned had thrown an object and there were extenuating circumstances, he decided to give him a break.

The many variations of useful core strength-based interventions provide child-guiders with numerous options that can have a range of desired effects leading to kids' improved behavior and well-being.

Figure 16–1

Summary of Verbal Intervention Techniques

TECHNIQUE	DEFINITION	EXAMPLE
1. Nonjudgmental Exploration	Gentle queries that promote engagement and open a dialogue	"What's up?"
2. Supportive Comments	Statements that support a child's feelings and position	"I don't blame you for feeling like this."
3. Repeating or Paraphrasing	Remarks that echo back or summarize a child's comment upset with the way you're being	"So you're saying no one cares. You're basically saying that you're treated."
4. Feelings Check	Gentle exploration or identification of possible feelings	"How does that make you feel? I'd feel angry if that happened to me."
5. Positive Recognition	Reinforcement for the acknow-ledgment of feelings and actions	"I like the way you owned up to that."

<cont.>

6. Praise		
General	Positive comments that acknowledge a person or accomplishment	"Excellent Job, Sam!"
Animated	Exuberant affirmations	"This is amazing!"
Specific	Acknowledgment of a particular success	"Your vocabulary, penmanship, and punctuation were outstanding."
7. Apologizing	Openly admitting to mistakes	"I'm sorry for yelling at you."
8. Sandwiching	Cushioning two positive comments around a more evocative one	"I'm really proud of you for telling me this. You know this means you can't go on the trip. You have it in you to make better choices. We've seen that."
9. Humor	The art of bringing on a smile	"If you don't want an extra chore, then laugh at this joke."
10. Reasoning Responses	"What if" statements that explain a forthcoming decision	"What if we let every kid…"

11. Connecting Statements

Reassurances that you are still in the child's corner

"Hey, it's not me against you. We're on the same side. I don't like having to ..."

12. Empowering Messages

Solicitations for input in a way that instills confidence and autonomy

"What do you think we should do?"

13. Explorative Responses

Fact-Finding

Questions aimed at ascertaining what has occurred

"What exactly did she say?"

Reflective

Questions that encourage a child to reflect on his actions

"Is that working for you?"

Psychological

Iinvitations to gently explore an underlying issue

"Is anything else going on?"

14. Plan Making

Creating or summarizing strategies to prevent issues from reoccurring

"So we decided you'll use the alarm clock and do more homework right after school. Good plan."

— CHAPTER 17 —

Strategic Verbal Interventions

The next set of tools needed to communicate effectively with at-risk kids is strategic verbal interventions. Slightly more advanced than the core strength-based verbal interventions described in chapter 16, these responses validate children for acting on their own behalf, even if such actions are deemed inappropriate, and provide hope and inspiration for their life's journey.

This chapter presents seven strategic verbal interventions that, with practice and vigilance, most child-guiders who work with at-risk youth can successfully implement. The challenge in using these interventions is to match the most suitable one to a particular child's needs and circumstances, a selection process that should be guided by intuition, creativity, and experience.

Reframing

Reframing portrays a negative behavior in positive terms, changing the way at-risk kids see themselves, which can reshape lives. Reframing is the second step in a three-step process of responding to challenging behavior. First, child-guiders try to understand it since behavior is always a message. Second, they attempt to reframe the function of the behavior in a positive light. And third, they sometimes try to direct, or "squeeze," the behavior into an appropriate context, a step we will examine in the next section of this chapter.

The power of reframing is twofold. First, reframing can counter the ill effects of negative labeling—a practice that erodes a child's self-esteem and the motivation to improve functioning. As mentioned, we use the term "stereotype myth" to describe this dynamic. Too many kids with emotional and behavioral challenges possess a deeply entrenched negative self-perception ("I'm a loser. Why try?"), which utterly erodes their motivation to be all they can be. If a child perceives himself in a negative way, that is how he'll likely function. Carol Dweck concurs, stating, "For twenty years, my research has shown that the view you adopt for yourself profoundly affects the way you lead your life."[1]

Reframing also helps kids understand why they act the way they do. For example, a youngster whose behavior has been reframed often discovers that her acting out has been serving a self-protective function, as reflected in the following example.

Fourteen-year-old Julia, a victim of repeated sexual abuse who had subsequently been kicked out of four foster homes, used obnoxious behavior to protect herself and keep people at a distance because she equated intimacy with pain. Considering her history, Julia was doing the best she could, and what she needed most was understanding and help. Jennifer, a junior high school guidance counselor, used reframing with her, explaining: "Julia, you seem very good at pushing people away. When you criticize your teachers, whine, and make disgusting comments about them, they don't want to get close to you, which is a shame, since you're a great kid. You really know how to keep adults at a distance." Jennifer's desire in reframing the obnoxious behavior was to loosen Julia's defensive posturing and enable the two of them to establish meaningful contact, thereby showing Julia that adults can be trusted. Her long-term goal was to gently nudge Julia into connecting her "pushing away" behaviors with her childhood experiences of pain and rejection.

Although reframing casts acting out in a positive light, it in no way condones misbehavior. A child who hears his misbehavior reframed knows his actions were inappropriate; yet he also feels buoyed by the praise, encouraged by a new sense of hope, and capable of gaining insights into the misbehavior, as demonstrated in the following scenario.

Walt, a sixteen-year-old dynamo with an electric personality, had an uncanny ability to irritate people and a tragic home life. His father, who had been physically abusive, had abandoned the family when Walt was six, and his mother struggled with drug abuse and couldn't properly care for him, which eventually led to his being placed at the residential center I worked at. Although he harbored considerable anger and was often rude, he could also be quite affable. Returning to the program after school one day, he announced, "Guess what, Charlie? The school secretary told me today that I'm the first kid in twenty-five years to get under her skin."

I pondered what he said for a few seconds and then proclaimed, "Wow! That's fantastic! Think about it. For twenty-five years, angry, pouting kids have been booted out of class, sent to the office, and you're the only one to get under her skin. What an amazing ability you have to affect people." He smiled.

"The problem is," I explained. "this amazing talent of yours is getting you in trouble, hurting people's feelings, and not helping anyone. We need to think of a way for you to use it to help you help the world." We discussed this issue for a while and finally figured out that he'd be a great talk show host. People would either love him or hate him, but they'd have to tune him in because he was so affecting. He walked away feeling great about himself, knowing he had a talent but one that should only be used in a specific type of place; otherwise, he'd have to pay the piper.

Months later, after a rough day, he and I had an evocative chat, and Walt was able to acknowledge that his rudeness might have something to do with having been neglected by his parents. By reframing his rudeness into an ability to affect people, I was able to get at this vital connection.

Casting acting out for attention in a positive light by reframing circumvents my greatest pet peeve in the child-guiding business—getting mad at kids for acting out for attention, saying such things as "That kid's just looking for attention!" and "She's an attention seeker!" During workshops I ask participants, "Have you ever worked with a challenging kid who you think got, or is getting enough, attention in life?" People laugh, and no hands ever go up. I then observe, "Yet every day we get mad at these kids for acting out for attention when we know they're not getting enough."

Many kids with challenging behaviors wear a scarlet letter *A* on their chests, a debilitating stereotype that many at-risk kids live with. Years ago when I was providing consultation to a psychiatric hospital on the East

Coast, the adolescent unit was out of control. One day we settled the kids down and held a group meeting, during which I asked all the kids to tell me something about themselves and ways we could improve the hospital. The first to speak were four adolescent girls who had been terrorizing the unit. Each one said the same thing: "I have this really bad habit of looking for negative attention." After the fourth girl spoke, I interjected: "I need to stop the group right now. If one more of you states that you have a bad habit of looking for negative attention, I'm going to puke on the rug. I think it's great you all look for attention—good or bad—because that means you haven't given up on yourselves. I'm not sure any of you ever got the attention you deserved. And I'm not blaming your parents. Maybe it was just bad luck all the way around. But when you act out for attention you are sending the message 'I'm someone of value, and I deserve more.' Are there good ways to seek attention? Sure. Are there not so good ways? Sure. But I don't want any of you to spend one more day of your life thinking there's something wrong with seeking attention."

I'll never forget how three of the girls then started sobbing. It was the first time in their lives they had thought, "You mean I'm not so bad for seeking attention." They left the meeting with less anger and a new way of thinking about themselves.

Reframing misbehavior (see examples listed in figure 17–1) can change a life, as reflected in the following story. I recently volunteered to speak to thirty at-risk students at a large high school after receiving an endearing email from one of their learning specialists, Kelly, who said the students were consumed with self-defeating thinking. I met with the kids in groups of ten, did some reframing, introduced dozens of metaphors and used other approaches to alter their negative mindsets, and promised to come back and celebrate with any kid who began working harder. Immediately, the kids started applying themselves with more vigor, and the feedback I got from Kelly was encouraging: "Many of them said they had never realized that there were alternative, more hopeful ways to think about their lives." Six weeks later I brought pizza for them all. Life isn't what you see, it's what you perceive.

Figure 17–1
Reframing

BEHAVIOR	REFRAME
Obnoxiousness	"You do an excellent job of keeping people at a distance; pushing people away. This behavior has probably made you feel more safe. But if you keep pushing like this we'll never get to see how wonderful you really are."
Learning disability	"You don't have a learning disability; you have a roadblock. Every major city in the world has lots of roadblocks, yet people get to work on time each day because they find a way around them. You can too. Some of the most successful people in the world have such roadblocks, but they find a way around them."
Rudeness	"When you choose to talk rudely, you make an impact. Maybe we can find a way to affect folks that doesn't cause them or you discomfort."
Swearing	"You're very expressive! You've got words I've never heard before. I think I'll use some of them at the football game on Sunday. Let's find a place for you to be this expressive without getting you in trouble."
Lying	"You're good at protecting yourself. If you're not entirely honest, then you can't get in trouble. Maybe you don't trust us yet. Protecting yourself is a good thing. Let's work on building the trust among us."

Refusing	"You're pretty cautious about trying things that you're not sure you can do. Who can blame you? You don't want to feel embarrassed or shamed. Why don't we take some baby steps and give this a try?"
Laziness	"You seem like you don't have the psychic energy to work as hard as I know you can. I think you've been going through a rough time. If you don't try things, you can't feel any worse. I respect you for that. But you might feel better about your situation if we gradually get you back to doing some of this stuff. What do you think?"
Tantrum	"I see you had a big message this morning. What were you trying to tell people? What was upsetting you? Let's work on expressing yourself in a better way."
Close-mouthed	"I think you're a really loyal son. I think you hold everything in to protect your family. And I think that's beautiful. But it's not us against your family. We're on the same side."
Stealing	"You're good at taking care of yourself. When you feel you need something, you figure out a way to get it. But we've got to work on ways for you to get what you need without stealing, because, as you know, stealing is wrong and makes everyone feel bad."
Provocative actions	"You're really good at getting me to experience how you feel. When you act in a way that gets me and others angry, what

	you're really doing is giving us a glimpse into your state of mind, letting us know how angry you are. You're a good messenger. But I think we can work on using your words better to relay this information."
Odd, different	"You're not odd or different; you're simply under-appreciated. I don't think the other kids really understand how cool you are and the strengths and talents you have."
Bossiness	"Man, you have great leadership qualities. We need to put you in charge of something. Of course, if you boss around your friends they may not stay your friends."
Restlessness, hyperactivity	"You guys have great energy levels. I wish I had such a motor! Let's downshift a bit until we go out later."
Arguing	"You are a fabulous arguer. You should be a lawyer. But where does a lawyer argue? Yes, the courtroom. This is not a courtroom. Save this talent for the right place."
Sexual behaviors	"Sexual feeling are good. Sexuality is a normal part of our lives. And there's nothing wrong with acting in a way that is self-pleasing. But this kind of behavior is conducted in private, not in front of others."

The Hydraulic Squeeze

Whereas reframing acknowledges a problematic coping behavior, the "hydraulic squeeze" moves it to a setting in which it can do no harm. This intervention, formulated by child psychologist Bernard Levine, PhD, "squeezes" a difficult behavior into a smaller, more clearly defined arena where it becomes benign, perhaps productive, and remains for further investigation. Such an option is far preferable to either letting the behavior get out of control or attempting to extinguish it, which may only give rise to more troublesome conduct. Misbehavior, after all, is a message, and messages need to be answered, not ignored or destroyed.

While reframing a child's acting-out behavior lets her know that she is valued and that people want to help her, applying the hydraulic squeeze helps her learn to channel her problematic behavior, showing her that it has meaning and may be indicative of a special ability but needs to be implemented in a more productive manner.

The hydraulic squeeze has many creative applications, two of which follow, along with a classic misapplication of this technique and a highly effective implementation of it in combination with others.

Using the Hydraulic Squeeze to Channel Expressiveness and Anger

Years ago I was asked to run a group of the eight toughest kids at a low socioeconomic middle school, whose behavior was so bad (truancy, profuse swearing, belligerence) that the school social workers and psychologist didn't want to meet with them. Initially I met with each kid individually for a few minutes, then starting the following week we met every Friday from noon to 1:30 p.m.

At the first meeting I said: "Okay, I know most of you guys and gals are very expressive. You've got words I've never heard before. I'm going to use some of them at the Patriot's game on Sunday. But here's the scoop: if you use such creative talk (swearing) on the bus or in school, you'll get in trouble. We're going to become good friends, and I don't like to see my friends get in trouble. So here's the deal: if you want to swear, save it for me. Every Friday from noon to 1:30 p.m. you can say anything you want in this group, as long as you haven't done so outside the group that week."

The first few group meetings were very colorful, with the kids saying such things as, "Pass the fucking chips, please!" "You're an asshole," "Hey, bitch, don't hog the soda!" I just ignored it.

After three weeks, one of the boys said to me, "Man, I hold it in every week, waiting for this fuckin' group. It's saved my life."

Each week every kid came up with one or two goals for the coming week. If they met their goals, they could get a pizza or sandwich on the following Friday. Every kid's behavior improved as well as their academic output. By the second month, there was very little swearing. Use of the hydraulic squeeze had channeled their expressiveness and anger to the point where they swore in a designated environment—the group—rather than in society, and eventually not at all.

Using the Hydraulic Squeeze to Control Undesirable Noises

Seven-year-old Freddy, like many kids his age, liked to make fart noises in public and soon became known for his meticulously timed disruptive flatulence. His therapist, Bernie, informed him that he could make all the fart noises he wanted when they were together but should otherwise try to hold them in. "When you make those noises in the presence of others, it gets you in trouble," Bernie gently explained. "That bothers me because I'm your friend." Weeks after applying this hydraulic squeeze Bernie reframed Freddy's noise-making as wildly musical and encouraged him to tape-record all his noises, labeling each one with a name, such as "Fabulous Flutter."

In time, Freddy's fart noises ceased altogether, and with Bernie's expert coaching he was able to see that farting had a lot to do with "pooping"—another of Freddy's fascinations—and that poops were messy. While exploring the "messiness" of his past and working through much of his underlying conflict, Freddy discovered that his fascination with farting had been his way of letting people know that his life had been fraught with despair and very messy as a result of power and control issues.

Misapplying the Hydraulic Squeeze to Physical Aggression

Counseling angry youngsters to strike an object, or providing a bag or pillow for venting purposes is not a good use of the hydraulic squeeze. Such responses may only reinforce their perception that they cannot control themselves without being physical and may thus promote future acts of physical aggression in moments of anger when they are not apt to have a punching bag or pillow at their disposal. Their anger should instead be channeled into sports or other physical activities, as reflected in the following scenario.

Eleven-year-old Gorman, who lived at a residential center, had poor impulse control and often acted out aggressively. One day he threw a lamp and, while on the verge of a tantrum, had to be removed from the unit until he regained control. I escorted him into my office and had him sit down. His body was tense; his face beet red; sweat was pouring from his brow; and his eyes had a glazed, wild look. "I need to punch something!" he screamed.

"I know you're upset, but you don't need to punch anything," I told him calmly, despite the fierce pounding of my heart. I then explained that I was not going to let him act aggressively and that if he tried I would have to hold him, which I did not want to do. It was touch and go for a few long minutes before he calmed down.

In future encounters with Gorman, I reminded him of the enormous self-control he showed that day and suggested that he divert some of his aggressive energy into sports or other physical activities, such as karate. He joined a community basketball league and gradually saw that he could control his anger without becoming physical.

Using the Hydraulic Squeeze in Combination with Other Techniques

Joel Shepherd, a juvenile justice officer working at an elementary school in Lexington, Kentucky, sent me this uplifting email a few years ago:

I attended your seminar recently and found it incredibly inspiring. This week I had a chance to use reframing and the hydraulic squeeze with a fifth-grade child who was angry and frustrated. This child has been dealing with a number of home issues and had become upset with a classmate. Teachers and administrators were tired of trying to correct her behavior. Seeing an opportunity to reframe and help her redirect what she was doing, I engaged her in conversation.

I explained that I was proud of her passion and how much she cared about her family (another student was making fun of her mother). I told her she was right to be angry, and we discussed why saying hurtful things to others really does hurt them. Remembering how you talked about students' dreams, I asked her what she wanted to be when she grew up, and she said a lawyer. I began to draw specifics out of her. Where do you want to go to college? What type of law will you practice? What kind of clients will you have? ("Wrongfully accused people who need others to stand up for them," was her answer.)

We then discussed her first victory and where she would take me to celebrate. We agreed on an expensive Chinese restaurant and that I could have Crab Rangoon puffs since she'd be able to afford them. She laughed. Finally, we talked about who she would come back to the school to thank for being a good guy (Officer Shepherd), for helping her along the way (Officer Shepherd), and for taking care of her (Officer Shepherd). We agreed to eat lunch together every week.

What a success! Charlie, I shared our talk with the school counselor. We are going to make that student a diploma and business cards. I also called the University of Cincinnati College of Law, and they are sending her a gift package of items. We want her to know we believe in her and support her dream!

I thought: "Not only did he help her channel her passion more productively using the hydraulic squeeze and reframe her arguing as evidence that she could someday be a great lawyer, but he used positive predicting and other interventions. I salute you, Officer Shepherd. And if I ever need a lawyer I'm calling the kid!" Nor was I the only one to salute him. At a recent day-long training for officers working in public schools in Kentucky, he was handed the School Officer of the Year award.

Positive Predicting

Years ago I created a technique called positive predicting to instill hope in kids with emotional and behavioral challenges by having them actively picture a positive future for themselves. To drive home the idea that they will indeed succeed I argue with them.

> Me: How should we celebrate when you have the best six weeks ever—pizza or Chinese food?
>
> Kid: Pizza.
>
> Me: Good! Pepperoni or cheese?
>
> Kid: Pepperoni.
>
> Me [looking slightly upset]: But I like plain. Could we do half and half?
>
> Kid: Yeah, that would be okay.
>
> Me [shaking my head]: No . . . that's not okay. Here you've had the best six weeks ever and I'm screwing up the celebration. If you want pepperoni, we're going with it. Thin or thick crust?
>
> Kid: Thick.
>
> Me [extending a fist bump]: I love it!

I want kids to walk away thinking, "Man, that guy really believes I can do this!" Talking about the future in positive terms makes the desired outcome more possible; and when it becomes more possible, it becomes more probable.

Victor Ortiz, the former director of an adolescent group home full of very aggressive and dangerous kids, used this approach one night after attending my trainer's workshop. He told me: "Upon entering my group home, I heard a two-hundred-pound hulking adolescent punching walls and swearing in his room. My staff, thrilled to see me, asked me to talk to him. As I approached his room, he screamed, 'Get the fuck away from me, Victor. Come close and I'll punch your fucking head, too!' Violating every rule in the de-escalation handout, I took three hard steps toward him and yelled, 'Hey!' He froze. Taking three more aggressive steps, I got right in his face and yelled, 'How should we celebrate when you win the Kid of the

Week award next Friday—pizza or Chinese food?' He turned to punch the wall again but instead, with his hand suspended in midair, looked at me and said, 'Well, I kind of like pizza.'

"'Pepperoni or cheese?' I asked him.

"I argued with him just like you said. He eventually sat down, chilled, and went on to win the Kid of the Week award the following Friday."

There are many other ways to use positive predicting to inspire hope in kids with emotional and behavioral challenges. Two time-honored applications of the technique are these:

- Have your kids create future business cards for themselves; post the cards on a wall under a banner reading: "Future Leaders of [your state]"; then ask the kids to sign a contract promising to send you their first real business card so you can compare the two.

- Inscribe a child's name and glue a photo of his face on a college diploma, then hang it on a wall under a sign that reads: "College-Bound Kids."

An eleven-year-old I once worked with, named Lester, was a talented artist but very down on himself as a student. He was making little progress in school and frequently acted out. After designing a business card that advertised his future art business and printing out several copies of it, Lester felt his prospects for the future going "from gray to multicolored." He excitedly gave every adult in the school his card, saying, "Use my art studio in a few years!"

It can be highly inspirational to use positive predicting the very first time you meet a kid or group. For even better results you could inject some realism into the dialogue, saying, for example: "We will be celebrating your accomplishment. Will you sometimes question your ability to get there? Sure, just don't give up. From struggle comes success."

The Millimeter Acknowledgment

Child-guiders often exert undue pressure on kids to own up to their mistakes or reveal the reasons for their behavior. Strength-based practice has a refreshing view of accountability, which is: kids should be accountable, but accountability is seen when they change, not when they admit to something. While it's preferable for kids to own their misbehavior, there are many times when change more than suffices.

A useful intervention to gain a minimal amount of accountability from kids is what I call the millimeter acknowledgment. It gently opens a small hole in the defensive shield of a child who is reluctant to admit something or disclose information for fear of increasing her vulnerability. It entails placing your index finger about one millimeter (less than one-twentieth of an inch) from your thumb and asking, "Do you think it's *slightly* possible that you might…?" all the while hoping the child will take a tiny bit of responsibility for her actions or feelings. It's often helpful to include percentages, if the child takes a little responsibility she is, in essence, aware that taking total responsibility.

The millimeter acknowledgment, while preparing child-guiders to expect defensiveness, also helps mitigate the frustration they may feel while conversing with youngsters who refuse to own, or reveal reasons for, their actions. This intervention is apt to ease kids into accepting more responsibility for their behavior and open the way for more direct communication.

Examples

> ADULT: Jonas, do you think there is a one percent chance that some of your behavior today has something to do with your mom's job?
>
> JONAS: I don't know. Maybe one percent.

The following scenario provides a more extensive example of the millimeter acknowledgment. Eight-year-old Jarrod, a challenged public school student and the product of a chaotic home life, had negligible self-esteem, a short emotional fuse, an unwillingness to take responsibility for his aggressive acts, and a reluctance to talk about serious subjects. One afternoon Bruce, the school counselor, heard screams coming from a distant hallway and went to investigate the commotion. He came upon Jarrod standing in the hallway with both the principal and a woman dressed in a blue uniform, hovering over him. He was yelling, "I *never* hit the monitor!"

"But, Jarrod, I *am* the monitor, and you definitely hit me," said the woman in blue.

Bruce quietly asked the principal if he could speak with Jarrod privately, and she agreed. Taking the boy aside, he asked, "Jarrod, what happened?"

"I got into a fight with Andy. He called my mother an asshole," explained Jarrod.

"Did the monitor try to break up the fight?" asked Bruce.

"Yeah," replied Jarrod.

Bruce bent down to talk to him at eye level. "Now, Jarrod, do you think it's *slightly* possible that you could have accidentally hit the monitor as she tried to stop the two of you from fighting?" he suggested, making the sign of the millimeter acknowledgment.

"Yeah, it's slightly possible," he replied.

"Okay, thanks for letting me know this. I'm sure it wasn't easy for you," said Bruce.

He motioned for Jarrod to accompany him as he returned to the two women. "Jarrod admits to accidentally hitting you," Bruce told the monitor. "He's very *sorry* about it."

"I accept your apology," the monitor said to Jarrod. "But tomorrow I want you to stay closer to me during the lunch hour."

"Okay," Jarrod replied.

As the foursome broke up, Bruce again praised Jarrod for admitting to his mistake. Jarrod beamed with pride and relief, then accompanied Bruce to his office to process the fight with Andy.

The millimeter acknowledgment also helped when I was working with a fifth grader who had made significant improvement but then I got an email from his school reporting that his single mother had lost her job and he'd been a mess all week. The next day, I visited him. After playing cards with him for a while, I asked, "Devon, is there a one percent chance that your tough week might have had something to do with your mom and her job?"

"No!" he shot back.

I had never seen him this distraught. I waited another five minutes and then asked, "Could your troubles this week maybe have a half of one percent chance of being related to your mom's situation?"

"No!" he yelled back.

I thought, "Don't even try to get this out of him. Just let him work it out. Come back tomorrow."

Ten minutes later we got up to go and he put his arm on my shoulder and said, "Maybe a quarter of one percent."

Although in this example a bit of bargaining was required, the technique nevertheless worked to gain some acknowledgment.

Shifting Responsibility

When dealing with an issue kids have most likely caused, it is often useful to temporarily shift the responsibility for it to someone else. In particular, when a child-guider has a decent relationship with the children, shifting responsibility becomes a backdoor approach to helping them curtail the problem behavior. For example, when I was the program director of a midsize residential setting a boy on my adolescent unit, Mario, was reportedly bullying some of the younger boys. One day I took Mario, a very angry, quiet, and intense young man, into my office and said: "Mario, I need your help, man. You're one of the oldest and most respected kids on the boys unit. I hear some of the kids are bullying others. I would like you to look into this and see if you can get the kids to stop. I like you, dude. And I can see that you have strong leadership skills. Will you help me out?"

"Okay," he replied. He soon stopped bullying.

Another time I used the shifting responsibility technique was with a fifth grader, William, who was reportedly teasing kids at the bus stop. "William, I hear there's a kid at the bus stop who is teasing some of the others. Can you look into this and perhaps get him to stop? The kids look up to you. You are a sweet kid with many talents. I need your help," I said.

"You think it's me, don't you?" he asked.

"No, I don't see you acting that way. I always see you being courteous and kind to the other kids and teachers. That's the real William. I don't think William teases kids."

Soon after, William stopped the teasing. Did I lie to him? Yes. Did he want me to lie to him? I think so.

The Exploration of Control

The exploration of control is a technique I recently developed from the writings and lectures of Robert Brooks, who suggests that child-guiders dealing with hopeless and depressed kids should get them to focus on what they can control as opposed to dwelling on a multitude of stressors and outcomes that can't be changed.[3]

This became clear when I was working with a fifth grader who was depressed about the prospect of being homeschooled the following year. I spoke with his parents and tried a number of approaches to lift his spirits, with no luck. I then decided to focus on what he could control.

I said, "It looks like you're going to be homeschooled next year, and you're not too happy about this, are you?"

"Not at all," he replied.

"Okay, you're in a lousy situation and it stinks. But if you are homeschooled next year won't you have a little more control about what you learn?"

"Yeah, I guess," he responded.

"You're a really bright kid. You're inquisitive and have a thirst for knowledge. Maybe over the summer you can look into topics that your parents can teach you that will be interesting. Heck, what you learn next year could be a lot more fun that what the kids at the middle school will get."

"That could be true," he said.

We went on to talk about his areas of interest and possible topics he could pursue. Subsequently, his mood during the last month of school was appreciably better.

Another example of the exploration of control is the following story. My brother, Howie, who is the host of a popular radio show in Long

Beach, New York, recently interviewed Joe Satriano, a retired teacher from the local school department whose wife, Susan, died a number of years ago from cancer. After her death, Joe established a scholarship fund for local high school students whose lives had been touched by cancer. The mother of one young woman Joe met with was battling breast cancer. The woman's spirits were low, and she was terribly worried about her mom. Joe told her that she couldn't control what happens to her mother, but that cancer patients do enjoy returning to a clean, warm, and neat home and that she *could* control. The young woman took Joe's words to heart and, despite the enormous demands of school and caring for her mother, made sure that their home was always nice and warm each time her mother returned from chemotherapy appointments. Helping out in this way lifted the spirits of the young woman and her mother, who is in remission and doing great. Joe gave this valiant young woman a scholarship. During her first year of college, she started a Cancer Cleaning Service. She's paying it forward.

Solution-Focused Communication

Bob Bertolino, PhD, a prolific author who specializes in guiding at-risk kids through strength-based, solution-focused communication, introduced me to a set of techniques that child-guiders can use to change the mindsets of kids who harbor self-defeating thoughts. Following are techniques from Bertolino's work that I have found to be particularly effective, though I have changed some of their names to make them more user-friendly. These techniques and many others can be found in his books *Thriving on the Front Lines: Strengths-Based Youth Care Work*[3] and *Working with Children and Adolescents in Residential Care: A Strengths-Based Approach.*[4]

Historical Exploration

When a kid utters a hopeless remark, an often helpful response is to ask him whether he has been in this situation before and, if he has, what he did to successfully navigate it. In essence, you are providing evidence to the child that he already has the skills and savvy to accomplish the difficult task at hand.

Example

MICHAELA: I can't do this assignment. It's too hard!

TEACHER: Michaela, let me ask you something. You're in eleventh grade, and you've passed every year. You've got a brain up there. How many other times have you been given a difficult assignment that made you nervous? Oh, and by the way they are supposed to make you nervous. If I give you something easy, then the message from me to you is: "Micheala's a dummy, and I've got to give her easy stuff." I give you hard stuff because you can handle it. It's a tribute to you. So, how many times have you received an assignment that made you nervous like this one?

MICHAELA: I don't know. Maybe twenty-five?

TEACHER: And of those twenty-five times, once you worked through the nervousness how many of them did you get a good grade on?

MICHAELA: Probably all of them.

TEACHER: All of them! Slap me five. So if you've been in this position twenty-five times and received a good grade each time what are the odds that you'll get a good grade this time? Ten—absolutely; one—no way.

MICHAELA: Probably ten.

TEACHER: Oh yeah! So let's look at any one of the hard assignments you got in the past that you completed. How did you do it? Did you go online for help? Ask a friend? Stay after school to meet with the teacher? Ask your parents for help? What did you do?

MICHAELA: Usually all of them.

TEACHER: All of them! So do you think you could do that this time?

MICHAELA: Sure.

TEACHER: It's in you to excel!

MICHAELA: Thanks.

Same-Situation Exploration

If a child hasn't been in the difficult situation he currently faces, then same-situation exploration is often helpful. This technique involves bringing up others who were in similar situations and successfully worked through them.

For example, a few years ago I was asked to assist a second grader who pooped on the school rug due to his anger over his parents' contentious divorce. After greeting him, I remarked, "What a great son you are for letting the whole world know how upset you are over your parents' divorce." I reframed his acting out, always a powerful way to begin a conversation. (I could have said, "for making a big stink," but I didn't want to go down that road.)

I then needed to instill hope. Since he had never been in this situation before, I used same-situation exploration.

> ME: Ernie, how many other kids were there in America one year ago today in your same shoes—great kids going through a painful divorce? There are, sadly, lots of divorces every year.
>
> ERNIE: Maybe ten thousand.
>
> ME: Okay. Let's say there were ten thousand upset kids just like you one year ago. Of those ten thousand, how many do you think have worked through the pain of the divorce and are back on track today?
>
> ERNIE: Maybe one thousand. (He wasn't very optimistic.)

ME: I think the number would probably be a lot higher, but let's say there are one thousand happy kids in America who were upset just like you are today. Well, if one thousand kids became happier, what are the odds that you can be one of those one thousand a year from now? Ten—definitely; one—no way.

ERNIE: Two.

ME: Right now you don't feel too hopeful. But how are you going to feel three months from now when you're at a four?

ERNIE: I guess I'll be feeling better about what's going on.

ME: And how come you'll get to a four?

ERNIE: Because you're going to help me.

ME: You bet! And how should we celebrate when you get to a four— pizza or Chinese food? (positive predicting)

We argued about how to celebrate and I, of course, gave in. Subsequently, Ernie's mood and attitude improved every month. After our three-month celebration we continued working on divorce issues, and by the time school ended in June he was the happy Ernie everyone knew and loved. After the summer break, Ernie saw me fifty feet down the hallway and yelled, "Hey, Mr. A! One thousand one, ka-ching, ka-ching!"

I also used same-situation exploration with my daughter when she took the road test to get her driver's license. She was incredibly nervous in anticipation of the test. On our way to the appointment, I tried a number of supportive verbal interventions, but they all crashed and burned. Finally, just before she entered the Department of Motor Vehicles I said, "Julie, how many kids in America with half of your intelligence and driving skills took the road test yesterday and passed?"

She replied, "Good point," and proceeded to ace the test.

Repeating or Paraphrasing with Qualifiers

Repeating or paraphrasing what kids say helps child-guiders better engage disgruntled kids. The technique is even more powerful if a qualifier is added.

Good

YOUTH: None of the kids like me!

COUNSELOR: So you're saying none of the kids like you?

Better

YOUTH: None of the kids like me!

Counselor: So you're saying none of the kids like you yet?

The movie *The Blind Side* models this technique. It is based on a true story about Michael Oher, a homeless youth who was adopted by a caring southern family who helped him realize his dream of playing in the National Football League. Near the end of the movie, Michael is assigned a tutor to help bring up his grades so that he can qualify for a college scholarship. Early on, when he gets frustrated and barks, "I can't do this!" the tutor calmly responds, "You can't do it *yet*, Michael."[5]

Examples

CHILD: I can't play this right.

INSTRUCTOR: So right now you can't play it the way you will in four weeks.

YOUTH: I'm stupid!

FOSTER PARENT: So at this moment you're not feeling too smart.

In a similar vein, it's also effective to partialize all-or-nothing problem statements. When kids are upset, they tend to present stressors in black-and-white terms, and by partializing their comments child-guiders help them see their problems in less ominous ways.

YOUTH: My parents always argue!

CHILD-CARE WORKER: So sometimes your parents argue.

CHILD: I always screw up at this!

ADULT: So from time to time you struggle with this—like we all do, eh?

Exception Questions

Despondency over an issue can also be addressed with exception questions, which lift the dark clouds of despair that envelop many at-risk kids.

Example

YOUTH: My father doesn't give a shit about me. He never does stuff with me.

COUNSELOR: That's too bad. Have there been any exceptions? Have you done anything with your dad recently?

YOUTH: Well, we went fishing a few weeks ago.

COUNSELOR: Really! Where did you go? What did you catch?

Scaling Questions

Scaling questions encourage at-risk kids to think about incremental improvements.

Example

COUNSELOR: On a scale of one to ten—ten meaning you'll get used to the new school and be happy there and one meaning the opposite—where are you now?

YOUTH: One!

COUNSELOR: Well, how are you going to feel when you're at four?

YOUTH: Guess I'll be feeling better about the new school.

COUNSELOR: And how might you get to four?

YOUTH: You and the school staff are going to help me.

COUNSELOR: Bingo. And how should we celebrate when you're at four?

YOUTH: Pizza!

COUNSELOR: Thin or thick crust?

YOUTH: Thick.

COUNSELOR: Love it. Slap me five!

Amplifying Change Using Speculation

Any time children or groups demonstrate the slightest improvement, to underscore positive developments and build self-esteem it is helpful to amplify the change using speculation you want the children to own.

Example

CHILD-GUIDER: Man, what a great week you've had! Everyone is talking about you. You really seem to be putting more effort into being respectful and taking care of your responsibilities. I'm actually kind of curious about why you've been doing so well. I could be wrong, but is it because you've figured out that being respectful and going with the flow opens more doors for you? Has that maturity thing kicked in, and you've decided to abandon some of the less mature ways of relating to folks?

Kid: I don't know.

CHILD-GUIDER: Who knows? But you're really making some great choices.

Perhaps the kid had simply been sick all week, but in speculating why he was doing better with a reason the child-guider wanted him to adopt, the child-guider encouraged positive change in the future.

Years ago I was asked to work with a very troubling second grader. For the first three months, I was of no help to him. It took me that long to figure out that he had been misdiagnosed. When we developed a better handle on where he was coming from, treatment progressed. During those initial months, he had one good week. Near the end of our session that week, I stated, "Man, you just had the best week you've had all year. Everybody is talking about you. And I'm really curious about why you had such a good week. Was it because you're getting older, more mature, and giving up some of that little kid stuff you've been doing?"

He responded, "Probably."

A few minutes later, I said, "Ooh, I just had a feeling over my entire body that next week is going to be even better, and I'm kind of curious about why."

He looked at me and replied, "Because I'm more experienced."

Changing Perspective Questions

Changing perspective questions can be used very effectively to suggest and encourage better behavior. For example, imagine a child-guider approaching the most difficult kid with whom she is working and saying: "Rayshawn, I've been thinking about you for two weeks. And I have a question I can't get out of my head. You've got to help me with it. Given all the tough stuff that's happened to you in your life—I maybe know one-tenth of what you've been dealing with—and given all the stress you've been under, why aren't you doing worse? You know, I think you make the bad decision to compare yourself to all the other kids. That's a crock. There's only one person you can compare yourself to: someone who's going through exactly what you are. And I'm telling you, man, if I could find ten more kids who have been through what you've been through you'd be up here (lifting her hand above her head) and they'd be down there (lowering her hand to knee level). Rayshawn, you have more courage in your pinky than I've got in my entire body. And the thing that really freaks me out is that I know you're going to do even better. You are my hero, and you will always be my hero."

The many strategic strength-based verbal interventions available to child-guiders offer endless possibilities for creative exchanges with at-risk kids. These types of exchanges encourage them to gain an expanded perspective, improve their mindsets and behavior, and attain greater success in learning and relationship building.

— CHAPTER 18 —
Relationship-Based Limit Setting

RELATIONSHIP-BASED LIMIT SETTING involves empathic connections combined with clear and firm boundaries that create needed structure in children's lives. In their book *No Drama-Discipline*, Daniel Siegel and Tina Payne Bryson sum up the importance of limit setting in child-guiding simply and poignantly:

> Our children need repeated experiences that allow them to develop wiring in their brain that helps delay gratification, contain urges to react aggressively toward others, and flexibly deal with not getting their way. The absence of limits and boundaries is actually quite stressful, and stressed kids are more reactive. So when we say no and set limits for our children, we help them discover predictability and safety in an otherwise chaotic world. And we build brain connections that allow kids to handle difficulties well in the future.[1]

The most critical factor child-guiders should consider when setting limits with children, particularly those with emotional and behavioral challenges, is sanctity of the relationship. Behaviors come and go, but relationships remain constant. Strong, trusting, and empathic relationships significantly curb problem behavior and serve as a springboard for improved functioning Therefore, every technique in this chapter has been created to reinforce the observation that for best results in setting limits child-guiders should say or do nothing to undermine their relationships with the individual children or the groups.

The Limit-Setting Continuum

Child-guiders refer to the progression of responses that can be applied to a misbehavior, regardless of its severity or the context in which it occurs, as the limit-setting continuum. Relationship-based limit setting progresses in five stages: supportive interventions, logical consequences, physical management, processing, and reintegration. The sequence of events occurring along this continuum is as follows:

- When a child (or group) begins to act out, warnings and other supportive interventions are used to encourage him to control his behavior and to support his capacity to make good decisions on his own. Of course, safety supersedes all else, which is why limit setting always takes context into account.

- If the problematic behavior continues or the child has broken an established rule, a logical consequence is often required. Once a logical consequence is administered, there should be no turning back since giving in to any protest against a logical consequence tends to increase the likelihood of more problems, as the child-guider becomes less predictable and trustworthy. However, there are occasions when ignoring a problem behavior and focusing on the good choices kids are making is the proper decision; the heat of problem behavior often dissipates when it isn't being fanned.

- If a child has trouble accepting a logical consequence and reacts in an unsafe manner, such as hurting himself or others, or acts in a dangerous way, physical management may be necessary.

- After logical consequences have been given and physical management, if needed, has been administered, it is time to process the incident with the child. This discussion should include a review of the event itself, the circumstances that led up to it, and consideration of healthier coping strategies to help the youngster and the child-guider avoid similar problems in the future. For serious behavioral incidents, further consequences might be discussed during the processing stage.

- The final task is to assist in the child's reintegration into his environment. This is accomplished by outlining how he will return to his life prepared to meet adult expectations, fulfill his personal responsibilities, and move on.

Tips for Effective Relationship-Based Limit Setting

When implementing relationship-based limit setting, it is useful to keep in mind these three tips.

1. Let context determine the best possible response. For example, if there are safety issues it's often prudent to set limits on low-level misbehaviors that, in calm times, might be ignored or gently addressed. Recall the example of the principal who kept students after school for any display of disrespect. When control was restored to the setting, less-stringent consequences for disrespect were applied. Think martial law: the imposition of extreme responses to a minor behavior is often appropriate in times of war and survival.

2. Follow the stages of the limit-setting continuum described in the following pages. In times of anger, resist the urge to start the process in the second stage, logical consequence, instead using strategies for self-management—such as telling yourself, "It's an injury, and it will heal"—and addressing the child or group with supportive interventions.

3. Keep focused on the goals of limit setting—maintaining the sanctity of the relationship; reinforcing core values such as safety and respect; and empowering the child to accept responsibility for his actions and to make better decisions.

The Five Stages of Relationship-Based Limit-Setting

Descriptions of the five stages of relationship-based limit setting follow, along with techniques and examples associated with each of them.

First Stage: Supportive Interventions

When kids begin to demonstrate unacceptable behavior, their greatest need is for supportive interventions that will empower them to take control of their actions. Supportive interventions help children become aware of their actions; learn the limits of acceptability; delay gratification; de-escalate unacceptable behavior; learn more productive forms of self-expression; and experience adults as caring people who are willing to assist them.

Supportive interventions, such as warnings, should *not* be cumulative: "That's your third warning today! Now you can't use the computer!" If a few supportive interventions get kids back on track, the limit-setting progression should start over thirty minutes later. Limit setting should always occur in the moment. This allows kids to earn multiple fresh starts and doesn't hold previous behaviors that have been resolved over their heads.

Following is a selection of time-tested supportive interventions. Child-guiders will quickly discover, through trial and error, which ones are likely to work best with which kids and in which situations. To become adept in the use of supportive interventions, practice them *all* and don't rely too heavily on "warnings." To get kids back on track, child-guiders should generally choose two or three of the supportive interventions when misbehavior starts to escalate. If the behavior persists, child-guiders should move to the next stage: logical consequences.

1. Establishing core rules

2. Verbal cues, reminders, and warnings

3. Distraction and redirection

4. Changing course

5. Voluntary move

6. Breaks

7. Humor

8. Nonverbal cues

9. Strength-based verbal interventions

10. Vicarious reinforcement of another child

11. Peer support

12. A class, group, or family meeting

1. *Establishing Core Rules.* Core rules, which ideally should be created by children and child-guiders together, support kids in making better decisions because the rules make them aware of expectations and empower the kids to abide by them.

During workshops, I often ask the following question: "If I walk into a room, hear a child swear, and give a consequence, am I starting the limit-setting continuum with a supportive intervention or a logical consequence?" In reality, the question can't be answered unless two critical pieces of information are ascertained: is there a rule about swearing and does the child know it? If the child knew there was a rule against swearing, then I started the limit-setting continuum with a supportive intervention. But if the child didn't know the rule or there was no rule, then I would have been starting the limit-setting continuum with a logical consequence, which often exacerbates tensions.

Establishing core rules can be seen as essentially issuing warnings. For example, Tim Murphy, a veteran residential treatment pro from Kentucky, often has the following dialogue with a kid he catches swearing.

> TIM: So you're telling me you didn't know about the rule against swearing?
>
> KID: No.
>
> TIM: Okay. Now you do, man.

When rules are established with kids, it encourages them to improve their behavior. At such times, it's easier for them to make good choices since they know what is expected of them and they helped develop those expectations.

Expectations that are *not* explicitly stated as rules can pose problems. For example, a student held responsible for using her cell phone will get rather angry if she wasn't aware there was a rule pertaining to cell phone use. On the other hand, stating too many rules can undermine relationships and kids' self-esteem. Child-guiders working with kids with emotional and behavioral challenges often overcompensate for the challenges by covering their walls with so many rules that they create an atmosphere intimating that the adults in charge are far more rule conscious than kid conscious and send the message "We expect you to act out."

Actually, when kids feel safe and nurtured in their relationships with child-guiders, there is little need for formal regulations; any time expectations are not met, adults can use their discretion, and the kids trust them to respond fairly. However, in settings where children have difficulty trusting adults a few established core rules help create a safe and predictable environment, which, in turn, helps dissipate insecurity-based anxiety. In most settings, three or four jointly composed rules are usually more than adequate.

It is not possible to formulate rules for all contingencies because forms of behavior that conflict with our unexpressed expectations arise from time to time. And that's okay. They become learning opportunities for the kids. For example, a child-guider and her group might establish the following rule: Treat all members with respect. In subsequent conversations, the child-guider and the kids can elaborate on what "respect" looks like and practice being respectful, as well as identifying swearing, teasing, put-downs, ignoring, and so forth as forms of disrespect. However, all these forms of disrespect do not need to be written on the wall. It's okay to have some ambiguity. If you've jointly established a group rule that calls for respect, then use of a borderline word can be a learning opportunity, as reflected in the following dialogue.

CHILD-GUIDER: We've talked a lot about being respectful and what that looks and sounds like.

KID: I didn't know I couldn't say the word *sucks*—it isn't swearing.

CHILD-GUIDER: You're right. But the way you said it felt disrespectful, and I wanted you to think about a better way you could have expressed your feelings.

KID: Bob lets us say the word *sucks*.

CHILD-GUIDER: Thanks for letting me know this. I'll talk with him to make sure we're on the same page.

It's often helpful to use driving metaphors to explain the nuts and bolts of limit setting, as is indicated below.

CHILD-GUIDER: Let me explain something to you, Ramone. If I'm driving down a highway where the speed limit is sixty-five miles per hour, there's a good chance I won't be pulled over if I'm going seventy-one miles per hour. However, once I choose to go over the posted speed limit, I give up control of what happens to me. I could be traveling seventy-one miles per hour, and a policeman hiding behind a tree might be thinking to himself, "I'm tired of people figuring they can go a little too fast without taking responsibility for their actions. I'm giving anyone who travels faster than seventy miles per hour a ticket today." We talk a lot about the importance of being respectful. Once you decide to cross that line in any way, you give up some control over what happens next. You don't know how someone is going to react. It's the way the world works.

Rules created jointly in the moment have the capacity to offer support and de-escalate tensions. You could say, for instance, "You kids seem upset about who gets to use the computer and for how long. Can we come up with some rules for computer use?"

In this day and age, child-guiders often struggle with rules about proper dress, piercings, language, hair color, and cell phone usage, among other issues. Child-guiders must continually balance the needs of the individual with group cohesion and safety. Checking with a number of other schools, programs, and homes to see what their policies are—reality testing—is always a good first step. It is also important to remember a key behavior management principle: Don't set limits that will be too difficult to enforce. I have visited many schools and programs where rules regarding dress and cell phone usage were being ignored because the child-guiders felt they were too difficult to enforce on a daily basis. Such environments are often fraught with tension.

Interestingly, Dana Brown, the former exceptionally talented principal at Malden High School in Malden, Massachusetts, a large inner-city school, related to me a year before he switched positions that the school dramatically changed its policy regarding cell phone usage and now allows students to use them in the hallways and at lunch, and that each teacher, along with the students, creates her own rules about usage during class. Principal Brown stated that consultants with expertise in trauma-informed care had told him that because some of his students were homeless and living in precarious circumstances, their phones were in essence a lifeline and that since the rule change the school had had few issues with cell phone usage. This positive, strength-based response had made a difference.

2. *Verbal Cues, Reminders, and Warnings.* When behavior begins to veer into undesirable territory, verbal cues, reminders, and warnings can help children get back on track. Having a child state the rule he is breaking often reduces behavioral issues. For greatest impact, child-guiders' verbal cues, reminders, and warnings should be delivered in a calm, supportive tone of voice.

Examples

"Elton, it's not such a good idea to run in the mall since you might bump into someone."

"Carmelita, could you please remind me about the running in the hallway rule? Thank you, dear."

"Class, it's getting a little too loud in here. I'm glad you're all bustling with energy. (reframing) Let's try to use quieter voices. Thank you. Remember, an indoor voice is…" The kids respond, "A very good choice."

"Howie, remember what we talked about—you were going to try harder to share with the other kids."

"Kerri, I love the way you prepare yourself every morning. (reframing) Remember, we spoke about wearing the right amount of makeup to school? What do you think about today's look? I'm a little concerned."

"Remember, we need to clean up the room before going to the park. Can't say hello to something new until we . . ." The kids respond, "Say good-bye."

"Guys, what do we always do before leaving the classroom? Yes, we line up and wait until everyone is quiet."

"Gang, we need to pick up the room and put everything away. If you got to do it . . ." The kids respond, "Just hop to it."

In the strength-based world, the focus is on what kids do right instead of what they do wrong. This principle can be effectively practiced by reminding kids of the desired behavior when improper choices are being made.

Examples

To a student who is calling out without raising her hand:

"Angelica, I *love* when you raise your hand to contribute."

To a kid who is procrastinating about getting his room cleaned:

"Isaac, when you get your room done fast, you end up with *a lot more* free time."

To a kid who is being disrespectful:

"When you talk to me in a respectful way, I really listen to what you have to say."

3. *Distraction and Redirection.* Distracting and redirecting kids who are beginning to misbehave are effective approaches to de-escalating, giving them a new focus and an opportunity to control their actions. Depending on the situation, try posing a challenge, introducing an irreverent object, changing the subject, doing something funny or odd with your body, or asking for opinions on a topic of known interest to the kids. As mentioned, I like to carry color cards from paint stores in my pocket, and when a kid becomes agitated I quickly approach, take out the cards, and loudly ask, "Which color would you paint my bathroom—mauve or fuchsia? I mean who paints their bathroom fuchsia? I can't even say it. What is my wife thinking? I'll get sick every time I enter." By the time I finish, the kids are chuckling and have forgotten they were upset.

Years ago I was consulting on a psychiatric unit for children. One of the boys, Gerald, was in the quiet room yelling. I opened the door, put my hands in a T position, and said to him, "Gerald, there's a group of young nurses coming for a tour in one minute. I don't want you to be embarrassed when they walk by. So when I give you a signal stop yelling. When I give you another signal, you can start again. Okay?"

"Okay," he said.

I gave him a signal, and he stopped yelling as the nurses walked by. A moment later I looked at him through the little glass pane on the door, smiling. He smiled, too, then came out and proceeded to have a wonderful day.

Redirection shifts the focus back to a more productive endeavor. For example, a teacher might suggest to a struggling student to switch his efforts back to work that was easier for him to successfully accomplish.

Examples

Distraction

Two children are arguing in the backseat of a car. The driver calmly asks, "Hey, kids, how many red trucks can you count in the next twenty minutes? I'll bet you can't count more than five."

A class is growing increasingly restless. The teacher intervenes by saying, "What kind of food would you like me to bring in for our Friday afternoon party?"

Dinnertime at a group home has become chaotic. The adult in charge draws the kids' attention to the latest sports results or the next field trip.

A student is becoming angrier. The teacher brings up his favorite music group's latest album, saying, "Didn't the lead singer fall off a stage and break his leg?"

My wife, daughter, and I were driving through Montana on vacation many years back. My daughter and I were arguing, and my wife yelled, "Oh look, wild cows!" My daughter replied, "Mom, there are no wild cows." But we stopped arguing and from that day the exclamation "Look, wild cows!" is uttered (get it) every time a distraction is needed in our home.

Redirection

To a student who is growing frustrated with a certain assignment:

"Hey, Billy, why don't you put that away and do the word search? Let's see how many you can find?"

To a youth in a group home who is arguing with a peer:

"Hey, Frank. Remember, good arguing occurs in a courtroom. This is the kitchen. I just bought some chocolate ice cream. You guys interested? It'll help you chill and talk."

4. *Changing Course.* In group settings, particularly those that guide kids with emotional and behavioral challenges, near the conclusion of an exercise or activity the kids often run out of steam, and their focus wanes. At such times, child-guiders need to be ready to change course.

As a former activity director of a large residential center, I learned this lesson the hard way. I'd have the kids playing basketball or softball, and then with ten minutes to go they'd lose interest and start getting on each other's nerves. At first, I tried every trick in the book to get them to finish. But in most cases they acted out and ruined what had been a very successful activity. I then learned to have filler activities at the end—fun, easy-to-do endeavors that held the kids' interest and let us finish in a positive way.

Examples

A teacher who has been using a didactic approach throughout a lesson quickly introduces an academic game or exercise that immediately engages her class.

A foster parent who has been supervising her daughter's homework senses the child would benefit from a more animated teaching approach.

Kids watching television at an out-of-home placement appear to be growing restless. A child-guider asks, "Hey, guys, anybody want to take a walk or do some cooking in the kitchen?"

As a workshop presenter, I occasionally sense that I'm losing the audience as more people chitchat, check their smart phones, or look at their watches. In response, I change course, get louder and more animated, or throw in more humor or an exercise to keep them active.

Child-guiders must always ask themselves, "How much of the behavior I'm seeing is related to my actions?" and then act accordingly. Often, changing course is the right supportive intervention.

5. *Voluntary Move.* Although the ideal strategy is to help children in conflict work out their problems, when time does not allow for mediation a voluntary move is often the best possible response. When two or more children begin quarreling, using the "divide and conquer" approach and suggesting a move is supportive, for it leaves the kids in charge of the decision. By contrast, asking a child to move is a consequence.

Examples

"Bob and Primo, you seem to be having a tough time together. Maybe you should think about choosing separate activities for a while."

"Sheelu, would you like to change seats until dinner is over? You and Mark both seem to need more space."

"Juan, you and David have been having a lot of trouble sharing a room lately. Do you think it would help if you slept in separate rooms for a few weeks?"

6. *Breaks.* Occasionally, a child or group that begins to misbehave simply needs a break. Offering a break is supportive because the child-guider is *suggesting* rather than ordering it. Ideally, we want kids to practice better self-management by learning to take breaks on their own. Classrooms and other settings can have calming areas to visit when kids need a break; suggesting a walk or specific activity works, as well. More and more schools and treatment settings now have sensory rooms that are full of calming apparatuses (mats, swings, mini-trampolines, squeezable objects, headphones, weighted vests, and so forth) that help kids regain emotional and physical balance, items that can also be in classrooms and program areas. In addition, more and more schools and child-guiding settings are engaging kids in mindfulness and yoga breaks, purposeful and recharging opportunities to maximize their strengths.

Examples

JUVENILE JUSTICE WORKER: Carl, do you think it might help to take a walk and clear your mind?

TEACHER: Sonia, do you think a few minutes at the computer will get you back on track?

JUVENILE JUSTICE WORKER: Amanda, would you like to take a break in the sensory room?

FOSTER PARENT: This hasn't been easy. Why don't you take a break and come back later? Maybe put the headphones on and relax. It's your call.

7. *Humor.* Humor used as a supportive intervention, including axioms, proverbs, and quotations, can significantly reduce the tensions prompting troublesome behavior. (For an in-depth discussion of humor, see chapter 13.)

Examples

Two first graders are throwing crayons across the table at each other. Their teacher winds up a small toy ostrich and sends it strutting from one end of the table to the other.

TEACHER: Jack, I would love it if you would put your clothes away. I would be sooo happy I might even cry tears of joy. Why, it could get so wet in here we'll need a boat and paddle to get out the door!

TEACHER: I'm not sure what I'm going to do about your behavior. I think I'll call the White House. "Mr. President, can you give me some advice today? Billy is not acting very democratic."

TEACHER: Kids, could we all just calm down and think about a pig in a mink coat? Please.

TEACHER: I've got a great joke to tell. When we're back on track, I'm going to throw it at you.

TEACHER: Look, we're not making good choices right now, and I don't know where this is going to lead us. But I do know that Yogi Berra, the famous New York Yankee catcher, once said, "You have to be careful if you don't know where you're going because you might not get there." Remember that, boys and girls!

8. *Nonverbal Cues.* Nonverbal cues, as described in chapter 15, can save the day when kids begin to misbehave, reminding them to take control of their troublesome behavior. Nonverbal cues include physical proximity; posters you can point to when the need arises; a "stop, think, and act" signal; creative facial expressions; ringing a bell or chime; rhythmic clapping; dimming the lights; and invented hand signals.

Examples

A group of third graders becomes boisterous. Their teacher circulates among them, sometimes positioning herself near an especially rowdy student.

A sixth grader starts eating pistachio nuts in class. The teacher slips a warning card onto his desk.

Fourteen-year-old Laura starts cursing under her breath. Her foster mother taps her forehead to remind Laura to "stop, think, and act."

The residents of a group home whisper as George, the adult in charge, spells out activities for the weekend. George stops talking.

A high school student seems agitated during class. His teacher, with whom he has a close relationship, lies on the floor next to his desk and makes an irreverent comment such as, "Why do they have square ceiling tiles instead of rectangular ones? Who sticks up for the rectangle?"

Distraction and nonverbal cue—A first-grade class gets too boisterous, so their teacher starts a rhythmic clap, which they copy. After a series of claps she plays Simon Says for thirty seconds and then responds, "Okay, it's time to clean up. Let's get going. Thanks."

If you develop a cue with a child or group that's attached to a set rhythm, then usually all you have to do when a problem behavior arises is tap the cue—Bum-bumpa-bum . . . bum, bum, bum—and they will get the message: "Here's some advice, talk real nice."

9. *Strength-Based Verbal Interventions.* All verbal interventions included in this book can be used in this first stage of relationship-based limit setting.

Examples

Nonjudgmental exploration—"What's up? Are you doing okay?" "What's going on, man?"

Support statement with concern—"I don't blame you for being upset. I'd feel the same way if I were you. Let's see if we can work together to help you make better choices. I'm concerned about you."

Repeating with qualifiers—"So you're saying I'm being unfair right now. Let's take a look at this."

Feelings check—"We've been dealing with many behavior problems today. It seems like some of you might have feelings that need to be talked about. What do you think? What's going on?"

Historical exploration—"Casey, you seem to be having the same problem you had yesterday. Do you remember what you did to turn your day around? It was a super move."

Same-situation exploration—"What have other kids done to get through this?"

Apologizing—"This hasn't been a very enjoyable class. I did say I'd bring in some snacks, but I forgot. I apologize." Occasionally an added comment is motivational: "So what's my consequence? Should I sing a song?"

Humor— "You know, you're acting just like a nine-year-old!" said with feigned anger to a nine-year-old child.

Reasoning response—"Hey, Gerry, what if we let every kid say those things? It wouldn't be a great place to hang out, would it?"

Connecting statement—"Jed, I don't want to give you extra homework. It's not me against you; we're on the same side. But if you don't start buckling down you may never learn this material, and it will really help you down the road."

Empowering message—"Bruno, do you think you could come up with a better way to ask for that?" "Sylvie, what would make you more comfortable? I can offer a few suggestions."

Explorative fact-finding response—"Let me make sure I know exactly why you're angry, Carl. What did Rick do to get you so worked up?"

Explorative reflective response—"It's getting pretty silly in here. Is something bothering you guys? Am I too boring?"

Plan making—"Shauna, I don't want to have to separate you and Taylor. Can we come up with a plan to get through math class without any more disruptions?"

Reframing—"I love your passion for the work, Ella. But let's try to let the others chime in, as well. What do you think?"

Millimeter acknowledgment—"Do you think there's a one percent chance that you could have made a mistake when you walked over there?"

Train metaphor—"Dudes, you've got steam bellowing, wheels spinning, oil seeping on the floor. Got any ideas to get this group train back on track?" Some child-guiders place a strip of Velcro behind a laminated picture of a locomotive and attach it to a laminated train track that's glued to the wall. If the kids start to act out, they simply walk over to the locomotive and turn it toward the floor. The kids get the message: "We're off track."

Eagle metaphor—"So you made a mistake. Big deal! What do we call a mistake? A chance to learn something new! Be the..." Kids: "Eagle!"

10. *Vicarious Reinforcement of Another Child.* Addressing a youngster's problem behavior may call unwanted attention to him, increasing his anxiety and distress; complimenting another child for the behavior you want the first kid to exhibit often does the trick. This principle holds true for groups as well as individuals.

Examples

Sarah is taking her time putting her books away. Julie is quicker at the task. Their teacher comments, "Julie, thank you for stacking your books so fast. You'll be one of the first to line up."

Several group home residents are making impulsive demands on a staff member. Their child-care counselor calls out, "Pete, I appreciate the way you asked so politely to see your point chart. I'll get it for you."

In the camp dining hall, Paul is bouncing in his chair and giggling; Kyle is sitting quietly beside him. Their counselor says, "Kyle, you are doing very well. You're showing me that you're ready to head outside. Great job."

11. *Peer Support.* Children can often be called upon to help a struggling peer. This intervention must be used with caution, however, because if the child fails to respond the others may take their frustrations out on him.

Examples

"Would those of you who have finished the assignment like to help the kids who are still working on it?"

"Hey, guys, Johnny is really angry about the cancellation of his brother's visit. He could use your help tonight. Maybe you could invite him to join you at the movies."

"We need to figure out how to get all these jobs accomplished. Can anyone think of a way to help Matt move the desks? Who else needs help?"

12. *A Class, Group, or Family Meeting.* Whenever tensions mount in a class, group, or family setting, an immediate well-run meeting can often de-escalate the situation and get the kids back on track. The more that participants share their feelings under the leadership of the adults in charge, the more they work through their conflicts, as opposed to acting them out. In addition, *regularly scheduled* meetings held on a daily or weekly basis can be extremely supportive, spawning a feeling of familiarity in which barriers and defenses begin to loosen and fall. Such meetings can also give kids a greater sense of control over their environment.

It can be equally helpful to have "check-ins"—regularly scheduled or in the moment—taking time to assess how a child or group is doing. Some teachers check in with their students by having each one write a number on a bulletin board when they enter the class in the morning, telling how they are feeling on a scale from 1 to 10. 1 = I'm feeling terrible; 10 = I feel great. This option has been found to be very helpful.

Examples

A teacher says to a class that is approaching chaos, "Please put your books away and join me on the rug for a class meeting. We need to talk about how the day is going."

A residential counselor explains to an agitated group of adolescents: "You guys seem to be on edge today. Why don't we step into the living room and have a short group meeting. I want you guys to come up with some solutions."

A mother announces to her three foster children who, for the past week, have been picking on one another upon their return from school: "I think it would be helpful to have a meeting every day after school from now on until we start getting along better. We need to talk more and argue less. Do you guys agree?"

"Abdul, let's do check-in for thirty seconds."

Setting good enough limits is an acquired skill. Consequently, most child-guiders are more comfortable in the supportive interventions stage of limit setting than in the second stage, logical consequences, so they at times overdo the issuing of warnings and other first-stage interventions. A memorable example of what can happen when the shift to logical consequences is delayed appears in the movie *Kramer versus Kramer*. A divorced father is sitting in the kitchen with his young son when the boy heads for the refrigerator, takes out a gallon of ice cream, and proceeds to eat it. The father tells him to put the ice cream back, but the boy ignores him and continues to tauntingly devour one spoonful after another. The frustrated father, meanwhile, spouts out warning after warning, finally becoming so angry that he forcibly yanks the ice cream away from his son.[2]

In this scenario, responding would have been better than reacting. After issuing two warnings, the father could have transitioned into the next stage of limit setting by saying, "Okay, son, I've asked you to stop eating the ice cream. I don't want you to ruin your appetite, so please put the ice cream away, or—," filling in the blank with a logical consequence. Afterward, the two could have processed the incident, at which point the father might have heard the message behind his son's behavior: he is upset about his parents' divorce. The shift to logical consequences would have both averted the father's anger and set the scene for more meaningful interactions.

Second Stage: Logical Consequences

The continued misbehavior of kids who do not respond to supportive interventions must be taken seriously since it usually expresses a need for greater child-guider assistance. Behavior is a message, and acting out behavior is a growing cry for help: "Something is bothering me" or "I've got some undetected wiring problems" or perhaps "I need a new way to get through this." When supportive interventions haven't quelled an escalating problem, logical consequences are often needed to provide the necessary control by holding children accountable for their actions in a respectful manner while reinforcing the values in question, such as respect, safety, and fairness. Limits issued using logical consequences make the world a safer, more predictable, and less stressful place in which to live. A good general guideline is: if two or three supportive interventions do not quell a problem behavior, it's time to follow up with logical consequences.

Unlike supportive interventions, which empower youngsters to alter their problematic behavior on their own, logical consequences attempt to transform it from the outside while giving kids an opportunity to reflect on their actions. All problematic behavior represents an opportunity to learn new ways of relating. Remember, consequences don't necessarily teach—adults do.

Administering Effective Consequences. Administering effective consequences requires foresight, determination, and a willingness to adhere to certain important aspects of implementation. One such aspect is to be prepared to *follow through* with any consequence set, because children need to know that you can predictably take care of them; that no means no; that protesting limits will only exacerbate the situation; and that they must learn to respect authority and rules of conduct. In addition to following through, administering effective consequences requires child-guiders to *counteract resistance* in the form of "But I didn't do anything. I have a right to be mad. I shouldn't have to leave the room!" Although kids should be permitted to protest anything they perceive as a misuse of authority, they must learn to do so at the right time and in the right manner.

The following examples illustrate the principles of being prepared to follow through and to counteract resistance. Although our first inclination as child-guiders may be to avoid confrontation as in option #1 below, determination to follow through and counteract resistance as in option #2 will more likely prompt a behavioral shift.

> ADULT: Jack, I've warned you repeatedly about skipping steps. I'd like you to walk up those stairs again.

> CHILD: No, Mr. Golden, I promise I won't skip steps anymore.

ADULT (OPTION #1): Okay, but next time——.

ADULT (OPTION #2): Jack, please come back and walk up the stairs again. Thank you.

> ADULT: Ed, will you please take a short break. I've asked you twice not to use that kind of language. You choose where you want to chill out. Thanks.

> CHILD: I didn't say anything. It wasn't me.

ADULT (OPTION #1): Well, it sounded like you. Please watch what you are saying.

ADULT (OPTION #2): Ed, please choose the comfy chair or the back table. You know what happens if you refuse. It's up to you, man.

In chapter 12, we introduced the term "pattern identification," and in fact most problem behavior occurs in patterns. Once we identify a pattern, our job as child-guiders is to explore the roots of the problem, make any necessary changes, and then empower the kids to be part of the solution. In terms of administering effective consequences, this often translates into encouraging kids to practice the desired behavior.

Resisting limits is a pattern we see in most settings focused on guiding children with behavioral challenges. As a result, it's critical for child-guiders to help the kids improve their abilities to accept limits. In her book *The Behavior Code Companion*, Jessica Minahan relates a clever anecdote in which she used pattern identification to turn the tables on a feisty young boy, Ned, with oppositional defiant disorder (ODD) who was resisting limits. Like so many kids, Ned didn't like hearing the word *no* and often acted up when denied something desirable.

> While I was visiting his home one day, Ned charged into the kitchen and yelled, "You forgot to give me a cookie! Can I have it?" She [his mother] looked at me with pleading, frightened, eyes. I stepped in front of Ned and said, "You are asking her a yes-or-no question and you can't handle the word *no*. That is entrapment." (Ned had just been telling me about spies and entrapment earlier in the day.) I said, "You need to change the question. You could ask, "When can I have a cookie?" Ned, still angry, snapped, "When can I have a cookie?" and his mother answered, "Right after dinner." He grunted and returned to the living room. Kat [his mother] used this technique daily after that with all of her children. She called it life changing.[3]

To improve kids' abilities to accept limits, it is also often helpful to discuss the issue with them: "Dudes, no one likes being told what to do. I don't. But part of growing older, maturing, and becoming successful is understanding that at times we need to do what we're told even though we don't want to. You'll have bosses and others whom you'll need to respect. Say no to them and you could lose your job, or other bad things can happen. Let's practice this. Shamir, you tell me what to do or give me a consequence, and I'll try to give the best possible response. Then we'll switch sides. Thanks."

In addition, it is possible to discuss the importance of accepting limits by using a highway metaphor. "Guys, imagine that I'm driving at sixty miles an hour down the highway—the posted speed limit—when a policeman pulls me over and gives me a speeding ticket. Of course, I'm pretty mad because I wasn't speeding; yet I know that if I swear at the officer he could arrest me for misconduct. Even though I have not broken the law, I have no right to act disrespectfully. So I tell the officer how fast I was going and then courteously accept the ticket, mentally planning to fight it later in court. You see, adults, like kids, are at times unfairly accused of things. Still, there's a right and a wrong way to deal with authority. We all need to make good choices in tough situations. Even though you might be correct about an injustice you suffered, it doesn't give you the right to act out or break a rule."

To help stand your ground after setting a limit, remind yourself of the golden rule of behavioral returns: Pay me now, or pay me more later. In other words, instead of worrying about how the child will respond in the moment think about how he might behave the next day, and the following month. Know that if you respectfully set firm and consistent limits he will learn to trust you, and you will both be better off down the road.

A third aspect of administering effective consequences is to think progressively. Ask yourself, "How often has this particular behavior occurred in the past?" The general guideline for progressive discipline is that the more often a problem behavior occurs, the stronger the response should be in terms of:

- Exploring the root causes
- Teaching and reinforcing the desired behavior
- Determining the consequence for the behavior

Although kids are apt to fume over stiffer consequences, the smoke will clear more quickly if they know in advance that consequences are administered progressively. Following are some examples of how to use progressive discipline when processing with children:

"John, you made a mistake when you punched Andy and pushed him down. We've had a good talk, and I know you're sorry. And I like what you said about dealing with him differently next time. So we've agreed that your consequence will be a one-day in-house suspension tomorrow. I don't like having to suspend you, but what if we allowed all the kids to act this way, even if they had good reasons to be angry? It wouldn't be safe around here, and safety is one of our most sacred values. John, this is the first time you've done something like this. If you should become aggressive again, what do you think will happen next time?"

John replies: "The suspension might be for a longer period."

"Jill, I've asked you three times in the last hour to take a break because you're choosing to bother people. I've tried to talk with you to see if something is on your mind, but you don't seem ready to open up. If in the next half hour you make another bad choice, you'll have to sit next to me for the rest of the class."

Like progressive discipline, it's always beneficial to factor in severity and frequency of the problem behavior when determining a consequence, considering how often it has occurred and how serious it is, perhaps using the highway metaphor to explain this: "Guys, if I get pulled over for speeding, before the officer issues a ticket, what does he do? He checks my record. If this is the fifth time in three weeks I've been pulled over for going a bit too fast, he's probably going to issue me a ticket. The *frequency* of my problem behavior warrants a stronger consequence. And in addition to the ticket I might need to go to driver education classes. My frequent driving problems indicate that I have some skills to learn. If, however, I get pulled over for going one hundred miles an hour in a fifty-mile-per-hour zone, that's called reckless endangerment, and I'm probably going to lose my license or end up behind bars due to the *severity* of my actions. This is how the world works. And this is how limit setting is carried out in this place."

Further, it's helpful to inform kids that after a bad choice, they can always make a good decision and that doing so will often factor in positively to the outcome. For example, a youth runs away from a group home, and after a few minutes of processing, the following dialogue occurs.

COUNSELOR: What do you think we should do?

YOUTH: I don't think you need to do anything. This is the first time I've ever run. And after thirty minutes I realized it was stupid to run so I came back. Look, I got a phone call from my mother. She isn't coming this weekend. I was pissed. I won't do it again.

COUNSELOR: I agree. But what if something ticks you off tomorrow and you run?

YOUTH: Then I probably should be grounded.

COUNSELOR: Yeah. Probably. Remember, use your words, man.

I always suggest to child-guiders not to have mandatory consequences for certain behaviors, such as hitting, running away, drug use, and vandalism since this may not encourage kids to self-regulate their behavior. For example, if a kid in a group home knows his level will be dropped for a week should he hit someone, he might, after a minor slap to a peer, decide he's got nothing to lose by inflicting some serious damage. If, however, the program has established minimum consequences for aggression, a youth who enters into an altercation might think to himself, "Stop! Walk away, don't make it any worse. If I walk, my consequences will be less. They say that after a bad choice I can always make a good decision."

Kids can also be told that there are no limits on the other end. "Yes, we have minimum consequences for serious behavior. However, keep in mind that if you do something incredibly unsafe or dangerous it could result in your being suspended, discharged from the setting, or arrested." Always factor in *severity* and *frequency*.

The fourth, and final, important aspect of administering effective consequences is to *avoid giving overly severe consequences*. Behavior is a message, and getting tough when kids seriously misbehave over long stretches of time, when calls for help are palpable, is usually not the answer. Better assessing the child, modifying or changing expectations, finding a more supportive setting, providing more skill-building and therapeutic assistance, and focusing more on strengths are responses that, in many cases, prove more effective. Remember, at McDonald's you expect to see burgers. Likewise, many child-guiders should expect to see misbehavior.

Types of Consequences. Child-guiders must use their judgment about which consequences to use with which kids. Factors such as age, maturity, emotional makeup, and context should all be factored in when deciding on the course of action. Any misbehavior could have a number of appropriate consequences based on context alone. The following types of consequences provide a basic structure for implementing discipline. Later in this chapter we will discuss response options to use when kids refuse to accept a limit, followed by a step-by-step progression that can be explained to children.

Redoing. If a child says or does something inappropriate or not up to established standards, she can be asked to redo it to practice the desired behavior (see figure 18–1).

Restorative Action / Reparation. When misbehavior physically or emotionally injures people or property, it's often helpful to have the child restore or repair the relationship or property by performing a task that gives something back and, at times, reconciling with the offended individuals (see figure 18–2). This consequence is like the community service sentence adult offenders often receive. Remember that children who act inappropriately frequently feel wounded themselves, and their misdeeds often fuel

Figure 18–1
Redoing Consequences

PROBLEM BEHAVIOR	RESPONSE
A child acts silly while lining up for a transition.	Ask the child to line up again and stand quietly.
A child speaks inappropriately to an adult or peer.	Ask the child to try again and express himself in acceptable terms. "I think you just called me staff member of the year, but I'm not sure it came out that way. Please try again. Thanks."
A child completes a chore unsatisfactorily.	Ask the child to do it again until it is properly completed. Help the child if she needs it. It's not the military.
A child runs through the hallway.	Ask the child to return and walk instead.
A student puts little effort into completing an assignment.	Ask the student to redo it. Offer assistance if necessary.
A child cuts into line.	Ask the child to enter again at the back of the line.
A child dresses improperly for an occasion.	Ask the child to return to his room and dress appropriately, providing assistance if necessary.

negative self-images, stifling motivation to improve their functioning, so this popular consequence also helps restore a child's self-image. I heard a well-known author praise this consequence, stating that it can actually build a child's self-esteem.

In the juvenile justice arena, and in a growing number of schools and youth-guiding programs, restorative justice is being implemented with impressive results. The Center for Justice and Reconciliation defines restorative justice as: "a theory of justice that emphasizes repairing the harm caused or revealed by criminal behavior. It is best accomplished through cooperative processes that include all stakeholders."[4] The editors of *Rethinking Schools* magazine, in an article titled "Restorative Justice: What It Is and Is Not," further describe this response to misbehavior as a replacement for the long-standing punitive zero tolerance response.

> Misbehave, get punished. That pretty much sums up the approach to "disciplining" students that educators through the decades have taken in schools and classrooms. The most extreme form of this law-and-order strategy is zero tolerance, described in *Rethinking Schools* by Bill Ayers and Bernardine Dohrn back in 2000, as these policies gained popularity:
>
> > Schools everywhere—public, private, urban, suburban, rural, and parochial—are turning into fortresses where electronic searches, locked doors, armed police, surveillance cameras, patrolled cafeterias, and weighty rule books define the landscape.
>
> In schools today, educators still respond to what they perceive as student misbehavior with punishment. However, schools and school districts appear to be abandoning the language of zero tolerance and in many places are introducing what is often called "restorative justice." This represents an enormous victory for the activists and organizations that for years have fought the school-to-prison pipeline. Zero tolerance puts school resources toward policing and push-out instead of toward teaching and support. The number of youth—overwhelmingly youth of color—out of school and incarcerated has skyrocketed; LGBTQ and disabled youth are also targeted.
>
> So we welcome the abandonment of zero tolerance.
>
> But simply announcing a commitment to "restorative justice" doesn't make it so. Restorative justice doesn't work as an add-on. It requires us to address the roots of student "misbehavior" and a willingness to rethink

and rework our classrooms, schools, and school districts. Meaningful alternatives to punitive approaches take time and trust.[5]

Figure 18–2
Restorative Action/Reparation Consequences

PROBLEM BEHAVIOR	RESPONSE
A youth bullies his peers.	Have the youth apologize to those offended and ask him to spend a few days helping disadvantaged kids in his school or community.
A child throws food during lunchtime.	Have the child apologize to the maintenance worker and ask her to help clean the cafeteria for a pre-determined amount of time.
A youth writes swear words on a wall.	Have the youth remove the swear words and repaint the wall. Perhaps involve him in a plan to decrease graffiti in the community.
A child breaks a valuable item.	Have the child do odd jobs to repay the cost of the item. (Unless it's exorbitantly expensive, limits should be placed on the upper end of a child's service.)
A youth is continuously rude in a home or child-guiding setting.	Have the youth give something back: "You took away a lot of the good feelings we have here by how you've talked to us. I'd like you to give something back. Please pick a few chores you can do to restore the good feelings we usually have in this place. Thanks."

If you're working with teens in any setting, you might want to explore restorative justice. At the very least, the restorative action consequence can be a meaningful addition to your repertoire of logical consequences.

I recently spoke with a woman who teaches the Love and Logic system, a very popular and successful approach to guiding children that uses restorative action consequences,[6] and she remarked, "Yes, it's an effective consequence. We call it a 'contribution.' The child who has taken something away by his actions now contributes something."

RESTRICTION. Children who behave responsibly enjoy privileges such as walking to stores by themselves, being unsupervised in a group setting, watching television, using the phone, playing unsupervised, hanging out with friends, riding their bikes, using the family car, taking public transportation, and staying out late on weekends. Abuse of these privileges leads logically to a restriction of these activities. Child-guiders should always factor in severity and frequency, as well as progressive discipline, when considering the restriction of a privilege.

> **RESTRICTION TRAPS.** Enticing though they may at first appear, limitations placed on certain privileges can be detrimental to a child's development and should therefore be avoided. One restriction trap to avoid is *restricting time with friends*. Although it may seem logical to say, "If you can't behave by yourself, how can I expect you to behave with a friend?" such a consequence is often counterproductive, for the power of friendship propels kids with emotional and behavioral challenges to improve their behavior. Take away opportunities for peer relating and we unwittingly promote what they serve to eradicate—misbehavior. In fact, because challenging kids often have difficulty making and sustaining friendships, and as a result have severely compromised self-esteem, it is incumbent upon us to facilitate friendships and find other consequences.
>
> If you are a teacher, for instance, consider allowing disruptive students to sit together on a provisional basis and offer them a second-chance option if things do not go well at first. You might say, "As long as you behave well, I'll let you boys sit together because I know you

are friends. If you get silly or have trouble, I'll need to separate you, but I will give you another chance to sit together next week." All the while, teach them the relationship skills they need. You may have to put up with some acting out in the short term, but the payoff for the kids will be well worth it.

A second restriction trap to avoid is restricting food intake. Many states that license residential and foster care programs prohibit the withholding of food from children—and for good reason. Such an act erodes their trust in adults and leads to physical pain as well as long-lasting rage. Most youngsters who have had food withheld from them and are fearful that it will happen again in fact hoard food. If a child misbehaves during a meal, simply explain that he will be served as soon as he calms down and that he need not worry about receiving the same amount of food as everyone else. If he is late for a meal, give him something else to eat, or ask him to make something on his own and clean up after himself. If he is repeatedly late for dinner, you could temporarily eliminate the privilege of going out on his own since he has not demonstrated an ability to manage his time well.

A third restriction trap to circumvent is restricting recreational time. At-risk kids desperately need recreational time for releasing pent-up emotions by moving their bodies and playing freely. Often this is the only time of day they feel good about themselves. Child psychologist Bruno Bettelheim equated taking recreational time away from an emotionally disturbed child with taking cough syrup away from someone with a sore throat.[7]

If you are a teacher, think twice about restricting a child from recess in response to misbehavior. For one thing, there is nothing logical about this consequence unless the child has been violent enough to receive a severe initial consequence or unless the problem behavior has occurred during recess, in which case a preferred option would be increased supervision. For another, a child who is told he may not attend recess is apt to continue misbehaving, since he has nothing to look forward to.

If you are a foster parent, do not to restrict your child from par-

Figure 18–3
Restriction Consequences

Problem Behavior	Response
A child uses a computer improperly.	Prohibit the child from using the computer for a specified period of time, or allow her to only use it when supervised by an adult.
A child racks up extra charges on a phone bill.	Restrict the number of minutes and amount of data the child can use.
A child rides a bike without wearing a helmet.	Prohibit the child from riding the bike for a specified period of time.
A child steals from a store.	Prohibit the child from going to stores unsupervised for a specified period of time. Also have him apologize to the store owner and make restitution.
A child refuses to do homework or chores.	Withhold the child's free-time privileges, such as watching television or playing outdoors, until the homework or chores are finished.

Note: Make sure you have a clear understanding about why a child struggles with these tasks. Lots of kids struggle with executive functioning issues and need help navigating these kinds of responsibilities. Remember, behavior is always a message. Factor in frequency and severity when restricting items, and encourage the child to help determine the duration of the restriction.

ticipating in sports or other forms of organized recreation because these pursuits enhance self-confidence and provide a sense of normalcy to kids who feel "different." Interestingly, some kids with low self-esteem misbehave in order to lose such privileges since they are afraid of being embarrassed on the field. "No homework, no sports," although a logical response, is often a self-defeating decree best replaced by "No homework, no TV till it's done—and if the problem persists we may need to devote more weekend time to your schooling."

REMOVAL OF TROUBLESOME OBJECTS. When objects play a role in problematic behavior, a reasonable consequence is to put them away for a specified period of time. Remember, though, that removing objects from children requires you to exert power over them—a dynamic that can unduly provoke those who are hypersensitive to the misuse of power. So make sure you have warned children about possibly losing a favored item, and freely modify the approach, such as by negotiating times when it is okay to use the object in question, as reflected in the following scenario. Eleven-year-old Justin relinquished his basketball with full understanding of his misdeed when his foster mother said, "Justin, I've asked you nicely not to bounce the basketball in the house, but you seem to be having a hard time following instructions today. Will you please hand me the ball—I'll return it after dinner. Thank you. Now, let's see if we can get you something else to keep your hands and body occupied that's indoor-friendly, okay?"

To apply progressive discipline, repeat a consequence like this but extend the period of relinquishment each time. Keep your options open by initially withholding the object for a short period of time, and make sure the maximum withholding period does not become unreasonable.

REMOVAL TRAPS. The strategy of taking away objects is often misused. One removal trap is *arbitrarily taking away personal possessions*, an approach to limit setting that is neither logical nor educational, but simply punitive. Examples include taking away a child's favorite doll for a day when she is rude; taking away a kid's electronic games for a while when he is fooling around at bedtime; or taking away a teen's car keys for being fresh. The adult's intent in such instances is to evoke within the child a sense of discomfort for having caused others grief.

But these punishments are a misuse of power and likely to arouse anger and exacerbate misbehavior. The only possession that should be taken away from a child is one associated with the problem at hand.

A second removal trap to avoid is *taking away allowance*. Making allowance contingent upon good behavior is a subjective practice experienced by many vulnerable kids as unfair and unpredictable. An unconditional weekly allowance is critically important, for it gives children a chance to exercise delayed gratification, money management, and other mature behaviors. When a child breaks or loses an item, rather than withholding his entire allowance to pay the costs of fixing or replacing it (a restorative consequence) it is more constructive to have him pay the nec-

Figure 18–4
Removal of Troublesome Object Consequences

PROBLEM BEHAVIOR	RESPONSE
A teen texts and uses a cell phone instead of getting homework done.	Remove the phone until the work is complete. If this is an ongoing issue, make a plan to allow for two-minute phone checks after thirty minutes of work, or something similar. Of course, for some kids occasional texting helps them navigate a homework assignment or chore. Every situation is different.
A child taps a ruler on a desk after being asked to put it away.	Remove the ruler for a specified period of time. (Perhaps give the child something else to tap that's soft.)
A child continues to wear clothing deemed inappropriate for a setting.	Put the clothing items away for a predetermined period of time. Allow the clothing to eventually be worn in an alternative setting.

essary costs through a brokered arrangement. One foster mother I know negotiated the following effective deal: "Geoff, you broke the window. You receive an allowance of five dollars a week. Do you think that paying three dollars a week for a month, combined with some extra work around the house, would be a good way to handle this?"

PROXIMITY MANIPULATION. A child who misbehaves is often sending the message "I'm not controlling myself very well. Keep me close." It is therefore logical to require such a child to stay within close proximity of you. You might explain: "Don, you've had a hard time getting along with people today. I've tried to help you out. But now I'd like you to please stay by me for the rest of the day. Thanks." The more problematic the behavior is, the closer the proximity should be. Through good behavior, the child can then earn back your trust and his autonomy.

Any time a child's problematic behavior raises serious concerns, it may be wise to assign him to one of the designated levels of supervision described below. When he shows an ability to maintain behavioral standards, allow him to move to a less restrictive level. As with any intervention, it is best to involve him in the decision making.

Following are three levels of supervision often used in settings for kids with serious behavioral challenges, appearing in order of increasing intensity.

- **Close supervision:** The child must let you know where he is at all times.

- **One-to-one supervision:** The child must remain in close proximity to you at all times.

- **In-sight supervision:** The child must remain within your range of vision at all times. This level is most appropriate for children who are abusing themselves or demonstrating other unsafe behaviors.

When using proximity manipulation, it is important to regularly assess the child's behavior and inform him of ways to move to a less restrictive level of supervision. Autonomy, to be reliably welcomed, must be regained gradually through actions that restore trust. Sadly, some kids, such as those with a history of sexually offending against others, require a high level of supervision until their autonomy is earned.

Figure 18–5
Proximity Manipulation Consequences

PROBLEM BEHAVIOR	RESPONSE
A child teases a sibling in the living room while a foster parent is cooking dinner.	Ask the child to come stay in the kitchen until dinner is served.
A high school student engages in self-harm.	Ask the student to check in with her guidance counselor a few times each day.
A student is bullying kids in the hallways.	Require the student to be escorted from class to class. Other consequences, such as restorative action may also be warranted.
A student is throwing objects in the cafeteria.	Have the student sit closer to the monitor for a predetermined period of time.
A youth is caught sexually touching another kid at a group home.	Place the youth in close supervision for a predetermined period of time. Other interventions may also be required.
A student is acting up at the back of class.	Have the student sit up front for the remainder of the class—if not longer.
Students are wandering too far during recess.	Require the students to stay on the hardtop the next day.

GROUNDING. Grounding is usually a good response to acts of aggression or violence, stealing, staying out without permission, suspension from school, running away, destroying property, inappropriate sexual activity, drug abuse, or other health or safety violations. Typically, a child who is grounded is required to remain at home or in his living unit for a set period of time, although he is permitted to attend school, watch television, and keep all essential appointments and team commitments. Grounding is essentially proximity manipulation conveying the message "We need to watch you more closely since you've lost our trust and need to restore it," as explained in the following scenario. "Mary, this isn't a punishment. You can watch TV and do all your normal stuff. You're grounded because you temporarily have lost our trust. You're a good kid who made a bad choice to steal the money. And we'll talk more about that. But right now, it's time to start earning trust back." A child who is grounded can also be asked to come up with a restorative chore or action to make amends.

The duration of a grounding should be based on the severity of the behavior along with the frequency with which it has occurred before, as well as other contextual factors, such as the psychological and neurological makeup of the child, the setting he lives in, and the reason the behavior occurred. Also, the length of grounding should be determined along with the youth. Effective groundings usually range from an hour to several days to as long as a few weeks, with longer durations reserved for repeated offenses or major safety or rule violations.

Child-guiders may at times inform their kids that good behavior during a grounding period, which might include various acts of restoration and amends, will reduce the duration. If child-guiders do make this an option, they should periodically check in with their kids to review their behavior and whether they are on track well enough to have their grounding period reduced.

It is important to remember that kids with emotional and behavioral challenges who are grounded often require a lot of attention and can easily become bored, antsy, and angry, so when an adult grounds a child it restricts the adult as well. Therefore, it is best to use this consequence only after a long talk with your observing ego. One good way to guard against

Figure 18–6
Grounding Consequences

Problem Behavior	Response
A group home resident runs away for the second time in a week.	The youth is grounded to the house for a week.
An eight-year-old punches a kid in a residential center for the fourth time in a week.	The child is grounded to the setting for twenty-four hours.
A foster teen comes home two hours late, a first-time offense.	The youth is grounded to the house for twenty-four hours.
A youth at a juvenile detention center spits at a worker, a first-time offense.	The youth is grounded to the unit for two days.

retaliatory reactions is to jointly decide on the duration of a grounding after all involved parties have taken time to collect their thoughts, even if this means the next day. Emotional distance is often needed to issue a fair consequence. Upon greeting her fifteen-year-old foster son when he returned home long past curfew with no explanation, one mother said: "Alex, you are going to be grounded for staying out until three a.m. You had us all worried sick! Tomorrow we'll decide how long you'll have to stay home—I'm too tired and upset right now. And the length of your grounding will be influenced by how you act from this moment on."

Kids often act up in a car. When this occurs, it is frequently difficult for the driver to respond. Here's a good response: "Guys, I've talked to you a couple of times about your actions. But people are still making bad choices, and I'm uncomfortable. What's happening is unsafe. I may need to pull the car over and wait until we turn things around. You will all have consequences when we get back. You might not be going out for a while. How long you'll be grounded will be decided by how well you behave from this moment on. It's up to you. Heck, behave like true gentlemen for the rest of the ride and there might not be any consequences. Remember, boys, after a bad decision you can always make—." And the kids say, "A good choice."

DIRECTED CHAT. When trouble is brewing, a meaningful one-on-one conversation held some distance from the turbulence can provide the increased attention a child or group needs to get back on track. This change of location serves a twofold purpose: it helps children gain emotional distance from the disturbance and, removed from an audience of peers who may be contributing to the problem, save face. Once a child-guider has isolated the child or group, the verbal intervention strategies already presented should be utilized, such as engagement through nonjudgmental exploration.

Figure 18–7
Directed Chat Consequences

PROBLEM BEHAVIOR	RESPONSE
A couple of students are acting disruptively during class.	"Guys, could you please talk with me outside class for a minute. Thanks."
A child is misbehaving during a meal.	"Garth, could I please talk with you in the hallway. Thanks."
A child is acting rudely to his foster parents.	"Larry, let's go into the living room and have a chat. You seem a bit off track. Thanks."
Youth are acting up during an off-grounds activity.	"Lorenzo, let's have a talk on the bench. It seems like something's going on. Thanks."

REMOVAL OF ATTENTION. If you are working with a child or group whose behavior becomes uncivil, a good consequence is to walk away. Your parting statement might be: "Jericho, I'm uncomfortable with the way you're choosing to talk with me. I'm going back to my desk."

EXAGGERATED KINDNESS. This consequence originated with the legendary author and practitioner William Glasser, MD. Glasser recounts a wonderful anecdote about a middle-aged single mother who was at her wit's end with her teenage daughter. The daughter wouldn't lift a finger to help with the cooking and cleaning in their home. The mother tearfully told Glasser that the two of them fought every day and that she had in fact slapped her daughter during a tense exchange that week. She pleaded for his help.

Glasser told her to go home and clean the kitchen her daughter had messed that morning and then greet her after school with a big smile, without mentioning a word about the kitchen—and to do this every day until her next session with him the following week. The mother was incredulous and complained that Glasser was letting her daughter get away with taking no responsibility for helping out. Glasser calmly told her to do as he suggested.

Seven days later the mother entered his office smiling and looking re-energized. She said she had done what he had suggested, and that on the very first day, for the first time in many months, she and her daughter had a wonderful talk after school. She said her daughter seemed suspicious, but they nevertheless connected. Over the next few days, the daughter continued to leave messes in the kitchen, but the mother repeatedly cleaned them up and greeted her with a smile. Eventually the girl began to do her share of the kitchen cleanup. The talks between the two grew even deeper. The mother ultimately reconnected with a daughter she felt she had lost.[8]

In this case, Glasser correctly determined that the most serious problem facing this family was not the daughter's reluctance to help out but the strained relationship between mother and daughter. Had the mother chosen a more traditional consequence, it might have backfired since their relationship—the all-important factor to consider when setting limits—was so damaged. The intervention Glasser suggested instead is similar to seeing is believing or a deliberate act of kindness, both described in chapter 6.

By contrast, I have a pretty good relationship with my teenage daughter, but from time to time she gets lax with helping out around the house. If I were to respond with exaggerated kindness, she'd be delighted, and it wouldn't change her behavior. Context always determines the best response.

BREAK. The customary term for this consequence is "time-out," which has a negative connotation. Consequently, more and more child-guiders now use the term "break," which better defines what the intervention is about and, rather than distancing children, bridges them since all people need breaks from time to time. I often tell kids: "If I'm in a staff meeting and get angry, the principal might tell me, 'Take a break, Charlie. You're getting too upset. Chill out, and come back when you're ready to discuss this.' I leave, cool off, come back, and contribute to the meeting. It's no big deal...NBD. We all need breaks to get back on track."

I recall sharing this anecdote with a group of feisty fourth graders on their first day of school, when I was called in to assist because in third grade they had "all been hellions," according to the principal. After I gave my "break talk," a particularly rambunctious student waved her hand wildly.

"Yes," I said to her.

"Wow! Last year time-out meant you were bad. This year it's not such a big deal!" she said.

"Yeah, NBD," I replied. They went on to have a super year.

A break for a child who is misbehaving and has not responded to supportive interventions ideally entails asking him to choose a chill-out area, such as a chair, desk, bean bag chair, couch, seat in a hallway, stairway step, sensory or break room, or bedroom, and to sit quietly and comfortably for an open-ended or specified period of time. With other kids it may take a walk or a run in the gym or outside, to help them get back on track.

This intervention is often more effective if child-guiders introduce choice into the equation: "Billy, could you please take a short break. You look like you could use some chill time. You choose where you want to sit. Thanks." After the break, the incident can be processed to help the child reintegrate it.

• *Why use breaks?*

There are a number of reasons to use breaks. First, a break gives a child who is misbehaving a chance to cool off and reflect on her actions, while reducing contagion issues if her behavior has been disrupting a group.

Second, a break is a quick response that helps children learn the boundaries of their actions and regain their sense of emotional balance, while giving child-guiders time to process the incident with the child. Learning theory dictates that the sooner a consequence is given for low-level misbehaviors—such as rudeness, obstinacy, minor aggressiveness, and silliness—the more likely it is to reduce future misconduct. During the processing phase, alternative responses can be suggested and self-management techniques reviewed.

Third, breaks can be repeated if a child continues to misbehave. By contrast, a delayed consequence for low-level misbehaviors may only escalate the problem behavior because the child may feel he has nothing more to lose. "Why should I behave? I've already lost my recess time," he may declare, or "I never do well enough to stay up late. I'm always in trouble."

Fourth, a break, unlike a delayed consequence, enables children to deal with an incident, put it behind them, and start over again with a clean slate. Delayed consequences, such as restoration and grounding, should generally be used only for more serious behaviors.

• *How long should breaks last?*

Breaks are most effective if they're open-ended, with their duration left to the child to decide, which is empowering.

Example

CHILD-GUIDER: Billy, could you please take a break.

(OPTION #1): You choose where you want to chill. Thanks. Please raise your hand when you're ready to talk with me.

Figure 18–8
Break Consequences

Problem Behavior	Response
A four-year-old foster child slaps her foster mother.	"Ouch! That hurt. Could you please come with me. I'd like you to chill out for a few minutes, and then we'll talk about using your words when you get upset. You can choose where to sit."
A teen in a group home swears profusely at a staff member.	"Whoa! What's going on? Could you please take a break. Come back when you're ready to talk with me. You seem really upset. Please cool off in your room or the study. Thanks, man."
A student angrily throws an object across the room.	"Devon, could you please take a break in the back of the room. That wasn't a good choice. Raise your hand when you're ready to talk with me about it. Thanks."
A kid meanly puts down a peer.	"Octavia, could you please chill out at one of the back tables for five minutes. Afterward, the three of us will try to work this out. Thanks."

(OPTION #2): When you seem calm, I'll come over and talk with you.

(OPTION #3): Come back when you feel ready to join the group.

The most appropriate of these responses would depend on the context in which the situation occurred.

In settings where breaks are used as a logical consequence, kids should discuss and practice taking them. For example, kids should learn that if they are asked to take a break they should not bolt back to their seat if the option is to return when they are ready.

CHILD-GUIDER: Remember, guys, if I need you to take a break, chill for a minute or so before coming back. It will help you. If the principal asks me to take a break, she'd be ticked if I come back three seconds later. Right?

When open-ended breaks prove problematic and consistency needs would be better served by having breaks with set amounts of time, child-guiders should choose this option instead. It's always best, however, to begin with the least restrictive, most empowering interventions.

For low-level misbehaviors, such as rudeness, silliness, ignoring demands, teasing, or minor aggressiveness, it's best to keep the break duration short. One to ten minutes based on age usually suffices. The younger the child, the less time she should be asked to sit. A minute or two is often plenty for kids under seven. Giving the kids timers has always been a questionable practice because the focus then shifts to how long they sit vs. the behavior in question. Resist using timers, if possible.

Some child-care experts recommend giving children who misbehave one minute of break time for each year of their lives. But that is a sad price to pay for growing older and an unwieldy guideline to follow while working with a mixed-age group.

• *How should breaks be served?*

To settle down and shift gears, a child taking a break should be relatively quiet and comfortable. Kids should never be forced to stand, face a wall, or serve the break in any way that is demeaning or uncomfortable. In general, it's best not to talk too much to a child who is taking a break, as it might reinforce the problem behavior.

A break isn't a punishment, so kids should be allowed to engage in activities that restore their balance, such as reading, listening to calming music, doing schoolwork, or handling sensory items. Above all, children should be told that breaks help them calm themselves and think about better decisions to make in the future.

Break Tips. Whether you are interacting with a strong-willed five-year-old or a teenager new to a group home, it is a good idea to keep the following points in mind.

1. Remember the core elements of *responding versus reacting*. Always say please and thank you when giving a break, and resist starting a command with *you*, instead using *I* or *we*: "Jasmine, we use our words to express ourselves. Could you please take a short break and think about a better way you could have handled that. Thanks."

2. Practice the affect scale. As they get louder, we get quieter. Also be careful to control the volume and tone of your voice, as well as your body language. Remember that a child will be most sensitive to the messages underlying your words.

3. When using set break times, do not restart a break if the child begins misbehaving partway through it. Instead, let him know that his time only counts when he's calm and quiet.

4. When a break is over, process the incident with the child, if only briefly. After a short break for a minor misbehavior, it is often sufficient to look in the child's direction and say, "Okay, Mary, you can get up. Let's try to talk more respectfully. Thanks." In more critical instances— for a child who has reacted emotionally to the intervention or who has performed a serious or recurrent misbehavior—process the incident in greater depth before he returns to what he was doing.

5. Expect to issue breaks over and over again for the same misbehavior. Viewing a break as a cure-all is a set-up for disappointment. When used correctly, breaks can keep disorderly situations under control and, over time, help children examine their coping styles and discover better alternatives. Of course, if a child or group exhibits the same

problem behavior(s) there should be a host of interventions introduced to help, of which a logical consequence should be a small part.

EXTENDED SEPARATION. Extended separation, a longer break to cool down and process a serious behavioral incident, lasts anywhere from thirty minutes to several hours. This consequence is used most often in settings where kids have serious behavioral challenges. It is usually issued to older kids who have committed serious acts of violence or other dangerous offenses.

This intervention requires important safeguards. First, no youngster should be asked to take an extended separation unless he is closely supervised and allowed to sit comfortably and engage in calming endeavors during the initial stages of the consequence.

Second, a person in a supervisory position, such as a principal, case worker, or unit director, should help determine the minimum duration of an extended separation because serious behavioral incidents often evoke intense feelings in child-guiders, occasionally causing them to become too emotionally involved to issue an appropriate consequence, as reflected in the following dialogue.

CHILD-GUIDER: Carlos attacked Jonny this afternoon. He went at him while we were watching TV. He's finally quieted down. We had to hold him for five minutes. We haven't explored the issue with him yet.

UNIT DIRECTOR: Thanks for letting me know. Keep Carlos off the unit for a few hours. Let's restore some calm to the group. After he's settled down and talked with you for a while, you can take him for a walk or go to the sensory room or study.

Calling a person in a supervisory role to help determine appropriate consequences for a serious behavioral incident, a third safeguard, should be instituted in all settings that deal with kids with serious emotional and behavioral challenges. In fact, in out-of-home placement settings it is often helpful to adhere to this rule: No consequence issued during a shift can extend into the next shift unless it is approved by a supervisor. Too often at the end of a brutal shift a youth-care worker will angrily bark: "That's it! You're grounded to the cottage for the next twenty-four hours." He then exits, leaving the new staff with a very disgruntled youth.

In addition to ensuring that extended separations meet these conditions, a home, program, or school should thoroughly document the extended

Figure 18–9
Extended Separation Consequences

Problem Behavior	Response
A seven-year-old in a residential setting punches staff member in the stomach.	The child is asked to take a break away from the group. If he's gained his composure, he can return to the group thirty minutes later after processing the incident with the staff member he hurt.
A youth in a special education school destroys furniture in a fit of rage, scaring some of his classmates.	The youth is asked to take a break in the quiet or sensory room. Once he calms down and processes the the incident, he's asked to hang out with one of the behavioral specialists for another hour before he returns to class. Upon returning, he clears the air with his classmates.
Two fifteen-year-olds in a group home get into a fight.	They are separated, and one is asked to chill out in the rec room, while the other is asked to cool down in her room. Once they've regained their composure, a staff member brings them together to process the incident.

separation, forwarding a copy of all records to pertinent individuals, such as lawyers, parents, state officials, and legal guardians. An extended separation that cannot be conducted in the fair and humane manner described above has no place in a setting's logical consequences.

The purpose of an extended separation is to help kids understand the seriousness of their actions, regain their emotional balance, process what occurred, and devise a reentry plan, which often involves reconciling with the offended parties and formulating appropriate consequences. During an extended separation, kids should settle in a comfortable, well-supervised location and, when they are ready, process the incident with a child-guider. In some settings, kids fill out a form asking why the behavior occurred, what better choices were available, and how these options can be used in the future. In addition, kids can be given an education assignment on a relevant topic. A youngster who has punched a peer, for instance, could be asked to read or write a story portraying the negative consequences of fighting and to compose an apology.

During or after an extended separation, child-guiders should process the incident with the youngster, giving him an opportunity to explain what happened and why; exploring his feelings and alternative ways he could have responded; and, in the case of serious misbehavior, spelling out further consequences, such as loss of privileges, intensified supervision, restoration, reconciliation with the offended party, or increased counseling to work on self-control and the origins of his anger. Processing also entails the child-guider owning up to any mistakes she could have made.

Numerous factors determine the minimum duration of an extended separation, including the age of the youngster, the seriousness of his actions, who he is (psychologically, developmentally, and neurologically), where he is, how soon he calms down, and the safety needs of the group. Once a child has regained his composure, he should not be required to sit in a designated place for the entire duration of the separation. He can do more productive things such as taking a walk, going to a sensory room, and, as with kids taking breaks, read, listen to music, and so forth. Other consequences, such as restoration and grounding, might also be part of the overall response. In addition, it's often important to have a group meeting when the kid returns after being away from the group, during which the kid can explain what happened, apologize to the group if he's willing, hear how his behavior made others feel, and get their okay to return.

In-House Suspension. An in-house suspension is issued for excessive tardiness, disruptive classroom behavior, acts of aggression, vandalism, and other dangerous or antisocial behaviors. A student given an in-house suspension is required to spend a predetermined amount of time in a non-stimulating location. As with an extended separation, the student should be allowed to sit in a comfortable chair, have appropriate snacks and lunch, and stretch her legs on a regular basis.

Because many kids who receive an in-house suspension need extra guidance, it is a good idea to structure it with this in mind. While a youngster is serving an in-house suspension, you may want to oversee the completion of her homework and also give her an assignment related to the targeted behavior, such as reading educational pamphlets or writing an essay on the negative outcomes of the misbehavior. You could also ask her to fill out processing forms about healthier actions and plans for doing better in the future.

In some instances, it is helpful to issue a restorative consequence, such as writing an apology or contributing to the school community by cleaning a designated area or by reading to younger students. Educational and therapeutic components added to an in-house suspension are likely to make a positive difference in the student's life and reduce the incidence of problematic behaviors.

Out-of-School Suspension. An out-of-school suspension is issued for bringing drugs or dangerous weapons to school, or otherwise infringing on the welfare of the student body. A child given this consequence is required to remain off school grounds for a specified time.

The decision to suspend a student is often motivated by lack of resources. For schools without sufficient personnel to conduct meaningful in-house suspensions, sending a child home for a number of days constitutes a best-possible response. The preferred approach, however, is to deal with troublesome behavior through in-house suspension. One reason is that kids who commit serious actions and are returned to their homes rarely receive the support and guidance they desperately need. Another reason is that many students with ongoing emotional and behavioral challenges experience out-of-school suspension as a rejection reminiscent of an earlier abandonment, which only reinforces their negative self-image. By contrast, a focus on in-house interventions and other remedial, preventative programs conveys the message "We care about you and don't want to send you away just because you've made a serious mistake. We want to deal with the issue here and help you make better decisions in the future."

EXPULSION. Expulsion is issued for a major violation that endangers the safety of a school community, such as selling drugs, bringing a gun to school, or performing repeated acts of violence. Many enlightened school officials are aware that students who are expelled for such infractions are in desperate need of help, and, rather than abandoning them to the streets, will arrange for them to get the help they need, such as enrollment in an alternative school or treatment setting.

Responding to Kids Who Refuse to Accept Consequences. Kids with emotional and behavioral challenges often have trouble accepting consequences. Some don't like being told what to do because they've repeatedly had power misused against them and are hypersensitive to being controlled in any way. Some come from homes where they are used to getting their way and must adjust to environments where child-guiders follow through with consequences for their own good. For others, temperament and neurological wiring can play a part. Remind yourself that there are no bad kids, just bad choices and bad luck, as you initiate the following responses.

EMPATHY, PRACTICE, WORDING. Child-guiders should expect their youngsters to challenge authority and have trouble accepting consequences. As a result, child-guiders should empathize with how the kids feel about being limited, explain why limits are important, and regularly help them practice how to accept consequences, as reflected in the following dialogue.

CHILD-GUIDER: John, if I ask you to take a break, what do you want to do—but what to you need to do?

JOHN: I want to fight it, but I need to take the break.

CHILD-GUIDER: Yes, my good man. After a bad choice…

JOHN: We can always make a good decision.

And when kids with oppositional tendencies accept limits, child-guiders should be quick to positively reinforce their actions.

CHILD-GUIDER: Great job, John! You chilled for a few minutes, and now you're cooking!

In addition to practicing the desired behaviors, child-guiders should be cognizant of the words they use with kids regarding oppositional issues since kids with emotional and behavioral challenges tend to respond better to less authoritative language and affect. For this reason, saying, "Could you please take a break. Thanks!" is preferable to "John, please take a break."

LIMIT-SETTING PROGRESSIONS. Ultimately, having a predictable limit-setting progression not only helps kids who struggle with accepting limits but also diffuses tension. With that in mind, every member of a setting, kids and adults alike, should know exactly what happens next if a child refuses to accept a consequence. In establishing a limit-setting progression, it is critical that child-guiders only issue consequences that have a high probability of being accepted by the child or group. In addition, child-guiders must be ready to adjust their limit-setting progressions based on the children's needs and capabilities.

Limit-setting progressions are also based on context. How a special educator responds to a child who is refusing a consequence might be very different from how a foster parent responds. Every child-guiding setting, from schools to homes to treatment settings, will therefore have different limit-setting progressions, all of which will be relatively effective. Following is a sample limit-setting progression that concludes with different contextual responses.

1. Helpful Advice

In explaining the limit-setting progression to kids, it's often helpful to say something like this: "We all make mistakes. And what are mistakes? A chance to learn something new. So if you make some bad decisions I'll try my best to turn you around by giving you helpful advice. I might warn you, have you state the rule you're breaking, give you one of my looks, or simply talk with you to see what's going on. If I try a few times to get you back on track and it doesn't work, then I'll probably give you a consequence since the behavior is getting worse and making everyone uncomfortable."

2. Logical Consequence

If kids do not respond to a child-guider's helpful advice, then it is usually time for a logical consequence and saying something like what I once said to a fourth-grade mainstream student: "Joanie, I've tried to help you get back on track. But you're still choosing to sit unsafely and make comments that bring down the group. Could you please take a break in the back. You can choose where you'd like to sit. Thanks."

3. Final Warning

If a child refuses to accept a consequence, there should be one final warning: "Joanie, I'll give you a minute to get back there. Make a good choice." The child-guider should then walk away and let the child save face. It's critical for child-guiders to avoid eyeballing kids at this stage in the limit-setting progression so that they may maintain dignity.

If after the predetermined time period the child still refuses to accept the consequence, then the child-guider should return and count: "Joanie, I've asked you to take a break in the back. Three, two, one…"

4. Contextual Response

If the child continues refusing to accept the consequence, then a contextual response must be given, such as the following.

IN A SCHOOL SETTING

"Joanie, could you please head to the office. You haven't been making good choices and have refused to deal with this in class. Thanks."

IN AN OUT-OF-HOME PLACEMENT SETTING

"Joanie, you know how it works: if you refuse to take the break, you won't earn your points for this period. I know you've been working hard to get some new privileges."

IN A FOSTER HOME

"Joanie, you know the house rule: if you refuse a consequence, I'll need to ground you to the house until you take care of it. C'mon, make the right choice. Thanks."

"Joanie, you know the house rule: no television until you get it done." (*Note:* The foster parent isn't taking TV away as a punishment but restricting TV watching until the consequence is served.)

IN AN AFTERSCHOOL SETTING

"Joanie, you know the rule: if you refuse the break, we'll need to talk with your parents when they pick you up."

In certain cases, the following response can be given to a kid who is refusing to accept a consequence: "Hey this isn't me against you. We're on the same side. But you made a bad choice, and I asked you to take a break. If you refuse, I'm not going to get into a battle with you. You know how it works. When a kid refuses, he loses some of his trust, which means he's not going to be at the top of the list when we are choosing kids to do things that require trust. It's your call." This kind of response tells kids that the refusal to accept a consequence affects trust and their future privileges.

Despite the importance of limit setting, it should not exacerbate already difficult situations. For kids with serious emotional and cognitive challenges, a good deal of their behavior should be ignored or sensitively addressed until the kids have developed good enough self-management skills to function in a world that generally uses motivational approaches—rewards and consequences—to manage people. Remember, the consequence for many kids with acute behavioral challenges is being sent to a residential program.

Third Stage: Physical Management

If a kid moves through the limit-setting stages and gets to a point where he is hurting himself or others, then physical management is often required. There have been many positive developments in physical management practices over the past twenty years. Universal guidelines for why, when, and how to physically intervene with kids appear to have now been established in almost every setting, state, and province that guides children. No longer can child-guiders physically hold or escort agitated children if they are destroying property or refusing to move—behaviors that resulted in many injuries to staff and children in the past. It has now become standard procedure to wait it out with kids who refuse to move. In group settings, if a child is being disruptive and physically threatening, child-guiders generally ask all the other kids to leave in order to help de-escalate the child who is struggling. Child-guiders should now only physically hold children if they are hurting themselves or others.

Restraint techniques have also improved, with most now requiring two or more people to hold a child, resulting in far fewer injuries. And most importantly, current restraint techniques often are applied while the kids remain standing. Since many kids who require physical restraint have been sexually abused, holding them while they are prone on a floor has the potential to retraumatize them.

Another development is that child-guiders who work in settings where physical management of kids still occurs are now more closely scrutinized, and every decision they make must be explained to the proper authorities;

in some states, improper restraint can result in a child-guider being arrested. Increased scrutiny is a positive development. I have visited a number of residential settings that videotape their daily interactions and have observed physical restraints that were unnecessary, prompted by child-guiders who failed to use proper de-escalation strategies. By the same token, progress in this area has raised the anxiety levels of many child-guiders. Knowing that they are under a microscope, some child-guiders wait too long to physically intervene or, in other cases, act too quickly. Fear, as well as other emotions such as anger, can often trigger reactive responses by a child-guider. But the fear factor is greatly reduced when settings that guide kids with serious emotional and behavioral challenges provide its workers with proper adult support. Child-guiding settings must continually assess the kids and staffing levels to ensure that child-guiders are well equipped to deal with the kids they serve.

When difficult emotions arise, to avert a physical encounter it is essential for child-guiders to employ their observing ego. It should always be activated any time a child-guider becomes engaged in an emotionally loaded situation such as the following.

KID: You're a fag. Why don't you drop dead?

ADULT'S OBSERVING EGO: This kid is really provoking you. You hate it when he calls you a fag. But that's your issue, not his. Don't overreact. Stay cool and look disinterested.

ADULT [CALMLY]: Steve, I'm worried about you, man. This has been a tough day. Let me know when you're ready to talk.

KID: Fuck you, asshole. I'm not gonna talk. Why don't you come over, and I'll give you my fist.

ADULT'S OBSERVING EGO: You're getting angrier. Relax—he doesn't really mean what he's saying. He's had a tough day and a tough life. Think about something else. Remember, it's an injury, and it will heal; respond instead of react. Distance yourself from him and his words. He can't keep this up much longer; he'll eventually run out of steam. Wait him out.

KID: You're a snot-nosed wimp.

ADULT'S OBSERVING EGO: Okay, he's got a point there. That's it…let the humor flow. Use the Force, Luke.

KID: What do I need to do to get out of this room and back to the kids?

ADULT'S OBSERVING EGO: Bingo!

ADULT: We need to talk about what happened outside, and create a plan for getting you back on track.

KID: I'm gonna knock over this table and punch you out!

ADULT'S OBSERVING EGO: You're scared. That's okay. Breathe. Don't look scared. Stay calm. Wait for others to arrive if you think he needs physical assistance.

ADULT: You seem pretty darn upset, Carl. Who can blame you?

KID [LIFTING THE TABLE]: Fuck you, asshole!

ADULT: Ah, man, that's the housekeeper's favorite table. She just painted it.

KID: Screw her!

The adult takes a step back, sits, and picks up a nearby newspaper, pretending to read it. He's sending a message to the kid that he's not that worried about what's going on, although he's acting. The kid eventually sits down and processes with the staff member.

Some child-guiding programs have a no-restraint policy. They will discharge a child who requires physical management. Although I can understand why programs institute such a policy, it seems ill-advised. To discharge a child who has been making progress after she hears tragic news from her social worker, prompting physical management, seems extremely unfair.

Settings that establish a positive, strength-based culture experience major reductions in the need for physical restraint. However, despite child-guiders' best efforts, some kids continue to require physical restraint. When physical restraint is done properly, it can be a brick in the child's road to recovery. Some kids actually want to be restrained because they haven't yet learned to ask for what they really need, such as a hug, or a better understanding of why they were so abused.

My advice to child-guiders who work with kids with serious emotional and behavioral challenges is the following:

- Know your craft. Almost every school and out-of-home placement in the child-guiding universe requires its staff members to be certified in this area by an established physical management and de-escalation program. Numerous programs teach child-guiders how to de-escalate kids and how and when to physically intervene, if necessary.

- Feel blessed to hold a position that helps society's most vulnerable children. Heed the sage words of Rachel Naomi Remen, author of *My Grandfather's Blessings*, who implores doctors working with cancer patients not to focus on the end result (the patient's probable death) but on the doing, to feeling blessed to be able to nurture and guide people when they are so vulnerable.[9]

After factoring in everything facing child-guiders who work with kids with serious emotional and behavioral issues, I consider them heroes who put their safety and reputations on the line every day, often for little pay and recognition. Feeling particularly moved one day, I wrote the following open letter to child-guiders:

Screw up and you hear about it. Gently and expertly de-escalate a youth who is threatening to throw a chair at your head and there's no guarantee you'll get the pat on the back you richly deserve. Yet, you folks show up every day and truly make a difference, and for that I thank and salute you.

Fourth Stage: Processing

If a child requires physical restraint, or is issued a more serious consequence, afterward it is essential for the child to process the entire incident with the child-guider—the factors leading up to it, the incident itself, and reentry plans. Processing gives kids the opportunity to properly express themselves and, most importantly, learn ways to use their strengths and problem-solving skills more effectively.

Prior to a processing session a child-guider conducts a pre-talk routine incorporating factors that he has determined will enhance a positive connection. Then during the session, the child-guider uses many of the interventions and techniques described in earlier chapters.

Processing itself can take many forms. Low-level misbehaviors, such as rudeness or excessive silliness, that have warranted a consequence might require only a brief period of processing, while serious misconduct, such as running away or acts of aggression, should be followed by more extended processing. During this stage, child-guiders explore with kids possible underlying issues that may have influenced the misbehavior, clarify what occurred, discuss alternative responses and possible modifications that would enhance functioning, and resolve interpersonal tensions that may have led to the incident.

Contextual Considerations. Behavioral incidents can be processed in any number of ways, depending on the context of the situation. To decide on the most effective approach in any instance, reflect on the following key factors.

THE SEVERITY OF THE ACTION. Following a short break for a minor misbehavior, a simple statement may suffice, such as "Jim, are you ready to rejoin the group? Let's save the silly jokes for recess. Thanks." After more serious actions and consequences, a longer and more comprehensive processing session is needed. For example, a special education student who has punched a classmate and has been sitting in the quiet room for half an hour requires a more profound level of engagement.

Nature of Your Relationship with the Child. Child-guiders must process behavioral incidents with kids they are not fond of in the same manner they would with the kids they enjoy being around, behavior that is called countertransference in the clinical world. As mentioned in chapter 11, child-guiders are like pies and every kid deserves an equal slice, a metaphor particularly poignant when it comes to processing.

Time Availability. The ideal time to process a behavioral incident is right after it has occurred, while the events and motivations are easy to recall. Immediate processing, however, is sometimes difficult in a busy foster home, shorthanded classroom, activity-driven summer program, or understaffed residential facility. If it is not feasible to process an incident immediately, make a plan to talk at a later time and apologize for the delay, letting him know he is important to you. As one seventh-grade teacher explained to a student who had just completed a ten-minute break, "Roland, I'm sorry I can't talk right now. Tomorrow we'll have a long talk after class. You are important to me."

Initial Assessment: Is the Kid Ready to Talk? Once you have factored in contextual considerations and are ready to process with a child, be sure he is ready to talk with you. Under no circumstances should kids be forced to talk when they are not ready to.

Years ago I came across a young man who had resided at my previous residential program. After leaving us, his behavior had regressed, and he was sent to a program in the Midwest with a national reputation. I had heard through the grapevine that they had subsequently kicked him out.

"Billy, how's it going?" I asked.

"Okay," he replied.

"So those bums discharged you, eh?" I asked.

"Charlie, I was doing great at their program. I was taking computer classes, and was all set to graduate with skills that would have landed me a super job," he explained. "Then one day my girlfriend called and broke up with me over the phone. I was devastated. I ran to my room, slammed the door shut, and sat on my bed in a daze. One of the staff came in and asked what was going on. I told him I didn't want to talk. But he wouldn't listen. He said, 'You know how we do things here. You've got to talk when you're upset.' I told him to fuck off. I wasn't ready to talk. He then got right in my face and said I had to open up to him. I was so pissed that I punched him on his nose. I was discharged the next day, and now I'm driving a truck sixty hours a week and barely see my family."

Sometimes a child will appear calm but refuse to talk or take responsibility for his actions. Such a child is best approached in a low-key manner and engaged through supportive comments and repeating statements. If he remains unwilling to talk but seems to have regained his composure, it's best to allow him to return to the group or home situation; however, step up his supervision until he is ready to process, explaining: "I'm sorry you won't talk with me, because this makes it harder to know how you're feeling and to discuss what happened. I really want to hear your side of the situation, but because of your silence I'm going to keep you close to me for the next few hours. (proximity manipulation) If and when you are ready to open up a bit, we'll talk—then you'll be freer to move around. It's up to you."

The Seven Steps of Processing. Most kids make good use of processing because, when properly conducted, processing invites them to safely explore a difficult interaction, examine underlying issues and feelings, and use the incident to find better ways of solving problems. Interwoven into the processing of an intervention are hellos and good-byes, helping kids say good-bye to the troubling incident and a good hello as they return for a fresh start. If serious behaviors are not properly processed, a child might feel anxious about getting back into the normal flow of things, as she will not be sure how the people involved in her episode feel about what happened: "Is Mr. Brison still mad at me? Does he think I'm a jerk for what happened?" "Are the kids going to jump down my back because I broke the Xbox?"

Kid-to-kid processing is just as important. If two kids got into a fight, they need to process the incident before returning to the group for a fresh start.

Following are seven steps that can be taken to effectively process problematic actions.

STEP #1: CLARIFYING THE INCIDENT. Exploring what occurred and why from the child's perspective is a highly effective way to start a processing conversation. Asking, "What happened?" or "What was that all about?" encourages the child to tell you her version of the episode and the factors that caused her breach of conduct. At this point it is important to listen carefully and empathetically, and avoid judging the child or her actions.

CHILD-GUIDER: No wonder you got mad. That would tick off a lot of people. Thanks for sharing the problem with me.

By contrast, you would not want to start off by asking, "Why did I send you to the break area?" or "What did you do wrong?" Such openers can prompt a sensitive and vulnerable child to think she is being treated unfairly, since the implication is that she alone is responsible for the problem. A youngster who has taken a brief break for a minor incident is apt to be less upset by such a direct approach, although she, too, would probably prefer the nonjudgmental question "What happened?"

STEP #2: CHILD-GUIDER OWNERSHIP. After empathically listening to the child's version, it's often helpful for the adult to admit to any mistakes he might have made.

CHILD-GUIDER: So I hear you say that I got to loud and that bothered you. I think you're right. I'm sorry. I'll work on that.

It is crucial for child-guiders to model humility. Kids have a hard time trusting adults who struggle with admitting their own mistakes.

Step #3: Exploring Underlying Issues. Once a child has relayed her version of what occurred and the child-guider has told his side and admitted to any mistakes, it is often helpful to explore factors that may have precipitated the behavior.

CHILD-GUIDER: Man, you really blew over a seemingly minor issue. Could something else be bothering you?

A lot of acting out is displacement, kids placing on child-guiders feelings that they harbor toward the significant people in their lives. Thus processing is often a time to get at a child's longstanding, pent-up issues.

CHILD-GUIDER: You were pretty mad at me today for letting you down. And you've been getting pretty ticked off at your teachers for also failing to meet your needs. Anyone you're mad at for letting you down?

CHILD: My fucking mother said she'd get me out of this hellhole by now. She never follows through with anything. I hate her.

Always, child-guiders must be very careful about interpreting behavior. It can rob a child of her defenses and, in many cases, be inaccurate.

CHILD-GUIDER: I think you're pretty upset because your dad lost his job!

CHILD: Fuck you! You don't know what the hell you're talking about!

On the other hand, gentle nudges are okay.

CHILD-GUIDER: What's up? Anything bugging you?

In addition, many of the verbal interventions presented in earlier chapters may be used at this time. The millimeter acknowledgment, for example, can be highly effective.

CHILD-GUIDER: Is there a one percent chance that some of today's actions has something to do with your dad's job? I don't know.

When exploring underlying issues, it's best to develop meaningful and trusting relationships with the kids and let their inner growth unfold in time.

STEP #4: SENSITIVELY PROVIDING THE CHILD-GUIDER'S VIEW OF WHAT TRANSPIRED. At this point in the processing, the facts as the child-guider sees them should be presented.

CHILD-GUIDER: You had a right to be angry, but it seems a bad choice to knock over the desk. Good kids sometimes make bad decisions. I'm just not a hundred percent sure it fell over by accident (the kid's version). Could I be one percent right about this? (millimeter acknowledgment)

If the child still refuses to accept responsibility, the child-guider could add something like the following.

CHILD-GUIDER: I'm sorry we can't come to an agreement about what happened right now. But this is how I saw it, and we need to discuss the best way to deal with it and the consequences.

STEP #5: JOINTLY DETERMINING ADDITIONAL CONSEQUENCES, IF MERITED. During this part of the processing, kids should be empowered to come up with appropriate consequences for their actions, if warranted.

COUNSELOR: This has been a good talk, Jared. I'm proud of you. So what should we do?

JARED: I don't usually poke holes in walls. Like I said, my girlfriend dumped me this afternoon, and I went crazy. How about I help fix the walls and am grounded for a few days?

COUNSELOR: I think that makes sense. Jared, girls can drive you nuts. We need to talk more about this!

STEP #6: REVIEWING ALTERNATIVE ACTIONS. As processing moves into this arena, it becomes a learning experience in self-management. Discussing alternatives to the problem behavior helps children make better decisions in the future. Child-guiders often ask kids to name the tools they could have used to better deal with the problems they were struggling with.

STEP #7: MAKING A PLAN FOR THE FUTURE. Creating a strategy for coping with upcoming events ideally gives the child a sense that things can improve.

> TEACHER: Okay, Kiel, thanks for sharing all that with me. So what's the plan? What do you need to do to get back on track? (short-term expectation)
>
> KIEL: I need to go to my seat and rewrite the vocabulary words. After that I can spend some time on the computer.
>
> TEACHER: And what's our plan to prevent the same problem from occurring again? (long-term expectation)
>
> KIEL: To not rush while I'm writing.
>
> TEACHER: Step after step…
>
> KIEL: That's the prep.
>
> TEACHER: No need to groan…
>
> KIEL: I can do this on my own.
>
> TEACHER: I'm going to start a temporary sticker chart to show when you've taken your time and correctly completed your writing assignments. I'm also going to send you home with a new notebook you can use for practice. I think we have a pretty good plan, don't you?
>
> KIEL: Yeah.

Fifth Stage: Reintegration

Reintegration, the final stage of the limit-setting continuum, prepares the child to return to the living situation via a brief preview of pertinent logistics: where to go, what to do, who to report to, and most importantly, how to function more appropriately. After securing a guarantee of the child's readiness and conducting the preview, it may be advantageous to reaffirm any plans she made during the processing stage.

ADULT: Okay, Akil, are you ready to return and get along with people in a better way?

AKIL: Yup.

ADULT: That's great. And what did we agree you need to do?

AKIL: I need to go back to the kitchen and finish my chore. Afterward, Mr. Kennedy and I will work on my class assignments.

ADULT: All right, head on back. That was a good talk we had. And remember, next time you get mad what are you going to try to do?

AKIL: Take a few deep breaths, count to five, and think about what will happen if I screw up.

ADULT: See you tomorrow.

Overall, relationship-based limit setting, while requiring understanding and mastery, offers a multitude of ways to make children feel safe and cared for, help them learn how to take responsibility for their behavior, and encourage them to develop in more positive ways for future success and well-being.

*** Reality Check ***

Limit setting is certainly influential in shaping effective child-guiding. However, a child's behavior does not occur in a vacuum; rather, it takes place in a particular context. Because this is so, the same behavior may call for a myriad of different limit-setting interventions, depending on the precipitating circumstances. For example, a youth might swear either because a brick just fell on his foot or because he is angry at his foster mother or upset that

Figure 18–10
The Limit-Setting Continuum

SUPPORTIVE INTERVENTIONS

Establishing Core Rules	Nonverbal Cues
Verbal Cues, Reminders, and Warnings	Strength-Based Verbal Interventions
Distraction and Redirection	Vicarious Reinforcement of Another Child
Changing Course	
Voluntary Move	Peer Support
Breaks	A Class, Group, or Family Meeting
Humor	

LOGICAL CONSEQUENCES

Redoing	Directed Chat
Restorative Action/Reparation	Removal of Attention
Restriction	Exaggerated Kindness
Removal of Troublesome Objects	Break
	Extended Separation
Proximity Manipulation	In-House Suspension
Grounding	Expulsion

PHYSICAL MANAGEMENT

PROCESSING

REINTEGRATION

his mother canceled a visit. Each situation requires a unique response.

With this mind, when implementing limit-setting interventions be sure to always consider the larger picture. Use the information provided in this chapter and the cues outlined in figure 18–10 as handrails to help guide your thinking; but let your knowledge of the children you work with and the context in which misbehavior arises determine the interventions you actually apply.

— CHAPTER 19 —

The Role of Incentives in Motivating Kids with Emotional and Behavioral Challenges

THERE IS CONSIDERABLE DEBATE about the use of incentives, or extrinsic motivation, to improve functioning in children and youth. Alfie Kohn, a prominent critic of standard behavioral practices such as rewards and consequences, writes in an article titled "Beyond Discipline":

> Even when children are "successfully" reinforced or consequenced into compliance, they will feel no commitment to what they are doing, no deep understanding of the act and its rationale, no sense of themselves as the kind of people who would want to act this way in the future.... To help students become ethical people, as opposed to people who merely do what they are told, we cannot merely tell them what to do. We have to help them figure out—for themselves with each other—how one ought to act. That's why dropping the tools of traditional discipline, like rewards and consequences, is only the beginning. It's even more crucial that we overcome a preoccupation with getting compliance and instead involve students in devising and justifying ethical principles.[1]

Likewise, Daniel Pink, the author of *Drive*, disputes the power of extrinsic motivation to improve the functioning of individuals, stating, "The secret to performance and satisfaction—at work, at school, and at home is the deeply human need to direct our own lives, to learn and create new things, and to better ourselves and our world." Pink further notes, "Rewards can deliver a short-term boost—just as a jolt of caffeine can keep you cranking for a few more hours. But the effect wears off—and worse, can reduce a person's longer term motivation to continue the project."[2]

The Benefits of Extrinsic Motivation for At-Risk Kids

There is no question that in almost every situation intrinsic rather than extrinsic motivation is the preferred way to guide children. We want kids to behave well and make good choices because it feels right to do so, not to earn a reward or avoid a consequence. And indeed, most of this book is devoted to offering tools and insights that improve lives from the inside out. However, Kohn's and Pink's critiques of extrinsic motivation are clearly written with "typical" children in mind, not those with emotional and behavioral challenges. When it comes to guiding such kids, the use of rewards and consequences not only is warranted but can at times be highly beneficial.

Although at-risk kids are often labeled unmotivated, in reality it is often fear of failing or being ashamed or embarrassed, as well as lack of skills and confidence, that holds them back. The good news is that these kids can sometimes break through their walls of fear and lack of self-confidence when enticed with incentives. And once they are on the other side of the walls they rarely go back. It is important to note, however, that neurologically impaired kids who are cognitively inflexible, such as those on the autism spectrum, as discussed in chapter 6, generally require the adults in their lives to accommodate their needs, such as creating user-friendly environments, in order to reduce pressure and anxiety, an intercession that ultimately enhances skill development and improved functioning; rewards and consequences often have a minimal effect on their mode of relating. But for cautious at-risk kids who do not suffer from significant neurological challenges a well-designed incentive plan can be transformative.

Kids who have suffered trauma overuse their survival brains and are consumed 24/7 with staying safe and not being exposed to further hurts. This dominance of the survival brain is like a herd of terrified elephants formed in a tight circle protecting their young in the middle, too afraid to venture into the higher regions of the jungle to enhance their lives. Similarly, due to fear and uncertainty, at-risk kids are often unable to access the higher regions of the brain that allow for more complex thought processing and happiness.

However, if kids stuck in their own elephant circle are motivated to step outside of it by incentives, once they are out and doing well they will rarely want to retreat to their cautious ways of functioning again. For example, I once promised Rick, a middle-school student who was skipping school four days a week, a pizza on Friday if he'd skip school only three times the following week. He skipped three, got the pizza, and was soon coming every day.

Daniel Willingham, author of *Why Don't Students Like School?*[3] in countering some of Kohn's assumptions, writes in an Encyclopedia Britannica blog, "Rewards can reduce motivation, but only when motivation was somewhat high to start with. If the student is unmotivated to perform some task, rewarding him will not hurt his motivation."[4] Since Rick was at rock bottom, offering a reward wasn't going to damage his psyche further. In fact, the reward and the ancillary work we did changed his life.

Years ago when I was having lunch with a physician who specialized in treating patients suffering from obesity, our conversation shifted to the use of incentives, and she said: "They work. We were treating twenty-five obese patients. Each desperately needed to start exercising. We had a treadmill, but none of them would get on. They were too afraid. We told each participant that if they got on for just one minute, they'd receive twenty-five dollars. Every one of them got on and ninety percent walked for thirty minutes."

Still, this doesn't mean child-guiders should always use incentives to motivate change. Incentives are tools, and through experience and wisdom child-guiders learn when to best utilize them. Clearly, the best way to reduce problem behavior is to create positive, strength-based environments that motivate kids to change from the inside out and to positively reinforce the desired behaviors. And since behavior is a message, child-guiders should always explore the root causes of behaviors and make necessary environmental changes.

In my own work with at-risk kids, I use far fewer incentive plans now than earlier in my career. Many of the tools described in these chapters do the job. But when all else fails and at-risk kids continue to struggle, a well-designed incentive plan can become a vital means for helping them cross their barriers of fear and venture into more enjoyable territories where help, achievement, and deeper relationships can be found.

Many years ago I toured a state-of-the-art residential program in Evergreen, Colorado, called Forest Heights Lodge. Some of their staff had attended my training. When Jody Olson, the assistant director, was showing me around, I asked him, "Do you use incentive programs with your kids?" He responded, "Oh yeah, if a kid needs one, we'll whip one up." I never forgot his words, because they echo my own thoughts about the use of incentives with at-risk kids as a boost to cross a barrier.

Months later when I questioned him further, he added this elegantly humane perspective:

> Incentives are indeed short term and we use them to physically demonstrate care to kids who are working toward internalizing the reality that the things they get are attached to the people who care enough to give them. It's always that people are more important than things. Things are tangible demonstrations of care.[5]

Over the years, I've successfully used a short-term incentive system with kids and found that, while I couldn't agree more with Daniel Pink, who concluded that rewards can deliver only a short-term boost, sometimes that is all a cautious kid needs. Often, as a kid progresses, he'll say to me, "Mr. A, I don't need the plan anymore." The greatest reward for an at-risk kid is to feel like a normal, productive kid, a reality reinforced for me by a troubled girl named Ophelia.

Years ago when I was working as a part-time behavior consultant at a large suburban school system in the Northeast, Ophelia, who had spent most of third grade in a self-contained stabilization class, was returned to her elementary school at the start of fourth grade with an aide, added supports, and appointments scheduled with me once or twice a week. For the first two months, she did well. During our sessions, we practiced the desired behaviors, played a lot of card games, used metaphors and recited self-talk ("Let it go, Joe. Just stay cool, no need to blow!"), and I positively reinforced her good decisions. But in early November her behavior began to regress. By December she was out of control. A few days before the holiday break, an emergency meeting was held to discuss her situation. The special education director, my boss, who had always been a big proponent of my work, attended. Midway through the meeting she looked at me and said, "You failed with this kid." My vacation was ruined. I couldn't stop thinking about Ophelia and how I had failed her. I had to do something, so I headed to Toys"R"Us.

On the first day back after vacation, I brought Ophelia into my office and showed her $250 worth of Bratz girl dolls and accessories, which she loved. We then created an incentive system that entailed her receiving them for agreeing to see the specialists she was refusing to meet, demonstrating improved behavior and gradually increasing her academic output. "Little changes often ripple into big solutions," I told myself.

Over a period of weeks, Ophelia resumed seeing the specialists, her behavior improved, and she felt increasingly comfortable tackling her academics. By June the Ophelia train was chugging along at a good speed, and she was feeling proud and happy. We had a warm final session, and I left school thinking, "I have failed with some kids—but not this one!"

The following September, on the first day of school, I anxiously approached Ophelia's class, thinking, "Am I going to have to spend a boatload of money on this kid again?" But Ophelia looked me in the eyes and said, "I don't need the dolls this year, Mr. A. I'm okay." And she proceeded to sail gloriously through the year.

From this experience I learned how vital it is for at-risk kids to feel normal and productive. I also learned that what propels kids forward is not only the incentive offered but the interaction and the aftereffects, both of which make incentives a valuable tool in child-guiding.

An important consideration when using incentives is how choice of words can either inspire or deflate children. In Shawn Achor's book *The Happiness Advantage,* he describes how words can have "a powerful effect on end results."[6] In recent years when discussing incentive plans with kids, I have stopped using the word *reward*, now regarding it as something to be offered for catching a crook, not for behaving better in a home, out-of-home placement, or school. Instead, I now use the word *celebrate,* which connotes a sense of warmth and connection. When kids start making better choices, an occasional celebration is certainly warranted.

Another benefit to using *celebrate* is the flexibility it offers. If a kid is promised a reward for earning a specified number of points by the end of the week but realizes on Thursday morning that he can't possibly earn that many points, he may lose his motivation to behave well; conversely, if on Thursday he realizes he has already earned enough points for his reward on Friday, he might exert less effort. But placing a child on an incentive plan, such as a daily point chart, and telling him that if he works hard, at the end of the week there could be a celebration gives the child-guider more opportunities to reinforce good effort even if the week has some ups and downs.

The child-guider could introduce the plan by saying something like, "Carlos, when I come in on Friday, I'll check your chart and talk with your teacher. If it looks like you've been trying real hard, we'll celebrate, buddy." Then, even if Carlos ends up having a rough day on Tuesday there could be a celebration on Friday because from a big picture, strength-based perspective, he accomplished a lot during the week and moved forward. By not adding up the points and by using the word *celebrate*, we provide a better path to higher functioning and happiness for these kids.

Creating and Implementing a Short-Term Incentive Plan

A short-term incentive plan is developed in collaboration with a child or group, and designed to be utilized for a specified time. Following are some key principles for establishing an effective incentive plan.

1. Reward improvement.

Because challenging behavior often results from years of psychological distress and its neurological ramifications, change is most often a slow, step-by-step process. Expectations that are too high at the outset are apt to dissuade the child or group from investing in an incentive plan. However, rewarding improvement offers kids opportunities to quickly enjoy success and is likely to inspire continued improvement. A good guideline is to offer rewards that a child or group has an 80 percent chance of achieving immediately, in keeping with the principle that little changes often ripple out into big solutions. I once worked with a fifth-grade student who had serious mental health issues, was on multiple medications, and hadn't picked up a book in over a year. I offered him a Big Mac if he'd read me one sentence from any book in the library. He read me one; I got him the Big Mac; and he was singing in the choir by the end of the year, a transformed young man.

2. Rate and celebrate serious behaviors more frequently; as behaviors improve, decrease the frequency of rating and celebrating.

Often a short-term incentive plan that rates out-of-control kids at brief intervals, such as every five minutes, and pays them off every half hour, helps child-guiders regain control of the group. I recall one third grader who was running through the hallways, refusing to do any work, and having tantrums throughout the day. We set up an incentive plan that issued him a check every five minutes for meeting his academic and behavioral expectations. If he earned two checks in a row, he was allowed to celebrate by using the computer for five minutes. Within a month, his behavior had stabilized, and we were able to implement a less-stringent motivational plan along with a regimen of self-management skills.

3. Use the best possible incentives and enticing mediums of exchange.

When deciding on the proper incentive, it's best to ask the children or group how they would like to celebrate some noteworthy corrective achievement, all the while preparing a number of options. Although at-risk kids should be afforded ample unconditional time with child-guiders and peers, in many instances the most desirable and corrective incentive option is additional time with an adult who can nurture the child and reinforce the good decisions they have been making. For example, a second-grade student who earns a bunch of stickers in a week for making better choices could trade them in for thirty minutes of one-on-one sports, game, or art time with the teacher's aide or the guidance counselor; if the student has trouble making and sustaining friendships, she could be offered an added bonus of inviting a friend to join them. An angry, defiant, or withdrawn child could be offered the chance to earn even more one-on-one time with an adult. Such extended interactions might boost her self-confidence, help reveal her underlying issues, and accelerate other gains.

The second most desirable incentive option is usually nonmaterial, such as a trip, additional free or recreational time, a later bedtime, extra computer time, more time to play video games, a welcome job, an invitation to choose music to be played for a period of time, or the chance to assist another group, class, or staff member. A group or class might enjoy a no-homework day, additional recess time, a field trip, or watching a video or YouTube, with popcorn.

In lieu of nonmaterial incentives, a material reward could be offered, such as school supplies, food (a granola bar, apple, trail mix, chips, candy, soda, or juice), a comic or crossword-puzzle book, a small action figure, money, DVDs, bus passes, iTunes and other gift certificates, books, or cards. Whenever possible, material rewards should be not only enticing but also healthy and wholesome. Celebrating a good week over lunch together with a kid or group is a powerful relationship-enhancing incentive that is often cherished by all participants. This has been one of my favorite and most successful ways of reinforcing movement in the right direction. Giving a kid the option to invite a friend or two to celebrate is extremely motivating. At times, these friends become cheerleaders for the kid!

Interestingly, what often motivates children up to age seven to improve their behavior is not so much a reward as the *medium of exchange*—the sticker, token, or ticket the child earns and trades in for the reward. And the more visually interesting the medium of exchange is, the more likely it is to inspire behavioral change.

An enticing medium of exchange for kids up to age twelve is fake money, especially with their image on it. In a fourth-grade class I was assisting, a challenging student named Billy earned fake dollar bills with his picture in the place of George Washington's; the teacher had taken a picture of Billy, cut it into an oval, taped it to the center of a dollar bill, then photocopied it multiple times. Hence Billy, by doing well, earned "Billy dollars," which he could trade in for a designated reward. One week the exchange rate was ten Billy dollars for ten minutes of extra computer time; the following week Billy was permitted to use his dollars to select from a menu of rewards. Likewise, a foster parent I know superimposes her own face onto dollar bills, allowing her two foster children to earn "Dotty dollars." From time to time, when confronted with a kid who is struggling, I take out my wallet, empty it, give it to him, and say, "Here's something to collect your dollars."

Similarly, years ago when asked to help a fourth grader with Asperger's syndrome who refused to practice skills he was learning in his social group, I gave him the option of earning a "William dollar" every time he practiced a technique. He so loved earning and collecting the William dollars that he refused to trade them in and made outstanding social progress over the course of the year. Just before the school year ended, I had an eighty-dollar plaque designed for him, designating him as the city's grand champion point earner for the year, which he loved.

For older kids, a good medium of exchange is often a ticket, suggesting that learning is a ticket to a good life. Or sometimes a silly or funny incentive will do the trick. A few years ago I watched a televised story of Ron Clark, an extraordinary teacher who, early in his career, taught at an inner-city elementary school where his students at first refused to work causing him to get creative. One day he entered the classroom with dozens of small milk cartons and told the kids that if they answered one of his questions he'd drink an entire carton. It worked. He drank carton after carton and started looking pretty sick, but he had engaged them, and they started working harder.[7] I've also heard of a teacher who sings a kid's favorite song each time she achieves a new goal.

4. Gradually raise expectations in response to improved behavior.

Gradually raising expectations in response to improved behavior enables kids to enjoy the success they've achieved without experiencing undue stress regarding future expectations. For example, if a teen is skipping school three times a week and receives an incentive for skipping only two times the next week, it celebrates her improvement. After keeping the incentive plan the same for a few more weeks to let her get used to coming to school more often, the child-guider may ask her to only skip once a week to receive the incentive. Weaning a child off an incentive plan slowly is often critical to success.

5. Keep the plan simple and easy to administer.

Keeping the plan simple and easy to administer involves taking into account the time available for record keeping and the resources available for granting the incentives. For example, if a child-guider has a busy schedule and is in charge of a large group of children, it might be hard to record a youngster's behavior every hour. A scaled-down plan that is administered well accomplishes more than a comprehensive one that is either carried out inconsistently or too complicated to remember.

6. Follow through, and make plans time limited.

The more committed a child-guider is to carrying out the plan, the more apt the child will be to invest in it and to trust the adult. If the child-guider forgets once to fill in a child's points or to pass out stickers with enthusiasm, she may lose interest. Occasionally, a youngster may test a child-guider's willingness to follow through by misbehaving just before receiving her incentive. In such instances, it is best to set an appropriate limit before following up with the incentive. If, for example, a child has earned a special trip to a local arcade but started a fight with her brother ten minutes before departure time, you could say, "You've earned a nice celebration. But I'm not comfortable taking you to the arcade given some of the choices you've been making. We'll set up a new time for the trip tomorrow."

Often a child or group will do well initially but later regress, at which point the child-guider truly needs to stick to the plan. The kids may be testing to see if the child-guider will revert to her old ways or they might be uncomfortable with their new mode of relating and the higher expectations that have been placed on them. Making an incentive plan time limited helps youth and child-guider alike apply the amount of energy needed to determine whether the plan is helping.

7. Discuss why children did or did not earn designated incentives.

To help reinforce the learning experience, child-guiders should make use of the strategic verbal interventions highlighted in chapter 17 to identify why incentives were or were not earned. Such discussions help fulfill the goals of incentive processing, which are to encourage a child to take responsibility for her positive as well as negative actions, to explore alternative behaviors, and to uncover the origins of her misconduct.

8. Award incentives as soon after assessment meetings as possible.

The consistent awarding of incentives provides structure and security. For maximum effectiveness, child-guiders should arrange for the processing and celebrating to take place as soon after their behavioral assessment as possible. For example, a foster child who earns points for afternoon behavior will benefit most from a 5:00 p.m. awarding of incentives. The longer the wait between behavioral assessment and provision of rewards, the less meaningful the plan will be.

9. Be flexible.

Be prepared to change the medium of exchange and rewards as needed to keep the plan effective and the children interested.

10. Create easy-to-read, kid-friendly inspirational behavior charts.

Young children usually respond well to colorful charts filled with interesting stickers or artwork. Older ones tend to prefer rather bland documents marked with points, checks, or other ordinary-looking graphics. There are a myriad of ways to construct a behavior chart. One popular approach is to draw a grid with boxes large enough to accommodate stickers, stars, tokens, chips, imitation gold coins, points, checks, or whatever the medium of exchange is. It is often a good idea to end with a column for total incentives earned and to spell out beneath the grid the target goal and terms of the plan.

A teacher I worked with recently helped a student named Joel, who frequently shut down during class, get on track by using the chart illustrated in figure 19–1. This kid-friendly chart contains trains, raps, pictures, and a growth mindset reminder: "The harder I try, the higher I fly." Whenever Joel went a good period of time without shutting down and was open to doing his work step by step, the teacher put a sticker in the appropriate box. During sessions and class, we all helped Joel learn new skills, practice the desired behaviors, alter his self-defeating mindset, and increase his confidence. He and I celebrated when he had collected a bunch of stickers. He finished the year working hard and feeling proud of himself.

For a child who is somewhat stuck and pessimistic about changing her ways or acquiring new skills, consider drafting a "Road to" chart. Such a chart proved to be a perfect catalyst for Jenn, a bright student with a high IQ who entered her third-grade inclusion class unable to read. She would often lament, "They've tried phonics and everything, but nothing works." She was frequently disruptive in class, in part because she felt cursed by her inability to read. Then

Figure 19–1
Joel's Good Choices Chart

I'm staying
on track, Jack!

Don't shut down,
bring the train back
to town. Earn some
fame… stay in the
game!

Here's a
cool rhyme—

Do my work
A little at a time.
Inch by inch
It's a cinch!

The harder I try,
the higher I fly!

Be the eagle.

Date		
Monday		
Tuesday		
Wednesday		
Thursday		
Friday		
Sticker = Good effort!		

one day Jenn's teacher taped together three sheets of green construction paper, cut out several one-by-two-inch "bricks" from light-
colored construction paper, drew a "road" about eight inches wide
down the three sheets of paper, and labeled it "Jenn's Road to Reading
Chart" (see figure 19–2). "Learning to read," she told Jenn, "is like

building a road—you do it one brick at a time." She went on to say that every time Jenn made a concerted effort to read she would receive a brick to glue onto the road, and that each time she completed four rows of cobblestones she would receive a reward for her accomplishment. Upon each brick was written her accomplishment. Soon Jenn began to read. Two months later she and her teacher decided that the "road" was complete and she no longer needed the chart.

To adapt this technique to other situations, child-guiders can draft a

Figure 19–2
Jenn's Road to Reading Chart

Target goal: Improve reading skills

Incentives: 1 cobblestone—made a good effort at reading

Reward: 4 completed rows entitle Jenn to a submarine sandwich for lunch

READING WITH MISS CAMBY ★	READING GROUP ★	★ SPELLING PRE-TEST	READING BUDDIES ★	READING GROUP ★	YEAH! LIBRARY TIME
★ ALPHABET WORK	READING BUDDIES ★	READING WITH MISS CAMBY ★	YAHOO! SPELLING TEST	READING WITH MRS. HAPSEN ★	★ LIBRARY TIME
LIBRARY WITH MR. CARMONA ★	★ READ COMIC BOOK				

Road to Writing (Learning, Spelling, Math Achievement) Chart and can reduce the number of rows, if desired. I once worked with a young boy with a certain trauma history who refused to do any schoolwork. We created a Road to Learning Chart, and months later, when I'd walk into his school he'd yell, "Go to the Learning Center, Mr. A." In the Learning Center were his Road to Learning Charts taped together, stretching twelve feet across. He loved looking at how far he had traveled.

A while back I volunteered to work with a young student with a brain tumor whose energy level was being affected by chemotherapy. During the first year, we constructed a Road to Learning Chart beginning in Boston and ending in California. When he got to Chicago, I brought in deep-dish pizza. The next year he greeted me on day one with these words: "Let's go to the universe this year, Mr. A." Consequently, I went home and cut out pictures of all the planets, glued them to a big poster board, and inserted ladders between them. Each time he put forth good effort, he got closer to the next planet.

Thirteen-year-old Kevin, who was having a hard time controlling his behavior, used a similar chart. His counselor labeled it Kevin's Good Choices Chart and gave him "bricks" for achieving self-control. After completing four rows of bricks, he celebrated with a pizza. By the time he finished his road, he had made major behavioral strides.

It is true that child-guiders can avail themselves of many strategies to help move kids forward without using extrinsic motivation. They can help the children better visualize their steps or modify their expectations, and so forth. Even so, as can be seen in the vignettes described here, a well-conceived incentive chart can make a difference.

11. Reward behaviors on a contingency basis.

As mentioned earlier in this chapter, it is important for child-guiders to let children know that if they have earned a celebration and then seriously misbehave, the celebration will be postponed. For example, if a child-guider has promised a lunch celebration with a child and right before lunch the child punches a peer, celebrating that day would send a mixed message. And if the child-guider takes away the celebration altogether, it would undermine the child's trust in him. In such cases, the child should be told: "You earned the celebration, and we will have it but not today. You made a bad choice to hit Frank. Today let's work through that. In a few days we'll celebrate the good work you've been doing." I often tell kids, "How would it look if I brought you lunch on a day you hit a kid?"

12. **Exercise honesty and discretion in settings where other children are not on an incentive plan. Frequently have the differences talk.**

In a classroom or other group setting, once a child's incentive plan is in operation other kids might ask, "Why don't *I* get incentives and extra privileges?" To explain this, child-guiders need to have the differences talk numerous times during the year: "Guys, I'm consistent, but being consistent doesn't mean that I treat you all the same. I do what you need." Most kids are fine with child-guiders creating special plans and altering expectations for the more challenging kids; they just need to be informed and perhaps be invited to help. Kids will, however, resent child-guiders individualizing plans and expectations for the neediest kids if they don't feel *they* are being treated fairly.

A Plan versus a Contract

Plans are often verbal agreements that serve to connect kids with adults; contracts are signed documents that appear to place kids and adults on opposite sides of a transaction. What's more, plans can be modified while contracts, as a rule, cannot be.

While a behavior plan is often recommended for nonaggressive offenses, a contract is routinely advised for more alarming behaviors, particularly those committed by adolescents. In such instances, kids who have acted violently toward themselves or others are asked to help design and then sign a contract ensuring that the dangerous behavior will not recur. The document usually lists rules to abide by and states the consequences that will follow any violation of the terms set forth in it. For example, for eighteen-year-old Sam, whose contract appears below (see figure 19–3), the penalty for breaking any of the stipulations he agreed to was expulsion from his foster home.

While it is understandable to want a violence-prone child to refrain from engaging in dangerous behaviors, the one-more-and-you're-out implication of a contract can, like the three-strikes-and-you're-out approach, place child-guiders in a precarious position: one more infraction and they must either follow through with an extreme consequence or be perceived as untrustworthy. Following through on a discharge notice such as Sam's is likely to eliminate their opportunity to help the youth, which may only

Figure 19–3
Sam's Contract

I, Sam, agree to:

(1) Refrain from hurting myself and others

(2) Take my medication without difficulty

(3) Attend group and individual therapy once a week

(4) Go to school every day

I understand that if I fail to meet any one of these conditions I will jeopardize my placement in this home.

Signed:_____

Program official:_____

Parent(s):_____

Date:_____

exacerbate his condition. Not following through is apt to magnify his insecurity and cause him to lash out in a cry for help. To guard against double-binds of this sort, child-guiders should consider creating a plan in lieu of a contract. In response to alarming behavior, they can then explain, "Let's create a plan to address these serious concerns."

Systemic Incentive Plans

Many special education and mainstream schools, residential programs, and juvenile justice facilities that guide kids, some with emotional and behavioral challenges, use a systemic incentive plan—an ongoing daily motivational program—to improve behavior and academic output and promote well-being among their populations. PBIS (Positive Behavior Interventions and Support), based on rigorous research evidence, offers a very successful systemic approach to "establishing the social culture and behavioral supports needs for all children in a school to achieve both social and academic success."[8] An essential component of PBIS is reinforcing positive behavior with some form of celebration, such as a class party for good academic and behavioral effort. PBIS is successful not simply because of the reward system it suggests but because of its positive, proactive approach to implementing a schoolwide behavioral support system.

The systemic use of incentives in settings designed exclusively for at-risk children and youth can help ensure the predictability and safety needed to help them grow emotionally, learn, and respond to other therapeutic interventions. In some inclusion or special education classrooms, teachers use point systems that allow students to earn stickers, points, or checks throughout the day and then trade them in for various rewards or privileges at the end of the day or week. The students often come to these settings with severe learning disabilities and other problems manifested by extreme cautiousness. Use of a daily incentive plan to navigate the stress of difficult academic work often helps produce the desired effects: improved functioning and academic achievement. Woven into the fabric of other milieu settings, however, this ongoing extrinsic motivation approach may be counterproductive in fulfilling a setting's goals and may not be in the best interests of the kids being served. Ongoing assessment is advised.

Strategic Applications of Systemic Incentive Plans

The use of a systemic incentive plan can be especially effective at routinely problematic times of day, such as bedtime, mealtimes, the preschool period, and chore time. Such strategic applications help diffuse stress by providing additional structure and stability. For example, to help close the day for a child with a trauma history who is often anxious about going to bed—the time of day when stimulation ceases and he is left to his horrific thoughts and images from past abuse—it is possible to use a bedtime star chart similar to the one illustrated in figure 19–4. Here a star has been entered for each day Carl, Fred, and Hank have gone to bed with no difficulty; each star adds twenty minutes to bedtime on Friday night and, if that goes smoothly, on Saturday night as well. Carl, for example, has earned a 10:10 p.m. Friday bedtime. If he gets a star on Friday night, he will have the same bedtime on Saturday night; if not, he will go to bed at his normal weekday

Figure 19–4
Bedtime Star Chart

Name/Bedtime	F	Sa	Su	M	T	W	Th	F	Sa
Carl 8:30	★	★	—	★	—	★	★	10:10	
Fred 8:30	—	★	★	★	—	—	★	9:50	
Hank 9:00	★	★	★	—	★	★	★	11:00	

bedtime of 8:30 p.m. Fred, who is the same age as Carl, also has a weekday bedtime of 8:30 p.m., whereas Hank's usual bedtime is later because he is older. Bedtimes should, of course, be based on age.

There are many variations on this theme. Some therapeutic facilities use a bedtime incentive system that rewards anyone who earns seven stars in a row by adding an extra half hour to the person's usual bedtime. The extended bedtime remains in effect until the child fails to earn a bedtime star, at which point her bedtime reverts to the original hour.

In years past, an early bedtime was often suggested as a consequence for misbehaving at bedtime, but this was an ill-conceived response. If kids have trouble getting to bed, child-guiders should attempt a myriad of strategies to make this a less anxious time of day, such as getting the child a nightlight; letting him listen to music; letting him go to bed later; making sure he gets a lot of exercise after dinner; or having a nice chat with him before bed. Of course, if the child misbehaves, the natural consequence is going to be that he'll be more tired the next day.

The bedtime star chart or some variation of it can be constructed to help children control their behavior at other times as well, such as during meals, while getting ready for school, or while performing chores. In such instances, each star they earn could entitle them to a certain block of time for a privilege related to the targeted behavior.

Level Systems

In many residential and other out-of-home placement settings, systemic incentive plans take the form of level systems that rewards kids for good behavior by raising their level. Kids earn points every day by making good choices, and then these points are tallied, usually on a weekly basis, to determine which level the child has achieved. Typically, a program has three or four levels, the highest of which allows kids the most privileges and autonomy.

There are major problems associated with this systemic approach to using incentives in out-of-home placement settings. One problem is that kids who act out the most in these settings tend to be relegated to the lowest levels for long stretches of time, which reinforces their negligible self-esteem. Another difficulty is the power the staff holds over kids, who too often are told, "Keep it up and I'll drop your level!" Additionally, in these settings there is often too much talk about levels instead of what really is going on.

In general, employing a level system is not, in this writer's opinion, the optimum way to manage a child-guiding milieu. For example, while visiting one residential program that wanted help eliminating its level system, I asked, "What's your highest level?" "Green," a staff member responded. "How many kids are on green today?" I asked. "None," she replied. "Actually, we've never had a kid earn green." The kids in that program could not help but feel like losers.

In one popular behavioral system used in far too many elementary schools, kids throughout the day are either at the green, yellow, or red level—red meaning they are not doing well. I heard about a mother of a challenging kid who picked her son up after school one day and asked, "Were you green today, Johnny?" The kid, who had been smiling, lost his cheery demeanor and responded, "Oh no, Mom, I'm not a green level kid. I'm a red level kid." Ouch.

This is not to say that schools and programs using level systems are bad and kids can't improve in these settings. Good, caring child-guiders can get kids to progress regardless of the system they employ. I, in fact, once quit a residential program because the director would not let me establish a level, or point, system. The kids were so out of control and the staff so poorly trained that I thought a short-term incentive system might have a settling effect on the milieu while I trained the staff to use a more strength-based, empowering approach.

I often tell child-guiders who work in schools and out-of-home placement settings that if they need to use a systemic group incentive system, to make it day to day not week to week, allowing every kid to wake up with a fresh start. I once instituted a daily level system at a detention center that was out of control; it helped immeasurably.

A question I hear a lot is: "So how do we control the kids without a level system?" The answer is quite simple. First, you create a strength-based culture in your setting that inspires kids to make better choices. Second, you offer lots of activities and opportunities for success every day. If a kid is acting up, a natural consequence is to not allow her to leave her space.

Third, you award privileges to each child based on her ability to handle them. For example, at my last residential program we had a privilege called store off-grounds, meaning that if we took a trip to the mall a kid with this privilege was allowed to go in a store unsupervised. Other privileges the kids could ask for included mall off-grounds, short on-grounds walk, short off-grounds walk, dating options, and job opportunities on grounds and off. And in each case the kids were awarded the privilege if on their best day they could handle it from a safety perspective. Thus, on any given day a kid might approach a staff member and ask to use his privilege. The staff member would say yes or no based on how the child was doing that day: "Charlie, you haven't cleaned up your room and have been making less than flattering comments to some of the kids. Let's clean the room and turn the attitude around a bit before asking me again. Thanks." This is an empowering and natural way to operate a milieu.

Fourth, you use logical consequences for all the kids and create individual incentive plans for kids who are struggling. Like Jody Olson stated, "If a kid needs one, we'll whip one up." This approach to running a milieu is similar to how a parent runs a home. We don't want kids leaving institutional settings and being unprepared for life.

I recall doing some training at a large residential program in California that employed a level system. While I was talking with one of the supervisors who knew I wasn't a big fan of level systems, she remarked, "You know, when a kid is ready to be discharged we take them off the level system two to three weeks before they leave us."

"Oh, that's interesting. Can you recall a kid close to discharge who was on a lower level that you took off?" I asked.

"Oh yeah, Ronnie left a few weeks ago. He was a big behavior problem. He actually went to another program," she replied.

"How did Ronnie do when you took him off the levels?" I inquired.

"He actually behaved real well for two to three weeks," she answered.

Some programs need a level system because the staff isn't capable of running a milieu that requires sufficient savvy and clinical judgment. But the goal should always be to get the staff the training they need and then implement a new, less power-laden approach to child-guiding that better prepares kids for life by replicating where many of them are going: to homes.

Conclusion

As stated in the introduction, the intent of this book is to help child-guiders decode the messages behind problem behavior and respond in ways that elevate children and youth to higher levels of functioning and happiness using effective strength-based tools and theories. The story of a courageous young man named Dave, who did just that, ultimately sums up the process and its value for at-risk children.

Years ago I conducted a workshop at a residential wilderness program for kids who had suffered severe trauma in their lives. At the conclusion of my presentation, a young man named Dave approached and asked, "Do you want to hear a good one?"

"Sure," I replied, and listened intently to his story:

I was terribly abused by my father as a kid. It was horrible. I ended up in a residential program for abused kids. Fortunately, the program was doing the kind of stuff you talk about. They got me to believe in myself. I turned my life around and eventually graduated from college with a degree in psychology. Wanting to give something back, I took a job working at a residential setting. At the time, I loved skateboarding and often frequented my local skateboard park. Early on, I noticed a scrawny little kid, Zack, who couldn't have been older than ten. He was there every day despite rain, snow, or heat. He wasn't very good, but he was tenacious. Over and over he'd fall, get up, fall, get up, and try again. I couldn't help but become a "big brother" figure to him. I'd give him tips, used equipment, and an occasional drink or ice cream.

Skateboarding was just beginning to take off in America, but there were no national skateboard magazines. So I decided to start one. I wrote to all the manufacturers and tournament hosts and received enough start-up and advertising money to get it off the ground. It became very popular and remained so for many years. Halfway through the first year, I did something that blew Zack away. For the first time ever I included a three-page pullout section in the middle of the issue. At the top I wrote, "America's Skateboarding Stars!" Below the title I placed full-length pictures of the top three skateboarders in America, along with Zack's picture cropped next to them.

I'll never forget the day I gave him that issue. He looked at it excitedly, like he always did, and then he opened up the pullout section and read the headline. He glanced left to right, seeing the first guy, the second, the third, and then the fourth—him! He did a double take, then again read the title and slowly looked at each picture. He couldn't believe it! He was so happy! I gave him ten copies of the magazine, and he ran home.

Zack became a darn good skateboarder. He won a few local events, and then I lost track of him. Years later I got a postcard from the Air Force Academy in Colorado Springs and found out Zack was flying jets. Sometime years later my doorbell rang, and a very tall, handsome man in uniform stood before me. It was Zack. After we exchanged greetings and a hug, Zack looked me in the eyes and remarked: "Dave, I've got to tell you something. Every day I was at that park I was being physically abused by my father. It was horrible. That park was the only place that made me feel good. You were the only person in my life who made me feel good. The day you put me in the magazine was the best day of my life. I still have the picture framed over my bed. Every night when I go to bed, I give my wife a kiss good night, look at 'America's Skateboarding Stars,' and ease into sleep with a big smile on my face."

Dave ended his account by repeating Zack's parting words to him, which I will remember for as long as I live: "Dave, you always treated me better than I am. And now I am better."

When we persistently try to help kids who need us in their corners, some really do soar.

Notes

Chapter 1

1. Charles Appelstein, *The Gus Chronicles: Reflections from an Abused Kid*, rev. ed. (Salem, NH: Appelstein Training Resources, 2012), 20.

2. James Garbarino (lecture, US Journal Training Conference, Las Vegas, NV, April 26, 2008).

3. Rick Miller, *Youth Development: From the Trenches* (Urbana, IL: Sagamore Publishing, 2012), 2, 122.

4. Emily E. Werner, retrieved from KidsatHope, http://gravycreative.com /clients/kah2015/wp-content/uploads/2015/05/Research-Synthesis.pdf.

5. Edward Hallowell, retrieved from http://www.drhallowell.com/add-adhd/.

6. Public Broadcasting System (PBS), http://www.pbs.org/.

7. Randall S. Sprick, *Discipline in the Secondary Classroom: A Positive Approach to Behavior Management,* 2nd ed. (San Francisco: Jossey-Boss Teacher, 2006), 6–12.

8. Larry Brendtro and James E. Longhurst, "The Resilient Brain," *Reclaiming Children and Youth: The Journal of Strength-Based Interventions* 14, no. 1 (2005): 52–61.

9. Ibid.

10. Ibid.

11. Francis X. Clines, "A Sandy Hook Parent Finds His Voice in Moving Beyond 'The Darkest Horror of It All,'" *New York Times*, May 9, 2013.

12. James Garbarino and Claire Bedard, *Parents Under Siege: Why You Are the Solution, Not the Problem in Your Child's Life* (New York: The Free Press, 2001), 43, 93.

13. Shawn Achor, *The Happiness Advantage: The Seven Principles of Positive Psychology That Fuel Success and Performance at Work* (New York: Crown Business, 2010), 15, 29, 44.

14. Ibid., 14.

15. Michael Durant, *Residential Treatment: A Cooperative, Competency-Based Approach to Therapeutic Program Design* (New York: W. W. Norton, 1993), 178.

16. Gabrielle Oettingen, *Rethinking Positive Thinking: Inside the New Science of Motivation* (New York: Penguin, 2014), quoted in Gabrielle Oettingen, "The Problem with Positive Thinking," *New York Times*, December 2014.

17. Ibid.

18. Serendipity, Miramax Films, 2001.

Chapter 2

1. Nancy Rose, *Raise the Child You've Got—Not the One You Want: Why Everyone Thrives When Parents Lead with Acceptance* (Napa, CA: Braeside Press, 2013).

Chapter 3

1. Rachel Naomi Remen, *My Grandfather's Blessings: Stories of Strength, Refuge, and Belonging* (New York: Berkley, 2000), 155–57.

2. James Whittaker and James Garbarino, eds., *Social Support Networks: Informal Helping in the Human Services* (Hawthorne, NY: Aldine de Gruyter, 1983).

3. Achor, *The Happiness Advantage*, 14, 18.

Chapter 4

1. Wayne Dyer, Segment on PBS.

2. Interview with Red Pollard's daughter on PBS.

3. *Cinderella Man*, Universal Studios, 2005.

4. Carol Dweck, *Mindset: The New Psychology of Success* (New York: Ballantine Books, 2006), 6–12.

5. Alfie Kohn, "The Perils of 'Growth Mindset' Education: Why We're Trying to Fix Our Kids When We Should Be Fixing the System," *Salon*, August 16, 2015.

6. Miller, *Youth Development*, 91–97.

7. Thomas Gordon, *P.E.T.: Parent Effectiveness Training—The Tested New Way to Raise Responsible Children* (New York: Peter H. Wyden, 1975), 171.

8. Ibid., 190–91.

9. Brendan Smith, *American Psychological Association* 43, no. 4 (April 2012): 60.

Chapter 5

1. David W. Winnicott, "The Capacity to Be Alone," *International Journal of Psychoanalysis* 39 (1958): 416–20; David W. Winnicott, *The Maturational Processes and the Facilitating Environment* (New York: International Universities Press, 1965).

2. Margaret S. Mahler, *On Human Symbiosis and the Vicissitudes of Individuation: Infantile Psychoses* (New York: International Universities Press, 1968); Margaret S. Mahler, "Rapprochement Subphase of the Separation-Individuation Process," *Psychoanalytic Quarterly* 41 (1972): 487–506; and Margaret S. Mahler, Fred Pine, and Anni Bergman, *The Psychological Birth of the Human Infant: Symbiosis and Individuation* (New York: Basic Books, 1975).

3. Edith Jacobsen, *The Self and the Object World* (New York: International Universities Press, 1964).

4. Heinz Kohut, *The Analysis of the Self: A Systematic Approach to the Psychanalytic Treatment of Narcissistic Personality Disorders* (New York: International Universities Press, 1971); Heinz Kohut, *The Restoration of the Self* (New York: International Universities Press, 1977).

5. John Bowlby, *Attachment: Attachment and Loss* (New York: Basic Books, 1969).

6. René A. Spitz, *The First Year of Life: A Psychoanalytic Study of Normal and Deviant Development of Object Relations* (New York: International Universities Press, 1976).

7. Abraham H. Maslow, *Toward a Psychology of Being* (New York: Harper & Row, 1962).

8. Mahler, Pine, and Bergman, *Psychological Birth of the Human Infant*.

9. Joyce Edward, Nathene Ruskin, and Patsy Turrini, *Separation-Individuation: Theory and Application* (New York: Basic Books, 1981).

10. Mahler, Pine, and Bergman, *Psychological Birth of the Human Infant*.

11. Edward, Ruskin, and Turrini, *Separation-Individuation*.

12. NIMH, "The Teen Brain: Still Under Construction," NIH Publication no. 11-4929 (2011), http://www.nimh.nih.gov/health/publications/the-teen-brain-still-under-construction/index.shtml.

13. Ibid.

Chapter 6

1. Michelle Garcia Winner, *Inside Out: What Makes a Person with Social Cognitive Deficits Tick?* (San Jose, CA: SLP, 2006), www.socialthinking.com.

2. Ross W. Greene, *The Explosive Child: A New Approach for Understanding and Parenting Easily Frustrated, "Chronically Inflexible" Children* (New York: Harper Collins, 1998).

Chapter 7

1. Marsha Linehan, *Cognitive-Behavioral Treatment of Borderline Personality Disorder* (New York: The Guilford Press, 1993).

Chapter 8

1. Anne T. Henderson, ed., *Beyond the Bake Sale: The Essential Guide for Family School Partnerships* (New York: The New Press, 2007), 1.

2. William P. Martone, Gerald F. Kemp, and Susan Pearson, "The Continuum of Parental Involvement in Residential Treatment," *Residential Treatment for Children and Youth* 6, no. 3 (1989): 11–37.

Chapter 9

1. Achor, *The Happiness Advantage*, 14.

2. Robert Brooks and Sam Goldstein, *Nurturing Resilience in Our Children: Answers to the Most Important Parenting Questions* (New York: McGraw Hill, 2002), 158.

3. Laura Hillenbrand, *Seabiscuit: An American Legend* (New York: Random House, 2001).

4. Scott Larson and Larry Brendtro, *Reclaiming Our Prodigal Sons and Daughters: A Practical Approach for Connecting with Youth in Conflict* (Bloomington, IN: National Education Service, 2000), 73.

5. Robert Brooks (lecture, Pollard Middle School, Needham, MA, November 21, 2015).

6. Robert Brooks, *The Self-Esteem Teacher: Seeds of Self-Esteem* (Circle Pines, MN: American Guidance Service, 1991), 85–86.

7. Boo McDaniel, HorsePower, 13 Pony Farm Lane, Temple, NH.

8. Marge Kittredge, Windrush Farm, 30 Brookview Road, North Andover, MA.

9. Richard Louv, *Last Child in the Woods: Saving Our Children from Nature-Deficit Disorder* (Chapel Hill, NC: Algonquin Books, 2008), 50.

10. Susan Cole et al., *Helping Traumatized Kids Learn: Supportive School Environments for Children Traumatized by Family Violence* (Boston: Massachusetts Advocates for Children, 2005), 57.

11. Robert Brooks and Sam Goldstein, *Raising Resilient Children: Fostering Strength, Hope, and Optimism in Your Child* (New York: McGraw Hill, 2001), 287–89.

12. David Crenshaw, Robert Brooks, and Sam Goldstein, eds., *Play Therapy Interventions to Enhance Resilience* (New York: Guilford Press, 2015).

13. Steve Baron, "Utilizing Strength-Based Strategies in the Schools—A School Psychologist's Odyssey" in ibid., 146–68.

14. Dachar Keltner, "Hands-On Research: The Science of Touch," *Greater Good*, February 24, 2011, http://greatergood.berkeley.edu/article/item/hands_on _research.

15. Judith Brook, quoted in Po Bronson, "How Not to Talk to Your Kids: The Inverse Power of Praise," *New York Magazine,* August 3, 2007, http://nymag.com /news/features/27840/.

16. Bronson, "How Not to Talk to Your Kids," http://nymag.com/news /features/27840/.

17. Paul Tough, *How Children Succeed: Grit, Curiosity, and the Hidden Power of Character* (New York: Mariner Books, 2012), 56, 74, 75.

Chapter 10

1. Michael Eric Dyson, "Punishment or Child Abuse?" *New York Times,* September 17, 2014, http://www.nytimes.com/2014/09/18/opinion/punishment -or-child-abuse.html?_r=0.

2. Brooks and Goldstein, *Raising Resilient Children.*

3. Robert Brooks, "Continuing Thoughts about Resilience and Caring: What We Can Learn from Military Veterans," November 16, 2015, http://www .drrobertbrooks.com/continuing-thoughts-about-resilience-and-caring-what-we -can-learn-from-military-veterans/.

4. Eric Greitens, *Resilience: Hard-Won Wisdom for Leading a Better Life* (New York: Houghton, Mifflin, 2015), 25–26.

5. George Sugai, "Positive Behavioral Interventions and Supports (PBIS)," http://www.pbis.org.

6. "Love and Logic," https://www.loveandlogic.com/.

7. "1-2-3 Magic," http://www.123magic.com/.

Chapter 11

1. Shawn Achor, *Before Happiness: The 5 Hidden Keys to Achieving Success, Spreading Happiness, and Sustaining Positive Change* (New York: Crown Business, 2013), 188–92.

2. George Kelling and James Wilson, "Broken Windows: Police and Neighborhood Security," *The Atlantic* (March 1982), http://www.theatlantic.com/magazine /archive/1982/03/broken-windows/304465/.

3. Dacher Keltner, "Hands On Research: The Science of Touch—How Everyday Forms of Touch Can Bring Us Emotional Balance and Better Health," *Yes! Magazine* (November 2010), http://www.yesmagazine.org/happiness/hands-on -research-the-science-of-touch.

4. Sprick, *Discipline in the Secondary Classroom.* 6-12

5. Richard Lavoie, *The Motivation Breakthrough: 6 Secrets to Turning on the Tuned-Out Kid* (New York: Touchstone, 2007), xix.

6. Ibid., 5.

Chapter 12

1. Tony Brown, *Tony Brown's Journal,* http://www.tonybrownsjournal.com/.

2. Robert Crichton, *The Great Imposter: The Amazing Careers of Ferdinand Waldo Demara* (New York: Random House, 1959).

Chapter 13

1. Edward Hallowell, ://www.drhallowell.com/add-adhd/.

2. Miller, *Youth Development,* 122.

3. Meghan Trainor, "All about That Bass," Epic Records, 2014.

Chapter 14

1. Gladwell, *Outliers.*

2. Miller, *Youth Development*, 85.

3. Bruce Perry, "Traumatized Children: How Childhood Trauma Influences Brain Development," *The Journal of the California Alliance for the Mentally Ill* 11, no.1 (2000), 48–51.

4. Miller, *Youth Development*, 86.

5. Sarah Ward, www.efpractice.com.

6. Oliver Sacks, *Musicophilia: Tales of Music and the Brain* (New York: Alfred Knopf, 2007), ix–xv.

7. Achor, *The Happiness Advantage*, 208.

8. Michelle Garcia Winner, socialthinking.com.

9. Jessica Minahan and Nancy Rappaport, *The Behavior Code: A Practical Guide to Understanding and Teaching the Most Challenging Students* (Cambridge, MA: Harvard Education Press, 2012); Jessica Minahan, *The Behavior Code Companion: Strategies, Tools, and Interventions for Supporting Students with Anxiety-Related or Oppositional Behaviors* (Cambridge, MA: Harvard Education Press, 2014).

10. Leah Kuypers, *Zones of Regulation: A Curriculum Designed to Foster Self-Regulation and Emotional Control* (Santa Clara: Think Social Publishing, 2011).

11. Katherine King, personal communication with author.

Chapter 15

1. Daniel Siegel and Tina Payne Bryson, *No-Drama Discipline: The Whole-Brain Way to Calm the Chaos and Nurture Your Child's Developing Mind* (New York: Bantam Books, 2014), xxii–xxv.

2. *The Horse Whisperer*, Touchstone Pictures, 1998.

Chapter 16

1. Remen, *My Grandfather's Blessings*, 156, 157.

2. Stephen Rollnick and William R. Miller, "What Is Motivational Interviewing?" *Behavioural and Cognitive Therapy* 23 (1995), 325–34.

Chapter 17

1. Dweck, *Mindset*, 6.

2. Robert Brooks and Sam Goldstein, *The Power of Resilience: Achieving Balance, Confidence, and Personal Strength in Your Life* (New York: McGraw-Hill, 2004).

3. Bob Bertolino, *Thriving on the Front Lines: A Guide to Strengths-Based Youth Care Work* (New York: Routledge, 2014).

4. Bob Bertolino, *Working with Children and Adolescents in Residential Care: A Strengths-Based Approach* (New York: Routledge, 2015).

5. *The Blind Side*, Warner Brothers, 2009.

Chapter 18

1. Siegel and Bryson, *No-Drama Discipline*, xxii–xxvii.

2. *Kramer vs. Kramer*, Columbia Pictures, 1979.

3. Minahan, *The Behavior Code Companion*, 140.

4. Center for Justice and Reconciliation, www.restorativejustice.org.

5. Editors of *Rethinking Schools*, "Restorative Justice: What It Is and Is Not," *Rethinking Schools* 29, no. 1 (Fall 2014), http://www.rethinkingschools.org/archive /29_01/edit1291.shtml.

6. Love and Logic, www.loveandlogic.com.

7. Bruno Bettelheim, *Love Is Not Enough* (New York: Avon Books, 1950).

8. William Glasser, *Choice Theory: A New Psychology of Personal Freedom* (New York: Harper, 1998), 197–206.

9. Remen, *My Grandfather's Blessings*.

Chapter 19

1. Alfie Kohn, "Beyond Discipline," *Education Week*, November 20, 1996, http://www.edweek.org/ew/articles/1996/11/20/12kohn.h16.html.

2. Daniel Pink, *Drive: The Surprising Truth about What Motivates Us* (New York: Riverhead Books, 2012), 8.

3. See Daniel T. Willingham, *Why Don't Students Like School? A Cognitive Scientist Answers Questions about How the Mind Works and What It Means for the Classroom* (San Francisco: Jossey-Bass, 2009).

4. Daniel T. Willingham, *Alfie Kohn Is Bad for You and Dangerous to Your Children*, Encyclopedia Britannica Blog, 2/2/09, http://blogs.britannica.com /2009/02/alfie-kohn-is-bad-for-you-and-dangerous-for-your-children/.

5. Jody Olson, personal correspondence with author.

6. Achor, *The Happiness Advantage*, 82.

7. *The Ron Clark Story* (made-for-television movie), January 13, 2006.

8. wwwpbis.org.

Recommended Reading

Achor, Shawn. *The Happiness Advantage: The Seven Principles of Positive Psychology That Fuel Success and Performance at Work.* New York: Crown, 2010.

Appelstein, Charles D. *The Gus Chronicles I: Reflections from an Abused Kid.* Salem, NH: Appelstein Training Resources, 2012.

Bertolino, Bob, Michael Kiener, and Ryan Patterson. *The Therapist's Notebook on Strengths and Solution-Based Therapies: Homework, Handouts, and Activities.* New York: Taylor and Francis Group, 2009.

Brendtro, Larry K., Martin Brokenleg, and Steve Van Bockern. *Reclaiming Youth at Risk: Our Hope for the Future.* Bloomington, IN: National Education Service, 1990.

Brendtro, Larry K., and Martin L. Mitchell. *Deep Brain Learning: Evidence-Based Essentials in Education, Treatment, and Youth Development.* Albion, MI: Circle of Courage, 2015.

Brooks, Robert, and Sam Goldstein. *Raising Resilient Children: Fostering Strength, Hope, and Optimism in Your Child.* New York: McGraw-Hill, 2001.

Brooks, Robert, and Sam Goldstein. *Raising a Self-Disciplined Child: Helping Your Child Become More Responsible, Confident, and Resilient.* New York: McGraw-Hill, 2009.

Clark, Lynn. *SOS Help for Emotions: Managing Anxiety, Anger & Depression.* Bowling Green, KY: SOS Programs and Parents Press, 2014.

Cole, Susan, F. Jessica Greenwald O'Brien, M. Geron Gadd, Joel Ristuccia, D. Luray Wallace, and Michael Gregory. *Helping Traumatized Kids Learn: Supportive School Environments for Children Traumatized by Family Violence.* Boston: Massachusetts Advocates for Children, 2005.

Durant, Michael. *Residential Treatment: A Cooperative, Competency-Based Approach to Therapy and Program Design.* New York: Norton, 1993.

Dweck, Carol S. *Mindset: The New Psychology of Success.* New York: Ballantine Books, 2006.

Garbarino, James. *Lost Boys Why Our Sons Turn Violent and How We Can Save Them.* New York: The Free Press, 1999.

Greene, Ross. *The Explosive Child: A New Approach for Understanding and Parenting Easily Frustrated, Chronically Inflexible Children.* New York: Harper Collins, 2010.

Lavoie, Richard. *It's So Much Work to Be Your Friend: Helping the Child with Learning Disabilities Find Social Success*. New York: Touchstone, 2005.

Lavoie, Richard. *The Motivation Breakthrough: 6 Secrets to Turning On the Tuned-Out Child*. New York: Touchstone, 2007.

Louv, Richard. *Last Child in the Woods: Saving Our Children from Nature-Deficit Disorder*. Chapel Hill, NC: Algonquin Books, 2008.

Miller, Rick. *Youth Development: From the Trenches*. Urbana, IL: Sagamore Publishing, 2012.

Minahan, Jessica. *The Behavior Code Companion: Strategies, Tools, and Interventions for Supporting Students with Anxiety-Related or Oppositional Behaviors*. Cambridge, MA: Harvard Education Press, 2014.

Minahan, Jessica, and Nancy Rappaport. *The Behavior Code: A Practical Guide to Understanding and Teaching the Most Challenging Students*. Cambridge, MA: Harvard Education Press, 2012.

Peters, Dan. *From Worrier to Warrior: A Guide to Conquering Your Fears*. Tucson, AZ: Great Potential Press, 2013.

Pink, Daniel H. *Drive: The Surprising Truth about What Motivates Us*. New York: Riverhead Books, 2009.

Remen, Rachel Naomi. *My Grandfather's Blessings: Stories of Strength, Refuge, and Belonging*. New York: Berkley, 2000.

Rose, Nancy. *Raise the Child You've Got—Not the One You Want: Why Everyone Thrives When Parents Lead with Acceptance*. Napa, CA: Braeside Press, 2013.

Sacks, Oliver. *Musicophilia: Tales of Music and the Brain*. New York: Alfred A. Knopf, 2007.

Seligman, Martin E. P. *The Optimistic Child: A Proven Program to Safeguard Children against Depression and Build Lifelong Resilience*. New York: Houghton Mifflin, 2007.

Whittaker, J. K., and James Garbarino. *Social Support Networks: Informal Helping in the Social Services*. Hawthorne, NY: Aldine de Gruyter, 1983.

Winner, Michelle Garcia. *Inside Out: What Makes a Person with Social Cognitive Deficits Tick?* San Jose, CA: SLP, 2006.

Index

About the Author

PROMINENT YOUTH-CARE SPECIALIST Charles D. Appelstein, MSW, a motivational speaker and author, teaches positive, trauma-informed, strength-based theories and techniques to parents and professionals who guide at-risk children and youth. He trains and consults internationally for treatment facilities, foster and adoption associations, parent groups, schools, mentoring programs, and juvenile justice agencies. His award-winning first book, *The Gus Chronicles I: Reflections From an Abused Kid*, is used as a training aid in hundreds of child welfare programs and colleges worldwide. Former program director of The Nashua Children's Home, a southern New Hampshire–based residential program for kids at risk and their families, Charlie lives in southern New Hampshire with his wife and teenage daughter.

To learn more about his work, including his training DVDs, self-help CDs for kids and parents, and speaking topics, visit www.charliea.com and Facebook.com/charlietraining.

Order Form

All items listed below were either written or produced by Charles D. Appelstein.

Quantity	Amount

Books

_____ *No Such Thing as a Bad Kid* ($24.95)   _____

_____ *The Gus Chronicles I* ($12.95   _____

_____ *The Gus Chronicles II* ($12.95)   _____

10% discount on orders of 10–24 books   _____

15% discount on orders of 25 or more books   _____

CDs

_____ *One-Line Raps for Girls and Chaps* ($12.95)   _____

_____ *Parent Rapsody* ($12.95)   _____

Training DVDS

_____ *The Power of a Strength-Based Approach in Reshaping the Lives of Children and Youth* ($195.95)   _____

_____ *Managing Number One and Staying Motivated to Do the Job* ($145.95)   _____

_____ *The Art of Communicating with Children and Youth Presenting Emotional and Behavioral Challenges* ($95.95)   _____

_____ *Strength-Based Parenting* ($59.95)   _____

Shipping and handling: for orders up to $25.00,
please add $3.50; for orders over $25.00, please add 8%.   _____

For Canadian orders up to $250.00, please add 18%;
for Canadian orders over $250.00, please add 15%.
Minimum Canadian shipping charge is US $14.50.   _____

Total amount enclosed   _____

Purchase orders are accepted.

Method of Payment

☐ Check or money order enclosed (payable to Appelstein Training
Resources, LLC, in US currency only)

☐ MasterCard   ☐ Visa   ☐ Discover   ☐ American Express

We do not accept credit card orders from Canada.

Account #_____

Expiration date____/____ CVC#_____ Zip code matched to card_____

Ship to:

Name _____

Address _____

City / state / zip _____

Phone / e-mail _____

**SOARING
WINGS
PRESS**

A Division of Appelstein Training Resources, LLC
12 Martin Avenue, Salem, NH 03079
Phone/fax 877-766-4487
www.charliea.com • charlieap@comcast.net